FINANCIAL TIMES
Mastering **Enterprise**

FINANCIAL TIMES

Sue Birley
Daniel F. Muzyka

Mastering

Enterprise

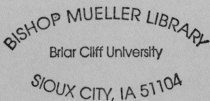
FINANCIAL TIMES
Prentice Hall

FTMasteringSeries

Executive Editor	Tim Dickson
Editorial Director	George Bickerstaffe
Academic Editors	Sue Birley, Imperial College Management School, London
	Dan Muzyka, INSEAD, Fontainebleau, France

Pearson Education Limited
Head Office:
Edinburgh Gate
Harlow
Essex CM20 2JE
England

London Office:
128 Long Acre, London WC2E 9AN
Tel: +44 (0)207 447 2000
Fax: +44 (0)207 836 4286

Website: www.business-minds.com

A Division of Financial Times Professional Limited

First published in Great Britain in 1997

© Compilation: Pearson Professional Limited 1997

Note: Licences have been granted by individual authors/organizations
for articles throughout this publication. Please refer to the respective
articles for copyright notice.

ISBN 0 273 63031 8

British Library Cataloguing in Publication Data
A CIP catalogue record for this book can be obtained from the British Library.

Illustration at the beginning of each Part © Michela Magas 1997

10 9 8 7 6

Typeset by Land and Unwin (Data Sciences) Limited, Bugbrooke
Charts and figures designed by Michela Magas
Printed and bound in Great Britain by Redwood Books Ltd, Trowbridge, Wiltshire

The Publishers' policy is to use paper manufactured from sustainable forests.

BK
£24.26

Contents

Preface

Mastering Enterprise was conceived as the first follow-up, or spin-off, of the *Financial Times'* successful 20-part series *FT Mastering Management* (also published in book form by Pitman Publishing).

There were several reasons for choosing entrepreneurship as the first in-depth examination of a single subject (*FT Mastering Management* covers all of the main management functions).

First, the creation and building of new companies and the fostering of the entrepreneurial spirit within large organizations has long been close to the newspaper's heart. It has for many years run a weekly 'Growing Business' page – launched under the editorship of Tim Dickson, now Director and Publisher of the *FT Mastering Series*.

Second, the subject leant itself ideally to the mix of academic theory and practical application pioneered in the original *FT Mastering Management*.

In this respect, *FT Mastering Enterprise* blazed something of a new trail, however. Rather than restrict itself to contributions from just three business schools as with the original series, *FT Mastering Enterprise* drew on a large number of geographically dispersed academics from a number of different institutions.

What they had in common, though, was leadership in the field. In the following pages you will find contributions from academics who are recognized 'gurus' in the area of entrepreneurship – Howard Stevenson, Bill Bygrave, Neil Churchill, Manfred Kets de Vries and Ian MacMillan. It also drew on a number of experienced practitioners, such as venture capitalists and bankers, to offer practical advice.

Two names stand out: Sue Birley of Imperial College Management School in London, and Dan Muzyka of INSEAD in Fontainebleau near Paris, who acted as Academic Editors to the series.

Through countless meetings, e-mails, faxes and telephone calls, they helped hammer out a synopsis and structure for the series and were indefatigable in networking their eminent colleagues to contribute. At the same time and in the middle of very busy schedules, they managed to write their own significant contributions. Great thanks are due to them and the other contributors.

FT Mastering Enterprise is merely the first development of *FT Mastering Management*. A new 12-part series – *FT Mastering Finance* – is planned for the newspaper and this, too, will appear as a Pitman Publishing book. Other series are likely to follow.

At the same time a new monthly subscription journal and an associated worldwide website are being planned.

As with the original series, all these innovations are dedicated to disseminating the latest academic thinking and discussion of practical issues to the widest possible audience with the aim of stimulating interest and thought and improving the skills of practising managers.

Appropriately enough, *FT Mastering Enterprise* is largely concerned with the creation of new organizations. It provides a solid foundation for the forthcoming series to build on.

George Bickerstaffe
Editorial Director, *FT Mastering Series*

The Academic Editors

Sue Birley

Sue Birley is Professor of Entrepreneurship at the Management School, Imperial College of Science, Technology and Medicine, London, and a non-executive Director of NatWest Bank. She has published numerous books and articles and sits on the editorial boards of a number of leading journals in the entrepreneurial and management fields. She is a Fellow of the British Academy of Management and the Royal Society of Arts.

Daniel F. Muzyka

Daniel F. Muzyka is IAF Professor of Entrepreneurship and Associate Dean, MBA, at INSEAD, Fontainebleau, France. His research interests include entrepreneurship and corporate strategy, especially as it applies to growing businesses. He has experience in finance and corporate strategy with the General Electric Company and as a strategy consultant. He has also been involved in starting up an entrepreneurial business.

Introduction

Today there is a great deal of interest from many quarters in the topic of entrepreneurship. In this world of downsizing, restructuring and techno-logical change, individuals are increasingly wondering whether they should strike out on their own, whether their fortune would be better realized through the pursuit of opportunities *they* believe and *they* have decided to pursue. At the same time, investors are wondering whether a better risk-return balance can be realized by backing these individuals. Corporate executives in search of ways to improve company growth, renewal and performance are pressing for more internal entrepreneurial activity. Government officials concerned with overall economic performance are asking themselves, 'Where is the next Bill Gates in my region and how do I help him emerge?' In short, entrepreneurship has many interested parties who need to understand it, to realize it, and to promote it.

This is a book dedicated to the subjects of entrepreneurship and entrepreneurs, no matter where they undertake their activities. Through the knowledge contained in the book, we hope that those with entrepreneurial ambitions will be better able to achieve successfully those ambitions.

Entrepreneurship

What exactly is entrepreneurship? Clearly, it describes the process and activities undertaken by entrepreneurs. These are individuals who organize, operate and assume the risks associated with a business venture they establish in pursuit of an opportunity they and others have identified. The entrepreneurial process is directed at capturing the value associated with business opportunities.

A major question that continues to exercise academics is the exact definition of 'entrepreneurship' and how far it extends. At one end of the spectrum are the 'Silicon Valley' or 'Route 128 (Boston)' group who see entre-preneurship as something related to founding and growing high technology businesses. These people see entrepreneurship as the creation of significant new wealth through the implementation of new concepts. At the other end of the spectrum are those who see any novel activity which creates organizational change and economic value as entrepreneurship. The one thing entrepreneurship researchers generally agree upon, however, is that 'entrepreneurship' is different from 'small business'. Most small businesses have limited growth potential and are primarily focused on creating a fair return for the efforts of the small numbers of those who work in the enterprise.

What is excluded from discussion in some narrower definitions of entrepreneurship? The answer is that some academics see topics such as entrepreneurial activity in the public sector or in larger organizations to not be a central part of entrepreneurship. Groups of 'new venture only' enthusiasts will not see anything short of independent, high-growth entrepreneurial activity as 'real entrepreneurship'. A broader audience accepts that there are a number of variations on entrepreneurial activity. Most will agree that the limited pursuit of opportunities, that is, capturing some of the value available still constitutes entrepreneurship. Life-style ventures, venture opportunities pursued by entrepreneurs in search of a different style of working, are commonly recognized as still being part of entrepreneurship. Some academics will accept that purchasing businesses for purposes of adding new value is also a form of entrepreneurial activity while others feel that such management buy-outs of existing businesses are not fully entrepreneurial in nature.

In this book we have accepted a broader definition and scope for entrepreneurial activity. We believe that the entrepreneurial process of identifying opportunity and realizing value is alive in both the public and private sector and in larger organizations. We take this broader perspective for several reasons. For example, in the case of the public versus private sector, the distinction between the two is increasingly unclear. Take for example, the notorious PSA (Property Services Agency) in the UK responsible for the management of the fabric of all government buildings bought by its management in 1994 and sold for many times the purchase price two years later. Value creation and privatization activities in eastern Europe have also blurred the line between public and private. In the case of larger organizations, it is clear that corporations are increasingly interested in promoting increased entrepreneurial activity. Furthermore, some 'entrepreneurial businesses' such as Microsoft and Branson's empire maintain their high levels of entrepreneurial activity despite their scale.

No matter what the definition of entre-preneurship we use, it is clear that the primary engines of the activity are the entrepreneurs themselves. Whether you are a corporate executive searching for more entrepreneurial activity, or a government minister attempting to deal with structural unemployment through the emergence of more entrepreneurial activity, you are attempting to mobilize more entrepreneurs.

Entrepreneurs

So who are these entrepreneurs? How can we recognize them? Is there a limited supply? Are they 'born or made'? Unfortunately the answers are not simple. We used to believe that they were drawn from those in society who were 'socially marginal' – the uneducated, the immigrant, or the poor – and who had an overwhelming need to prove themselves, had a strong 'need for achievement'. Consequently, early studies in the field describe the characteristics of those who started businesses in terms of both demographics and motivations in an attempt to arrive at an 'identikit entrepreneur'. Often-cited examples of successful entrepreneurs in the US only reinforce this model. Examples of immigrants who have 'made it big' are abundant, especially on the East Coast and New York areas and in California's rich entrepreneurial climate.

We have come to realize that these early attempts at classifying entrepreneurs and their motivations were incomplete, at best. It did not work because the environment changed and their characteristics changed. Take, for example, the experience in the United Kingdom. Studies have shown the successful entrepreneur is just as likely to be highly educated, and have worked in a large corporation in a senior management position before becoming an owner-manager, than to have left school and started a business at the age of 16. In other words, the supply of entrepreneurs is marvellously diverse and variable over time. It is influenced in part by genetic powers, by family background and early business experiences, and by the economic environment. To put it another way, the population can be viewed as having a range of inclinations towards enterprise with those in the middle most susceptible to change from employee to owner.

We know that the socio-economic climate (in the case of 'external' entrepreneurs) and the corporate environment (in the case of 'internal entrepreneurs') can significantly influence the emergence of entre-preneurs and entrepreneurial activity. Economic and tax policy, the provision of low-cost resources, appropriate training, and high-profile role models are all mechanisms which have been shown can move the goal posts. Indeed, that is exactly what most governments throughout the world are attempting to do. Organizations are similarly looking at their 'macro environment' in terms of whether it supports or suppresses entrepreneurship.

The book

We have four wishes with regard to the book's value to entrepreneurs. First, we hope we can encourage those with entrepreneurial ambitions that it is never too late nor entirely inappropriate for anyone to think of themselves as a potential entrepreneur. Second, we also hope that they will realize that there are many paths to entrepreneurship, from new ventures to buy-outs, to realizing opportunities within larger firms. Third, we hope they will recognize that there is no such thing as a perfect opportunity. Whether an opportunity is successful depends more on how it is implemented rather than its pure economic characteristics. Finally, but most importantly, we hope that entrepreneurs will realize that pursuing an opportunity should bear a health warning: it will not be easy. There are always problems to deal with and challenges to overcome.

The series of topics covered in this book explore the process of founding a venture and highlight some of the issues faced by those creating or remoulding an organization, the commercial problems which they confront, the family dilemmas which emerge as the business grows, and the decisions which they make. As such, the book is concerned with exploring the creation and management of those new ventures, which result in significant wealth for the owners. In other words, the focus is upon the development of new or reformed significant businesses rather than the development of new products or services. Clearly, this includes entirely new businesses developed by high-profile entrepreneurs such as the Tata Family, Richard Branson or Ted Turner, and by others less well known but equally successful.

Entrepreneurial process

Creating a new opportunity does not usually happen overnight. Whatever the eventual form of organization which emerges, whatever the route to market, the study of entrepreneurship is the study of the *process* through:

● identifying and developing an opportunity in the form of a vision

● validating and conceptualizing a business concept and strategy that helps attain the vision (for example, start-up, buy-out, franchise, etc.)
● marshalling the required resources to implement the concept
● implementing the business concept or venture
● capturing the full opportunity through the growth of the enterprise
● extending the growth of the enterprise through sustained entrepreneurial activity; and
● capturing the value through a business exit.

All of these activities take time and there are no rules as to how long each stage may take. In addition, it is often the case that entrepreneurs have to 'loop back' as they engage in the process. For instance, they find their business concept needs refining in light of what the potential resource suppliers want. An idea can be in gestation, perhaps through the process of invention, for many years or it may emerge in an instant. A manager may have a growing awareness of the possibilities of a buyout through press coverage but may be unsure how his or her employers would react – until they suddenly announce that the business is for sale! The embryo entrepreneur may always have carried a latent desire – until the right opportunity came along.

A certain set of behaviours must accompany the identification and pursuit of the opportunity. Entrepreneurs normally do not have the resources, power or 'authority' in hand that is required to just go and implement a venture. They must engage others in their ideas. They must leverage resources they do not control – or use 'other people's money' in the popular language. They must focus on growing rather than being particularly efficient. All of this suggests that there is a very clear reality driving the behaviour we see in entrepreneurs.

Given the powerful underlying logic of entrepreneurial activity, the sequence and contents of the book are modelled on the entrepreneurial process. The book first begins by considering entrepreneurship and entrepreneurial behaviour but immediately moves to the entrepreneurial process. The early parts of the book deal with identifying the opportunity, while the final stages deal with the entrepreneurial exit.

The topics
The entrepreneurial territory that is covered in the book includes a wide variety of activities, beyond the classic entrepreneurial new venture. The following are addressed both directly and indirectly within the book:

● **Management buyout (MBO):** the process by which the incumbent management team buys the business which they are managing, often a subsidiary, from the owners. In the process, it may have changed size, have new systems, or new arrangements with customers. It will certainly have new 'owner-managers' and it will probably have new investors in the form of venture capitalists.

● **Management buy-in (MBI):** the process by which a management team from outside the company purchases the company or the subsidiary from the owners. Often, they will involve the incumbent management in the acquisition, a process sometimes called a 'Buy-out/Management Buy-In'.

● **Franchising – the franchisee**: in Europe this has usually been seen as a 'small business activity' whereby individuals purchase a single franchise outlet. This is certainly not the case in the United States where 'Franchise Entre-preneurs' have built their business through the acquisition of multiple outlets, territories, and franchises. So, for example, in a single town they may own both Pizza Hut and Burger King as well as non-food Jiffy Lube. As a result of a recent EU Directive, which required the possibility of the ownership of multiple units in all member states, this is now a phenomenon which is emerging in Europe and that is certainly present in Asia.

● **Franchising – the franchisor**: The franchisee opportunity is not the only reason we include franchising in the series. Clearly, it is also one of the mechanisms available to entrepreneurs to build wealth based upon a business or product concept. Indeed, one third of retail businesses in the USA are franchises. Franchising is a way that many entrepreneurs can rapidly grow their businesses. This is particularly true of service businesses where the service is delivered locally. Franchising the business concept permits the growing entrepreneur to involve further entrepreneurial energy in the form of franchisees in pursuing the opportunity and permits the lead entrepreneur to leverage off the resources of franchisees in promoting and extending the business concept.

● **Corporate venturing**: an activity which some large organizations have used as a way of injecting enterprise and so revitalizing the business portfolio. The aim is to find new 'windows of opportunity', evaluate their potential, and invest in them for the long term. The latter may be through investing in existing early stage businesses needing development capital, joint ventures, or new subsidiaries within a 'venturing division'. For the large, mature organizations this means grappling with the questions of motivating and rewarding those directly involved, the 'corporate entrepreneurs'. However, this is just the tip of the iceberg.

● **Entrepreneurial corporation:** form of larger organization which provides an extension beyond those companies involved in promoting increased entrepreneurial activity through corporate venturing. More interestingly, the series will touch on the ways in which a number of companies trying to create new managerial systems in a rapidly changing environment are attempting to become 'entrepreneurial organizations'.

● **Family businesses**: here we are interested in those businesses owned and managed by a family through more than one generation, and the stresses and strains that this places upon both the family and the business relationship, particularly during the succession times. Clearly, the ways in which the business is managed and the extent of involvement of both children and extended family will vary according to the particular family culture.

In parts of the world, the family business and network are a primary mode of building and extending entrepreneurship. As Narissa Chauvidal of Imperial College found, in Thailand, more than 80 per cent of the top 100 companies are owned and managed by their Thai-Chinese founders and, of these, 97 per cent by the second generation.

The book seeks to address entrepreneurship in its many forms with the recognition that the primary vehicles for entrepreneurship do vary around the globe. In the US, the classic start-up is the much-vaunted vehicle for 'real' entrepreneurs. In Europe, many entrepreneurs prefer buying a business as a basic vehicle for their ambitions.

Interest

Who might be interested in this book? In short, it contains something for almost every constituency, for everyone interested in pursuing their entrepreneurial ambitions and those who are interested in promoting and supporting entrepreneurs. The book and the chosen content was designed and selected from the outset to appeal to multiple audiences, including:

- *Potential entrepreneurs*: Wish to consider 'taking the plunge' and become an entrepreneur? Think you have identified a business opportunity that others are not pursuing? Considering buying out the business you are managing within that holding company? For individuals in these circumstances, you will discover a wide spectrum of information, ranging from how to test your opportunity, to opportunities for exiting the business. Many of the articles will build your knowledge and experience in the field, leading to a more successful entrepreneurial experience. You will also find some insight into 'what it takes' to be successful. This book should help you answer the question: 'Do I have the right stuff?'
- *Existing entrepreneurs*: Managing the growth of the business is always a challenging opportunity. Owner-managers of existing businesses will find some insights into common challenges in growing the business. Additional insight will come from

observations about how to preserve entrepreneurship as you grow and how to make money on exit. For the owner-manager, this book becomes a helpful compendium of information about the collective experiences of other owner-managers.
- *Investors*: Private investors, bankers, and others directly involved in financing, evaluating and supporting entrepreneurs, including venture capitalists, can benefit in two ways. For those with limited experience with entrepreneurs and entrepreneurial business, the book provides a well-rounded briefing on entrepreneurial behaviour, entrepreneurial business and entrepreneurial challenges. For those with extensive experience, the book can help frame and share existing experiences and will help raise additional questions for investigation.
- *Advisers*: Consultants, accountants, and bankers who are interested in supporting entrepreneurs would find some helpful insight into the challenges faced by entrepreneurs. Furthermore, they should find some ideas on how to frame and present common entrepreneurial opportunities and problems.
- *Business partners*: Those who are suppliers, customers or alliance partners of entrepreneurial businesses will benefit significantly from this book. Further understanding about their behaviour, patterns and needs can aid in building a better business and personal relationship. Insight can further aid in negotiation leading to a 'win–win' for all parties.
- *Policy-makers*: Policy-makers can benefit from this book by understanding the objectives, motivations and needs of an entrepreneur and entrepreneurial business. This can lead to more appropriate public and tax policy. Government officials may also benefit through ideas on how to support entrepreneurs and entrepreneurial initiative in their own organizations.

Finally, the book can also appeal to the simply curious who will benefit through understanding their friends, neighbours and associates as well as an important sector of the economy.

The Authors

The people who have contributed to the series of articles in this book were chosen from among the world leaders in their fields. The group includes both academics and practitioners from entrepreneurship and related fields. They come from institutions and organizations from around the world, from Wharton and Harvard in the US to Imperial College and INSEAD in Europe. We also draw on the experience and insight of an inter-national cast of consultants, investors and entre-preneurs. While the study of entrepreneurship is a relatively new field of endeavor for academia, the individuals who have contributed their knowledge to this series often have ten or more years of experience and insight which they have brought to bear in preparing their contributions. We all hope you will find our insights to be helpful and will use the book as an on-going resource; a place you can regularly return to for clarification and support.

Book structure

As mentioned earlier, the book was organized to consider entrepreneurial topics from formation to exit: from framing the original business concept, to assembling the team and resources, to planning and capturing the value. Part 1 begins with a consideration of the nature of entrepreneurship and entrepreneurs. Particular emphasis is placed in the beginning on the nature of entrepreneurial behaviour, a key element in the successful pursuit of entrepreneurial opportunity.

Parts 2, 3, and 4 are all focused on the early stages of an entrepreneurial pursuit. Part 2 deals primarily with the nature of entrepreneurial opportunity. This is followed very naturally by Part 3 which deals with the sources and structuring of financial resources.

Part 4 contains a series of articles focused on issues of getting started: managing the beginning of your venture.

Parts 5 and 7 contain knowledge and insights on topics related to the successful pursuit of the venture opportunity. Part 5 addresses the important topic of teams and people in entrepreneurial initiatives.

Successful entrepreneurs are rarely found without a profoundly dedicated and powerful team aiding their pursuit of the opportunity. Part 7 aids our understanding of growth by pointing out the stages of growth and the challenges associated with growth.

Part 6 discusses several topics related to the nature of entrepreneurship around the world. Entrepreneurial challenges and practices, as well as the environment for entrepreneurs, are somewhat different in the various parts of the world. We hope you will find this section insightful in identifying the underlying regional differences in entrepreneurial perspectives and ambitions.

Parts 8 and 9 deal with issues of entrepreneurship and larger organizations. Part 8 is focused on the theme of management buy-ins and buy-outs. Many entrepreneurs find a foundation for their entrepreneurial ambitions in existing businesses that are part of larger firms. They may choose to purchase an existing business as an outsider (buy-in) or purchase part of a firm from the firms they currently work for (buy-out). These activities can create value by aiding existing companies or pieces of companies in achieving their full potential by pursuing existing or new opportunities to their fullest. Part 9 deals with the full spectrum of topics surrounding entrepreneurial activity in larger organizations: how to build and preserve a high level of such activity, as well as alternative modes of pursuing opportunities outside of the existing organ-izational processes (for example, corporate venturing).

Part 10 focuses on the topic of entrepreneurial exit. What are the options for entrepreneurial exit? How can you capture the most value? This, we believe, is the fitting end for any work dedicated to entrepreneurship: capturing the value.

We hope you will find this book useful both as something that is worth reading from cover to cover and as an overview of the field of entrepreneurship. In style, we have attempted to balance the work between something that is completely journalistic in nature and an academic work, full of content but less easy to wade through. In content, we have tried to commission and select pieces that answer a broad variety of questions and sometimes take very different perspectives and that deal with some common problems and opportunities facing entrepreneurs. We also hope it will serve as a reference. The ability to move from distinct article to distinct article as well as to navigate among the chapters, we hope will provide for a strong framework to index the work. Finally, we hope that it will inspire you as a 'would-be' entrepreneur to act. The challenge, fun and reward in entrepreneurship are found less in reading about it and more in doing it. As the saying goes: Just do it!

Sue Birley
Daniel Muzyka

1

☞ **Introducing enterprise**

Contents

Contributors

Manfred F. R. Kets de Vries is the Raoul de Vitry d'Avaucourt Professor of Human Resource Management and Clinical Professor of Management and Leadership at INSEAD, Fontainebleau, France. He is also a clinical psychoanalyst.

Juan Roure is Professor at IESE, the business school of the University of Navarra in Barcelona and Madrid, Spain, a Visiting Professor at INSEAD, France, and Academic Co-ordinator of EFER and Europe's 500 Association.

Howard H. Stevenson is Sarofim-Rock Professor of Business Adminstration at Harvard Graduate School of Business, Harvard University, USA. The Sarofim-Rock Chair was established at Harvard Business School in 1982 to provide a continuing base for research and teaching in the field of entrepreneurship.

Introduction

Part 1 is about those fascinating people, the entrepreneurs. We begin by posing the commonly asked questions – who are they, where do they come from, how do they behave, do they take risks, and can we pick them? Reassuringly, we are left with the conclusion that there is no simple answer and, more important, that there is no such thing as an 'identikit' entrepreneur. Those who take the path of enterprise are marvellously heterogeneous.

Creative rebels with a cause

Manfred Kets de Vries details the unique – and sometimes aberrant – behavior traits that make up an entrepreneur.

What are entrepreneurs like? What distinguishes them from other business people? What makes them so special? Although as a group they are not easy to get a handle on, some characteristics seem to be common to all of them.

Entrepreneurs seem to be achievement oriented, like to take responsibility for decisions and dislike repetitive, routine work. Creative entrepreneurs possess high levels of energy and great degrees of perseverance and imagination, which combined with a willingness to take moderate, calculated risks enable them to transform what often began as a very simple, ill-defined idea into something concrete.

Entrepreneurs can instill highly contagious enthusiasm in an organization. They convey a sense of purpose and determination. By doing so, they convince others that they are where the action is. Whatever it is – seductiveness, gamesmanship or charisma – entrepreneurs somehow know how to lead an organization and give it momentum. Most importantly, entrepreneurs are the driving force of any country's economy; they represent the wealth of a nation and its potential to create employment.

An extremely successful entrepreneur is Richard Branson, the Chairman of the Virgin Group, an empire that encompasses travel, communications (books, radio and television stations, computer/video games), retail and hotels. The story of Branson and Virgin is covered in detail on p.18.

Branson's leadership style is a unique combination of energy, originality and shrewdness. He is the major driving force in the company, a master of motivation and knows how to get the best out of his people. Furthermore, he is aware of some of his weaknesses and has hired others to compensate for these, having in the process created a highly effective executive constellation made up of executives with diverse skills.

Branson, however, is an exception in the way he has taken on the entrepreneurial role. Entrepreneurs are not a homogeneous group. They come in all shapes and sizes, each with his or her own characteristics. In some cases entrepreneurs possess personality quirks that, while originally may have been a source of great strength, can – when excessive – cause serious problems for the entrepreneur and the enterprise.

The entrepreneur's inner theatre

The need for control

A significant theme in the life and personality of many entrepreneurs is the need for control, a preoccupation that inevitably affects the way they deal with power relationships and their consequences for interpersonal action.

Some entrepreneurs are strikingly ambivalent when an issue of control surfaces – they are filled with fantasies of grandiosity, influence, power and authority yet they also feel helpless. They like to be in control but fear being controlled by others.

Some entrepreneurs have serious difficulties addressing issues of dominance and submission and are suspicious towards people in positions of authority. This attitude contrasts greatly with that of managers. While managers seem able to identify in a positive and constructive way with authority figures – using them as role models – many entrepreneurs lack the executive's fluidity in changing from a superior to a subordinate role.

Instead, entrepreneurs often experience authority relationships and the accompanying structures as stifling. They find it difficult to work with others in structured situations unless, of course, *they* created the structure and the work is done on *their* terms.

Listening to entrepreneurs' case histories, one can find many situations where it was their inability to accept authority and organizational rules that drove them to become entrepreneurs in the first place. Many are 'misfits' who need to create their own environment.

People who are overly concerned about being in control have little tolerance for subordinates who think for themselves. In an organizational context this desire for control can go to extremes – for example an entrepreneur wanting to be informed about every minute operation of the company. Such micro-management – appropriate as it may be in the start-up phase of a company – will increasingly become a burden as it stifles the information flow, hampers decision-making, and inhibits the attraction and retention of capable executives.

The late Robert Maxwell was a good example of an entrepreneur obsessed with control. In his companies there was only one way of doing things. It was his way or the highway. He had to control everything around him, whether people or companies. Everything, however trivial, had to be approved by him. There was no management structure; everything revolved around and depended on him. Through this kind of fragmentation, which created a considerable amount of obscurity, he kept control over all decisions.

A sense of distrust

Closely related to the need for control is a proclivity toward suspicion of others. Some entrepreneurs have a strong distrust of the world around them. They live in fear of being victimized. They want to be ready should disaster strike.

Paradoxically, quite a few feel best when their fortunes are at their lowest. When at the top of the success wave, they imagine themselves incurring the envy of others. No wonder that they respond that business is only 'so, so' or 'not too bad' when they are asked how things are going. But if their fortunes turn and they are close to bankruptcy, it is as if they have paid the price, done their penance for being successful. As this produces a sense of relief, their predicament can have a positive effect. With the alleviation of anxiety, they have the energy to start anew, which they do with enthusiasm and a sense of purpose.

As some entrepreneurs have a pervasive fear of being victimized, they are continually scanning the environment for confirmation of their suspicions. This behavior pattern does, of course, have its constructive side: it makes them alert to moves by competitors, suppliers, customers or government that affect the industry. Anticipating the actions of others protects them from being taken unaware.

But such vigilance can also lead them to lose any sense of proportion. Focussing on certain trouble spots and ignoring others, entrepreneurs may blow up trivial things and lose sight of the reality of the situation.

When a strong sense of distrust assisted by a need for control takes over, the consequences for the organization are serious. Sycophants set the tone, people stop acting independently and political gamesmanship is rampant. Such entrepreneurs can interpret harmless acts as threats to their control and see them as warranting destructive counteractions.

The problem in contending with such distorted form of reasoning and action is that behind the false perception that leads to fear and suspicion, one can always find some confirmation. Unfortunately, the person who manages in this way forgets the price the company pays in deteriorating morale, low employee satisfaction and declining productivity.

The need for applause

The heroic myth begins with the hero's humble birth, his rapid rise to prominence and power, his conquest of the forces of evil, his vulnerability to the sin of pride and finally his fall through betrayal or heroic sacrifice.

The basic symbolic themes here – of birth, conquest, pride, betrayal and death – are relevant to all of us. Some entrepreneurs act out the same myth, as we have seen, with a Greek chorus in the background applauding their achievements but warning them about pride.

Perhaps the myth explains why so many entrepreneurs live under a great amount of tension. They feel they are living on the edge, that their success will not last (their need for control and their sense of distrust are symptomatic of this anxiety) but they have also an overriding concern to be heard and recognized – to be seen as heroes. Some entrepreneurs experience a strong urge to show others that they amount to something, that they cannot be ignored.

A manifestation of this strong narcissistic need is the interest some entrepreneurs show in building 'monuments' as symbols of their achievements. Sometimes the monument is an imposing office building or production facility; sometimes it is a product that takes on a symbolic significance.

Maxwell, for example, was indefatigable in seeking (and getting) attention. He constantly needed an entourage and an audience. He was a great self-promoter and was irrepressibly boastful. His objective was to be in the news constantly. The *Daily Mirror* was turned into a kind of family album, with Maxwell writing his own headlines. He even acquired a soccer club, another highly effective way to stay in the public eye.

Defensive operations

Some entrepreneurs also resort to some peculiarly primitive defensive processes, which can lead to a great discrepancy between the narrative truth and the historical truth; facts are arranged to suit the individual's needs. Splitting – a behavior pattern whereby everything is seen in extremes, black or white, friend or foe – is a defense mechanism used by some entrepreneurs. Maxwell was no stranger to this way of dealing with others. If you disagreed with him, you were his enemy. He did not take easily to different points of view. He did not forget or forgive his enemies' 'crimes'. On the contrary, he had a memory like an elephant and would go to great lengths to get even.

Some entrepreneurs also have a tendency to blame others for what goes wrong. They do not see their own responsibility in the matter. Scapegoating is an excellent way of blaming others while feeling virtuous oneself. In assigning blame elsewhere, entrepreneurs may rationalize away whatever responsibility they have for questionable events. Their capacity to delude themselves can be tremendous.

Many entrepreneurs are also incapable of sitting still. There is a cyclical quality to their behavior. They are prone to great mood swings. They have difficulty in controlling their impulses and managing anxiety and depression. They fear that being passive would make them overdependent and in the end fall victim to control by others. Moreover, passivity evokes depressive reactions.

Managing for creativity

We have seen that entrepreneurs come in many different shapes and sizes: some manage for the good, others can become quite destructive. Some of the darker notes of entrepreneurship are quite real, however, and pose serious quandaries for those working for them. Managing an entrepreneur is not always one of the easiest tasks. But although the extremes stand out, most situations do not go that far.

Entrepreneurs do not necessarily have more personal problems than other people, nor do they inevitably have personality disorders. What one can extract from the previous comments, however, is that entrepreneurs have their own unique ways of dealing with the stresses and strains of daily life.

In saying this, I want to emphasize that the boundaries between the very creative and aberrant behavior can be blurred. The mix of creative and irrational is what makes entrepreneurs tick and accounts for many of their positive contributions. Entrepreneurs create new industries and stimulate the economy. Their visionary abilities and leadership qualities make it possible for their employees to transcend petty concerns and accomplish good work.

There are three kinds of people in this world: those who make it happen, those who see it happen, and those who wonder what has happened. We all know where entrepreneurs fit in. ■

The six dimensions of entrepreneurship

Entrepreneurship, argues **Howard Stevenson**, is neither a set of personality traits nor an economic function. Rather it is a cohesive pattern of managerial behavior that can be measured.

Entrepreneurship is an approach to management that we define as *the pursuit of opportunity without regard to resources currently controlled*. The description can be refined by examining six critical dimensions of business practice: strategic orientation; commitment to opportunity; commitment of resources; control of resources; management structure; and reward philosophy. We shall define these dimensions by examining a range of behaviors.

At one extreme is the 'promoter', who feels confident of his or her ability to seize an opportunity regardless of the resources under current control. At the opposite extreme is the 'trustee', who emphasizes the efficient utilization of existing resources.

While the promoter and trustee define the end points of this spectrum, there is a range of managerial behavior that lies between them, and we define (overlapping) portions of the spectrum as entrepreneurial and administrative behavior. Thus, entrepreneurial management is not an extreme example, but rather a range of behavior that consistently falls at one end of the spectrum.

Strategic orientation

Strategic orientation describes the factors that drive a company's formulation of strategy. A promoter is truly opportunity driven. His or her orientation is to say: 'I am going to be driven only by my perception of the opportunities that exist in my environment and I will not be constrained by the resources at hand'. A trustee, on the other hand, tends to say: 'How do I utilize the resources that I control?'

Within these two poles, the administrator's approach recognizes the need to examine the environment for opportunities but is still constrained by a trustee-like focus on resources. An entrepreneurial orientation places the emphasis on opportunity.

It is this dimension that has led to one of the traditional definitions of the entrepreneur as opportunistic or – more favorably – creative and innovative. But the entrepreneur is not necessarily concerned with breaking new ground. Opportunity can also be found in a new mix of old ideas or in the creative application of traditional approaches. We do observe, however, that organizations tend to look for opportunities where their resources are.

The pressures that pull a company towards the entrepreneurial range of behavior include:

● *Diminishing opportunity streams*. Old opportunity streams have been largely played out. It is no longer possible to succeed merely by adding new options to old products.

● *Rapid changes in:* technology – creates new opportunities, at the same time it makes old ones obsolete; consumer economics – changes both ability and willingness to pay for new products and services; social values – define new styles and standards; political roles – affect competition through deregulation, product safety and new standards.

Pressures that pull an organization to become more administrative include:

● *The 'social' contract*. The responsibility to use and employ people, plant, technology and financial resources once they have been acquired.

● *Performance criteria*. How many executives are fired for not pursuing an opportunity compared with the number that are punished for not meeting return on investment targets?

● *Planning systems and cycles*. Opportunities do not arrive at the start of a planning cycle and last for the duration of a three or five-year plan.

As we move onto the second dimension it becomes clear that the definition of the entrepreneur as creative or innovative is not sufficient. There are innovative thinkers who never get anything done. It is necessary to move beyond the identification of opportunity to its pursuit.

Commitment to opportunity

The promoter is willing to act in a very short time frame and to chase an opportunity quickly. The duration of their commitment, not their ability to act, is all that is in doubt. Commitment for the trustee is time consuming and, once made, of long duration. Trustees move so slowly that it sometimes appears they are stationary; once there, they seem frozen.

It is the willingness to get in and out quickly that has led to the entrepreneur's reputation as a gambler. However, the simple act of taking a risk does not lead to success. More critical is knowledge of the territory they operate in. Their familiarity with their chosen field means they have the ability to recognize patterns as they develop and the confidence to assume that missing elements will take shape as they foresee. This early recognition enables them to get a jump on others in commitment to action.

Pressures that pull a business towards this entrepreneurial end of the spectrum include:
- *Action orientation*. Enables an organization to make first claim to customers, employees and financial resources
- *Short-decision windows*. Due to the high costs of late entry, including lack of competitive costs and technology
- *Risk management*. Involves managing the organization's revenues in such a way that they can be rapidly committed to or withdrawn from new projects
- *Limited decision constituencies*. Requires a smaller number of responsibilities and permits greater flexibility

In contrast, administrative behavior is a function of other issues:
- *Multiple decision constituencies*. A greater number of responsibilities, necessitating a more complex, lengthier decision process
- *Negotiation of strategy*. Compromise in order to reach consensus and resultant evolutionary rather than revolutionary commitment
- *Risk reduction*. Study and analysis to reduce risk slows the decision-making process
- *Management of fit*. To assure the continuity and participation of existing players, only those projects that 'fit' existing corporate resources are acceptable.

Another characteristic we observe in good entrepreneurs is a multi-staged commitment of resources with a minimum commitment at each stage or decision point.

Commitment of resources

The issue for the entrepreneur is this: what resources are necessary to pursue a given opportunity? There is a constant tension between the amount of resources committed and the potential return. The entrepreneur attempts to maximize value creation by minimizing the resource set and must, of course, accept more risk in the process. On the other hand, the trustee side deals with this challenge by careful analysis and large-scale commitment of resources after the decision to act. Entrepreneurial management requires that you learn to do a little more with a little less.

On this dimension we have the traditional stereotype of the entrepreneur as tentative, uncommitted or temporarily dedicated – an image of unreliability. In times of rapid change, however, this stepped, multi-staged commitment of resources is a definite advantage in responding to changes in competition, the market and technology.

The process of committing resources is pushed towards the entrepreneurial domain by several factors:

● *Lack of predictable resource needs.* Forces the entrepreneur to commit less up front so that more will be available later on if required

● *Lack of long-term control.* Requires that commitment matches exposure. If control over resources can be removed by environmental, political or technological forces, resource exposure should also be reduced

● *Social needs.* Multi-staged commitment of resources brings us closer to 'small is beautiful' by allowing appropriate levels of resource intensity

● *International demands.* Pressures that we use no more than our fair share of the world's resources.

The pressures within large corporations, however, are in the other direction – towards resource intensity:

● *Personal risk reduction.* Any individual's risk is reduced by having excess resources available

● *Incentive compensation.* Excess resources increase short-term returns and minimize the period of cash and profit drains – typically the objects of incentive compensation system

● *Managerial turnover.* Creates pressures for steady cash and profits gains, which encourage short-term, visible success

● *Capital allocation systems.* Generally designed for one-time decision-making, these techniques assume that a single decision point is appropriate

● *Formal planning systems.* Once a project has begun, a request for additional resources returns managers to the morass of analysis and bureaucratic delays. Managers are inclined to avoid this by committing the maximum amount of resources up front.

Control of resources

Entrepreneurs learn to use other people's resources well and to decide over time what resources they need to bring in-house. Good managers also learn that there are certain resources you should never own or employ. Very few real estate companies employ an architect. They may need the best but they do not want to employ him or her because the need for that resource, though critical to the success of the business, is temporary.

The stereotype of the entrepreneur as exploitative derives from this dimension. The entrepreneur is adept at using the skills, talents and ideas of others. Viewed positively, this ability has become increasingly valuable in the changed business environment. It need not be parasitic in the context of a mutually satisfying relationship. Pressures towards this entrepreneurial side come from:

● *Increased resource specialization.* An organization may need a specialized resource such as a hi-tech patent attorney or state of the art circuit test equipment but only for a short time. By using rather than owning, a company reduces its risk and fixed costs

● *Risk of obsolescence.* Reduced by using rather than owning an expensive resource

● *Increased flexibility*. The cost of exercising the option to quit is reduced.
Administrative practices are the product of pressures in the other direction:

● *Power, status and financial rewards*. Determined by the extent of resource ownership and control in many corporations

● *Co-ordination*. The speed of execution is increased because an executive has the right to request certain action without negotiation

● *Efficiency*. Enables an organization to capture, at least in the short run, all the profits associated with an operation

● *Inertia and cost of change*. It is commonly believed that it is good management to isolate the technical core of production from external shocks. This requires buffer inventories and control of raw materials and distribution channels. Ownership also creates familiarity and an identifiable chain of command, which becomes stabilized with time

● *Industry structures*. Encourage ownership to prevent being pre-empted by the competition.

The promoter wants knowledge of his or her progress via direct contact with all of the principal actors. The trustee wants relations more formally, with specific rights and responsibilities assigned through the delegation of authority. **Management structure**

   The decision to use and rent resources and not to own or employ them requires the development of an informal information network. Only in systems where the relationship with resources is based on ownership or employment can resources be organized in a hierarchy. Informal networks arise when the critical success elements cannot be contained within the bounds of the formal organization.

   Many people have attempted to distinguish between the entrepreneur and the administrator by suggesting that being a good entrepreneur precludes being a good manager. The entrepreneur is stereotyped as egocentric and idiosyncratic and thus unable to manage. However, although the managerial task is substantially different from that of the entrepreneur, management skill is nonetheless essential. The variation lies in the choice of appropriate tools.

   More entrepreneurial management is a function of several pressures:

● *Need for co-ordination of key non-controlled resources*. Results in need to communicate with, motivate, control and plan for resources outside the organization

● *Flexibility*. Maximized with a flat and informal organization

● *Challenge to owner's control*. Classic questions about the rights of ownership as well as governmental, environmental, health and safety restrictions undermine the legitimacy of control

● *Employees' desire for independence*. Creates an environment where employees are unwilling to accept hierarchical authority in place of authority based on competence and persuasion.

At the other end of the spectrum, pressures pushing towards more administrative behavior include:

● *Need for clearly defined authority and responsibility*. To perform the increasingly complex planning, organizing, co-ordinating, communicating and controlling required in business

● *Organizational culture*. Often demands that events be made routine

● *Reward systems*. Encourage and reward breadth and span of control.

Reward philosophy

Finally, entrepreneurial companies differ from administratively managed ones in their philosophy regarding reward and compensation. Entrepreneurial organizations are more explicitly focused on the creation and harvesting of value. In start-up situations, the financial backers of the organization – as well as the founders themselves – have invested cash and want cash out.

As a corollary of this value-driven philosophy, entrepreneurial companies tend to base compensation on performance (where performance is closely related to value creation). Entrepreneurial companies are also more comfortable rewarding teams.

More administratively managed companies are less often focussed on maximizing and distributing value. They are more often guided in their decision-making by the desire to protect their own positions and security. Compensation is often based on individual responsibility (assets or resources under control) and on performance relative to short-term profit targets. Reward in such organizations is often heavily oriented towards promotion to increased responsibility levels.

The pressures that pull companies towards the promoter end of the spectrum include:

- *Individual expectations*. Increasingly, individuals expect to be compensated in proportion to their contribution rather than merely as a function of their performance relative to an arbitrary peer group. In addition, individuals seemingly have higher levels of aspiration for personal wealth
- *Investor demands*. Financial backers invest cash and expect cash back, and the sooner the better
- *Competition*. Increased competition for talented people creates pressure for organizations to reward these individuals in proportion to their contributions.

On the other side a variety of pressures pull companies towards more trustee-like behavior:

- *Societal norms*. We still value loyalty to the organization and find it difficult to openly discuss compensation
- *Impacted information*. It is often difficult to judge the value of an individual's contribution
- *Demands of public shareholders*. Most public shareholders are simply uncomfortable with compensation that is absolutely high, even if it is in proportion to contribution.

Summary

In developing a behavioral theory of entrepreneurship it becomes clear that entrepreneurship is defined by more than a set of individual traits and is different from an economic function. It is a cohesive pattern of managerial behavior.

This perspective on entrepreneurship highlights what we see as a false dichotomy: the distinction drawn between entrepreneurship and intrapreneurship. Entrepreneurship is an approach to management that can be applied in start-up situations as well as within more established businesses. As our definition suggests, the accumulation of resources that occurs as a business grows is a powerful force that makes entrepreneurial behavior more difficult in a larger company. However, the fundamentals of the behavior required remain the same. ∎

Ten myths about entrepreneurs

Juan Roure details research that shows that, while some entrepreneurs in Europe are thriving, our ideas of entrepreneurial companies in general may need revising.

Which companies are the real job creators in Europe? Who are the entrepreneurs building them? What is the profile of these successful entrepreneurs? What strategies are they following?

These are some of the questions that we have been trying to answer at the European Foundation for Entrepreneurship Research (EFER) since 1987. One of the latest studies conducted by EFER under the patronage of the European Commission – 'Europe's 500 Dynamic Entrepreneurs: The Job Creators' – has helped confirm many of the general beliefs about entrepreneurship in Europe but also has led us to question some of the more common myths about job creation and growing successful companies.

This article contrasts some of the myths and expectations that we had before starting the study with the realities that we discovered through detailed research results and interviews with 500 successful entrepreneurs, identified from screening ten million companies from 16 different countries.

The research sample was limited to mid-sized companies with less than 500 employees in 1989 (the beginning of the period under study) and more than 40 by 1994 (the final year under study). In all the companies the entrepreneur(s) held a significant percentage of ownership.

Myth 1: Small and medium-sized enterprises (SMEs) are the job creators.

Reality: Only a certain type of SME – the 'dynamic companies and entrepreneurs' – are the high growers and job generators.

In the period under study, the number of net jobs in Europe, counting all companies, decreased by nearly two million, with most of the losses attributable to large organizations and about 700,000 losses attributable to SMEs. In contrast, the sample of 500 companies that we identified were able to create more than 100,000 jobs. The average annual growth of the 'dynamic companies' identified was about 21 per cent in employment and 29 per cent in turnover. Therefore, in Europe, as supported by a similar study in the US, a small proportion of SMEs is responsible for creating the majority of new jobs.

Myth 2: New companies are the fundamental source of growth in employment.

Reality: High job growth is produced by both old and new companies.

Much attention has been paid to the problems of starting up new companies. However, very little is known about managing the 'transitions' that are usually linked to strategic moves to new products or markets and to changes in ownership, such as incorporating new partners, family successions or merger and acquisition.

Europe's 500 'dynamic' companies have been in business for 17 years on average. Four companies were actually first established in the 19th century, and only 14 per cent were less than five years old by 1994. The spark for growth in many already existing businesses seems to come from the successful management of some of these 'transitions' and from a persistence in pursuing new opportunities.

Myth 3: Growing companies come from new and high-growth sectors.

Reality: Dynamic companies come from all sectors.

These results seem to demonstrate that there are no successful sectors but, rather, successful entrepreneurs and organizations. The sectoral distribution of Europe's 500 is quite similar to that of all SMEs. However, the service sector as a whole seems to provide a more fertile ground for growth than manufacturing.

Myth 4: Entrepreneurs of growing companies are young and well-educated.

Reality: Dynamic entrepreneurs are of all ages and educational levels.

Three-quarters of Europe's 500 entrepreneurs are in the 35 to 65 age range. Only seven per cent are under 34 and 18 per cent are over 65. 'Dynamic' entrepreneurs come from a wide range of educational backgrounds, with less than one-third having a university degree. These types of entrepreneurs consider themselves as 'constantly trained professionals' and rate themselves most highly on skills such as strategy, negotiation and communication.

Myth 5: Growing companies are developed by an energetic and self-sufficient entrepreneur.

Reality: Dynamic companies are built by teams or a partnership of entrepreneurs with a professional approach to management.

Most of the entrepreneurs studied seem to have great self-confidence in their own ability to identify and then capitalize on opportunities, overcoming all kinds of obstacles. However, they realize the challenges involved in growing a business in today's competitive environment and, therefore, they form teams or partnerships to complement themselves in managing the company.

Myth 6: Growing companies target large and growing markets.

Reality: Dynamic companies target market segments where they can be leaders or strong challengers.

More than 80 per cent of Europe's 500 entrepreneurs consider themselves to be the market 'leader' or 'challenger' in the segment in which they compete. These companies try to avoid competition by concentrating on segments or 'niches', which they sometimes create themselves, where they try to play a significant and influential role by applying proactive strategies.

Myth 7: Growing companies target mainly domestic markets where they can dominate such markets.

Reality: Dynamic companies target a significant proportion of their sales to export markets where they can learn and grow.

About 80 per cent of Europe's 500 are active in export markets. On average, the share of exports is 44 per cent of turnover, the final destinations mainly being other EU member states. These dynamic companies export a much higher percentage of their turnover than European SMEs in general, using mainly direct distribution channels and, to a much lesser extent, foreign investment, joint ventures or licensing.

Myth 8: Successful growing companies use low-cost strategies to compete.

Reality: Dynamic companies compete with high-quality products and superior service.

Europe's 500 entrepreneurs have opted for differentiation strategies far more frequently than for low-cost strategies. They seek to differentiate mostly in the quality of their products and in the service that they provide to their customers. These strategies are supported by the high involvement of employees and customers in the improvement process and the high commitment to quality of the entrepreneurs themselves.

Myth 9: Successfully growing companies rely primarily on unique technology.

Reality: Dynamic companies rely primarily on people, whom they carefully recruit, train and develop.

Even though Europe's 500 entrepreneurs consider technological knowledge an important asset to reduce cost and take advantage of new opportunities, they pay a high level of attention to human resources policies, particularly to recruitment, training, employee recognition and team building. Dynamic entrepreneurs, in contrast with other SMEs, may have been stimulated by fast growth in employment, which forced them to adopt a more formal and professional approach to people management.

Myth 10: Growing companies use sophisticated sources of financing to build their companies.

Reality: Dynamic companies are predominantly self-funded, with assistance from bank loans.

Europe's 500 entrepreneurs seek to remain financially independent as much as possible. In 87 per cent of the companies, the major entrepreneur controls more than half of the shares. The most important source of financing for this type of company is from retained profits. Bank loans are the only other significant source of finance. Venture capital and private investors had some importance only in approximately 10 per cent of the companies that have gone public. However, another 30 per cent are considering listing in the future; this may lead to an increased importance being placed on developing capital.

In conclusion, dynamic entrepreneurs have had and expect to continue to have a profound impact on Europe's wealth and job creation. Europe's 500 is only a small sample of a large number of other dynamic entrepreneurs already existing, but hidden, or with the potential of becoming high growers in the future.

The study of these entrepreneurs is still in the early stages. The first results seem to challenge many of the entrepreneurship myths that have been developed through the years. Europe's 500 Association has been recently created with the purpose of becoming the 'voice' and releasing the enormous potential of 'dynamic entrepreneurs' in Europe. ■

◆ CASE STUDY

Richard Branson: the enigmatic entrepreneur

*This case is extracted and edited from 'Branson's Virgin: The coming of age of a counter-cultural enterprise' prepared in 1995 by **Robert Dick**, research associate at INSEAD, under the supervision of Manfred F. R. Kets de Vries, Raoul de Vitry d'Avaucourt Professor of Human Resource Management at INSEAD.*

Family and early life

Richard Branson was born in July 1950, the first child and only son of Ted Branson and his wife Eve. He was later joined by two sisters, Lindi and Vanessa. The family has remained close, all enjoying what Richard was later to describe a 'happy and secure' childhood.

Both Ted and Eve came from comfortable establishment backgrounds. Ted was the son and grandson of eminent lawyers. Eve came from a family of clerics, farmers and stockbrokers, whose womenfolk were expected to have horizons beyond the home.

Eve had decided views on child-rearing. While she was never a martinet, she pushed her children to be self-reliant and responsible, to take control of their own destinies rather than relying on others.

One summer afternoon, as she and four-year-old Richard were on their way home after visiting his grandparents, Eve told Richard to get out of the car and try to find his own way back. The farmhouse where they were staying was not far but Richard got lost, ending up at the neighbor's farm.

Eve Branson now admits that she may have been overly enthusiastic about encouraging Richard's independence but she has never regretted it. She considered her children's ability to overcome challenges would encourage the kind of spirit she wanted to see in them. Accordingly, she used her own considerable energy to organize activities, games and projects for her children that were not only fun but also served a useful purpose.

Holidays, weekends and other free time were used productively. The Branson household had no television since it was 'time wasting'; shyness in children was simply bad manners and self-indulgence to be discouraged; if money was short (as it was in the early days when Ted's father cut off his allowance in protest at his precipitate marriage), then a solution could always be found in small money-making schemes that Eve thought up.

Ted Branson was never a strict and remote father figure. Sympathetic and supportive by preference, a half-hearted disciplinarian if really necessary, Ted was less directly ambitious for his children than Eve, who expected, for example, that 'Richard [would] one day be prime minister'.

Richard grew up to be the archetypal naughty boy. Frequently in minor scrapes, scolded for innumerable misdemeanors and hyperactive in all he did, his parents found him both endearing and fatiguing. According to his father, Branson began his first business venture when he was around 11 or 12 years old. He planted a thousand seedlings and then went back to school convinced he would make a killing selling Christmas trees. Rabbits ate the trees. About a year later he tried again. This time the scheme involved budgerigars. Another failure.

Richard's parents were particularly concerned about his progress at school, where his main accomplishments were on the sports field, thanks to a strong physique and competitive spirit. His schoolboy heroes were sportsmen, particularly cricketers, and adventurers such as Scott of the Antarctic, the British explorer and a distant relative by marriage.

His indifference to schoolwork (not helped by long-undetected poor eyesight) meant he achieved only average results, which ruled out a legal or other professional career. By contrast *Student* magazine (Branson's first successful business venture) excited Branson with its possibilities and offered a timely and convenient exit. So, with his parents' reluctant blessing (his father's support was particularly influential), he quit school.

Branson left few friends behind him. While not unpopular, his energetic and single-minded pursuit of that which pleased him left little room for others. His indifference to the contemporary social mores and allegiances common at a school like Stowe (an exclusive private school with a liberal reputation) left him somewhat isolated. His few friends were those inveigled into his various and numerous projects. Commenting on the end of his schooldays, Branson said: 'Having left school without going to university, I decided to make money . . . I never considered failure'.

The 'hippy entrepreneur'

Having in some respects commercialized the anti-establishment life-style of the 1960s, it was not surprising that Branson was labeled 'the hippy entrepreneur' by the business and musical press. His alternative image was reinforced by the company's operating style where, from the start, informality and equality were essential principles – rarely found in the business world at the time.

When Virgin started out, everyone received the same low salary, there was an absence of hierarchy (Branson was, and is, 'Richard' to everyone) and personal attire was casual to the point of idiosyncrasy. Even when the company had expanded massively, this style was very much in evidence; Branson and his staff are rarely seen in conventional business clothes, preferring sweaters and jeans even on formal occasions. Similarly, the company's offices, accumulated over time, were a collection of modest, often dilapidated, buildings scattered about northwest London from which the sound of rock music could usually be heard.

For a long time Branson's office and home was a canal houseboat where he worked alone apart from two secretaries. Eventually Branson was forced to move to a larger home since his two children 'started to answer the phones' but he kept the houseboat as an office.

His wife, a down-to-earth Glaswegian from a working-class background, has no interest or role in his business life. This is something of an anomaly at Virgin since Branson, contrary to conventional wisdom, is a great believer in working with family and friends, seeing only the advantages and not the risks.

His cousins, aunts, school and childhood friends, parents and former girlfriends have all been drawn into his various business activities. Only his first wife found the situation difficult to accept but even she is now in a joint venture with Branson developing hotels in Spain.

The charges of nepotism that such arrangements usually engender were muted at Virgin because Branson adopted a promote-from-within policy, giving many of his staff opportunities that their lack of experience and training would have precluded in more conventional companies.

Virgin was unconventional in other ways too. Somehow Branson created the impression that people worked at Virgin for fun and excitement rather than simply as a means of earning a living. Notoriously indifferent to material possessions and unconcerned about everyday financial matters, Branson saw no difficulty in paying modest salaries provided people were enjoying themselves, feeling part of an idiosyncratic enterprise that had a heart. If people were down, a party would revive spirits and, incidentally, give Branson the chance to play a practical joke on newcomers, an embarrassing rite of passage at Virgin that is maintained to this day. Much of this operating style was established not so much by design but by the exigencies of the time when Virgin was getting started. It has proved to be a successful model that Branson can replicate.

His philosophy is to immerse himself in new ventures until he understands the ins and outs of the business and then hand it over to a good managing director and financial controller who are given a stake in it and are then expected to make the company take off.

He knows that expansion through the creation of additional discrete legal entities not only protects the Virgin Group but also gives people a sense of involvement and loyalty, particularly if he trusts them with full authority and offers minority shareholdings to the managers of subsidiaries. He is proud of the fact that Virgin has produced a considerable number of millionaires. He has said that he does not want his best people to leave the company to start a venture outside. He prefers to make millionaires within.

He sees similarities in the Japanese *keiretsu* system (small companies interlocking in a collaborative network) to the structure he has created at Virgin, with more than 500 small companies around the world operating quasi-independently.

Richard Branson has become an international celebrity, the subject of numerous profiles in gossip magazines, the business press and television programs. In the UK he has achieved folk-hero status. He is frequently cited as a role model by young people wanting a successful business career that does not compromise personal ethics.

The 'real' Richard Branson

In material terms Branson is undoubtedly successful. He became one of the UK's richest people before he turned 40 and recently ranked as the 11th wealthiest person in the UK, with an estimated net worth of £895mn.

Asked to explain the strategy that got him to this point, he will talk of minimizing risks – 'protect the downside, always be ready to walk away' – and seeking out opportunities to build 'the largest entertainment group outside the US'. Over the years he has made a few strategic statements that, with hindsight, do not relate very much to subsequent events. Most frequently, however, he says he simply wants to enjoy himself.

But can a strategy for fun really explain the creation of a music company by a founder who, paradoxically, has little interest in or knowledge of music? Equally, it is difficult to explain how a shy man, ill at ease when speaking publicly or in private conversation with strangers, can become a supreme self-publicist; how an establishment-born figure with intrinsically conventional views can become the champion of radical and libertarian causes; or how the man who is almost obsessive about fair play can negotiate ferociously for the last penny in a deal.

A London *Sunday Times* report on the British Airways affair (the so-called 'dirty tricks' affair) quoted Lord King (at the time BA chairman) as saying: 'If Richard Branson had worn a pair of steel-rimmed glasses, a double-breasted suit and shaved off his beard I would have taken him seriously. As it was I couldn't . . . I underestimated him'. Perhaps Lord King is not alone in being misled by the hippy entrepreneur image that surrounds Branson. But if that image is not the real Richard Branson, then what is? ■

The above case is an abridged version. Copies of the complete case may be obtained from the European Case Clearing House, telephone (+44) 01234 750903; fax (+44) 01234 751125; E-mail ECCH@cranfield.ac.uk.

2

☛ The opportunity

Contents

Contributors

Peter Saunders is Lecturer in Accounting and Entrepreneurship at Imperial College, London.

David Molian is Lecturer in Marketing and Entrepreneurship at Imperial College Management School, London. His research interests include general marketing, new ventures marketing and the marketing of innovation. He is a partner in Euro Group Consulting specializing in corporate restructuring for the single European market.

Rita Gunther McGrath is Assistant Professor, Management Organizations Division, at Columbia Business School, New York. Her research focuses on how competitive advantages are gained through innovation and new venture management.

Stephen Spinelli is Assistant Professor of Entrepreneurship at Babson College, Wellesley, Massachusetts. His research interests include franchising, multiple outlet operations, retailing and new venture creation. He is a former franchisee of Jiffy Lube in the US, developing 47 stores in eight years, a founding shareholder of Jiffy Lube International, and founder, Chairman and CEO of American Oil Change Corporation.

Peter Kelly teaches MBA courses in entrepreneurial management at London Business School and the University of Notre Dame. He is currently pursuing his Ph.D. at LBS and his doctoral research focuses on the informal market for venture capital in the UK.

Introduction

Part 2 is concerned with finding a new business opportunity. Clearly, a swift scan of the high street, or any new product catalog, will quickly show that there would appear to be very few new ideas – just old ones repackaged and relaunched. So how do you spot where the opportunity lies, or when a change in legislation has opened a new 'window'? This part deals with these questions, with how to assess a new opportunity, and how to decide on the right market entry strategy.

Spotting the market opportunity

Daniel Muzyka looks at the way entrepreneurs identify opportunities. The related question of what makes a good opportunity is tackled in the article on assessing opportunities on p. 33.

The key to entrepreneurship is the ability to identify, pursue and capture the value from business opportunities. Entrepreneurs exist to pursue opportunity. Without it, they have no *raison d'être*. No one can call him or herself an entrepreneur until they have identified and at least begun the pursuit of an opportunity.

The problem in addressing the topic of opportunity – and particularly the question 'what makes a good opportunity' – is that it is hard to generalize. The underlying nature of technologies and the way they are adopted by customers and specific industries and competitive dynamics make the construction of a checklist of opportunity characteristics difficult.

It is even harder to generalize about where entrepreneurs find opportunity. For some entrepreneurs, opportunity comes as a result of extended thought and exploration. For others, it is the product of a fortunate set of circumstances and a quick response to a lucky phone call from a desperate potential customer.

However, having said that, we can draw from entrepreneurship research over the past 15 years. We can also draw from research on those who bet on entrepreneurs for a living: private investors and venture capitalists. Their reflections provide us with some guidelines on opportunity. In reviewing these sources, you will find some consistent themes regarding the characteristics of 'good' opportunities.

However, we begin our discussion of opportunity with a note of caution. The one thing we do know about entrepreneurial opportunity is that the opportunity models developed by strategy and marketing researchers may not fully apply to new-venture opportunities.

More than once, existing strong competitors in industries such as computers (for example IBM) have asked themselves how these young upstarts have been so successful in pursuing opportunities that did not appear on the radar screen of corporate staff groups.

The problem may lie in the underlying source of the models used by large competitors: they were taken from observations of long-run market competition in *established* markets not from *establishing* markets.

Despite the difficulty in generalizing from the experiences of successful and unsuccessful entrepreneurs regarding opportunity, we will make an attempt to summarize what we know.

Opportunities themselves are something that exist on paper or as an idea. Realized opportunities are those that individuals have turned into profitable and functioning businesses. Opportunity, in practical terms, may therefore be defined as a business concept that, if turned into a tangible product or service offered by a business enterprise, will result in financial profit.

Are there any general points we have learned about opportunity by observing entrepreneurs? The answer comes in a few cautionary points.

What is an opportunity?

Opportunities are about creating value, not necessarily lowering cost

Some would-be entrepreneurs become fixated on whether their product is cost competitive or the lowest-cost product. The name of the game, however, is not necessarily about low cost, despite what some popular production strategy gurus have said. It has been, and always will be, about creating value. Does the opportunity help increase the customers' effectiveness and efficiency? It is simple economics: if it is worth it, people pay. The failure of some entrepreneurs who believe they haven't come in at the right cost is that they have not communicated value.

One example is a productivity software package that came out in the early days of microcomputer software. It was priced below $90 per copy. The company selling the product was doing poorly vis-à-vis other packages available. What did consumers tell it? – 'You cannot provide value since all you do is communicate through price'. It brought the price closer to $120 per copy and used the additional revenue to advertize in order to communicate the value of the product. Turnover climbed precipitously.

Opportunities are not the same for everyone

Many economic and business models suggest that somehow opportunity is 'out there' and that it simply 'happens'. The only problem is who will invest in it and then catch it. Don't get caught in this perspective. If there is one truth that comes from the experience of entrepreneurs, it is that not everyone is equally equipped to perceive or capture an opportunity.

The experience of each individual or team makes them more or less able to identify and capture opportunity. In addition, each individual's perspective (which is a product of their products, services, markets or skills) is different.

What does this mean? It means that although you may be worried that someone else, will pursue 'your' opportunity, it is not necessarily perceived as an opportunity by anyone else. They may not have your advantages.

This also means that even though something may be an opportunity for someone else, perhaps you ought to avoid it. In the end, any measure of whether something is a real opportunity must take into account whether you can implement it.

Not everyone pursues opportunities, even if they are obvious

How many times, when someone else started a business and made money out of it, have you said to yourself, 'I had the same idea'?

Profit is left to those who wish to show initiative and actually pursue rather than just think about a business opportunity. Creative thought is wonderful but if it does not lead to action it is only an expenditure of energy. Most people and companies do not pursue opportunity, especially if they are reasonably satisfied with the status quo. You must show real initiative to pursue opportunity.

Complex opportunities break down

It unfortunately appears to be a fact of life that the more complex an opportunity is – for example, involving a large number of parties and integrating numerous steps and components for it to work successfully – the more it is *un*likely to come to fruition or to work in the long-run.

Some entrepreneurs have ideas but, as they try to pursue them, they find they must involve more and more parties. Sometimes entrepreneurs get caught up in the 'artistry' of the opportunity and forget how vulnerable they become when so many components must work together. These are the entrepreneurs whom one subsequently often hears lamenting that they had figured out the opportunity but it was just one little problem that ripped it apart.

Opportunity is not always (rarely?) found in well-documented growth markets

Too many entrepreneurs and venture capitalists have been lured into effort and investment in pursuing opportunities that everybody else has seen. For example, an excessive number of companies were established, virtually simultaneously, in the hard disk drive industry in the US to pursue the new 'Winchester drive' technology. Only a few survived.

A simple rule might be that if an opportunity is discussed in all its details on the front page of the *Financial Times,* you might take the time to determine whether it is going to be a real value-added opportunity for you. I always enjoy those advertisements in business journals that note an undiscovered entrepreneurial opportunity that has been successfully pursued by thousands.

Opportunities are not necessarily the result of inventions by the entrepreneur

Despite the comment that entrepreneurs are not necessarily inventors, many entrepreneurs are determined to invest their time and effort in searching for opportunities based on some kind of technological breakthrough. This may be admirable, even desirable, but is not necessary.

Where do opportunities come from?

Entrepreneurial opportunities come in many ways, shapes and forms to those who pursue them. Some individuals are gifted in identifying and throwing off ideas for products and services at a rapid pace. Others conceive how they can make money from an idea they get from a newspaper or hear about from a friend or acquaintance.

Most entrepreneurs have to show a modicum of creativity, although a particularly creative mind is not required. The role of entrepreneurs is not to be people of 'ideas'. Their role is to be creative in structuring a business around an opportunity and then implementing their ideas.

What we have observed, however, is that the business opportunities they identify are usually related to past experience. It is rare that someone has a lightening bolt out of the blue and identifies a new blockbuster opportunity in a field with which they are not or only slightly familiar. Opportunities are usually related to our work experience or social environment.

In other words, ideas for opportunities come from within the realm of our existing knowledge and usually result from our mind connecting seemingly unrelated ideas. The simple rule is: if you want to develop a new concept in a specific, unfamiliar business, go to work in that business so that you know how it functions and can see the linkages.

What types of opportunities are there?

Opportunities are not all the same in either their potential or their risks. We often glorify the individuals who identify and pursue the radical new technologies. However, the reality is that these types of entrepreneurial opportunities are the exceptions and not the rule.

Some individuals seek to identify and pursue such high-potential, high-risk opportunities. Others look for opportunities that have lower risk/return profiles, that is, the entrepreneur accepts somewhat less profit for the sake of a lower-risk project. This may involve not the pursuit of some new high-density, silicon-based chip but the transplanting of a franchise operation from one country to another.

Most successful entrepreneurial opportunities involve the pursuit of relatively simple ideas. For example, entrepreneurs have made significant sums from mass merchandizing carpets in more attractive stores, producing appropriate bakery buns locally to supply McDonald's or locating convenience shops in emerging, high-traffic areas.

In looking for opportunity, consider not only the risk/return relationship but also, and probably more importantly, your own objectives. Some people are looking for the opportunity of a life-time with massive potential. For them, such an opportunity will define their life. They will pursue it to the fullest. These are often the entrepreneurs we hear about. The Bransons (Virgin) and Gates (Microsoft) of this world fit into this category.

Others are interested in what we often refer to as 'lifestyle' opportunities and businesses. If you are looking for a business opportunity that will help you realize a desired pattern in your life, then you must be careful to define the limits you wish to impose on the nature of the business that will result from pursuing an opportunity.

There are many people who start everything, from specialist hotels to mail-order firms, because the daily operation of such businesses also enables them to pursue a certain lifestyle. Many individuals who, for example, wish to spend more time, or more structured time, with their families are looking for a different balance between the opportunity and their potential profit. ∎

The search for a good idea

How do you come up with a good business idea? **Peter Saunders** lists some ways to help your creativity.

The aim of this article is to help you build an inventory of creative resources and help you identify a personal strategy for opportunity search.

Essentially there are only two ways in which you can create business ideas – generate your own or develop someone else's. The second is far more common because virtually every successful business is a development of an earlier business concept. These areas, such as management buy-outs/buy-ins, corporate spin-offs, franchising and buying an existing business, are covered in detail in other articles.

In terms of generating business ideas, there are three sources of opportunities: adverts, agents and opportunity spotting, or watching out for businesses that you find match your objectives.

All people and organizations have needs that they fulfil in many different ways. When you can meet these needs better than they are currently being met, then you will almost certainly have a business opportunity.

One common route is the employer as an 'idea generator': you might duplicate what your employer is currently doing, or service a new market that the employer has not bothered to exploit.

Other ways of recognizing people's needs include 'the complaints department', where you listen to people whinging to see if you can find ways of reducing their problems; asking yourself 'what do people want?'; spotting trends (the growth of home personal computers has led to an enormous number of new businesses from hardware to software, along with magazines and books); and identifying market gaps.

There are some established thinking techniques such as visualization, brainstorming and morphological analysis that can be used to generate ideas.

Visualization is a technique that has been used successfully by many, including Conrad Hilton of Hilton Hotel fame whose autobiography even has a chapter called 'You've got to dream'. The process is to day-dream – to visualize a picture of your own future. Does it include your own company? If so, what is it? Visualization is good at helping determine long-term goals, idea generation and idea evaluation.

Everyone has heard of brainstorming. When used well, it can create large numbers of ideas. To work well, you need between five and ten people and you need to have planned the session in advance. There is insufficient space in this article to cover best practice, so you will need to read up on the topic before using.

Morphological analysis – dividing a complex problem into elements – can also help generate ideas. As an example one might take skin care products: sun cream, anti-wrinkle and tanning lotion, to suggest just three. The potential market for these might be segmented by age – teenage, 20-something and 30-plus. By combining the two, you have nine ideas. Skin tone may be relevant as well. If you have only three skin tones, you are up to 27 ideas already. Once a box has been developed in this way, the more important elements can simplified into a morphological matrix with only two axes.

Finally, there are some experts in corporate creativity who can help in idea generation. The most well known is Edward de Bono whose book *Opportunities: a Handbook of Business Opportunities Search* includes some excellent suggestions. It contains a 'start point checklist', which has you listing your intrinsic assets, operating assets and your situation assets. He suggests one looks at what other companies have left behind and to segment markets farther than they have traditionally been.

Many businesses have been started as a result of a search process that followed traditional routes, such as improving on existing businesses or a geographical change.

Improving on existing businesses can take many forms. You need to look at existing businesses and ask yourself: 'Can I do that and do it better?' What constitutes 'better'? Suggestions include quality improvements, simplifying the product or service, improving customer appeal, making it more cost effective, production efficiencies, making it more reliable, better marketing or greater convenience.

Another traditional approach is to shift the geographical base of a business. This requires you to find a business that you can both put into action and transfer.

In conclusion, much of the research into new enterprise creation links greater creativity with the size of the prospective entrepreneur's networks. The implication of this is that you should, like politicians, go out to the masses. Press the flesh and *talk* to people. ■

An opportunity – but is it worth it?

Starting a business depends on spotting an opportunity. But more important, says **Sue Birley**, is assessing just how good that opportunity is.

New business opportunities arise constantly. You only have to walk down the high street to see new shops opening all the time, stroll down the supermarket lanes and test the new products on offer, buy your favorite computer magazine and send for the latest piece of software or browse through your local paper to find any service you care to desire.

Moreover, you can probably convince yourself without too much difficulty that you had the idea first but simply did not have the time or inclination to put it into practice. After all, what is so very clever about an idea for a chain of hamburger restaurants, a new record label, a new specialist publisher, an accounting firm offering services tailored to the small firm, an even smaller personal computer? It must be easy.

Well, you only have to look at the closure rate of those self-same shops, the number of inventions that never achieve even one sale, or the shelf-life of those new products or services, to see that all too often people simply get it wrong – and at great financial cost and personal pain. Why does this happen? It is due to a multitude of factors.

Eighty-seven individual reasons were listed as contributing to the failure of an owner-managed firm. These were reduced to 24 themes:

1 Capital structure	**9 Pricing**	**17 Obsolescence**
2 Management team	**10 Suppliers**	**18 Reliance on grants**
3 The economy	**11 Marketing**	**19 Family succession**
4 Customer diversity	**12 Growth**	**20 Legislation**
5 Financial management	**13 Quality**	**21 Cost of money**
6 Owner attitudes	**14 Adverse publicity**	**22 Personnel problems**
7 Rising costs	**15 Ill health**	**23 Fire, flood**
8 Lack of planning	**16 Partnership problems**	**24 Industrial injury**

Clearly, more than one factor contributed to the failure of a business, and seven combinations emerged:

1 The unlucky (35 per cent) businesses that were obviously under-capitalized but less so than the rest. There was no obvious overriding feature to explain their failure.

2 Those with poor systems (21 per cent) had a wider customer base than the rest and suffered less from the effects of the economy. Nevertheless, an inadequate capital structure and a poor management team was combined with poor financial management.

3 Those with marketing and market problems (14 per cent) tended to have a narrow customer base and a management team with poor marketing skills.

4 Those out of balance (11 per cent) had been seriously affected by a general rise in costs, an under-capitalized balance sheet, poor financial management, inadequate market planning and, in some cases, a reliance on grants.

5 Those out of control (9 per cent) had poor financial management, an inadequate management team, and tended to underprice and overtrade. This was often compounded by poor quality and poor labor relations.

6 The niche businesses (9 per cent) suffered from narrow customer and supplier bases.

7 The disasters (1 per cent) suffered more than the rest on all except one of the dimensions – financial management.

Source: Sue Birley and Niki Niktari: *The failure of owner-managed businesses: the diagnosis of accountants and bankers,* The Institute of Chartered Accountants, London (1995).

Figure 1

A recent study asked 486 bankers and accountants to give the reasons for client failure (*see* Figure 1). Respondents to this study were also asked the question: 'Could the failure have been avoided? '; two-thirds replied 'yes'. In their view, many businesses had been launched with a weak business concept and a lack of planning. In other words, the opportunity was not properly assessed.

Opportunity assessment is a continuous process of gathering data, reviewing the proposition, and reformulating the business concept. Most entrepreneurs will tell you that the business that was eventually created bore little resemblance to the one they had originally envisaged.

Market potential

The place to start is the market. After all, common sense tells us that without customers who are prepared to buy the product there is no prospect of a business.

Unfortunately, exploring the market can be complicated. How is it defined? Is there more than one? How big is it? How many potential customers? Where are they located? Do you have a piece of technology with many potential applications? (*see* Figure 2).

But more important, is there a genuine need – and is it already recognized? By now, you should begin to see the potential elephant traps. It is very easy to convince yourself that you would like to have it – so others must too. You would love to have your groceries delivered at 6.30 on a Friday evening – and the

Internet now makes it possible to place an order. But how many people in your street or locality have access to the Internet and could be persuaded to switch their buying habits – and what would they be prepared to pay for the service?

The potential market may be large and there may be a genuine need, but what **Market share** percentage of customers do you think you can persuade to switch to your product? Indeed, who are the customers?

We all buy washing powder in the supermarket but we do not decide which brands are displayed on the shelves. That is the role of the supermarket buyer, who may prefer to deal with large suppliers offering a range of reliable, quality products than a new business offering a new, untried product.

In other words, you need to think about routes to market and the barriers you may encounter. Of course, this means looking at the competition and their likely reaction to your entry. For example, will they reduce their prices, increase their advertising or develop a similar product in order to try to squeeze you out?

> Pam Murphy had a slurry problem on her farm. The slurry pit was leaching into the local river. So, she had a machine designed that would separate the slurry into solid and liquid. This made storage much easier.
>
> However, leaving a batch of solid for a couple of weeks, she found it had heated up, destroyed all the germs and 'cooked' into a perfect, friable fertilizer.
>
> Pam thought: 'I am going to sell that' and so the concept of Cowpact was born. In the first year, she sold 25,000 bags by mail order. But that was just the beginning. Pam had a product that could be sold to either the gardener or farmers or both, and the copyright on a process/machine that could be sold in the farm equipment market.
>
> What should she do? Where was the greatest opportunity?

Part of the answer will depend upon how much of a threat you are likely to be **Figure 2** to them – and this is often a function of size and market power. Clearly, the more diverse the competition and the smaller your target share, the greater your chances.

How do you find out? You do not need to invest in expensive market surveys – although it may be necessary later on – just ask a few commonsense questions. In other words, you should be looking to establish the 'ball park' to see if it is worth spending time in more detailed market research. You are trying to 'prove the concept'.

Certainly you will be expected to answer these questions, and many more, if you are seeking to raise money. Investors need to be convinced that you understand your market-place and are realistic about your chances – and so do you. In the end, however, investors are usually more convinced by names and orders than by market surveys.

Establishing that there is a market is only the first stage. You now need to think **Routes to** about the potential ways to capitalize on the idea – and it may not be to start **market** your own business.

The market may be highly concentrated, dominated by two or three global companies that also control the channels of distribution. So you may be advised to sell the patent, license it or become a partner in a joint venture.

For example, would you advise Pam to set up as a farm equipment manufacturer?

In other words, there are two questions to be answered:
- Is there a market?
- Is there potential for an independent business?

If you decide to continue with a new start, remember that competitors are rarely inactive. The best that you can hope for is that they are slow and/or ineffective. You need to think about how much time you may have before competitive reaction will have a serious effect on your business – and what you can do to protect yourself.

Protection

Fundamental to the process of assessing the opportunity is the need to talk to potential suppliers, customers and subcontractors. 'But what if they steal my idea?' is a constant concern. 'What can I do to protect myself?'

Clearly, being first to market and establishing your brand is one way, as is asking your contacts to sign confidentiality agreements. However, there are three other legal forms of protection to consider:

● *Patents:* This refers to the invention of a tangible item, which incorporates novel features involving an innovative step and which is capable of industrial application. In the UK, it must not have been disclosed before the patent application, although this requirement varies by country. Granting of the patent gives the owner a monopoly on its use for a specified number of years. Patents are granted on a country-by-country basis.

● *Registered design:* Covers designs that are attractive. They may include a shape, configuration or pattern for a specific, manufactured article such as a car.

● *Copyright:* Prevents the copying of original works, although in any court action it must be proved that copying has actually taken place. Great minds do sometimes think alike.

Business viability

So far you have been looking at market opportunity. Alongside this you should also be thinking about the business opportunity. Evaluation of this will depend upon how you intend to arrange the business – to what extent are you going to subcontract the manufacture of the product or the provision of the service?

Clearly, the answer to these questions will, in turn, depend upon issues such as your skills, availability of subcontractors, quality and funding, but eventually it will depend upon your financial analysis. Quite simply, you need to know the answer to two deceptively simple questions:

● What are the likely costs of the business and can you sell at a price that will produce a viable profit? Think about the possible margins – how much room for manoeuvre do you have if your estimates of either the price or costs are wrong?

● Is the forecast cash flow sustainable? Too many businesses have failed with positive margins but no cash simply because others would not or could not pay in time.

Unfortunately, there are no simple answers to these questions. So you need to think about what may go wrong – sales take longer to take off or be only half your expectations, customers take longer to pay or suppliers are not as reliable in quality or delivery as you had been led to believe. Your licence to operate as a restaurant does not arrive until after Christmas.

What would these do to the build up of your sales? In short, what are the critical success factors for your business, how likely are they to happen, how can you mitigate against them and how fatal could they be?

Is it worth it?

By now you must be wondering. However, remember that you will already know many of the answers or have access to help through your business contacts, friends and family. You simply need to take a cold hard look at all aspects of your idea in order to convince yourself and others that it might work.

One final question – what are you prepared to lose? What are the crawl-out costs **The crawl-out** if things go wrong? This is the dreaded issue of risk. There are four types: **costs**

- *Financial*: can you afford to lose your investment?
- *Career*: can you return to your previous job or career?
- *Family and social*: how will it affect your social reputation?
- *Psychic*: how afraid are you of failure?

Which of these worries you the most – and would it stop you? In reality, few successful entrepreneurs think in these terms. They simply see the 'upside' of an opportunity and provide contingencies to 'manage the downside'. ■

Market research

Daniel Muzyka provides a few basic observations regarding market research that are often made by entrepreneurs.

- **Get your hands dirty**

Even if you do have the money to get others to carry out some of your market research, it is better to do at least part of it yourself. By interviewing, speaking with and observing potential customers, you get very important information about their behavior that can help you fine tune and better sell your concept, both to the customer and to possible sources of finance.

- **Focus on the quality of research rather than quantity**

Certainly, you must interview a sufficient number of people concerning your product and market ideas. However, do not just focus on the quantity of individuals you interview. Ask yourself about the quality of the information you are gathering.

- **Be prepared and flexible in undertaking research**

Always be clear about what data you need to gather and whom you wish to speak with. At the same time, be prepared to change techniques (for example, move from surveys to focus groups) and to include others in the process as required. The research is a learning process. All along the way, you may receive information that points you in other directions and to other sources. Follow your instincts and be willing to probe and experiment as required.

- **Use an iterative approach**

What this means is that you should plan to go out, collect information, return and reflect and plan to go out again. Do not see your evaluation process as a single event that provides you with a 'yes' or 'no' answer. Reflection on what you are learning is key.

● **Even if you are excited, do not lead the witness**

One problem entrepreneurs sometimes get trapped in is that they cross the boundary between testing their ideas with potential customers and selling their idea. You want honest evaluation. If you signal that you are only interested in getting people to accept what you are saying, you will be defeated in your evaluation. You may get positive results but they are meaningless.

● **Be prepared to change the product or service**

Part of not trying to sell your ideas is that you must be open-minded about the possibility of modifying your product or service. Test alternative combinations of features in the market. Part of the iterative process is that you may modify the product or service during the course of the market research and evaluation.

● **Do not get frustrated at the lack of data**

Do not think of yourself as directly answering a question. You are assembling information to complete a puzzle. It is rare that you will find information directly affecting the evaluation of new opportunities. It should be more not less common that you do not find appropriate information directly impacting your opportunity. In the end, you just want to make sure you are approximately – not exactly – correct and that you have big margins for error even if your forecast is a little off.

● **Realize that you also learn after initial introduction**

The actual product introduction process is also an opportunity for evaluating opportunity. You should prepare methods of collecting information around the introduction so that you can make quick adjustments that will maximize your potential for success. ■

The parsimonious path to profit

Rita Gunther McGrath explains how and why entrepreneurs pursue opportunity at the lowest possible cost.

The entrepreneur had a problem. He needed several thousand color advertising brochures in time for a crucial trade show. The best price quote so far had been around $1,500 but even this amount would challenge his already pressured bank account. What was he to do?

The answer eventually presented itself in the form of a forklift truck. Our entrepreneur's uncle, who ran a small manufacturing operation located in an industrial park, possessed a forklift. It also seems that a modest printing company located at the same site did not have a forklift and was in the habit of

The dust and heat of the foundry proved lucrative for one entrepreneur – in the shape of a 'robust robot'.

© BG plc

borrowing the uncle's now and again. A few telephone calls later and our entrepreneur had his brochures, without the daunting price tag.

This story reflects three fundamental habits of successful entrepreneurs. First, a strict discipline of asset parsimony. Second, use of all the resources at the entrepreneur's disposal, in particular social capital. And finally, an approach to making investments of time and money that is analogous to the taking and exercising of financial options.

Asset parsimony

Most start-ups are chronically short of resources. So it is not surprising that entrepreneurs attempt to contain costs. Those of us who study entrepreneurship, however, observe that using the minimum possible amount of assets to deliver their outputs is not something that entrepreneurs do only under situations of cash starvation.

We see even very wealthy entrepreneurs adhere to the same stingy ways with which they began their careers. It seems that being conservative with expenditures is not merely dictated by the situation; it is an overriding philosophy regarding the creative use of assets that permeates the successful startup.

Consider the case of one of our recent graduates, who decided to get into the import/export business, trading from New York to his native Brazil. The first difficulty was that, being new to the business, it would be difficult to create credibility in the minds of potential customers. Using his small New York City apartment as a base, for example, was unlikely to instill a great sense of confidence in people who would have to entrust him with considerable advance business if he was to succeed. Clearly, a reputable office address seemed called for.

He could of course have simply taken a lease on such a space or rented shared space in one of those multiple-business complexes that have sprung up to serve exactly this kind of need. Doing so, however, violates one of the cardinal rules of asset parsimony: never incur fixed costs if they can be avoided.

How then to avoid incurring fixed costs on New York City real estate? The answer appeared in the form of an old school friend from Columbia days with an extremely fashionable Fifth Avenue address. The friend eventually agreed to let our entrepreneur borrow an unused desk and receive mail at his address. Within a month, this was extended to include access to telephone and fax equipment, delivery vans and secretarial support – all paid for but on a strictly variable basis. What is interesting about this arrangement is that both parties benefited. The entrepreneur acquired a valuable location and his host was paid for underutilized fixed assets.

Where the conventional corporate approach is often oriented toward maximizing returns on a net present value basis, entrepreneurs willingly sacrifice some potential returns in order to minimize fixed investments and maximize flexibility. This has the effect of limiting their exposure if the venture does not, after all, succeed as expected.

Successful entrepreneurs show genius at unlocking value tied up in underutilized assets. Renting computer time at night, laboratory equipment during the weekend and access to databases already owned are examples of how entrepreneurs, simply by being flexible enough to work when others aren't, can obtain access to resources at a fraction of what it would otherwise cost.

Successful entrepreneurs are also expert scavengers. Every day, corporations literally throw away valuable assets. One of my favorite stories in this regard is told by a former colleague at the Wharton School of the University of Pennsylvania, Ed Moldt.

At a time when the state of the art in computers was switching from card-read data input and storage to tape-based technology, companies began to aggressively shut down their card-reading operations and to throw away the equipment. So anxious were many to get the readers off the premises that not only were they not sold, good money was actually paid to have them removed.

In the midst of all this, Moldt recognized that the conversion from cards was unlikely to be complete and that even the companies making the leap to tape technology were likely to have a need for some card-reading for several years still to come. He then began quietly acquiring card-reading equipment.

As he hoped, the need for card-reading had not been eliminated but few suppliers remained with capacity to do the work, leaving him in possession of a near-monopoly. This is surely a case of asset parsimony taken to the extreme – not only did he not expend capital to acquire his assets, he was actually paid to take them on.

The same philosophy that applies to the use of physical assets can be seen in the entrepreneurial use of human talent as well. Salespeople, for example, will often be generously paid but on a commission basis not a salaried one. Rather than use high-priced consultants to do market studies or develop proposals, entrepreneurs might call on friends or family or volunteer to sponsor a student project. In these cases, the basic idea is to bring cash flows in before allowing major expenditures.

The moral of the asset parsimony tale is one coined by Ian Macmillan, director of Wharton's acclaimed Snider Entrepreneurial Center, some years ago:

- *Never buy new what can be bought secondhand.*
- *Never buy what can be rented.*

- *Never rent what can be borrowed.*
- *Never borrow what can be begged.*
- *Never beg what can be salvaged.*

Together with being choosy about how they invest their money, successful entrepreneurs are brilliant at leveraging social capital into valuable opportunities. They tend to be inveterate, energetic and continuous networkers. **Social capital**

Consider the approach to opportunity spotting utilized by Per Lovgren, a Swedish founder of many companies based on his knowledge of sophisticated CAD/CAM technology. The worst return on investment Lovgren has ever enjoyed is in excess of 500 per cent, to give the reader a sense of the power of his approach.

Lovgren travels extensively and on his travels frequently arranges social evenings out with members of his network of management consultant acquaintances. While he is quite happy to pick up the bill for an evening's entertainment, the consultant will be pressed to articulate a problem that his clients are facing that requires a technical solution.

One problem that surfaced on such an occasion was the labor difficulties being experienced by foundry owners in Northern Europe. Foundries are dirty, hot, uncomfortable places to work in and finding labor willing to endure these conditions was becoming increasingly difficult.

While a logical alternative would be to automate as far as possible, explained the management consultant, robots don't do well in the foundry environment either. The grit, dust and heat bring their mechanical control systems to a halt in short order.

Lovgren then set out to find whether something like a 'robust robot' was technologically viable. He tapped into a second network, this time of professors of engineering. Over breakfast, the professor evaluated the problem, declared the technology to be a non-issue and offered to make a prototype for a budget of something like $300,000. At this juncture, Lovgren could easily have written a personal cheque and gotten the project underway. But wait – that would have violated the philosophy of asset parsimony.

What he did instead was to use his management consultant network to obtain access to their companies' foundry consultants. Using these contacts, he was able to convince foundry managers to each contribute a small sum to the development of the prototype. Note that not only did this allow him to proceed without investing his own money but it also ensured ready acceptance of the first prototypes and subsequent installation of the final product in a critical mass of foundries.

Memberships in networks, in other words, creates a form of 'social' capital, which, much like economic capital, can be used to create productive assets.

A final observation about entrepreneurial resource acquisition strategies is that they can be likened to the taking and exercising of options. In financial economics, options contracts represent small investments made against an underlying asset that yields the opportunity, but not the obligation, to purchase that asset at a later date. Options thus provide access to opportunities at relatively low cost. **The options approach**

In pursuing their business opportunities, successful entrepreneurs adopt a similar pattern of investment. By building social capital, they begin to lay the foundation for gathering the information and ultimately insight that generates new business opportunities. They can then mobilize their networks to acquire resources at minimum cost and subsequently validate their initial assumptions.

This has the effect in real terms of making incrementally more significant commitments to the business as better and better data are revealed. Should the indicators at any point suggest that the business is not viable, the entrepreneur can simply stop pursuing it or redirect attention into other areas without having incurred huge losses in plant and assets.

The options logic allows us to pinpoint how asset parsimony and social capital help create wealth. If assets are acquired sequentially, with minimum possible investment, they limit the downside losses in the event of failure, just as financial options do.

By deftly mobilizing their social capital through unique information and friendship networks, entrepreneurs can eliminate uncertainty as to the value of the underlying business in ways that are idiosyncratic to them.

Thus, only someone with Lovgren's access simultaneously to those who could identify the source of the problem (the management consultant), could define the technical solution (the engineering professor) and could provide financing (the foundry managers) is likely to have started this particular business. Only someone with Lovgren's skill at maintaining rock-bottom investment amounts would enjoy his level of substantial returns on equity. This has the effect of simultaneously allowing him to build a substantial business from an ordinary-looking labor problem while preventing competitors from simply copying what he was able to do.

In sum, we see in successful entrepreneurs not so much sudden flashes of inspiration and great good fortune as a consistent set of conscientiously applied disciplines that ensure the minimum possible investment for the maximum possible returns. ∎

The discussion presented here has benefited enormously from conversations with Ian C. MacMillan of the Wharton School of the University of Pennsylvania and Sue Birley of Imperial College, London.

Catching the punter's eye

Peter Kelly details the criteria venture capitalists and private investors set when they are considering whether or not to risk their cash.

'There is no question that irrespective of the horse (the product), horse race (the market), or odds (financial criteria), it is the jockey (the entrepreneur) who fundamentally determines whether the venture capitalist will place a bet at all.'
Professor Ian MacMillan, Wharton School of the University of Pennsylvania

Any experienced 'punter' will tell you that there are two fundamental facts of life in trying to predict the outcome of any race. First, it is a simple truth that the future cannot be predicted with accuracy. Second, there is inevitably an element of luck involved in 'picking winners'.

Having said this, before placing a bet, experienced punters often gather as much information as possible on the condition of the horse, the track and the jockey in the hope that the additional insights provided will enhance their ability to overcome these given facts.

This horse racing analogy applies equally to the world of the venture capitalist. Any experienced 'investor' will tell you that there are two fundamental 'facts of life' when trying to determine which ventures to back.

First, the only thing that is known for certain is that the projections upon which an investment decision is based are 'wrong'. Investors and entrepreneurs alike hope that the venture's performance will exceed projections. However, in reality, Murphy's Law often holds true – whatever the problems encountered along the way may be, the venture inevitably takes longer to develop than planned. Second, timing and luck can, and do, influence the level of returns achieved by investors.

Venture capitalists make 'informed bets' on the basis of information presented to them in a business plan that outlines the nature of the opportunity, the strategy developed to exploit it profitably and on a sustainable basis, and the credentials of the management team that is going to 'make it happen'.

In the course of due diligence, investors will seek out additional information to satisfy themselves that:
- all elements of the plan 'hang together'
- relevant risks have been identified and accounted for whenever possible
- prospective returns offered adequately compensate for the risk being borne by the investor and entrepreneur alike and, most importantly
- the management team has the skills, drive and ambition to succeed, particularly in the face of the inevitable pitfalls associated with building and managing a business.

Investors work under the presumption that through gathering additional information and insights, their ability to identify 'winners' is enhanced.

For an entrepreneur seeking external equity from either venture capitalists or private individuals (so called 'business angels'), it is important to understand the

Spotting the winner. Experienced investors, like the punters, will do their homework before parting with their money.

© Philip O'Mara, FT

various criteria investors use to evaluate potential investment opportunities.

In many ways, investors are like the Yukon panhandlers of the gold rush days. Panhandlers spent a great deal of time and energy sifting through silt and gravel in search of gold nuggets. Likewise, investors sift through a great number of potential opportunities to identify those of truly high potential that are worthy of further detailed consideration.

A vast majority of proposals, typically 80 per cent or more, are rejected after a cursory review of the business plan. When an investor chooses to review a proposal in greater detail, relatively few are actually funded. For every hundred proposals received, perhaps two or three receive backing.

How do investors decide which proposals to back? Venture capitalists and private investors tend to rely on similar decision-making processes in determining which proposals to support. The two markets are in many ways distinct, however, and thus it is useful to discuss the approach of each separately. (*The private investment market – so-called 'business angels' – is discussed in detail in Part 3 – see p. 86.*)

The venture capital perspective

Generally speaking, venture capital funds screen proposals on the basis of a number of generic criteria including: a) the minimum size of the investment they are willing to consider (usually over £1m); b) the industries that they are prepared to back; c) the stage of development of the business (seed, start-up, expansion); and d) the geographical focus of the venture's operations.

It is important for entrepreneurs seeking venture capital to identify the 'right' venture capitalist(s) to approach by ensuring, as far as possible, that their proposal 'fits with' the investor's profile. Fortunately for entrepreneurs, venture capital associations in many countries publish comprehensive annual directories that provide contact and fund-specific information to aid the search process.

There has been a marked shift in the industry away from the provision of small amounts of capital (less than £500,000) to ventures in early stages of development to the financing of larger, later-stage management buy-in and buy-out transactions.

Having said this, a small number of funds do focus exclusively on small, early-stage deals and other major market participants, most notably 3I (Investors in Industry) in the UK, continue to invest in these situations.

The message for entrepreneurs seeking relatively modest infusions of capital to finance early-stage development is that it is not impossible to secure venture capital funding but it is highly improbable.

Assuming for the moment that your proposal meets the fund's general screening criteria, venture capital companies are still left with the daunting task of separating the 'wheat from the chaff'.

At this stage of the process, the business plan is briefly reviewed by a fund manager with the aim of forming an opinion on certain key aspects of the plan including:

- the nature of the opportunity
- the potential size of the market; and
- the strategy proposed to exploit it.

If the investor is not satisfied that the opportunity is in fact 'real', that the market growth projections are unrealistic and/or that there is no meaningful basis upon which to create a sustainable and profitable competitive position, the proposal will likely be rejected.

Simply put, investors will focus their efforts on those few plans that fit their investment criteria, are well thought out and offer the prospect of achieving compound annual returns on investment ranging from 30 per cent for management buy-outs to 50 per cent or more per annum for early-stage investments.

In the minority of situations where a more detailed investigation is warranted, venture capitalists will invest a great deal of time consulting with internal and external sources of objective information about key aspects of the plan. They will talk to potential customers, suppliers, patent lawyers, technology experts and the like.

Venture capitalists will also test out the financial viability of the plan by conducting a sensitivity analysis on the assumptions upon which the plan is based.

During this due diligence phase, the 'management capability factor' takes on added importance. Regular meetings are arranged between fund representatives and members of the management team. Aside from being able to question specific aspects of the plan presented to them, through regular interaction with the management team, investors are able to gain a better understanding of the team's true capabilities, their ability to work together as a team and their commitment to the venture.

Testing management resolve to deal with the inevitable setbacks and challenges associated with building a business is often a decisive factor in the final decision to invest. Additional information obtained in the course of due diligence narrows the opportunity set down even further – at the end of the process a 'typical' venture capital fund will invest in only two or three opportunities from every 100 received.

**The private
investor
perspective**

Private investors rely on a similar process in deciding which proposals to back. However, unlike venture capital funds, which maintain a highly visible, public presence, private individuals prefer a degree of anonymity, both as a means of controlling the volume of their deal flow and of protecting sensitive personal information pertaining to their private investment activity.

Approaching the 'right' individual investor is inevitably a hit-or-miss affair for ventures seeking private equity.

From our discussions with private investors, potential investment opportunities are screened on the basis of size, location, and venture needs. In general, private individuals invest:

● in smaller amounts than do venture capital funds (usually in amounts between £5,000 and £500,000)

● in ventures that are located in close proximity to their home base of operations; and, often,

● in situations where the business can directly benefit from the expertise of the investor.

Most private investors have managerial experience in the area of the new venture and are prepared to back promising proposals in a variety of different industries, particularly if they choose to invest as part of a syndicate of investors. Entrepreneurs seeking private equity need to be very clear about what contribution they want the investor to make and are well advised to seek out potential investors located in close proximity to their operation.

As the process unfolds, the quality of the entrepreneur/management team becomes an increasingly important consideration. Working as closely as they do with the venture, the personal chemistry developed between the investor and the management team is an absolutely vital consideration. In the words of one investor: 'No matter how good the opportunity appears, if I cannot get on with the people, there is *no* deal!'

**Advice for
entrepreneurs**

What is the point of investing the time and resources into developing a business plan if there is only a two per cent or three per cent chance that the entrepreneur will be successful in raising funds?

In my experience, a great many business plans fail to pass an initial screen for a number of reasons, some of which can be easily dealt with, others less so. *(A checklist of the main issues that need to be covered in a business plan appears in Part 4, p. 116.)*

In some cases, it is not altogether clear to the investor what the nature of the opportunity is or, for that matter, how much capital is required and for what purpose. There should be no doubt in the mind of the investor 'what' they are being asked to fund. This information should be conveyed in the executive summary of the plan in clear and unambiguous terms.

The real challenge for entrepreneurs is to prepare a plan that 'captures the investor's imagination'. Business plans are marketing documents – the messages conveyed should encourage the reader to 'continue reading'.

Many entrepreneurs I have met are passionate believers in their idea or concept. Enthusiasm creates excitement and interest on the part of investors but, when taken to an extreme, passion often gets translated by entrepreneurs in their business plans as 'preaching the upside' and 'ignoring the downside'.

In my experience, investors want 'a balanced view' assuring themselves in the process that the entrepreneurs:

- know what they are talking about
- have identified and considered potential risks from their perspective; and
- are committed to see the project through.

But a clearly articulated and convincing business plan alone is not enough. The plan must be carefully targeted to the appropriate audience. In guiding their decision to seek venture capital or, alternatively, equity from private individuals, entrepreneurs should address the following questions.

Is the amount of capital required large enough to be of interest to venture capital funds? If so, which funds have a stated preference for investing in ventures operating in my industry and/or at my venture's stage of development? If not, do I have a clear idea of what type of expertise and involvement I am seeking from a private investor?

These guidelines are little consolation for the many business plans that fail to secure funding for no other reason than that the two parties hold irreconcilable differences of opinion – situations where the entrepreneur sees an opportunity and the investor does not. In this respect, one can only conclude that opportunity is, indeed, in the 'eye of the beholder'. ■

How to build a strong launch pad

Traditional market entry strategies adopted by large corporations are increasingly unsuitable for today's turbulent times. In this respect, new ventures have some advantages. **David Molian** sets out the current position and offers some appropriate new venture strategies.

'Is launching new products harder or easier today than it was ten or twenty years ago?' Ask this question of a brand manager in a large consumer goods company and almost certainly the response will be 'harder'.

Probe for the reasons why, and the usual suspects emerge: intensified competition; consumers who are both more value conscious and less brand loyal; dwindling product life cycles; and increasingly powerful retailers.

Estimates vary for the rate at which new products fail in the market-place but the consensus seems to be that most new products in most markets will fall by the wayside. In some industries, such as the software business in the 1980s, the failure rate can be as high as 90 per cent.

The problem is compounded by the increasing pressure to innovate, partly as a result of fast-changing consumer tastes and behavior and partly because of the possibilities arising from enhanced or novel technologies.

In the case of established brands, managers search for ways to exploit the 'equity', or market strength, of a brand through product variants (the mini and maxi chocolate Mars bars, for example) or via diversifications into adjacent segments (Mars milk drinks and Mars ice cream). New products that come to market without a parent brand must make their own way in a world that, if not actively hostile, is usually indifferent.

If market conditions are tough for established organizations, how much more difficult the environment must be for the new venture, especially the start-up. Well, yes and no.

Compared with existing businesses, the typical new venture has fewer resources of every kind, fragile or embryonic networks, and a need to build trust and credibility among both customers and suppliers. It carries more inherent risks. Yet it also possesses certain intangible assets that do not appear on the balance sheet. Speed, or the ability to adapt rapidly, and a capacity for flexibility are two of the more important ones. A management that is hungry is a third asset. And *not* being burdened by the weight of corporate history may well be a fourth.

The management of risk

One of the major themes of *Mastering Enterprise* is the management of risk. How exactly to get into business is frequently one of the major areas of uncertainty in most new ventures. To highlight the options faced by a new venture, it is worth examining how large businesses have traditionally managed the risks associated with entry into new markets or taking new products to market.

For big business, geographical expansion typically followed a pattern: first, importing agencies were used; then, as demand was established, a subsidiary was created or purchased. The overseas businesses would expand through the transfer of product and process technology from the parent as and when the market was ready.

New product introduction, or entry into new market sectors, also followed clear guidelines. Large consumer companies were interested in products with mass market potential, not niche items. The planning, testing and introduction cycle was an extensive one, supported through qualitative and quantitative market research, with the decision to launch normally dependent on a successful 'test market', from which national market performance could be predicted. Finally, if the project was sanctioned, large resources in terms of advertising, salesforce and marketing support were committed to minimize the risk of failure.

Not surprisingly, the time between product concept and full-scale launch could be measured in many months if not years. This was acceptable in a stable environment of steadily rising, predictable consumer demand in which all the players played by the same rules – a description that fits the quarter century that followed the Second World War.

Today, relatively few markets (in the developed world at least) conform to that description. Markets that are growing are frequently turbulent and hard to forecast. Those markets that are static – such as mature commodity sectors like soap powder or mass cosmetics – may contain a few pockets of niche activity but are generally a battleground in which a few dominant competitors wrestle each other for an extra quarter per cent of market share.

The upshot of all this is that big business has had to rethink radically its approach to innovation and new product launches. Extended periods of commercialization, where an innovation is handed from research to development to marketing like a baton in a relay race, are just too long. In too many markets the window of opportunity is lost. Yet trying to compress that time to market can create its own risks, as Unilever's recent experience with Omo Power (Persil in the UK) shows. **The rules have changed**

Second, confidence and certainty of success can no longer be attained in the same way. Firepower is no guarantee of victory. IBM's PC Jr and Kodak's Disk Camera are just two examples of failed new product launches supported by hundreds of millions of dollars.

In turbulent times, market risk is closely tied to the dynamics of the supply or value chain. Within any industry there is a sequence of transactions that take place between the raw materials producers and the final consumers. This may be complex, as with most manufacturing activities, or it may be simple, as is the generally the case with services. **The value chain and opportunity**

To succeed, the new venture must create value for which a customer is prepared to pay. In each stage of the chain, value is added, the profitability and relative power within the chain varying for each player. The market entry decision is closely related to the position within the value chain that the new venture adopts.

In dynamic markets, opportunity can be seen as the outcome of *changes within* the value chain or the *capacity to create change within* the value chain. Consider two examples. First, the groceries sector.

In the UK 30 years ago, creating and sustaining a national grocery brand meant conforming to a certain set of criteria. The manufacturer had to be able to deliver to thousands of small retailers nationwide and to handle the associated invoicing and account management. It also had to create and support national advertising campaigns backed by point of sale promotions or neighborhood coupon drops.

Large companies tackled the problem by integrating their activities right along the value or supply chain: from agreeing long-term contracts with suppliers, to running fleets of trucks and delivery vans and maintaining a national network of regional and local delivery depots. Smaller organizations used intermediaries such as wholesalers and brokers, which could achieve economies of scale through aggregating product lines and breaking bulk further down the supply chain.

Fast forward to the 1990s. Today, a small grocery producer can achieve nationwide penetration through supplying just a single big retail account. Delivery can be contracted out and is usually restricted to a handful of large drops each week at the customer's central warehouses. And building brands through million pound advertising campaigns is not an issue since the retailer is marketing the product under its own label (*see* Figures 1 and 2 for examples of changing value/supply chains).

This transformation has taken place, of course, because of the change in the balance of power between the manufacturer and the retailer in the UK as the grocery trade has concentrated into the hands of the multiples. Established

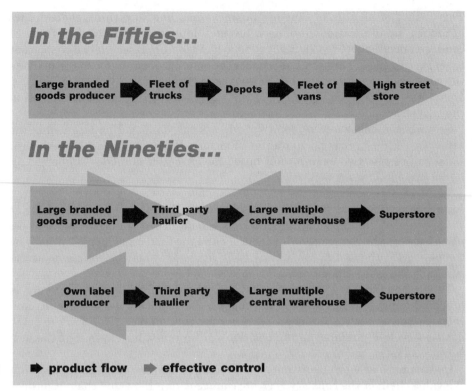

Figure 1: Changing
the balance of
power in the supply
chain

branded-goods producers see themselves under threat and point to diminishing consumer choice.

But the other side of the equation is that opportunities have been created for literally hundreds of new suppliers to gain entry into the market because the value chain has been transformed. Indeed, certain expanding groceries sectors, such as ethnic foods, are dominated by such enterprises.

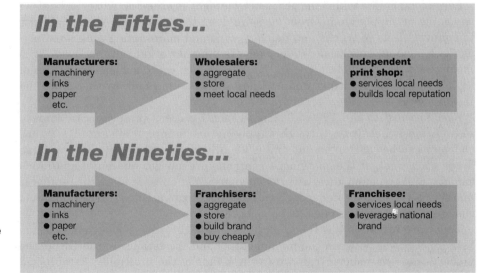

Figure 2:
Reconfiguring the
value chain: the
high street print
shop

The second example illustrates how enterprising new businesses create market opportunities using the potential created by shifting social behavior.

Mail order has its roots in the 19th century. In the UK, it became primarily a mechanism for providing the poorer classes with cheap credit for clothing. Up until the late 1980s, mail order expenditure by the wealthier ABC1 socio-economic groups remained disproportionately tiny. Then something happened. The middle classes became comfortable with the idea of buying from a catalog.

Large US companies, such as Land's End and LL Bean, began to operate in the UK. Traditional catalog specialists moved up-market and new ventures, such as Cotton Traders, Racing Green and Boden, rapidly carved niches for themselves. This change in social attitudes had lowered the barriers to entry: such companies could get into retailing without tying up their working capital in a high-street presence.

They were assisted by the emergent technology of low-cost computerized databases and widespread adoption of the credit card. In the late 1990s we shall see more and more new ventures that get into direct marketing or shopping from home via the electronic equivalent of the print catalog, the Internet web-site.

The value chain and risk management can be usefully brought together as a two-dimensional framework in which to view market entry strategy. Given that each new venture occupies a position somewhere in a value chain, a choice has to be made as to *how much of the marketing risk the new venture assumes, and how much is in some form shared by other players in the chain.* **Risk sharing versus market access**

For all ventures there is a spectrum of risk sharing. At one end are businesses such as biotechnology laboratories whose discoveries are normally licensed to large pharmaceutical houses for downstream exploitation in new drugs. Like an author, this kind of company lives on a royalty income generated by its intellectual property, while the risk of taking the discovery to market is very largely borne by the counter-party.

At the other end of the spectrum are organizations that sell direct to the market, who position themselves in the final section of the value chain, such as catalog retailers. Between the two extremes lies a huge variety of risk-sharing arrangements, covering agencies, wholesaling, franchising, subcontracting and so on.

The second dimension is access to the market, which also runs along a spectrum from the immediate relationship with the end customer enjoyed by the direct sales company to the very remote connection of the biotechnologist. **Figure 3**

As Figure 3 shows, there is typically an inverse relationship between a high degree of risk sharing and access to the market. Note that we are not talking here of *absolute* risk: if the essence of an opportunity is a company's capacity to react swiftly to customer demand, as in the fashion business, assuming the entire marketing risk may well be less risky than laying off that risk via a counter-party through whom contact with the customer is filtered.

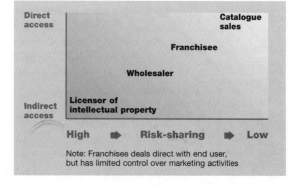

Note: Franchisee deals direct with end user, but has limited control over marketing activities

51

Conversely, if a direct line to the ultimate buyer is of no importance in the business concept, selling direct is unlikely to make much sense.

Equally, we are describing *entry strategies* rather than the long-term shape that a business assumes. It is hard to envisage how an organization could employ business format franchizing (for example, instant printing) as a means of getting into business, since the concept has to be tested and made to work before it can be replicated. Franchizing is a very effective means of expanding certain kinds of business more rapidly than through organic growth or acquisition. On the other hand, from the perspective of a franchisee, purchasing a franchise can be a very appropriate method of using risk-sharing to get into business.

Prototyping and flexibility

Selecting the appropriate risk-sharing arrangement is a *strategic* decision. Marketing risk can also be managed *operationally* by consideration of the process by which a new venture is brought to market.

It was observed earlier that traditional large organization approaches to the innovation process can be too protracted and cumbersome a way of responding to market changes: and, in any case, the typical new venture does not have the resources to emulate this process.

There is, however, a very important element of good innovation practice that the new venture should focus on, namely the notion of *prototyping*. The term comes from large engineering projects but it has application to all sorts of new ventures. A restaurant business can be prototyped – that is in a format that is acknowledged (by the management at least) as provisional, to be modified in response to market reaction. So can a service.

This concept is valuable for the following reasons:

● Prototyping is a means of containing risk through limiting the commitment of resources. This is especially critical in markets of great uncertainty, such as high-technology sectors, where customer demand or market potential cannot be known or even guestimated in advance of entry.

● Prototyping allows the new venture to test the robustness of the product or service concept, often through giving target customers access in advance of the launch. This is common practice in the software industry, where new software is routinely tested by selected customers (who benefit from privileged access) prior to full release. One of the UK's premier health and fitness clubs adapted this approach. While the club was still under construction, local residents were mailed invitations to tour the site. Those who accepted were shown the plans for the final design and invited to comment, with the result that a number of suggestions were incorporated while it was still possible to do so. The club also, it need hardly be said, acquired a useful database of prospective members.

● Prototyping fosters a mentality of flexibility and responsiveness to customers. Some new ventures start with the advantage of an advance order book. The first wave of customers may represent the core clientele of the business in the medium and even the long term. The first product or service may constitute the main business activity. Equally, neither condition may apply, and within a short space of time the business may be looking both for new customers *and* new products if it is to grow and prosper.

● In many new venture environments, conventional market research methods may not apply. The costs alone of a professional research agency are often prohibitive. But an even greater obstacle may lie in the product/service concept. Where demand is latent (or believed to be latent), the only way to prove it exists is to test the market by offering an early version of the concept in the full knowledge that it may change as a result of customer exposure.

Hand-in-hand with prototyping goes the notion of incremental commercialization. Traditional modes of innovation are based on a clear separation between development and launch – at a certain point development was frozen and the finished product entered the market.

Incremental commercialization

Clearly, in a manufacturing business (unless it is making bespoke products), a time is reached when mass production to a specification must start. However, even the established approach to new product development includes an element of incremental commercialization in the form of test markets, which allow a company to modify the product either in its physical form or in the way in which it is marketed before a full launch.

For many new ventures, attempting to keep development and launch as distinct processes is inappropriate. For one thing, in line with the rest of the economy, most new ventures today will be service-based at least as much as product-based.

Marketing doctrine states that the way to sell a service is to make it, as much as possible, into a product. But the beauty of a service-based business is the speed and flexibility with which the service can be modified in response to the market. At the point of entering the market, the new venture needs to exploit that inherent advantage and avoid undue rigidity in advance of feedback from customers.

A further consideration is that in many sectors the boundaries between research, development and launch are fuzzy because of the nature of the business. Take software, which is a product category in continuous evolution. The point at which a piece of software is 'finished' is, in a real sense, arbitrary. Customers are purchasing not a one-off product but a stream of upgrades and new versions, which arrive at ever-shortening intervals.

Summary

A management team should bring to the market entry decision the same skills that characterize the successful entrepreneur – the capacity to determine where in the marketplace the opportunity lies; the ability to work with that opportunity and shape it in response to customers' needs; the feel for managing risk to acceptable levels through the use of partners or suitable intermediaries; and, above all, the ability to smooth the path into the market through the limited exposure offered through techniques such as prototyping and incremental commercialization. ■

Marking the key points on the opportunity map

Daniel Muzyka provides guidance on what makes a good opportunity.

The name of the game in entrepreneurship is adding value. This includes value added for all parties, especially for the business pursuing the opportunity. The product must add clear value in the eyes of the customer, and distributors and retailers, if they are involved.

How do we measure value-added in real terms? The rule of thumb shared by venture capitalists and other risk capital investors is that you should have a gross margin of 35 per cent to 40 per cent or better. This means that in the financial evaluation of an opportunity, the turnover, less the direct cost of labor and materials to produce a product or deliver a service, should produce a number that is at least 40 per cent of the turnover. This is the real value-added of your product.

Why does this matter? Well it is obvious that a higher gross margin translates into a higher potential 'bottom line'. Furthermore, gross margin indicates how much value is being added by unique intellectual, design and marketing resources. If not much value is being added, why do it? Without this value-added, you are taking on a significant risk while not creating much, despite the hard entrepreneurial work of assembling people and assets that the opportunity requires.

The magnitude of the opportunity

How big does an opportunity have to be? This question is a little akin to asking how many angels can dance on the head of a pin. The more serious, and right, answer is: 'it depends'.

It depends upon the magnitude of value you wish to create and that will attract and retain your interest. It depends upon the size of opportunity that will attract investors who are of interest to you. (Risk capital investors usually have a minimum value in mind.) It depends upon the value that is required for you to position yourself in the market to be an effective and growing competitor. It depends upon that famous economic factor 'minimum efficient scale' – how big do you have to be to be efficient in the use of required assets? And it depends upon the magnitude of the business necessary to attract the key team members you require to make the business successful.

Growth-oriented entrepreneurs do not only consider the magnitude of the opportunity but also the basic expected growth rate. True growth-oriented entrepreneurs are very focused on the potential growth rate. Some realize that too fast a growth rate over an extended period is a negative aspect of opportunities. It is difficult to manage, it attracts competitors like ants at a picnic, and it requires extensive and continuous financing to provide adequate working capital. They also realize that too low a growth rate will not permit them to create their desired value and will not attract key stakeholders.

What are the required growth rates? This varies considerably and obviously depends upon the context. However, we can generally say that sustained single digits are too low and sustained triple digits are very difficult. Obviously, this question also depends upon just how big a business you want to build. A 'lifestyle' opportunity probably should not grow too big.

Business economics

In this context this simply means profit. There are two important issues for the would-be entrepreneur: How much profit and where exactly is the profit created? If a business does not add enough value, you cannot have a reasonable profit.

Beyond this, the question is: where in the income statement and balance sheet do you create value? How do you make money? Where does the profit come from?

You need to know the key levers in the business that make money for you. You also need to know whether these levers are sustainable. For example, do you make money because you are able to move quickly to supply shops with bread when they under-ordered from their regular suppliers (who visit them once a day only) and their customers are demanding more?

The ability to move quickly and fill spot demand (at a premium price, of course) may be the basis of the business. Understanding these levers makes you understand what your focus should be in managing the business and permits you to test whether it is sustainable and appropriate for you.

One business I knew had a tendency to upgrade every neighborhood it entered. The business itself made a solid though not terribly exciting profit. The entrepreneur would go in, buy a property in which the business was located, upgrade it, start up business and later sell out to a franchisee. Other businesses were attracted to the area and would also contribute to upgrading the area. When an evaluation of the worth of the property was made for sale to the franchisee, the entrepreneur would invariably make a large capital gain.

Where did he make his money? In the real estate conversion. He was clear on where he was dedicating his time and energy. He didn't fritter away time on trying to squeeze major improvements in the profitability of the underlying shop. Rather, he would move on to look for new locations.

How long can you pursue the opportunity?

No opportunity lasts forever. In fact, I encourage you to contact me if you find a highly profitable (legal) opportunity that lasts forever. First, I might like to invest. Second, I would like to record it so that others would know it. The real question is how long does an opportunity last before everyone else decides to jump in and shift competition to a cost base rather than value base, or worse?

What are the determinants of how long you can uniquely pursue an opportunity? First, do you have some contract that makes a technology uniquely available to you? It may not be a technology that you have unique control of but, rather, a unique source of supply or a unique distribution channel. Second, are you addressing some niche opportunity that substitutes for existing products or provides a strong but unique base for development? Customers whose needs you specifically meet represent a powerful source of competitive advantage. Third, do you have some unique relationship that provides you with a competitive advantage? Fourth, do you have some way of creating 'post-entry barriers' (something someone has to spend money on to overcome) for other organizations who follow you into the business?

Your fit and belief in the opportunity

It is often the more emotional side of any opportunity that makes that marginal difference in the success of one entrepreneur and the failure of another. You alone can assess these factors. Do you like the opportunity? Do you really believe in the opportunity? These factors matter because therein lie your level of likely persistence in the face of all the normal difficulties encountered by entrepreneurs.

What are some of the finer aspects of good opportunities?

There are a few lessons about opportunity that long-term successful entrepreneurs have learned.

● *This opportunity leads to others.* To build up a profitable, value-creating business in the long term, an original opportunity must lead to other opportunities.

● *The opportunity helps you build leverageable skills.* Another characteristic of a good opportunity is related to the skills developed and exercised within the organization. Good opportunities are those that force an organization to develop a skill that can be leveraged for the pursuit of many new ideas.

● *Opportunity should not be evaluated or pursued alone.* Investigations of 'serial entrepreneurs' and how they identify successive successful opportunities suggests that the saying 'two heads are better than one' may be true. Successful serial entrepreneurs usually seek out other individuals, but often just one, with whom they work from business to business. The partner adds new skills to the mix and permits a more robust evaluation and implementation of opportunities.

The final points you may wish to consider encourage you to review the competitive environment and how you compete.

● *Are near competitors 'sharks'?* There are some opportunities that involve competition (or near competition) with companies and individuals that are not very aggressive. On the other hand, in some industries, existing competitors 'eat their young'. Look around and see if there are any new companies that have actually survived in the broad industry you are considering.

● *How you compete is more important than where you compete.* Worry about your model of competition and don't get fixated on the question of where you are going to compete. Searching for location is important, and needs to be undertaken, but only after you have assessed how you will compete and make money in your business. ■

The pitfalls and potential of franchising

Stephen Spinelli argues that as long as both sides contribute appropriately then franchising can be a key enterprise success story.

Is franchising entrepreneurship? Certainly, most people would agree that Ray Kroc, founder of the giant restaurant chain McDonald's, or Anita Roddick, The Body Shop founder, were entrepreneurs. But their companies are the franchiser, the owner of the trade mark and system. What about the franchisees, those individuals who buy a franchise, implement the concept on a local basis and serve customers? Are they entrepreneurs?

The question revolves around more than linguistics. The central issue regards the ability of the franchisee to create wealth. Clearly, there are no guarantees of wealth when a new venture is founded. Return *and* risk are key ingredients of the entrepreneurial process, and therefore the potential of failure looms in any business start-up. However, if the buyer of a franchise is simply purchasing employment, then a franchise is no more than an alternative to an employment agency.

The franchise industry

Franchising is a major part of the US economy and is substantial in the UK and other western European countries. More than one-third of all retailing in the US, worth almost $750bn annually, is generated through franchised outlets. As much as ten per cent of retailing in the UK is generated by franchises.

Franchising is generally divided into product franchises and business format franchises. The product franchise is characterized by franchised dealers who concentrate on a company's product line and, to some extent, identify their business with that company. A car dealer selling one manufacturer's models is an example. Business format franchising accompanies the trademark and distribution rights with information provided by the franchiser to the franchisee on the production processes and delivery system. Business format franchising usually includes a marketing plan, documented and enforced procedures, process assistance, and business development and innovation. This article concentrates on business format franchising.

The belief that franchising is an entrepreneurial venture is supported by the phenomenon of multiple-outlet ownership by franchisees. Some individuals are buying more than one outlet of any given franchise and even purchasing different types of franchises. They achieve growth and diversification through franchising.

One of the largest franchisers in the world is UK conglomerate Allied Domecq, which owns Dunkin Donuts, Baskin Robbins, Firkin Pubs and others. Bob Rosenberg, head of Allied Domecq's franchise operations, believes that Allied Domecq franchising has substantial growth remaining, much of it in Europe. 'We can double our size in the US, and the potential in Europe is exponential,' he says.

Confident of growth in the US and Europe: Bob Rosenberg, head of franchise operations at Allied Domecq, one of the world's largest franchisers.

Allied Domecq is not alone. Over 50 per cent of members of the International Franchise Association (an association formed by franchisers) have international departments and 93 per cent of those companies expect to increase international expansion. Research indicates that 22 per cent of franchisees own more than one outlet. The Kwik Kopy group sees franchising and multiple store franchisees as a key aspect of the growth in entrepreneurship in Europe. The company argues that its franchise owners are with customers every day, focussing on their needs and sharing better ways to fill those needs with their franchisee colleagues. 'That is why franchising works. We are not interested in just growing, we want greater success.'

Franchisees are becoming larger and more sophisticated. KFC (formerly Kentucky Fried Chicken) has granted franchise rights to Mitsubishi in Japan. In 1991, the European Community approved a block exemption to anti-trust regulations so that franchisers may now sell in larger geographic territories, allowing franchisees to build a number of outlets.

Keeping the franchisee satisfied?

According to US franchise lawyer Eric Karp: 'The relationship is evolving. There is clearly an understanding that building equity is an important aspect of the franchise purchase decision. That means the productive franchisee-franchiser relationship is a long-term strategic relationship that builds wealth for both parties. When franchisees can't do better than a salary, the relationship breaks down'.

Figure 1

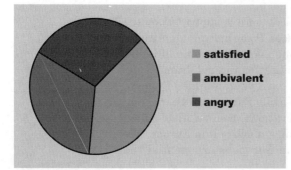

- satisfied
- ambivalent
- angry

While the International Franchise Association proclaims a 95 per cent success rate for franchisees, recent research at Imperial College (Steve Spinelli and Sue Birley: *An Empirical Analysis of Conflict in the Franchise System,* Imperial College, London) indicates that almost 30 per cent of franchisees are dissatisfied.

Franchisee satisfaction appears more linked to the manner in which the relationship is conducted than to issues involving finance.

Most franchise contracts are long term (five to 20 years) and, generally, there should be a delineation of responsibilities between the franchiser and the franchisee based on competitive advantages. Those centralized functions that carry economies of scale, such as the acquisition of supply and the creation and purchase of advertising, are assigned to the franchiser. On-site implementation, including real estate, hiring of employees and the local sales effort, is left to the franchisee.

It is not surprising that our research finds most franchisees would like more services that are provided better. Figure 2 is a list of the key activities involved in the franchisee-franchiser relationship showing those that franchisees view as important and how adequately they regarded them as being provided. We used a 1 (clearly not important or clearly not adequate) to 5 (most important or completely adequate) scale.

More important in our research was defining which of these service 'gaps' caused dissatisfaction in the relationship. Clearly, the bundle of marketing functions (national advertising, promoting new products and services, market information and analysis, and organizing local advertising co-operatives) are the most sensitive issues for franchisees. Good franchisers are good marketers in the view of franchisees. In general, however, franchisees have a clear tolerance zone of acceptable franchiser behavior.

Service variable	Importance Mean	Adequacy Mean
Resolving disagreements fairly	4.47	3.02
Effective national advertising	4.46	3.10
Promoting new products & services	4.36	3.10
Developing new products & services	4.33	3.11
Clearly defined operating procedures	4.11	3.38
Market information & analysis	4.07	2.39
Programs & procedures for training employees	4.07	2.94
Access to franchiser management	3.99	3.35
Acting as a supplier of products	3.90	3.36
Training in management skills	3.90	2.58
Organizing local advertising cooperatives	3.77	2.40
Support in new store development	3.76	2.90
Advice on management problems	3.76	2.80
Financial assistance and credit	3.74	2.53
Training in accounting & bookkeeping	3.53	2.48
Advice on financial management	3.52	2.30
Provision of standardized equipment	3.49	3.31
Advice on inventory control	3.45	2.75

**Figure 2:
Franchiser service variables – importance versus adequacy**

The franchise method of growth is predicated on the assumption that value has been developed through the careful operation, testing and documentation of a commercially viable idea. The essence of franchisee due diligence is to verify the ability of the franchise to create wealth through a business format and for that format to be transferred for local execution.

What franchisees should look for

Prospective franchisees must answer two questions:
● Is risk sufficiently mitigated by the trademark value, operating system, economies of scale and support process of the franchiser to justify sharing equity with it (via the payment of an up-front franchise fee and on-going royalties)?
● Is personality and management style amenable to sharing decision-making responsibilities in the business with the franchiser and other franchisees?

For those of a more quantitative bent, does the franchisee fee and the present value of the royalties equal the increased net income from the value of the franchiser trademark? In other words, how many more hamburgers will I sell with a golden arch in front of my restaurant (and the systems and advertising that support the arch) than I would going it alone?

(It appears that franchisees tend to be so consumed with start up, survival and growth in the initial years of operation that building equity is only obliquely regarded as important. But, around the seventh year of operation, their piece of the value of the brand seems to take on greater importance. If the franchisee does not internalize the value of the franchise by then, there is a dramatic up-turn in dissatisfaction.)

A new franchisee should be assured that the franchiser has the income stream and/or is capitalized well enough to provide the support services required to transfer its knowledge base to the franchisee. The list of franchiser-provided services in Figure 2 is an appropriate starting point.

Is there sufficient quantity and quality of resources, applied to the specific support area, to fulfil the franchiser obligations?

The chronology of store development indicates the critical path of service support. Starting with an intimate understanding of the primary target customer, is there a specifically documented guideline for acquiring (through lease or purchase) a location that makes the customer reachable? Are there blueprints or fitting-out plans to guide the construction process?

While a facility is being built, the business format must be taught to the franchisee. Therefore, a training mechanism must be in place. The methods of training and the level of sophistication of franchisers vary dramatically. This is an extremely important issue. Once the franchisee is trained, what about staff? Employee turnover in an existing operation may not necessarily correspond to the scheduled training programs of the franchiser (if they are offered), and the franchisee often becomes the trainer for his or her staff. How well he is trained for this task not only impacts profitability but affects quality of life issues.

Long hours are a reality in most entrepreneurial ventures. But poor training schemes may cause a franchisee to spend inordinate amounts of time and effort in operations and little time managing the growth of the franchise.

The international dimension

A common problem with franchizing in Europe is that a trademarked system is 'imported' from the US with little attention to the small but significant differences in customer demand and the detail of how the business format will address that demand. Therefore, understanding the amount and sophistication of franchiser support services when a franchise is brought from another country takes on even greater importance.

The degree of effort to rationalize differences in adjustments to the business format and having the resources in place to react to changed customer demand can ameliorate the difficulty of recognizing and reacting to cultural differences. Malls in the US versus the high street in Europe is a distinction that dramatically affects franchise success. Again, our research has shown that delivery by the franchiser to the franchisees of the bundle of marketing services required to grow a venture is essential for a successful franchise relationship.

Part of the thinking behind the importance of the marketing services is a thorough understanding of the franchises target customer. Not understanding who the customer is may lead to improper outlet location, among other important decisions. Often it is difficult or impossible to relocate a business without significant financial hardship. Franchisees' businesses can get trapped in a bad real estate deal.

The importance of information

One of the significant advantages of a franchise is the availability of an abundance of information to complete a due diligence of the opportunity. In the US there are numerous federal and state laws regulating franchising, including a disclosure document called a Uniform Franchise Offering Circular.

There are no similar disclosure requirements in Europe, but European buyers of US franchises might be well advised to read the Uniform Franchise Offering Circular, which includes such things as franchiser-audited financial statements, a list of existing US franchisees and current franchise litigation. Additionally, visits to existing franchise outlets and interviews with current franchisees provides a wealth of information.

Technical issues of support and logistics are easily discovered. However, the more important issue is the way in which the franchise relationship is managed. Our research clearly indicates that the advantages of franchising, including economies of scale in purchasing, supply and marketing, result from rapid growth and overall size of the franchiser. Buying power increases and competitive advantages in cost are manifest. However, size can be a double-edged sword.

Franchisees see themselves as partners with the franchiser in a strategic relationship. Partners require communication to develop decision-making synergy and co-ordination to properly execute plans. When communication and co-ordination result in a co-operative attack on the marketplace, franchisees are overwhelmingly satisfied. It is essential that investigation of a franchise includes an understanding of the processes by which communications occur and changes are implemented. Often the conduit from the franchiser to the franchisee is a 'field representative' of the franchiser.

As we began this article with a discussion of wealth creation as a key to the entrepreneurial process, it is important to report that our research indicates that many franchisees are making money. The average franchisee in our study at Imperial College had a profit of around £40,000. However, it is equally important to recognize that the 'average' does not necessarily describe any individual franchisee and that returns cover a wide spectrum. ■

●◇ CASE STUDY

Jiffy Lube International Inc.

This is a summary of three case studies – Hindman and Company, Bridge Capital Investors, Inc., and Jiffy Lube International, Inc. They can be found in New Venture Creation, 4th edition, 1994, McGraw Hill/Richard D. Irwin and forthcoming 5th edition, 1998, by Jeffry A. Timmons, F.W.Olin, Distinguished Professor of Entrepreneurship, Babson College, USA.

After graduating from the University of Minnesota with a master's degree in health care administration, Jim Hindman worked for ten years as a hospital administrator. In 1967, he started Hindman Associates, specializing in building nursing homes and, by the mid-1970s, his ownership interests in these and a variety of other unrelated businesses were collectively worth several million dollars. However, after a spell as head football coach of Western Maryland College, he became restless and, by 1979, he was again looking for new business opportunities. Ed Kelly and Steve Spinelli joined him.

The fast oil change business caught his attention. Demand in this market was growing as the number of full-service gas stations had halved over the previous ten years. Jim's brother-in-law knew a man who operated a 'Jiffy Lube' franchise and, after several meetings with the owner in Utah, Jim bought the Jiffy Lube trademark and the rights to seven franchises. He then set about growing the business. Their goal was to get to 100 units by the end of 1982 through both the sale of new franchises and the acquisition of existing service centers and small franchise chains. Revenues would come from four sources:

1 Royalty fees from franchisees.
2 Rental income on property leased or sub-leased to franchisees.
3 Initial fees from new franchisees
4 Sales by company-owned centers.

By March 1983, the company was projecting 96 centers in operation. However, this growth was not without its costs. Revenues in 1982 had been $3.5m with losses of $1.4m. Financing of the operation was through a combination of loans and sale of stock to directors, employees and other investors and, most significant, through the sale of 29 per cent of the company to Pennzoil, the supplier of oil for the majority of the Jiffy Lube centers. In return, Pennzoil agreed to guarantee $6.3m of real estate financing.

Unfortunately, the relationship with Pennzoil was far from perfect. They soon discovered that the two companies had different objectives that resulted in different strategies for Jiffy Lube's expansion. Jiffy Lube's business plan emphasized 'clustering' and 'franchising' whilst Pennzoil advocated 'wide coverage' and company-owned service centers. Hindman decided that the relationship simply wasn't working and he would have to buy Pennzoil's stock and find other sources of finance. With Jiffy Lube's worsening financial status. . . . 'They wanted out. Maybe they thought we were going bankrupt, and they could pick up the service centers when we went under'.

Not so. In 1984, the company made a profit for the first time. During the first few years, the company had sold franchises one at a time. But this was not sufficient. Individual sales did not saturate areas quickly enough to achieve name recognition and make advertising cost effective. So, in 1983, they began to sell 'area development rights' to investors and entrepreneurs. In return for an up-front, non-refundable fee, Jiffy Lube gave investors the exclusive right to build a certain number of franchises within a specific geographical location. Fees varied depending on the market potential. For example, Tampa, Florida cost $150k, whilst San Francisco cost $250k. In addition, the company continued to collect the initial franchise fee of between $20,000 and $25,000 for each individual unit developed. As the company grew, management expected the rights to become more valuable, eventually selling for as much as $1m in larger markets such as Los Angeles.

This sale of large area development rights increased the need for real estate and construction financing. To fund this, Jiffy Lube had signed an agreement in 1983 with Old Court Savings and Loan to provide $16m for the purchase and development of 37 new centers. This was not to end happily. The morning headline on May 6, 1985 – *Local Savings and Loan Collapses, State Takes Over* – saw the closure of Jiffy Lube's primary real estate lender. Clearly, they couldn't assume that funding from Old Court would resume, nor could they afford to wait. Development of the service centers could not be put on hold since Jiffy Lube would default on real estate purchases if cash payments were not made on time. Contractors were waiting to start, and new franchisees depended on the service centers being completed for their livelihood.

Throughout the summer, the management team battled from one crisis to another using short-term borrowings and stopgap measures. Unfortunately, their problems were not confined to finance. Competition for market share was getting fierce. In August, Quaker State Oil bought Minit Lube, the number two company in the quick-change industry after Jiffy Lube for $35m. Jim Hindman said '*This put us up against the big boys for the first time*'. But Quaker State had not finished. In September, Jim received a call from the president of the company, '*Look, we just bought Minit Lube and I think we should talk* '. Contingent on future earnings, they made a formal offer of $53.9m.

Jim's reaction was simple. He must grow. '*We will become the MacDonalds of the quick oil change business. With approximately 270 service centers open in late 1985, these goals require the opening of over 1000 new centers by 1990*'. But such rapid expansion would need funding, and so in July 1986, the company raised $28m through an initial public offering and between 1986 and 1987 increased the number of centers from 348 to 561. At the same time, the company broadened the scope of services to franchisees. Training and maintenance of company programs and policies were high priorities; a certification program for technicians was developed; formal procedures were established for employee selection; and a 'mystery shopper' scheme introduced. Steve Spinelli, now a franchisee owning a significant east coast area and president of the Association of Franchisees, explained that . . .' *There are always points of contention in a franchise relationship and we had our fair share. However, Hindman had an ability to intercede personally at strategic moments and to force communications between top management and franchisees. His open door policy included making sure that our door was open too.*'

Year	Revenue	Service centers	
	($'000)	franchised	company operated
1986	7,683	361	23
1987	10,169	578	31
1988	14,218	805	39
1989	18,840	1,047	47
1990	22,210	1,297	47
1991	23,954	1,427	47

Table 1

The results were dramatic: 1987 sales revenue exceeded the original business plan. In March, the company had become the first quicklube company to advertize nationally. Touting the slogan, 'We'll take care of you like family', a $5m television campaign featured Dick Van Patten's family. Additionally, regional and local franchisees planned to spend $15m on local advertising. Just as Jim Hindman had expected, the IPO had raised public awareness and, by 1991, there were more than 1400 Jiffy Lube outlets operated throughout the USA (*see* Table 1).

Postscript

In 1991, Steve Spinelli sold his 47-store franchise to a major oil company. His interest in entrepreneurship and especially franchising led him to pursue his Ph.D. at Imperial College of Science and Technology in London. He graduated in 1995 and now teaches, researches and consults in the fields of new venture creation and franchising at Babson College, USA. ■

The above case is an abridged version. Copies of the complete case may be obtained from the European Case Clearing House, telephone (+44) 01234 750903; fax (+44) 01234 751125; E-mail ECCH@cranfield.ac.uk.

Finance

BANK

Contents

Contributors

William D. Bygrave is the Frederic C. Hamilton Professor for Free Enterprise and Director of the Center for Entrepreneurial Studies at Babson College, Wellesley, Massachusetts, Visiting Professor at INSEAD, France and Special Professor at the University of Nottingham, UK. He teaches and researches entrepreneurship, especially financing of start-up and growing ventures.

Peter Kelly teaches MBA courses in entrepreneurial management at London Business School and the University of Notre Dame. He is currently pursuing his Ph.D. at LBS and his doctoral research focuses on the informal market for venture capital in the UK.

Jonathan Levie is a research fellow at London Business School. His research interests focus on strategy and resource acquisition in young, growing companies. He is engaged in an eight-nation study of the relationship between entrepreneurs and their bankers, sponsored by the Foundation for Entrepreneurial Management at LBS.

Colin Mason is Reader in Economic Geography at the University of Southampton.

Richard Harrison is Professor of Management Development at the Ulster Business School, University of Ulster at Jordanstown.

Hugh Richards is a director of 3i and is responsible for 3i's investment business in London.

Herwig M. Langohr is Professor of Finance and Banking at INSEAD, Fontainebleau. His research interests include corporate finance, money and banking.

Martin Binks is Senior Lecturer in Economics and Entrepreneurship in the School of Management and Finance at the University of Nottingham.

Christine Ennew is Professor of Marketing in the School of Management and Finance at the University of Nottingham.

Introduction

Part 3 is about the various sources of money which you may need to start a new venture. The part is in two sections. First, the authors discuss the merits of sources such as family and friends, bankers, venture capitalists, and business angels. Their articles also give some handy hints as to the criteria which each of these 'lenders' may use in assessing business. The second section looks at the overall financial structuring of the emerging business.

Section 1
Sources of finance

Calling on family and friends for start-up cash

William Bygrave provides an overview of the kinds of financing decisions that need to be faced by the new entrepreneur.

For would-be entrepreneurs, there are two types of start-up capital: debt and equity. Simply put, with debt they do not have to give up any ownership of their businesses but they have to pay current interest and eventually repay the principal; with equity they have to give up some of the ownership to get it but they may never have to repay it nor even pay a dividend. So it is a trade off between paying interest or giving up some of the ownership. This is discussed in more detail in the following accompanying article by Peter Kelly. Debt and equity funding are discussed separately on pp. 75 and 82.

In practice, what usually happens depends on how much of each type of capital an entrepreneur can raise.

Most start-up entrepreneurs do not have much flexibility in their choice of financing. If it is a risky business with little on no assets, it is impossible to get any bank debt without putting up some collateral other than the business's assets – most likely that collateral is personal assets. Even if entrepreneurs are willing to guarantee the whole loan with their personal assets, the bank expects them to put some equity into the business, probably equal to 25 per cent of the amount of the loan.

It is no surprise that the vast majority of entrepreneurs have to start their businesses on a shoestring and leverage their own savings and labor. And they start with remarkably little capital. For example, one quarter of the *Inc.* 500 – *Inc.* magazine's annual list of its 500 US small business stars – began with less than $5,000, half with less than $25,000 and three-quarters with less than $100,000. Fewer than 5 per cent began with more than $1m.

Typically, entrepreneurs start their businesses with 'sweat equity' and personal savings. Sweat equity is ownership earned in lieu of wages. Then a wealthy investor who knows something about the entrepreneurs or the industry, or both – sometimes called an informal investor or 'business angel' – invests some personal money in return for equity.

When the company is selling product, it may be able to get a bank line of credit secured by its inventory and accounts receivable. If the company is growing fast in a large market, it may be able to raise capital from a formal venture capital company in return for equity. Further expansion capital may come from venture capitalists or from a public stock offering or a merger with a larger company.

Most new companies are not high-potential businesses and will never be candidates for formal venture capital. Nevertheless, they must find some equity capital. In most cases, it comes from the 4Fs – the Founders initially dig deeply into their personal savings (often to the point of exhausting them) then they turn to Family, Friends and Foolhardy investors.

It can be a scary business. Entrepreneurs often find themselves with all their personal net worth tied up in the same business that provides all their income. It is double jeopardy because if their businesses fail they lose both their savings and their means of support. Risk of that sort can be justified only if the profit potential is high enough to yield a commensurate rate of return.

How can the owners of private companies get a satisfactory return on their investments without making their companies public or selling them? The two ingredients that determine return on investment are the amount invested and the annual amount earned on that investment. Hence, entrepreneurs should invest as little as possible to start their businesses and make sure that their companies will be able to pay them a 'dividend' big enough to yield an appropriate annual rate of return.

For income tax purposes, that 'dividend' may be in the form of a salary bonus or fringe benefits rather than an actual dividend paid out of retained earnings. Of course, a prudent company ought to be generating cash from its operations – rather than by borrowing more money externally – before that 'dividend' is paid.

It is said that happiness for an entrepreneur is positive cash flow. However, if a company is growing rapidly, every penny of internally generated cash is plowed back into the enterprise to sustain its growth, leaving nothing to be distributed to the entrepreneur and the investors.

Sources of seed capital for the *Inc.* 500 (%)			
● Personal savings	78.5	● Venture capital	6.3
● Bank loans	14.4	● Mortgaged property	4.0
● Family members	12.9	● Government	
● Employees/partners	12.4	guaranteed loans	1.1
● Friends	9.0	● Other	3.4

Note: more than one source was used in some cases
Source: *Inc.*, October 1992

Figure 1

Perhaps, it is more correct to say that real happiness for an entrepreneur is free cash flow – the internal generation of more cash than a business needs to sustain its optimum growth rate. Free cash flow can be distributed as dividends to the owners or used to buy back shares from owners who want to realize their investment in the company or be retained in the business.

No wonder Bill Gates is smiling a lot these days. Microsoft, the company he started on a shoestring in the late 1970s, is generating so much free cash flow in the late 1990s that it adds millions of dollars daily to its $7bn war chest while Netscape, its arch rival in the battle for supremacy of the Internet software market, has had to sell more equity to raise $96m with its second public offering in less than 18 months. ■

From blueprint to reality: the quest for resources

Peter Kelly provides an overview of the kinds of financing decisions that need to be faced by the new entrepreneur.

The identification and assessment of entrepreneurial opportunities (covered in Part 2) are necessary ingredients to develop the 'blueprint' for a new business. The next challenge faced by aspiring entrepreneurs is to secure the necessary resource commitments to transform their 'blueprint' into a 'business reality'.

From the entrepreneur's viewpoint, the 'ideal' structure for a new business would be one that requires no commitment of capital to secure the use of necessary assets, where customers pay for the product or service in advance, and suppliers provide ready access to unlimited trade credit on generous repayment terms.

Assuming that sales were made on a profitable basis, there would never be a need to establish a line of credit at the bank or inject equity into the business. In theory, the only 'problem' the entrepreneur would have to face in this situation is deciding how best to use the cash generated from the business.

In reality, entrepreneurs need to think through very carefully the financial implications of their business plan as resources will be required to:
● secure the use of assets necessary to 'make it happen'
● finance the ongoing working capital needs of the business.

Your capital signals credibility

In the very early stages of venture development, access to established channels of funding such as banks, leasing companies or private investors is likely to be restricted.

To provide evidence that the business concept works and that demand exists, entrepreneurs have little choice but to rely on their own personal resources, supplemented by funds provided to them by close friends and relatives – so called 'love money'.

This should not be altogether surprising. It is unreasonable to expect outside parties to provide resources to support the development of a business in the absence of any tangible support being demonstrated on the part of the entrepreneur.

Establishing a business on the basis of often limited personal financial resources has been referred to as 'bootstrapping'. Two guiding principles of successful bootstrapping are:
● spend only as much time and as much capital as is needed to credibly demonstrate to other resource providers, such as banks and investors, that the opportunity is commercially feasible
● free up capital from any readily available source.

Many entrepreneurs have successfully launched their businesses by raising funds from the following sources:
● personal savings

- severance packages
- personal overdrafts
- credit cards
- pension plans
- mortgaging the house
- sale of personal assets
- 'compassionate' relatives and friends
- developing the business on a 'moonlight' basis by maintaining outside employment.

Having successfully demonstrated that a profitable opportunity exists, the financing needs of the business will often change dramatically. Building a business often implies on-going investment in plant, equipment and working capital. Ideally by this point, the entrepreneur will have established a credible track record to convince banks or investors to support the development of the venture.

Securing the use of assets

Before considering the financial implications of securing the use of assets, entrepreneurs are well advised to carefully assess the rationale for acquiring rights to them in the first place.

They should address a number of questions. Why is it necessary to secure the use of this particular asset? Are the qualities and attributes of the asset suitable for the venture's needs? Will the asset base provide a platform for future growth? How far in advance should we build up the venture in anticipation of rising consumer demand?

I am not suggesting that these questions can be resolved. However, it is important for the entrepreneur to be very clear about the choices made in terms of a venture's asset composition – choices that bear inevitable financial implications.

Financial advisors will tell you that 'the value of any asset is in its use and not in its ownership'. Leases – where one party maintains legal title over the asset but negotiates an agreement with another to use the asset over a set period of time and for a specific amount of consideration – are an increasingly popular financing vehicle in today's business environment.

The 'lease' versus 'buy' decision is often guided by tax considerations but irrespective of whether a business chooses to lease an asset or purchase it outright, the important point to note is that both routes have cash flow implications for the business.

Most leases require the payment of a deposit and involve contractual payments at regular intervals for use of the asset. Ownership reverts back to the lessor at the end of the period if the lessee decides not to exercise the 'purchase option' that is often included as part of the original lease agreement.

Similarly if an asset is purchased outright and financed with debt, lenders will often finance only a portion of the acquisition price and will often require that the purchaser make up the remainder in the form of a down-payment. In the very early stages of venture development, deposits and/or down-payments will often come from the proceeds raised from issuing equity.

Working capital

A desirable objective for any business is 'to get the money in before you have to pay it out'. But this is impractical for many new businesses. In order to induce some customers to order, credit terms often have to be offered.

On the payables side, however, until the entrepreneur establishes a track record for prompt payment with key suppliers, the venture may be required to conduct affairs on a cash-only basis.

The financial implications of this situation are quite clear. Indeed new ventures will often require additional up-front capital to finance the working capital requirements of the business in the early days as the venture builds credibility with key resource providers.

The evolution of a financial structure for a start-up

As we have seen, in the formative stages of venture development, the financial structure of the business is often 'unidimensional' – that is, 100 per cent equity financed. The business often lacks the asset base to pledge as collateral and the cash flow to service debt obligations.

However, with the passage of time and the development of a track record of performance, additional sources of finance other than equity become available. These include trade credit, debt finance and government-funded support programs.

In determining the appropriate financial structure for a given business, it is important that the interests of the entrepreneur, debtors and other investors are aligned to the greatest extent possible. This is a persistently difficult exercise in practice as each of the parties face significant trade-offs.

Equity is a necessary prerequisite for successfully raising debt finance. Unlike debt, which requires regular cash outlays in the form of principal repayments and interest, there is a discretionary element built into most forms of equity with respect to the payment of dividends and redemption of capital.

Difficult trade-offs are faced by an entrepreneur in situations where additional equity is required to finance growth and this capital needs to be raised from outside sources. External equity providers may take steps to limit the freedom of action of the entrepreneur by maintaining veto rights over major business decisions. In some instances, entrepreneurs may choose consciously to forgo growth to retain 'control' over their venture.

Aside from issues related to 'loss of control', entrepreneurs are also reluctant to raise outside equity because the 'perceived cost' is too high relative to debt. Most entrepreneurs consider debt finance to be 'cheap'. After all, the return to debt holders is often 'fixed' for substantial periods of time and interest costs are a tax-deductible expense. Importantly, debt has an obvious 'control appeal' for entrepreneurs – they often perceive that they can obtain the necessary resources while retaining equity control.

However, debt also has drawbacks. Among other considerations, lenders look at the value of the security pledged in support of their advances and the stability and level of the cash flows being generated by the business to meet ongoing interest and principal repayments.

In addition to security, lenders will often impose specific conditions that can restrict the freedom of action of the entrepreneur. 'Equity control' is little consolation if the business defaults on its obligations to pay interest and principal on time. 'Effective control' may pass to lenders in the event of default when decisions are taken by them to wind-up the operations or sell the business to recover their advances.

Here again, choosing an appropriate financial structure raises a difficult trade-off for the entrepreneur. The use of debt in the financial structure results in 'leverage effects' to equity holders. They stand to benefit from the 'unlimited upside' of their investment decisions that are, in turn, financed, in whole or in part, by debt holders whose return is essentially fixed.

However, employing too much debt results in an undercapitalized business that may be unable to weather downturns in operating performance that, in turn, could impair the ability of the venture to meet its on-going debt obligations to the point where the very survival of the business might be at stake. ■

Convincing the cash-conscious banker

Jonathan Levie describes some of the sensitive issues involved in persuading a bank to part with money to fund a new venture.

Most large banks provide excellent information packs on how to open a new business account and how to make a loan proposal.

Here we aim to shed light on these issues so that the entrepreneur can take informed decisions on whether and how to seek debt finance and present a proposal in the best possible way. The following sections describe the nature of lending; the benefits, costs and risks involved to both parties; and critical success factors in forging a banking relationship for a new venture.

Few entrepreneurs understand the nature of lending. As Adam Smith noted over 200 years ago, they tend to think that banks could and should 'extend their credits to whatever sum might be wanted without incurring any other expense besides that of a few reams of paper'.

The nature of lending

This view enrages bankers, who typically reply: 'If you become successful we cannot share in your success, so why should we lose if you lose?' In this long-running shouting match, both sides miss the point.

Banks make the bulk of their profits on net interest income. This is the difference between the interest they pay on money 'borrowed' from depositors or other banks and the interest they receive on *the same money* 'lent' to borrowers (such as entrepreneurs). Very little (say five per cent or so) of the asset base of a bank consists of shareholders' funds, or equity, and they operate on very narrow net interest margins.

For example, let's assume that, for commercial lending, fees cover expenses and that the net interest margin is three per cent. A customer defaults on a one-year term loan and the entire principal (amount loaned) is lost. As the bank must

How and why bankers make lending decisions, is rarely clear to entrepreneurs.

© FT Pictures

repay its depositors, the loss reduces the equity portion of the bank's balance sheet. Even worse, because it is allowed to lend only in proportion to its equity base, the loss reduces its ability to lend.

Yet to just make up the principal in that one bad loan, the banker must earn the full three per cent net interest margin on over *33 new loans* of the same type. (It takes more than 33 three-hundredths to make one.) This is why bankers do not like high-risk loan proposals, why loans must be repaid and why security in support of an advance is often sought 'just in case'.

Experience and statistics have led bankers to believe that new ventures are, on average, relatively high-risk lending propositions. However, the long-term rewards to bankers on new venture lending can be high also. A young company that grows into a successful strong business creates an ever-increasing potential source of income to its bank – from fees, loan interest, deposit interest, foreign exchange, leasing, factoring, venture capital, merchant banking, insurance, extra personal accounts for an expanding and increasingly wealthy workforce and increases in local business activity.

Bankers are well aware of this and attempts to poach 'star' accounts in the medium-sized corporate sector are legion. However, research in several countries has indicated that entrepreneurs who have a good banking relationship are surprisingly loyal to the banker who helped them to start up and that attempts to poach are often resisted.

No one can predict precisely which new businesses will succeed; banks may well have to accept an increased level of bad debts among their new venture accounts in order to capture the stars of tomorrow. The good news is that failure rates are highest early on, when the amount of debt a company carries is relatively small.

Why should entrepreneurs borrow? Debt finance only makes sense if the returns to be made on the extra business financed by the debt considerably exceed the costs and risks of borrowing. In that case, the entrepreneur can make more money with bank finance than without it and can even write off the interest against tax.

Benefits, costs and risks

The costs of borrowing include search costs, interest costs, and fees and conditions attached to the use of the debt. These conditions can place considerable restrictions on the future management of the business and even on the private life of the entrepreneur's family.

The risks of borrowing include wasted time in shopping around to no avail, interest rate rises, unexpected charges, a new bank manager with a different perspective, a change in bank policy and the bank's reaction to a 'temporary' downturn in the business (which might include freezing the current and deposit accounts and calling the loan in early).

Bankers are constantly asked to put up virtually all of the finance for a new venture. This suggests that the real reason why so many entrepreneurs seek debt finance is that they desire to minimize their own financial investment while maximizing their 'control', defined as share ownership (*see 'From blueprint to reality: the quest for resources'*, p. 72).

Bankers are well aware of this. If a banker does entertain such a proposal, the loan will have so many conditions attached to it that the banker will not just 'control' the business but also the entrepreneur.

Personal loans are now routinely screened in many countries using computerized credit scoring techniques. Commercial loan decisions, in contrast, are still heavily influenced by the personal impression the entrepreneur leaves on the loan officer.

Critical success factors

Research suggests that bankers form an impression of an individual quickly and tend to stick to it. It is for this reason that the entrepreneur must impress at the first meeting. The aim should be to project confident professionalism. Entrepreneurs should dress conservatively, turn up on time, emphasize their relevant experience and management skills, be ready to produce documentary evidence to support their argument, articulately argue the case for debt finance using the banker's language and not give in too easily.

Remember the banker needs to be sure that the entrepreneur can negotiate with his/her other resource providers and overcome unforeseen obstacles to pay back the loan. Asking tough questions is one way of testing these skills. Research also shows that overblown attempts to impress can leave a negative impression.

The banker's language is the language of finance – and surprisingly few entrepreneurs speak it. This means that the financially literate and articulate entrepreneur has a real competitive advantage in the market for debt finance. In the interview, the banker will probably question key assumptions behind the numbers in the financial plan. They are well aware that projected sales figures can be derived to cover the loan instead of the other way around. Financial honesty is just as important as financial literacy.

Bankers often assess debt proposals using simple checklists. Figure 1 shows two widely used checklists. Some banks have introduced more complex checklists that are closer to credit scoring systems. They assess the management, market, strategy and general competitive environment using a statistically determined weighted scoring system. Opinions vary as to the value of these for new venture proposals. Many bankers place more weight on their judgement of how the entrepreneur will cope in any eventuality than on their assessment of the venture's strategy, which may evolve considerably.

Remoulding the proposal

The banker may suggest changes in the entrepreneur's proposal to reduce the bank's exposure to acceptable levels. In debt/equity terms, 'acceptable' usually means roughly equal contributions to the capital base of the business by the promoters and the bank.

Bankers need to see that the entrepreneur is putting as much as is necessary into the company. They also need to be sure that the finance is actually needed in the amount and type requested. Although factoring (the sale of receivables) is not usually an option for a new venture, the leasing of some assets may be and leasing can sometimes improve cash flow and the debt/equity ratio.

Security

Security is probably the most contentious issue in the entrepreneur/banker relationship. Bankers need at least one and preferably two alternative sources of repaying the loan other than cash flow. Land, buildings, vehicles, government stocks, quoted shares, insurance policies, stocks and receivables all have security potential but only at their distress sale value. Often the only fall-back security available at startup is in the form of a personal guarantee backed by assets, usually the family home.

The 5 Cs
Character of borrower
Capacity to repay
Conditions (product, industry, economy)
Capital provided (debt/equity ratio)
Collateral, or security

CAMPARI
Character of borrower
Ability to borrow and repay
Margin to profit
Purpose of the loan
Amount of the loan
Repayment terms
Insurance against non-payment (security)

Figure 1: Two common banker's checklists

The practice of requesting personal guarantees varies from country to country. Entrepreneurs hate them because they wipe out the advantages of limited liability. Bankers like them because they feel the entrepreneur will work that much harder to ensure the loan is repaid. On the other hand, having to call on a personal guarantee in the event of a shortfall from the sale of business assets is one of the most difficult and stressful ones a banker must make.

Bankers tend to be sceptical of government-backed business loan guarantee schemes for situations where insufficient security is available. They infringe on their profession, may have politically-motivated conditions attached (such as a prohibition on personal guarantees in the UK scheme), carry a higher paperwork load and have a higher failure rate.

It may be smarter to portray a proposal as a 'regular' banking proposal, in which sufficient security is available, and keep the personal guarantee option open initially in the hope of negotiating it away later. Creative thinking about security, such as obtaining options from suppliers to repurchase assets in principle, getting revaluations on land or buildings, or positive data on the marketability of assets, can help meet the banker's requirements. Separating cash flows into 'definite' (for example, secured orders, royalty or service payments from secured orders) and 'probable' (future sales) may reduce the amount of security required.

To offset the risk and security issues in a new venture proposition, the entrepreneur should ensure that the banker recognizes all the profit possibilities to be gained from this new account.

Negotiating hard on fees or the interest rate may not be in the entrepreneur's best interest. If the banker stands to gain say 30 per cent more interest income by charging 1 per cent more, and if that 1 per cent represents only 10 per cent of the entrepreneur's tax-deductible interest charges, then why should it stand in the way of securing the loan?

Let's assume that after shopping around, and several near misses, an entrepreneur has secured a loan commitment.

Aftercare of bankers

The banker's enjoyment of the up-front fees will soon fade and nervousness will set in. Bankers hate 'surprises' and often assume the worst when they hear nothing. To offset this, the entrepreneur must keep up a steady stream of good news and warn the banker of possible bad news before it happens.

The banker will probably want regular (such as monthly) balance sheets, profit and loss, and cash flow accounts. The entrepreneur should also send press releases, customer endorsements, export sales leads, invitations to exhibitions, whatever good news he or she can muster. Enquiries related to other high-margin banking products, which have some likelihood of being needed (such as large foreign exchange transactions or letters of credit, for example) will keep the banker focussed on the future profitability of the account rather than on its present riskiness.

If an entrepreneur has continued to keep the bank abreast of developments, and the worst happens, the banker will at least feel informed. In addition, if the banker moves on and a new banker takes over, the file will show that some progress is being made. Often, what entrepreneurs need in a crisis is a little more time from their banker. Time is granted on trust. Keeping up that stream of information can create a small reserve of trust, which one day could save the life of the business. ■

What venture capitalists look for

Daniel Muzyka and **Sue Birley** describe the factors venture capitalists look at when they consider investing.

One group that spends a great deal of time screening business ventures for appropriate opportunities is the venture capital industry. Indeed, they may review as many as a hundred before investing in one. During this process, as is the case with any professional group, they develop implicit models of what makes a good opportunity.

Entrepreneurs need to recognize and understand these models as part of their search for funding. Even though venture capital in Europe and the US represents only a small percentage of total capital invested in entrepreneurial business, and may not be directly relevant to all entrepreneurs, these investors have had a major impact in influencing the evaluation models of other classes of risk-capital investors simply because of their experience. As such, they provide guidance as to the relevant factors to consider when evaluating an opportunity.

This is a complex area with multiple factors to be taken into account – and, of course, every business is different. So, the investor is likely to be faced with the need to weigh up the relative importance of, for example, market potential, forecast financial performance and management skills.

Curious as to whether there was some generalized decision model used in the industry, we asked 70 venture capitalists to tell us about the factors they considered – and the trade-offs they made – in their investment decisions. As we review these factors, it is important to keep the phrase 'all else being equal' in mind since we assume that there is data available to support each of the criteria listed. A lack of information on any may arouse suspicions and propel it to number one for purposes of evaluation. The criteria used are listed under seven headings:

● *Product-market factors* involving various aspects of the nature of the product and the market, such as projected market size, growth and seasonality.

● *Strategic-competitive factors* related to the classic notions of strategy and competitive dynamics and including the nature and degree of competition, strength of suppliers and distributors, and the ability to create 'post-entry' barriers (the ability to block others from coming into a market).

● *Management team factors* involving the leadership capabilities and track-record of the lead entrepreneur and the management team.

● *Management competence factors* including organizational and administrative abilities, marketing, sales and production capabilities.

● *Financial factors* including, for example, time to break-even and the projected rate of return.

Figure 1: Order of factors considered in assessing venture capital opportunities

1 Leadership potential of lead entrepreneur.	19 Degree of market already established.
2 Leadership potential of management team.	20 Time required to pay back the investment.
3 Recognized industry expertise in management team.	21 Ability to influence nature of business.
	22 Importance of unclear assumptions.
4 Track record of lead entrepreneur.	23 Stage of investment required.
5 Track record of management team.	24 Ease of market entry.
6 Sustained share position.	25 Strength of suppliers and distributors.
7 Marketing/sales capabilities of team.	26 Nature and degree of competition.
8 Organizational/administrative capabilities of team.	27 Location of business.
	28 Business and product fit with venture capitalist's portfolio of investments.
9 Ability to get the cash out of the investment.	29 Projected market size.
10 Degree of product market understanding.	30 Sensitivity to economic cycles.
11 Expected rate of return (return on investment).	31 Ability to syndicate (or bring others into the investment) deal.
12 Time to break-even.	
13 Financial/accounting capabilities of team.	32 Number and nature of co-investors already in the deal.
14 Ability to create post-entry barriers.	
15 Business meets funds constraints.	33 Seasonality of product market.
16 Process/production capabilities of team.	34 Scale and chance of later financing rounds.
17 Uniqueness of product and technology.	35 Location of business relative to fund.
18 Market growth and attractiveness.	

- *Fund factors* reflecting the relationship of the opportunity to the nature and location of the fund. Venture capitalists must be conscious of their portfolio and the commitments they have made to their investors regarding the type of investments they will consider (for example, early-stage start-ups, management buy-outs and so on).
- *Deal factors* relating to the specific nature of the investment, the stage of development of the business, and the ability to syndicate the deal and to invest in later rounds (that is, at later stages in the growth of the investment).

Is there a common view and, if so, what is the relative importance of each of these factors when venture capitalists are asked to trade one off against another? The answer to the first is 'yes'. European venture capitalists generally have the same model for evaluating potential investment, whatever the stage of development of the business – and these are the same as those used by their colleagues around the world. Figure 1 lists the overall rankings and indicates that venture capitalists are primarily interested in whether the lead entrepreneur and the team have the required leadership and managerial capacity to be able to deliver the opportunity. Their logic is clear. If they are absent, then everything else is problematic.

Financial projections receive some weight but are overwhelmed by considerations of the team and the market opportunity. Again, this makes intuitive sense. Financial projections are only realized when a good business proposition becomes a reality, not when it is forecast. The actual nature and degree of competition in the market is less important than the team's apparent ability to sustain and protect market share.

The implications for entrepreneurs when seeking external finance are clear. Who implements what is most important. How and where they will implement it is secondary. So entrepreneurs need to worry about themselves, their skills and the fit of the management team in relation to their proposed venture. They need to make sure they can convincingly demonstrate leadership ability and the appropriate competencies to potential investors.

They should focus on presenting a clear product-market strategy, incorporating a unique product or service that can create post-entry barriers.

In addition they must make sure they have credible financial projections that are clear about the time to operating break-even (which for venture capitalists should be relatively short) and show a way for investors to get their money out (the all important exit route).

The entrepreneur should not become obsessive about presenting copious, well-packaged financial information. Real risk capital investors know that these are all fantasy without the rest of the opportunity being in line.

In fact, these guidelines are relevant whatever the situation – whether you are seeking funding from a bank, from a private risk capital investor or venture 'angel', from your family and friends, or whether you are simply trying to convince yourself of the viability of your proposal. After all, you have almost certainly invested time and, probably, money already and it makes sense to see if it is worth continuing! ∎

For a full report of the study see Muzyka, Birley and Leleux, 1996 'Tradeoffs in the Investment Decisions of European Venture Capitalists' Journal of Business Venturing Vol. 11, no. 4, July, 273–288.

How the venture capitalists work out the financial odds

Equity financing is the riskiest form of new venture investment and investors require significant provisions to reduce their risk. **William Bygrave** explains.

Every business has equity financing. Initially it is money that entrepreneurs put into their ventures to get them launched. Some entrepreneurs augment their personal capital with money invested by family and friends. A few expand the equity in their business by selling shares to wealthy individuals, 'business angels'. A tiny elite group of high potentials raise equity capital from formal venture capital companies. Of the two million or so ventures started annually in the US, about 95 per cent get all their equity funding from the founding entrepreneurs and their immediate family and friends. No more than 5 per cent get funding from angels; and less than .05 per cent get it from formal venture capitalists.

The most sophisticated private equity investors are professional venture capitalists. By examining how they evaluate, value and finance entrepreneurial companies, we can learn a lot about the process of private equity investing. Granted, this is a group of sophisticated investors, but they set the standards for good practice when it comes to equity investments in private companies.

Entrepreneurial folklore says that professional venture capitalists do not invest in a company until their rising greed overcomes their declining fear. Put differently, it means that they do not put money into a company until they are convinced that there is a reasonable probability that the potential financial returns measure up to the risks. As a rule of thumb, this means that they expect to get a return of between five and ten times their initial investment in about five to seven years. In an ideal case the company will grow rapidly and float an initial public offering of its shares within five years of the first venture capital investment.

Common shares are the riskiest equity – none more so than shares in a young, private company. Besides the fact that common shareholders stand last in line to get paid when a company fails, investment in a private company lacks liquidity because there is no public stock market where the shares can be readily traded. But there are many other risks to contend with.

Consider the example of Apple Computer. Founder Steve Jobs first approached a professional venture capitalist in the autumn of 1976. At that time, the company was selling Apple I microcomputers to hobbyists. The total market for microcomputers was minuscule and no company had a commercially viable product. What's more, Jobs and partner Stephan Wozniak were college drop-outs with modest work experience. The venture capitalist turned them down because Jobs and Wozniak were neophyte entrepreneurs without significant management experience with an introductory product in an embryonic market. At the venture capitalist's suggestion, they approached Mike Markkula, a semi-retired

Intel veteran, who made an angel investment in Apple and brought much-needed management savvy. The company introduced the Apple II in 1977. Next year, when Apple sales were about $10m a year, the first professional venture capital was invested. By then the infant microcomputer industry, propelled by the VisiCalc spreadsheet, was no longer exclusively the domain of nerds; early adopters were actually using microcomputers for real business applications.

When venture capital was invested in Apple, the management, market and technological risks, although still high, were much lower than they had been 18 months earlier and were outweighed by the potential financial returns. How do venture capitalists evaluate those risks and what kind of returns do they expect from the companies in which they invest?

First and foremost, venture capitalists invest only in companies with first-class entrepreneurial leaders in markets that are big enough for a company's sales to grow to at least $50m with pre-tax profit of 20 per cent within five years. Experience shows that a company like that will be able to go public, or be bought by a larger company, and will return five to ten times the venture capitalist's original investment. A tenfold return in five years yields an annual rate of return of 58 per cent and a fivefold yields 39 per cent, which are within the range of satisfactory risk-adjusted returns.

Next, venture capitalists hedge their bet by staging the financing in more than one round. Suppose an early-stage company projects that it requires $5m of equity financing before it will be able to go public. If a venture capital group decides to invest, it will usually split the financing into two rounds of say $2.5m each.

Provided that the company meets its projected sales and profit milestone with the first round of $2.5m, the venture capitalist will almost certainly want to invest the second $2.5m. Typically, if the first round is sold at $1 per share, the second round will be about $3 per share. Hence, with two rounds of financing, the company sells only 3,333,333 shares (2.5 million plus 833,333) to raise $5m, rather than 5,000,000, if it had raised all the financing in one round.

However, if the company falls hopelessly short of its milestone, the venture capitalist most likely will not invest any more money and, in the worst case, will be prepared to write off the first $2.5m. So by staging the investment, the venture capitalist hedges his risk and the company, provided that it meets its projections, reduces the number of shares that it sells.

If this were a real-world case, it's likely that the venture capitalist would syndicate the deal with two other venture groups because another way that venture capitalists manage their total financial risk is by investing in a portfolio of different companies.

Finally, venture capitalists reduce their financial risk by purchasing convertible preferred shares, which give them very specific rights and preferences compared with holders of common shares. The final investment agreement can run to 200 or more pages but the key provisions of the agreement are summarized in a term sheet of a few pages.

Those provisions protect the venture capitalist's investment in the event of both negative and positive future events. The venture capitalists have rights to convert preferred shares to common shares, dividend rights, redemption rights, registration rights, protection from ownership dilution in a recapitalization, rights to maintain pro rata ownership in future rounds of private financing, and rights to approve the issue of any equity security, the liquidation of the company and the acquisition of or investment in another company.

They also have ways of controlling the company through both ownership of equity and seats on the board of directors. If they hold 51 per cent of the common shares, they have outright voting control. Although they initially might not have a majority of the board seats, they have the right to appoint a majority of the board of directors if specified negative events happen.

In addition, the term sheet places significant requirements on the management and employees of the company. These include issuing timely annual audited financial statements and monthly or quarterly unaudited statements, non-compete agreements, key person life insurance, a stock vesting agreement that any employee who leaves prematurely has to sell a portion of his or her shares back to the company at their nominal price, an agreement that while the company is private any employee cannot sell shares to a third party without first offering them to the preferred shareholders, a limitation on the stock option pool and limits on managers' salaries.

Due diligence, financial prudence and legal agreements notwithstanding, it is impossible to eliminate the risk inherent in equity investing. In general, investments in younger companies are riskier than those in older ones because they have shorter track records and investments in them have to be held longer. Hence, venture capitalists classify companies according to their stage of development.

A *seed-stage* company is one with not much more than a concept; a *start-up* company is one that is already in business and is developing a prototype but has not sold it in significant commercial quantities; a *first-stage* company has developed and market tested a product and needs capital to initiate full-scale production. *Second-stage, third-stage and mezzanine* financing fuels growing companies; and *bridge* financing may be needed to support a company while it is between rounds of financing, often while it waits to go public.

The younger a company, the greater the risk and the higher the expected return. The expected annual return declines from about 80 per cent for seed-stage financing to about 30 per cent for a third-stage financing (*see* Figure 1). It is the expected returns, combined with the valuation of a company, that determines the price per share a venture capitalist will be willing to pay to buy equity in it. Since venture capital is invested in growing companies, the venture capitalist wants to know what the value of the company is likely to be at some future time when it can sell its investment and realize a capital gain. It estimates the valuation of the company at some future date then discounts it back to its present value.

Stage	Expected annual return
Seed	80%
Startup	60%
First-stage	50%
Second-stage	40%
Third-stage/Mezzanine	30%
Bridge	25%

Figure 1: Expected returns on venture capital equity investments

Here is a simplified illustration of the most commonly used method. A one-year-old company is seeking $2m of start-up financing. Its projections show that it will have earnings (net income) of $5m five years in the future. The venture capital group believes that the company can have an initial public offering in five years and that the price to earnings (P/E) ratio will be 20. Thus, the future total valuation of the company will be $100m (20 × $5m).

The venture capitalist wants a 60 per cent rate of return; so the present value of the company is \$9.54m [\$100,000,000/(1.6)^5]. Hence, for an investment of \$2m, the venture capital group needs 21 per cent [(\$2/\$9.54) × 100] of the company's equity to achieve a 60 per cent return. There are huge uncertainties in that computation. The earnings are only projections and even if the company achieves its projections five years hence it might not be able to go public if the market for initial public offerings is in a slump. And who is wise enough to foresee what the P/E ratio will be five years in the future?

Figure 2 shows how the percentage ownership required to yield a 60 per cent return on a \$2m investment varies with the future valuation of a company and the holding period. It contains some simple messages for entrepreneurs seeking venture capital. First, they should think big enough when making their projections because the greater the future valuation of the company, the less equity they will have to sell to raise their venture capital. Second, they should propose an early public offering because the

Holding period	Future valuation of the company (\$ million)				
	20	**40**	**60**	**80**	**100**
2 years	26%	13%	9%	6%	5%
3	41	20	14	10	8
4	66	33	22	16	13
5	NA	52	35	26	21
6	NA	84	56	42	34
7	NA	NA	89	67	54
8	NA	NA	NA	NA	86

Figure 2:
Percentage equity required to yield a 60% annual rate of return on a \$2 m investment

shorter the expected holding period for the investment, the less equity they will need to sell. Third, they should grow their companies as big as possible before raising venture capital because the longer they wait, the lower the required rate of return and the shorter the holding time to harvest the investment.

In this example, if the company were a first-stage instead of a start-up investment, the required rate of return would be 50 per cent instead of 60 per cent, and it might be ready to go public in four years instead of five. Hence, the company would need to sell only 10 per cent of its equity instead of 21 per cent.

Target annual returns that can go as high as 80 per cent seem to be outrageously exorbitant to new entrepreneurs. But they have to keep in mind that returns from good investments have to compensate for losses on bad ones. In a successful venture capital portfolio, out of every ten investments, two will make or exceed the target rate of return, two will be total write-offs and the remaining six will range from the 'walking dead', where the companies never get big enough for a significant harvest, to the 'walking wounded' that need refinancing if they are to have a chance of making it.

The average annual returns on venture capital since the birth of the professional industry in 1946, have been, at best, in the mid-teens, which suggests that this industry is not making excessive returns on a risk-adjusted basis. Indeed, some financial observers might argue that the returns are not adequate compensation for the risk involved.

No doubt about it, private equity is the most expensive type of capital for entrepreneurs. What's more, when it comes from sophisticated investors, such as professional venture capitalists, it has numerous covenants and restrictions. When things go badly wrong, venture capitalists exercise their rights and intervene in managing the company, often removing one or more of the founding entrepreneurs in the process. It's those situations that lead to the derogatory term 'vulture capitalist'.

However, when things go well, everyone wins. Entrepreneurs get the capital that enables them to grow their companies faster; venture capitalists get a return commensurate with the risks they take; and society gets exciting new products and high-quality jobs. What's more, the best venture capitalists such as Arthur Rock, John Doerr, and Ben Rosen bring much more than money to the deal. They bring the wisdom, earned by advising and observing entrepreneurs in whom they invested, to build tiny companies such as Apple, Sun Microsystems, Netscape, Lotus and Compaq into industry giants. ∎

Ben Rosen, venture capitalist behind Compaq Computer, the world's largest PC-maker.

'Business angels' – heaven-sent or the devil to deal with?

Most funding for new business ventures comes not from conventional sources but from informal, and often idiosyncratic, sources. **Colin Mason** and **Richard Harrison** explain.

There is a widely held perception that venture capitalists are the main source of equity finance for new and young entrepreneurial businesses. However, the reality is that the vast majority of venture capital funds specialize in providing development finance to established businesses and to financing management buy-outs and buy-ins. Entrepreneurs seeking less than £250,000 are likely to be wasting their time in approaching venture capital funds. By far the main source of what has often been termed 'classic' venture capital – that is, small amounts of high-risk, early-stage equity financing provided by patient investors who provide value-added advice – is the so-called informal venture capital market.

This comprises high net-worth individuals, the majority self-made with substantial business and entrepreneurial experience, who are prepared to invest, either on their own or with others, directly in entrepreneurial businesses. They are often termed 'business angels' (although many dislike this term). Most are relatively infrequent investors making an average of one investment every 18 months, although a small minority of investors are considerably more active, making three or more investments a year.

Business angels tend to keep a low profile. They are not listed in any directories and there are no public records of their investments. It is therefore impossible to say how many business angels there are or how much they invest in aggregate. Best estimates of the scale of the informal venture capital market suggest that there are about 250,000 business angels in the US who invest $10bn-$20bn every year in over 30,000 ventures. This is at least five times the size of the institutional venture capital market in terms of dollars invested annually and is at least 20 times larger in terms of the number of ventures financed. In the UK, the informal venture capital market is estimated to have invested at least twice as much in the small and medium-sized (SME) sector as venture capital funds.

Business angels are a heterogeneous group and making generalizations about them and their investment activity is problematic. Nevertheless, the research that has been undertaken in the UK, Nordic countries and North America suggests that angel investments have the following characteristics.

Size of investment
The majority of business angels invest less than £50,000 per investment although some will invest more than £100,000 per deal. However, around half of all business angel investments involve co-investors, usually other business angels (generally trusted friends and business associates) but occasionally venture capital funds, and thus deal sizes can be larger. The business angel, or syndicate, will sometimes provide additional follow-on finance. Because of the effect of the business angel's investment on a company's balance sheet, many entrepreneurs are also able to negotiate additional loans from their bank.

Business angels make investments in virtually all industrial sectors but predominantly in start-ups and early-stage ventures (although they occur across all financing stages). **Business characteristics**

Investment structure
The majority of investments involve equity finance. However, business angel investments may also involve loans (generally unsecured), guarantees and debt-equity arrangements either alongside equity finance or on their own. Equity investments typically involve straightforward financing instruments (ordinary shares). More complex instruments (for example, types of preference shares) are relatively unusual except in large investments (over £100,000).

Business angels normally do not take a controlling interest. It is more common in larger deals, which typically involve more than one investor, for the investor(s) to take a majority shareholding. However, these deals are often structured in a way that allows the entrepreneurs to regain majority control if the business meets performance targets.

Value-added contribution
Informal venture capital is 'smart money'. Business angels are value-added investors. They contribute their commercial skills, entrepreneurial experience, business know-how and contacts through a variety of hands-on roles to make a wide range of strategic, monitoring and supportive inputs.

Entrepreneurs who have raised finance from business angels report that their most valuable contribution is as a sounding board for the management team. Despite the obvious potential for this involvement to lead to inter-personal conflicts with the entrepreneur, the available evidence suggests that in most cases relationships are consensual and productive.

Geographical distribution

Informal venture capital is a local marketplace. Business angels can be found in virtually every town and city. The majority of their investments are local, typically within 50 to 100 miles of where they live. This is because of the hands-on nature of their investing and consequent need for frequent contact. However, business angels who have very specialist investment preferences (for example, a particular sector or technology) are likely to invest over longer distances.

Holding period

Business angels are fairly patient investors, with a majority willing to hold their investments for more than five years. Successful exits are normally achieved through a trade sale.

Motives

Most business angels are motivated first and foremost by the opportunity for capital gain. Thus they are only interested in investing in businesses that have the potential to achieve profitable growth that will generate returns of 30 per cent or more a year (averaged over the life of an investment) on start-ups and at least 20 per cent for investments in established businesses. However, there are some investors who are also seeking income from their investment, either by working full-time in the business or else by being paid a regular fee for their value-added contribution.

Business angels are also motivated, in part, by non-financial considerations from which they derive 'psychic' income, notably the opportunity to play a role in the entrepreneurial process and the fun of making informal investments. They gain personal satisfaction and excitement from being involved with an entrepreneurial business and helping it to get started and grow and in seeing their judgement vindicated by the success of their investee companies. Some business angels are also motivated by various 'hot buttons' – for example, an interest in a particular technology.

Altruistic considerations also play a role: these include the opportunity to bring a socially useful product or service to market, assisting in the economic development of their community and supporting the free market system that enabled them to prosper by helping the next generation of entrepreneurs.

Approach to investing

Business angels' approach to investing is influenced by three key considerations. First, since they are investing their own money, they do not need to refer decisions to others for approval. Second, they typically allocate only a relatively small proportion of their wealth to their informal investments. Thus, it will not seriously affect their lifestyle if they lose their money. Equally, they are sufficiently wealthy not to *need* the returns from a successful investment. Third, the business experience and financial sophistication of most business angels means that they are capable of evaluating the merits and risks of prospective investments, especially those in industries in which they have had experience.

Investment criteria

Investors reject well over 90 per cent of the investment proposals that they see at the initial screening stage – where a potential investor comes across an investment opportunity and decides whether it is of sufficient interest to invest some time to investigate it in detail or to reject it out of hand.

The attitude of most business angels at this stage is suspicious and even cynical. They are looking for reasons not to invest. Although the identification of one or two perceived weaknesses in the proposal is unlikely to be sufficient to make the investor stop reading, the accumulation of several weaknesses will lead to the investor deciding to reject the proposal.

The first question that an investor considers is whether the opportunity meets his or her, often idiosyncratic, personal investment criteria in terms of the industry/market, amount of finance required, location of the business and stage of business development. Having established that the proposal is a good fit, the investor will begin to consider the content of the proposal in more detail.

Advantages and disadvantages of raising finance from business angels

Informal venture capital has a number of attractions. Although business angels seek a financial return on their investments in the form of capital appreciation, they are, nevertheless, often motivated in part by non-financial considerations and so may be willing to accept lower returns. Business angels are often prepared to invest in an opportunistic way, often without too much study or investigation, particularly if the business is in a market or technology area that they are familiar with. Business angels are generally quick to make an investment decision and to write the cheque. US studies indicate that the time between first meeting and receipt of funds is less for private investors than venture capitalists (2.5 months compared with 4.5 months). There is limited involvement by fee-based professionals, thereby minimizing the costs involved for the entrepreneur. Business angels are normally prepared to take a longer term view of the investment.

Most business angels play a 'hands on' role in the companies in which they invest. Thus entrepreneurs are able to benefit from the substantial commercial skills, entrepreneurial experience, 'know how' and contacts of their investors. In some cases they may even play an active management role.

But there are also some disadvantages that should not be ignored. They are less likely to become involved in later financing rounds. Although most informal investors are happy with a minority stake, they may nevertheless expect to have an active involvement in the business and a significant say in strategy. Some angels may be meddlesome. In some cases, business angels may turn out to be 'devils' with ulterior motives for investing.

How to find a business angel

Most business angels rely upon networks of trusted friends and business associates to identify investment opportunities and are more likely to invest in opportunities that come from these sources. Other referral sources include accountants and, less often, bankers, lawyers and stockbrokers. Some angels also identify investment opportunities through their own personal search.

Entrepreneurs can maximize their chances of finding business angels by using the following strategies:
- search locally
- look for successful entrepreneurs who are familiar with the industry or market
- many business angels are active in charitable and civic affairs
- participate in networking organizations such as business clubs, industry and professional associations, university alumni associations as well as social organizations such as golf and tennis clubs
- use 'gatekeepers' such as lawyers, accountants and venture capitalists
- consider joining a business angel network. These provide a channel of communication between informal investors and entrepreneurs seeking finance. Their objective is to enable entrepreneurs to bring their investment proposals to the attention of a number of private investors simultaneously and to provide investors with a convenient means of identifying and examining a range of investment proposals while retaining investor anonymity until the due diligence stage.

Most operate on a not-for-profit basis, with state or quasi-state bodies underwriting the gap between their operating costs and the revenue that they derive from registration fees charged on investors and businesses and, in some cases, a success fee levied on the business. There are others that operate on a commercial basis, either on a free-standing basis or as part of accountancy or corporate finance practices.

Business angel networks are still relatively minor players in the informal venture capital market and many business angels are sceptical of the quality of the investment opportunities that come through such networks. However, network staff are often able to help entrepreneurs improve the presentation of their opportunity (for example, by ensuring that it contains the type of information that business angels seek). Some networks claim that 15 per cent to 20 per cent of opportunities that they circulate to investors receive funding. The feedback that entrepreneurs receive from network staff and from the angels to whom they are introduced but who do not invest can also be helpful. ∎

⚯ CASE STUDY

Stantret: A private cargo airline in the USSR

This case was originally prepared by Dr Igor Touline of the Institute of World Economy and International Relations, Moscow. It was subsequently edited by Dr Abby Hansen in collaboration with Professor Derek Abell, IMD. Financial support was provided by the European Foundation for Entrepreneurship Research (EFER).

In the early 1990s all forms of transport in the USSR had become severely inadequate. Railways were in need of modernization; roads were in disrepair; in the trucking and civil aviation industries there was a serious lack of both spare parts and gasoline. Aeroflot, the largest air carrier in the world, put little emphasis on maintenance and flew its planes until they wore out. Moreover, these inefficiencies were not confined to transport. The food storage and processing facilities were also in poor condition. In the spring of 1990, all these problems were thrown into stark relief when it became clear that the country was likely to reap a bumper harvest. Vegetables and fruit grown in the Crimea would be left to rot whilst demand in distant places like Siberia suffered from shortages.

This was an ideal opportunity for Sergei Slepstov. Aged 25, he had risen from a factory worker in his native town in the Urals to become a senior marketing manager with a construction concern that was participating in the creation of a computer information network. Its role was to disseminate supply and demand information about surpluses and shortages of construction materials around the country. Working with this information gave him an idea:

The idea of organizing an effective brokerage activity got stuck in my mind. Nothing could be more straightforward. If someone has a surplus of something and another person or organization has a shortage of the same thing, all one has to do is to organize a mutually beneficial exchange.

Sergei concluded that sellers and buyers could profit handsomely if swift transportation of produce could be ensured. But how could he make it work? Quite simply, he found an 'angel'. Within days of conceiving the idea for an air transport service, friends introduced him to Ustas Lamin, president of a large Soviet-American joint venture in the entertainment business, called Stanlet. Sergei recalled that Ustas said to him:

I shall give you the possibility but nothing else.

Stantret was established as a subsidiary of Stanlet and, with this as a credible business base, Sergei approached the bank for a 600,000 rouble, three-month credit facility. He had forecast that, given the difference in price between tomatoes in the north and south, one aircraft could make enough deliveries in three months to yield 141,000 roubles in earnings. All he had to do was to find an aircraft, pilots, fuel, flight paths, landing slots and, of course, customers.

He first went to ARI, a subsidiary of the Ministry of Aviation Industries [MAI], located near Moscow, which had several dozen planes sitting idle most of the time. He told the ARI managers that he had a large order to ship fruit and if they could provide an equipped plane and arrange its reception along the route, they could share the profits. After some delay they agreed. Lack of fuel was, however, a major problem. But Sergei knew that report-padding and double counting were routine and he suspected that fuel reported as having been consumed was, in fact, still available. So, he decided to barter. In northern parts, he offered fresh produce and elsewhere consumer goods like video equipment, which he bought in Moscow using the company's bank credit.

When putting together a deal with a large scale buyer of agricultural produce he would arrange for the free use of one or two tons of a 40 ton shipment of fruit in the interests of 'ensuring the smooth operation of the air bridge'. The one–two tons cost little to the buyer, compared with the selling price in the north and, in return, the buyer was guaranteed a timely delivery. U. Umarov, managing director of a large joint venture in Tashkent:

When I attempted to use an Aeroflot plane there was such a prolonged delay that I never dispatched the consignment of fruit. When I tried sending another consignment by motor transport, two trucks disappeared and I had to hire guards and sustain losses. With Slepstov, there was neither problem, nor any losses . . . With Aeroflot; arrival on time is an exception. Even when Slepstov charges more than Aeroflot, I gain.

By September, 1990, Stantret had far exceeded the forecasts in the business plan, flying the aircraft for twice the number of hours projected; and by the end of the first quarter, 1991, the company was showing a gross profit of 18,410,100 roubles. During this time, he had continued to arrange the cargo flights with creative deals that often involved an ad hoc mix of regular payments and barter, a skill which he later taught his employees. However, this was part of his downfall.

At the end of April 1991, he noticed that two large contracts showed a customer price five per cent below the price he had negotiated and, upon close inspection, he found that the rest of the contracts included similar discounts. Checking with friends at the bank, he found that large sums had been paid to the accounts of managers responsible for his air shipment operations:

It was a real blow. I didn't catch them red-handed, but I could no longer believe them. I still can't see what went wrong.

The final blow came when he learned that a new joint-stock company, Volga-Dnieper, had accumulated 270 million roubles – enough to buy several large cargo planes. Even more worrisome, it had forged relationships with MAI.

Sergei faced a major strategic decision. Should he turn Stantret into a joint-stock company and orient it towards long-term projects? Should he accept the invitation of a US commercial company to become its official representative in the USSR? Should he leave the company, raise money on the strength of his own good name, and start a new business of his own? Where was the new opportunity? ■

The above case is an abridged version. Copies of the complete case may be obtained from the European Case Clearing House, telephone (+44) 01234 750903; fax (+44) 01234 751125; E-mail ECCH@cranfield.ac.uk.

Recipe for a capital cake

Hugh Richards explains how financial structures for new ventures are put together.

Much of the classic thinking about financial structuring was developed for large, stable businesses, particularly quoted ones. It tends to draw heavily on historical track record and stock volatility in determining the cost of capital. That thinking has little place in helping a young company, where the uncertainty is such that informed guesswork and compromises are the order of the day. This article will examine some of the ground rules and then look at practical examples by way of illustration.

The starting point is to establish how much capital is required and for what purpose. This may sound obvious; but the younger the business, the higher the level of uncertainty and the more difficult the funding requirement is to estimate.

We can start in the classic business planning sense by considering the market and the likely level of sales, and work back through variable costs of sales to fixed-cost requirements. This builds up a picture of the overall cash requirement, for what purposes it will be required and how its shape changes over time. These cash flows can then be tested by working a series of 'what if' scenarios and examining the impact on the funding requirement.

The key principle in funding is matching – the provision of capital must mirror the purpose to which it is being put. Put simply, you would not wish to finance a major factory development with three-year money nor a personal computer with a 25-year mortgage. Most businesses have some more or less permanent requirement for capital, best funded by equity and retained earnings, some longer-dated requirements best matched by term debt and some fluctuating requirements most easily funded by overdraft.

Business owners are concerned to keep the cost of capital to a minimum. The principle choice is between debt and equity (discussed in detail on pp. 75 and 82) although in practice the cost can be altered by mixing the two in varying quantities. To recap briefly. Debt is cheap, usually costing one per cent to three per cent over the bank's cost of capital. Though cheap, it also has teeth and the old adage – 'debt gets you up in the morning, equity lets you sleep in late' – is relevant. Debt brings with it obligations – interest payments and capital redemptions that have to be made – and the consequences for not doing so are severe.

So there must be a sensible and prudent relationship between the reliability of a series of cash flows and the amount of debt being used to finance them. For example, a fully let portfolio of 12 office properties let to good quality tenants could be financed almost entirely with debt, while the long-term working capital requirement for the launch of a new product in an overseas market would be more prudently financed with a high level of equity.

The principal difficulty with equity is that it is expensive. It is the most valuable resource that the owner has to sell and once sold is difficult to repurchase. To make the sale worthwhile, the owner has to believe that he can use external capital to build a business more quickly and more soundly, ensuring that his reduced level of shareholding in a bigger business is more valuable than the retention of all of it in a smaller one.

Risk and return

The provider of capital starts by analyzing the various risks that he or she faces. Perhaps the most important is one that the entrepreneur rarely considers, and if he does, even more rarely has a full perspective on, *managerial risk* – to what extent does the team have the ability to deliver? There must be a mix of relevant skills, the experience and the determination to succeed. Much better a good team with a marginal idea than a marginal team with a good one. The former will survive, the latter probably will not. (These issues will be considered in Part 5, p. 170.)

Despite large amounts of work, there is little evidence of correlations between particular backgrounds and entrepreneurial success . The biggest danger is the temptation to back people with similar backgrounds to your own or people that you like. This is almost universally disastrous! There is a limited amount that you can deduce in an interview type of environment. You have to see people *in situ* in their businesses, talk to their team, to those around them, to those for whom they have worked in the past.

Where you believe you have identified shortcomings, it is important to fill them with complimentary skills from others rather than hoping that people will change fundamentally. This may require full-time additions to the team or support of a more non-executive variety. The single most critical appointment from an investor's perspective is that of chairman. That person's responsibility is to ensure the competence and capability of the team as a whole and he is more likely to have a proper perspective than a shareholder alone.

The *commercial risk* that an investor faces is a function of a company's circumstances and potential within its particular environment and is identical to that of the entrepreneur.

The *financial risk* is not the same, if only because the amount of capital and the forms in which an investor proposes to make it available will be different to those of the entrepreneur. The key from the investor's perspective is to understand the potential returns from an investment and to weigh those against the amount placed at risk on the one hand and the chances of losing it on the other.

Returns to investors can be by way of income (for example, interest on loan stocks, dividends) and/or capital (for example, redemptions, profit on sale of shares). But usually the potential for a capital profit on an eventual sale of the investment is by far the most significant of these.

Shareholdings, particularly minority ones, in unquoted companies are usually wholly illiquid so an assessment of the potential value of the company as a whole at some stage in the future needs to be made. If the investment is a minority one, then equally importantly the chances of the majority wishing to sell at all needs to be assessed. That potential must be weighed against the risks.

First, the quantum of exposure needs to be understood. If the investee company fails, how much would be lost? The answer is almost invariably the whole of the investment. It may be possible, however, to enjoy security for at least part of the investment, for example, a loan secured on a factory or on the company's debtor ledger. The chances of realizing that loss links back into the assessment of the managerial and commercial risks that an investor faces.

Let us now look at applying these ideas in two strongly contrasting situations. **Examples** First, the start up company. The risks are at their greatest. Managerially, you probably have a group of people who have not worked together before and who have not started up a company before. Commercially, you will be unclear about the product's potential in the market; you may not know whether the product 'will work'; you may not even know whether the company can manufacture or supply it.

3i's practical experience is that such companies usually take three separate rounds of finance and an average of seven years before they become independently cash positive. One in eight is a huge success; two in eight fail within a short timescale; and five in eight limp along. As a rough rule of thumb, an investor must believe that there is the possibility of multiplying his or her original investment by a factor of ten, if everything goes according to plan, to justify taking risks of this magnitude.

Take Geoconference Limited as an example. Teleconferencing is the process by which three or more parties are involved in the same phone call, using either normal audio phones or video facilities. The company aims to provide a service co-ordinating such calls, which can be a logistical headache for companies even when few parties are involved. Where more than four or five parties are connected, normal corporate exchanges fail to cope and a third party agent is required. Calls of several hundred parties can be accommodated with the aid of special equipment. The company will use a top of the range bought in 'bridge' to provide its service.

Geoconference's clients will predominantly be large corporations. In 1995 the UK audio market was worth around £13m and is reported to be growing at 50 per cent per annum. The video market is still nascent, but with the wider incorporation of cameras into desktop PCs, the potential could be considerable. Competition comes from the large international telephone companies, and Geoconference will compete by offering a wider range of add-on services, and most importantly, by providing a better quality of service.

The management is a key attraction. The proposed managing and operations directors have worked together in the telecommunications industry for the past 16 years, and are now keen to build a business of their own. A sales manager and financial controller have been identified, and a chairman with previous start-up experience has been appointed.

Demand is almost impossible to forecast with any accuracy, but the directors believe that sales could reach more than £5m per annum within four years. To fund capital expenditure and initial losses, some £2m is required. The directors have £100,000 available to invest. Would you provide the balance, and if so, on what basis?

It should be clear by now that decisions such as this are not straightforward. Commercial risks include extended delays in getting new equipment operational, the need to recruit suitable staff quickly, and critically, how rapidly new customers can be gained. Existing service providers could respond by cutting price and new entrants could enter the market.

The potential, however, in a growing market is considerable and the experience of the management is encouraging. So, if we are inclined to invest, what terms would be appropriate?

A proportion of the requirement can be met with a Regional Selective Assistance grant from the Scottish Office. The balance of around £1.5m is to be subscribed in a mix of equity and loan stock by 3i and one other institution in exchange for a 60 per cent shareholding. Thus our risk is some six times that of the management for an equivalent level of equity. A good investment? We will have to wait and see. All that we can say at this stage is that we believe there is at least a chance that Geoconference could be worth £25m.

Compare the start-up situation with that of a management buy-out of an existing concern. The buy-out is the process by which incumbent management effect the purchase of the business for which they are presently working. (Buy-outs will be covered in detail in Part 8.)

There are two principles common to all buy-outs. The first is that the management team invariably has but a fraction of the amount of money required – so it effectively borrows the balance. The second is that it is the cash flow of the company concerned that is utilized to pay for and redeem the capital that was borrowed to effect the purchase.

So there must a be a sensible and prudent relationship between the purchase price of the business and its underlying ability to generate cash that is surplus to its ongoing requirements. In contrast to the start-up situation, there is a management team with an established track record, and the commercial circumstances of the company do not change.

The risks are principally financial ones, a function of the new leveraged structure that is being imposed on the company. As a guide, eight out of ten of all buy-outs backed by 3i are broadly successful and the possibility of doubling your money if everything goes according to plan would be a practical rule of thumb.

Take CareCo, a company that operates nine homes for elderly dependent patients with a total of 360 beds. They are located in 'character' properties and the company aims to provide a premium quality of care to private patients and those able to top up state-provided funding. Occupancy levels reached 95 per cent three years ago but have now fallen to 87 per cent, affected in part by the uncertainties surrounding new legal requirements.

A number of the homes would benefit from capital expenditure, with the opportunity to take the number of beds up from 360 to 410. In the medium term, modest growth is forecast from the acquisition of additional homes on the back of demand arising from the company's reputation with municipal authorities.

The management team is long established and has been responsible for building the business over the years. The matrons in charge of each of the homes play a key role and are heavily committed to CareCo's philosophy.

Turnover in recent years has been broadly static at £5.1m with falling occupancy levels matched by a tight control on costs. Profits of about £1m look to be a maintainable minimum, rising progressively over five years to £2m as a consequence of the capital expenditure program. An acquisition price of £7.5m has been set by the vendor. A further £3.1m is needed for capital expenditure and the management has £200,000 to invest.

The key to the financing of this business is the strength and reliability of its cash flow. The maintainable earnings of £1m a year translates entirely into free cash flow, enabling a bank loan repayable over 12 years at a fixed rate of nine per cent per annum to be accommodated comfortably.

The balance of £2.3m to effect the purchase must come from the management's backers. But on what basis? More debt would not be appropriate but nor do the growth prospects for the business justify locking up large amounts of ordinary share capital.

In practice, the majority of the requirement is invested by way of preference shares, offering a cost of money yield and redemption over five years, starting in five years' time. The core equity is made up of the management stake of £200,000 for 40 per cent, and £300,000 from 3i for 60 per cent. The capital expenditure requirement would be met by providing a mix of bank debt and additional preference capital.

The effect of this structure is to provide the bank with a well-covered loan, the investor with a total investment of £2.3m, composed in the main by preference capital but including a stake of 60 per cent in CareCo and the management with a highly leveraged stake of 40 per cent at a cost of £200,000.

The relationship between the management's cost of equity and that effectively paid by the investor (in this case, a factor of around seven) is often known as the envy ratio, for obvious reasons. If all goes according to plan, the bank loan and then the preference capital will be progressively redeemed, providing for a rapid rise in the value of the core equity holding.

Leverage of course also works in reverse. If the company struggles to achieve its forecasts, the yield on the preference capital will be threatened and then potentially the company's ability to redeem it at all. The value of the core equity would be worthless.

To sum up, the potential for entrepreneurial companies and the uncertainties that they face make traditional structuring techniques inappropriate. The important principles are to match the funding profile with the requirement and to weigh the potential for returns against the risks that are faced. ■

Valuation as a source of insight

Herwig Langohr explains how discounted free cash flow valuation works and its important relationship to business realities.

Entrepreneurs are in business to build value. The question is: how much value is actually being built?

Valuation is a process that assists the formation of an answer based on business judgment. More than a technique, it is a benchmarking exercise, typically done before making major decisions such as selecting a business strategy, starting a new line of business, expanding an existing one or before entering important transactions such as buying or selling a business, spinning off a bundle of activities from a larger organization, getting outside shareholders in for the first time, attracting a strategic partner, raising new equity or going public.

What the entrepreneur needs to realize is that he or she will typically know much more about the business than the equity investors he or she is trying to attract. This, one might think, should be reassuring to investors. In fact, it is often frightening to them. Why? Because the entrepreneur may not only know the good news about the business much better but also the bad news. While investors know that there will always be some lemons around, they don't always know which they are.

Valuation is part of the due diligence process that tries to sift the wheat from the chaff. It therefore helps parties to reach agreement about a price at which they are willing to transact without being clairvoyant about the true risks and returns of doing so.

Principles

The key in the valuation process is the point of view of investors. The decision to part or not to part with their money in exchange for a security is theirs. They are fully aware of the information asymmetry in the situation. This perspective generates our seven valuation principles.

1 *The purpose of valuation is to gain understanding* – not to get a number. No diligent investor will pay a number without understanding what is behind it. Once understood why, how and when the business is expected to make profit, the problem of what value to place on the profit stream is already largely solved.

Through analyzing the profit equation, valuation helps reach a sound business judgment about the value of the business. Therefore, it cannot be disconnected from the critical aspects of the business context and requires due transparency of the profit drivers and their mechanics. Otherwise, valuation is a garbage-in and garbage-out exercise not worth undertaking.

2 *For investors, only the future pays – never the past.* Valuation attempts to simulate the future; not to settle up the past. Information about the business

past and the management track record help in assessing expected future performance but the buyer will only pay for the future.

The entrepreneur has probably made considerable sacrifices and entrepreneurial efforts. Investors only count the business prospects these create, not their costs. That is why these are called sunk costs. In entrepreneurship, endeavors bear no entitlement for compensation; only prospective benefits do. It is sometimes hard for entrepreneurs to come to terms with this merciless reality. If some errors have been made in the past or bad luck has struck, it could very well be that prospective value falls considerably short of historical value.

The worst that could happen then is that the entrepreneur sticks to these sunk costs as value benchmarks. This could prevent the business from attracting the equity oxygen it needs to grow, to develop, sometimes even to survive. More than one business has run into this ground of sunk costs. It is always better to cash an actual market price that is low than not to cash a historical value that is high.

3 *Cash is king.* For the purpose of valuation, the future prospects of the business must be laid out in cash flow terms. Again, this is because we look at the business from investors' perspectives.

To buy business assets or shares in the business, the investor gives up a scarce resource: cash. If financed with a loan, the investor uses the cash purchased with the loan to pay for the investment. Even if the means of payment is a security given up in exchange for the investment, the resource cost that the investor sacrifices in this transaction is the cash value of the security handed over the day the deal is executed. Buying into a business is in that sense no different than buying groceries: you don't pay with accounting numbers but with cash.

What the investor wants back eventually is also cash. He or she needs to know how much cash the business is expected to free up that could be returned to investors while maintaining the business in optimal shape. This is called free cash flow (FCF). Valuation must provide insight into the FCF generating power of the business and determine its current market price for the investor. Accounting data will be useful inputs in this process but are not the output.

4 *Cash today is worth more than cash tomorrow.* No entrepreneur acutely aware of his or her immediate cash needs will argue with that. So future FCFs must be discounted back to the present to determine what they are worth today, that is, their present value (PV). Discounting means computing how much cash is needed now to produce the expected FCFs through interest, interest on interest and returning the cash invested. The PV is an amount that produces a cash flow stream equal to the FCF stream.

Of course, the higher the interest rates, the lower the PV. This 'time value of money', which incorporates inflation, is given by the yield on a default-free government bond with equal length as the FCF stream. For a five-year pound sterling stream, this would currently be around seven per cent, making £1,000 in five years worth £713 today, and £1,000 during five years in a row, £4,100.

5 *To take more risk, investors want higher expected return.* In other words, there is no free lunch. Again, no entrepreneur will take offense at this. But an interesting paradox arises. Where is the risk if you get higher return? The answer is that while we are pretty sure about the amount of the risk that we are taking now – that is, the amount that could be lost and the likelihood of loosing it – we remain pretty uncertain about what the actual future return is going to be. The price is what you part with and risk. The return is only what you expect.

The higher these risks, the poorer the quality of the FCFs and the more the market will downgrade these to a low PV. The deeper PV is downgraded for poor quality, the higher the expected return that these cash flows represent relative to that PV. In other words, the worse the possible downside, the higher the upside must be to offer an attractive deal. It is not unusual to find discount rates of 60 per cent to 80 per cent per year for start-ups or first-round equity financing to reflect these uncertainties. (See *How the venture capitalists work out the financial odds*, p. 82.)

Risk-adjusted discount rates are what are called the cost of capital, known as 'k', or the expected return after corporate income taxes that a prospect must offer to attract investors. Investors establish their requirements on the basis of the alternative risk return opportunities available in the market, the actual marketability of the project and their own relationship to its management.

To compensate for general equity risk, the market has paid on average over the last 70 years an arithmetic premium of around 7.5 per cent over the bond rate. To compensate for the risk of a particular company relative to the stock market, that premium must be adjusted by a factor from 0.40 for businesses with relatively highly stable revenues and low operating leverage to 2 for equity that is highly exposed to the business cycle because of commercial, operating and financial risks. A 'safe' project would currently command a 'k' of around 10 per cent, a 'risky' one 22 per cent.

But entrepreneurial projects are more often than not illiquid. Selling them may require considerable time and effort. This illiquidity imposes additional costs and risks to investors for which they want additional compensation. This can easily increase the discount rate by 5 per cent to 10 per cent.

In addition, suppliers of risk capital often offer advisory, monitoring and networking services along with their capital. These consume a lot of time and could risk damage to reputations. They must be compensated. Fees are out of the question. Capital gains are not. This adds an additional 20 per cent to 40 per cent to the discount rate.

In short, the illiquidity, service and reputation considerations tend to swamp competitive capital market risk return requirements in the downgrading of expected FCFs to determine the PV of an entrepreneurial project.

6 *The business entity creates the value, not the securities that distribute it.* This simple but powerful principle helped two famous economists, Miller and Modigliani, earn the Nobel prize.

The entity approach to valuation starts with valuation of the business as a business, regardless of how it is financed. It discounts the FCF from operations at the 'k' of the business cost to obtain the PV of the business entity. In the absence of any financial debt, this would correspond to the value of the company's shareholder equity. In the presence of such debt, its market value is deducted from the business entity value to obtain the PV of the equity.

7 *While it is good to be with the right company, it is better to do the right thing.* Investment bankers and dealmakers typically use some form of 'comparables' to price cash flow forecasts. This valuation against peers is a legitimate due diligence consideration for intermediaries and a useful consistency check. But it should not become an alibi for lack of scrutiny.

The entrepreneur sells a unique proposition and the investor expects to collect returns from a specific business. While market-based, the valuation method should provide sufficient insight into these unique characteristics.

The discounted FCF approach applies these principles extensively and involves six steps:

Application

- forecast FCFs during the forecast horizon
- estimate 'k'
- estimate the continuing value, that is, the value at the horizon
- discount all these to the present to get the business PV
- add cash and marketable securities
- deduct financial debt to get the equity PV.

This building block approach makes transparent where value comes from and is therefore popular. It also links easily to regular business information and circumstances.

For example, the FCF of a particular period is nothing more than net operating profits minus taxes paid on these (NOPLAT), plus depreciation minus the investments that had to be made during the period to generate the cash. These investments are the increase in working capital requirement (the investment necessary to operate the fixed assets, such as increases in receivables or inventory, which tend to be proportionate to sales) plus net capital expenditures. In other words, the FCF approach recognizes realistically that to create more value, most businesses require investment. No investor can eat the cake (withdraw cash) and have it too (leave cash in the business to create more value).

Take as another example a company that stops growing after a few years. At the horizon, the company plans simply to replace assets without any further investment. In this case, FCF will coincide with NOPLAT and NOPLAT will never grow. It becomes like a perpetuity and its value at the horizon is simply NOPLAT divided by 'k'. If the company is expected to grow after the horizon, a realistic long-term sustainable growth rate of FCF will have to be built in to estimate continuing value.

Further, consider a company that operates under perfect competition – unlikely for start-ups or initial financings but not unrealistic sometime down the line. In that case, you pay for what you get and get what you pay for: the cost of further expansion investments (I) will be equal to the PV of the FCFs that these investments will generate. This is like buying bonds in an efficient bond market: they earn the competitive return but nothing more.

The cost of such investments is equal to the present value of their expected free cash flows: $I = PV(FCF)$. The difference between the PV(FCF) and I is called the net present value (NPV) or, synonymously, the economic value added (EVA) of an investment. Under perfect competition or in an efficient bond market it is zero: $NPV = EVA = PV(FCF) - I = 0$. Under these circumstances, expansion does not add value and FCF is also equal to NOPLAT. It is as if the company were only replacing its existing assets.

Alternatives: the comparables approaches

While discounted cash flow is the best way of organizing valuation according to our seven principles, price to earnings (P/E) and price to book value (P/B) ratios are second best variants to it.

The P/E ratio tells how 'expensive' one unit of earnings really is. Naturally, i) the more that unit of earnings can grow without asking for more cash from the shareholders, ii) the more that unit pays out in cash to the shareholders without reducing its future growth, and iii) the lower the 'k', the better the quality of that earnings unit and the more expensive it will be.

The P/B ratio tells how many currency units of shareholder value one currency unit of shareholder investment has created. It is a measure of what management has done with a unit of shareholders' money: create value (P/B>1) or destroy it (P/B<1). Naturally: i) the more the prospective profitability of the business exceeds its 'k' and ii) the more there are such profitable investment opportunities, the higher the market value of that capital will be relative to its original cost.

The comparables approach to valuation multiplies the earnings (E) or book value (B) of the business to be valued with the P/E or P/B ratio of a 'comparable' company to determine what the business would be worth if it would command these P/E or P/B ratios.

If applied properly, these approaches should reach similar valuation results because they also work with forecasts about the business, its cash flows to investors, growth and cost of capital. Unfortunately, they rely extensively on accounting numbers and are used often as an alternative to proper analysis by simply plugging in a P/E or P/B ratio without due investigation of the true comparability between the businesses. Further, because accounting data involve many discretionary adjustments and few businesses are really comparable at all times, this method can lead to confusions.

Actually, P/E and P/B ratios are highly variable within industries and over time. Companies in the publishing sector in the Netherlands recently had P/E ratios ranging from 8.3 to 24. Between 1949 and 1995, the average S&P 500 P/E ratio was 13.9, ranging between about 6.9 in 1980 and 22.5 in 1961. The S&P 400 P/B ratio ranged from about 0.4 to 1.9 between 1960 and 1994 with an average of slightly less than 1.1.

Conclusion

Discounted FCF, P/E and P/B approaches should all lead to the same valuation results if applied equally analytically. The more a situation is complex, the more the profit equation and the uncertainties surrounding it require thorough analysis to gain insight. The discounted FCF method forces that analysis. That is why some people criticize it for requiring too many estimates and approximations and for being 'too academic'. But in our opinion, it is always better to be approximately right than to be exactly wrong. Diligent investors know this. That is why the more complicated the discounted FCF is, the less they will be satisfied with shortcut methods. The financials of a business plan are a check on its overall consistency and attractiveness. Discounted FCF analysis is a simple exercise to help determine how much value the business is actually expected to build. And isn't this what valuation is all about? ■

Profiting from a closer banking link

Most enterprises are funded by the banking sector. **Martin Binks** and **Christine Ennew** explain the importance of a two-way information flow to maintaining a good relationship.

However well developed a local venture capital industry may be, it is still the banking sector that is the main supplier of finance to growing businesses. The dependence on bank finance is evident in both the UK and the US, where there are well-developed venture capital providers, and is even more extensive in countries such as Germany and Japan where venture capital is less well developed.

This heavy reliance on bank finance (in the form of either long or short-term debt or some mixture of the two) means that any problems or inefficiencies in the provision of such finance can result in the loss of growth potential from enterprising businesses. Aside from the negative impacts that this may have on individual entrepreneurs, there may also be a significant cost to the economy if enterprising businesses are unable to grow and develop.

When banks consider the provision of debt to an entrepreneur, they are effectively making an investment in the enterprise concerned and looking for a return in the form of interest payments and the repayment of the initial capital. In deciding whether to provide finance, a bank must evaluate the potential of the proposed project and the likely commitment of the management to ensuring the success of the project.

This process is by no means straightforward and provides a classic example of the problems that may arise when contracts are being negotiated in the presence of what economists refer to as 'asymmetric information'. Asymmetric information is a situation in which one of the parties to a contract does not know or cannot observe some of the information that is necessary to the contracting process. In the case of bank finance, this is present because a bank typically cannot perceive the true abilities of the entrepreneur and the real prospects for the proposed project. This is a problem that arises in advance of contracting and may be compounded by monitoring problems once finance has been provided.

Specifically, having provided finance, a bank may not be able to ascertain whether the entrepreneur is actually devoting the necessary amount of effort to ensuring the success of the project. Such information problems are not unique to entrepreneurial companies but are considerably more prevalent because these businesses tend to be smaller and the costs of information collection higher.

Credit rationing

Economists have evaluated the existence of these problems and their implications for the provision of debt finance from both theoretical and empirical standpoints. One perspective suggests some form of credit rationing will arise and that potentially viable projects will fail to obtain funding. However, an alternative viewpoint argues that the result will be an oversupply of credit rather than a 'debt gap'. Others have suggested that the extent of these problems may be overstated and that decisions to lend or not and the price of funds only reflect a bank's knowledge of the entrepreneur and his or her business.

Clearly, the current state of our knowledge is very partial and there is a need for further work to understand the existence and effects of information asymmetries. However, there is evidence to suggest that some of the apparently conflicting views may not be mutually exclusive. A study of lending decisions to smaller US businesses, for example, suggests that while the macro effects of credit rationing may be small, credit may still be rationed to some entrepreneurs and be more readily available to others. In particular, this result may be related to the role of collateral in debt finance.

Companies may overcome bank uncertainty by offering sufficient collateral to both secure the debt and provide reassurance that the business will perform to the best of its abilities in undertaking the project. Offering collateral, in the form of either personal or business assets, can be seen as an entrepreneur signalling the quality of a project; and the willingness to accept the risk of surrendering collateral in the event of failure ensures that he or she is fully committed to the venture.

However, if collateral is in limited supply, debt gaps may still exist and valuable projects may be lost. Lack of collateral may be particularly prevalent among smaller and more enterprising businesses. In addition, the provision of personal collateral in the form of a guarantee or house deeds effectively erodes limited liability status and the protection it provides. This can be expected to discourage investment at the margin, given the additional personal risk it implies.

Information flow

While collateral provides one mechanism by which the problems of debt access may be reduced, an alternative approach is to consider how to improve the quantity and quality of information flows between the bank and the business.

Although perfect information is an unobtainable goal, the quantity and quality of information available to a bank will be influenced by the nature of the relationship with each business. A close relationship has the potential to provide a bank with a better understanding of the operating environment facing a particular business, a clearer picture of the managerial attributes of the owner and a more accurate overview of the prospects for the business.

Thus, from the perspective of the bank, the relationship provides the basis for understanding customer needs and resources and identifying the most appropriate ways of meeting needs. This relationship is not simply a one-way process. An effective banking relationship requires a positive contribution from both parties. The ability of a bank to meet customer needs requires that the owner/manager provides the bank with appropriate and timely information and is receptive to suggestions and advice from the bank. This process imposes costs on both sides, and each party may only be prepared to invest in the development of a relationship if the benefits are expected to outweigh the costs. Furthermore, a close relationship may not be necessary or appropriate for all businesses. The established, stable, smaller business with no aspirations for growth and limited financing needs may have little to gain from investing in improving the flow of information to its bank.

☞ A cautionary tale of collateral

In many countries, banks make significant use of collateral to ease the information problems associated with a lending decision. As well as signalling the quality of a project and incentivizing managers, collateral also provides a means of recovering at least some of their investment should a venture fail.

In practice, realizing security in the event of default can be difficult and may attract adverse publicity. Banks are nevertheless careful to ensure that the realizable value of collateral is greater than or equal to the value of the loan.

This can present problems particularly in relation to business assets. In the event of default these commonly command a much lower price (at auction for example) than their value to the company as a going concern.

Thus the value of collateral required will often be much greater than the finance provided. One consequence is that companies purchasing plant and equipment add far more to their costs than they do to the value of business assets for collateral purposes.

The more rapidly companies expand, the larger the gap between the two and the more likely their

proprietors are to rely on personal assets (houses, shares etc) to secure additional debt.

Businesses often resist the idea of surrendering control over personal assets, particularly where this means limited liability status is eroded. The tables show the pattern of 'collateral taking' over the past eight years based on data provided by the UK's Forum of Private Business. Although the use of purely personal collateral has declined, the use of personal and business collateral has increased.

The UK's Small Business Loan Guarantee Scheme was introduced in 1981 in order, among other things, to address the collateral issue. Despite many changes in the scheme's design, it is primarily concerned with providing debt to businesses where all available security is already pledged. It does not tackle the question of personal as opposed to business asset collateral except in as much as some personal assets may be deemed unavailable if a partner or family not involved in the project has a claim on the assets.

The scheme is still available, though possibly underutilized because companies and some bankers are not aware of it. ∎

However, for the entrepreneurial business with significant financing needs to fund growth, a relationship may be essential for success. Equally, banks may perceive significant benefits from investing in the development of a relationship with such a business because of the impact of its current and future success on bank performance.

The changing nature of the relationship between small businesses and their banks has been closely monitored in the UK since the Committee to Review the Functioning of Financial Institutions (the Wilson Committee) reported in 1979. This monitoring has been continued through regular surveys of the membership of the Forum of Private Business (FPB), which have taken place every two years since 1988. The Forum of Private Business is a representative body for businesses similar to the National Federation of Independent Businesses (NFIB) in the US.

These surveys provide evidence of an initially poor relationship between banks and smaller businesses but also show that significant improvements have occurred since 1992. More significantly, recent surveys have shown that businesses that are more participative in their relationship with their banks may benefit in terms of better financing terms and conditions and a better quality of service.

Banks, too, appear to benefit from closer relationships since customers are generally more satisfied and appear to be significantly more loyal. The 1996 FPB survey received responses from nearly 4,000 companies. On the basis of these it is possible to categorize companies and their banks into Participative (P) and

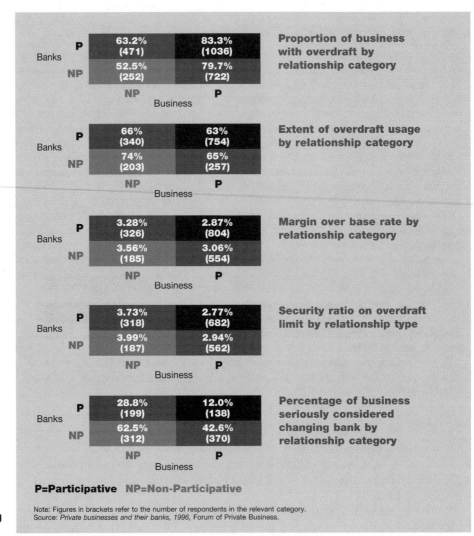

Figure 1: Financing characteristics

Note: Figures in brackets refer to the number of respondents in the relevant category.
Source: *Private businesses and their banks, 1996*, Forum of Private Business.

Non-Participative (NP) and observe the respective financing conditions (*see* Figure 1).

The increasing emphasis on the relationship between entrepreneurs and their banks is particularly apposite now because of changes in technology and the competitive environment in which bankers operate.

As established above, the relationship is seen to be important because it determines the effectiveness of communication between the two parties and, therefore, the exchange of information. In the past much has been made of the contrasting experiences of Anglo-Saxon banking methods in the UK and US and a more relationship-based 'industrial banking' approach such as that operating in Germany, Japan and, to some extent, France.

Some of the claims for the supremacy of the industrial banking systems have been exaggerated in that the benefits of such a longer-term approach were usually enjoyed more by medium and larger-sized businesses than by smaller

Type of collateral on overdraft (% of respondents)					
	1988	1990	1992	1994	1996
Personal	n/a	31.8	32.4	30.2	24.4
Business assets	n/a	24.9	28.2	25.1	26.9
Business and personal	n/a	25.5	30.7	30.3	32.0
None	n/a	17.9	8.7	14.4	16.7
Number	n/a	3315	4692	3486	2642
Collateral ratio on overdraft	-	4.78	3.48	2.35	3.14

Type of collateral on loan (% of respondents)					
	1988	1990	1992	1994	1996
Personal	23.2	28.5	27.1	25.8	21.2
Business assets	27.2	31.5	32.3	31.3	31.7
Business and personal	22.4	23.5	29.4	32.2	35.8
None	27.3	16.5	11.2	10.7	11.3
Number	872	1721	2603	2142	1371
Collateral ratio on loan	-	3.85	2.09	1.92	2.00

Note: collateral ratio = value of collateral divided by value of loan it secures
Source: *Private businesses and their banks, 1996,* Forum of Private Business.

Figure 2

entrepreneurial organizations. Nevertheless, these traditions have appeared to engender a longer-term perspective on the growth and development of businesses as well as more highly qualified bank staff. The actual outcome of these alternative approaches to banking relationships is hard to measure but should be apparent in qualitative differences in the exchange of information undertaken by banks and entrepreneurs. Certainly there is evidence to suggest that information flows in the UK bank/business relationship are improving and developments in information technology have the potential to enhance this process significantly, both by improving the quality of information sharing and by reducing the costs of so doing.

The impact of new technology on the banking industry has been augmented by the growing emphasis upon cost reduction as a result of increasing competition in their traditional markets. At the same time, the pressures towards engendering a more effective relationship have also grown.

Countries such as Germany, in which banking relationships were traditionally more effective, may be slower to embrace the potential offered by new technologies. Changes in the UK and the US may lead to the integration of information exchange between entrepreneurs and their banks with rapidly developing management information systems, credit-scoring decision-support models and expert or knowledge-based systems. This may enable businesses and banks to be much more accurate in tailoring the closeness of the relationship to the needs of both parties. The resulting efficiency gains could lead to significant advances in the competitiveness, both of the banking industry and the enterprises they serve. ■

Getting started

ENTIRE 1st FLOOR OFFICES
TO LET
BRAHAM GOOD
+ partners
01·935 1653

Contents

Contributors

Alice de Koning is a Ph.D. candidate, strategy and entrepreneurship, at INSEAD, Fontainebleau, France.

Jean-Louis Barsoux is a senior research fellow in strategy and management at INSEAD.

Robert M. Johnson is Lecturer in Entrepreneurship at London Business School. Previously he was a successful entrepreneur in both the US and UK.

David Norburn is Director of Imperial College Management School and London University Inaugural Professor of Management. His research focuses on corporate governance, cross-border acquisitions and joint ventures. He is a director of two entrepreneurial companies, Whurr Publishing and Newchurch & Co.

David Grayson is Director of the Prince of Wales Award for Innovation and Chairman of the Business Link Accreditation Board.

Howard E. Aldrich is Kenan Professor of Sociology at the University of North Carolina, USA. In his study of the role of social networks in entrepreneurship, he focuses particularly on gender differences.

Albert Angehrn is Associate Professor and Director of the Center for Advanced Learning Technologies (CALT) at INSEAD.

Amanda Brickman Elam is a graduate student in sociology at the University of North Carolina, USA. Having worked several years for a start-up software firm in the Research Triangle Area of North Carolina, she takes a special interest in business ownership.

Introduction

Part 4 deals with the process of getting started and the various stumbling blocks along the way. The authors remind you of some simple but crucial universal truths – that it always takes longer than you think, that you will inevitably face many obstacles, that you need to think about corporate governance issues, that there is always help around, and that often that help comes from your personal and social network, your family and friends. You are also reminded of new 'network' opportunities through which to market your services – the Internet.

A business plan to entice backers

Alice de Konig provides a checklist for what to put into a business plan and how to present it.

Gather the information first

A business plan includes many elements, most of which will require careful research. Depending on the country or region you live in, you will be able to rely on a combination of libraries, government databases open to the public, lawyers or accountants, and personal contacts. Interviews with potential customers and suppliers give your plan credibility and will probably improve your business idea and strategy.

The easiest way to build the business plan is to collect the information first, before writing the plan. European Venture Capital Association suggests this list:
- Resumés of founders and key managers
- Statistics relating to sales and markets
- Names of potential customers and anticipated demand
- Names of and information about your competitors and your assessment of them
- Financial information required to support your project
- Research and development information
- Production process and sources of supply
- Information on requirements for factory and plant
- Magazine and newspaper articles about your business and industry
- Regulations and laws that could affect your business
- Product and process protection (patents, copyrights, trademarks).

Why are you writing a business plan?

Remember to write for your readers. Who will read your plan? Is it potential investors, customers? Think about what questions they will have and what aspects of the business are important to them. When you write the sections and design the layout of the plan, imagine you are speaking to your audience.

Business plans are useful for existing businesses, too. If you plan to turnaround a business or start a new phase of growth for your existing business, a business plan is a great tool to articulate your ideas while at the same time convincing investors and other people to support your project.

Communicate your passion. Whatever your great concept, it's your responsibility to explain the idea in a clear and lively fashion. Let others catch your enthusiasm. In fact, the very process of researching and writing the business plan will help you clarify your ideas.

Most important, don't let your audience get bored: keep it interesting and concise, all the way through.

Make it look good

The business plan speaks for you. The better it looks and the clearer the ideas in it, the more results you'll get. A clean professional look means your business plan will be read seriously. If you don't have the computer skills to prepare the plan, hire a service that does.

A business plan isn't a novel – try to keep it within 20 to 40 pages, including a three to five page summary (see below). Obviously, a sophisticated high-technology manufacturing business may require extra pages to cover the necessary details. Include enough detail to demonstrate you have done your homework and you understand the market and the business. Remember, if your audience is venture capitalists, you just need to convince them to invest.

Start off the business plan with the executive summary, which should give the essential elements and excitement, to entice the reader into looking at the full plan. Investors get lots of proposals – they won't read for more than five minutes if you can't intrigue them.

Organize the information into logical and clear sections. Short sections of two to three paragraphs with informative headings are easier to read and to review. A detailed table of contents also helps.

Use the business plan to help your readers 'see' your business in the future. By including all the critical elements (which are here organized in three main sections) the business plan should answer your readers' unspoken questions about how your business will actually work. These sections are summarized from EVCA research, which asked venture capitalists what they wanted to see in a business plan.

The contents of the plan

Management and organization information – who are the people?
Like potential employers, potential investors need to be convinced that you and the other people in the venture team have experience, skills, talents and integrity. A synopsis of each person's background, with special attention to any successes in managing high-growth projects, should be included.

Besides the people you have, what specific skills are missing in the management team? Acknowledge the gaps and show you understand what kind of people the business needs to succeed. In fact, your readers might be able to help you find that key person.

How will you structure the organization? In terms of the board, what kind of directors do you need or want? In terms of employees, describe your vision of reporting relationships, incentives and recruiting.

Product information – what is the product or service?
Describe both the features and the benefits to the customer of the product. Insert a photograph or artist's impression. Relate your product or service to existing products and technology and clarify the distinctions. If you have a technological idea, explain the product and its uses in plain language.

Is more R&D required? Write up a research plan, including specific development objectives, a budget and schedule. What are the risks in the technology? How likely is it that another company is working on similar ideas? Can this R&D be leveraged into a range of products? What about patents?

How will you deliver the product? A detailed analysis and plan for producing the product should be generated. Don't just include the factory or shop but also describe how and where you will get your raw materials and notice whether any problems might occur (for example, delay in overseas delivery). What will be the production costs? How will you control quality?

Review government regulations for your product (national and at least regional) and be sure to identify required approvals or environmental restrictions. What plan do you have for getting approvals or permits?

Marketing information – how will you market your product?

The bottom line for any business is converting an idea into a product that people will buy. Is there a market for your product? Do you understand the market forces that will affect your business? Do you have the ability and resources to sell and distribute your product?

● *The market*: The first priority is to clearly specify the target market segments, explain why your product is suitable and what advantages it offers over existing products.

How will you position your product for the target segments? Discuss all the relevant factors – your proposed marketing policy for the price, quality and design of the product, the type, style and content of advertising and public relations, the sales force, service and so on.

Estimate both the size of the market, and the cost in people and finances for reaching it. The marketing strategy and customer benefits should work together. For example, your pricing strategy should be based on the value of the product to the customer, not on your manufacturing costs.

● *The competition*: The business plan must describe who your (potential) competitors are, including companies overseas. You should also prepare a defensive strategy based on probable reactions of your future competitors. Beware of competitors with lots of money – they have the resources to fight hard and long if they decide you threaten their future.

● *Sales and distribution*: The first decision is whether to work with outside agents or to have your own sales force and distribution system. Both have advantages and disadvantages.

Think about ease of reaching customers, size of orders, number of customers and need for customer support as you decide on a system. If you will depend on only a few customers for most of your sales, you must plan how you will manage that relationship profitably.

Consider export sales separately – the costs and benefits of outsourcing distribution may be very different. Many private companies and public services can help your business expand internationally at a reasonable cost.

● *Advertising and public relations*: Many products require advertising to create sales. Explain your advertising philosophy, budget and plan, making sure to link the advertising to your overall market positioning strategy.

Your options include using public media for 'free' advertising. An agency can help create a winning strategy but select an advertising or PR agency carefully – check the work they have done in your industry.

Financial information

How will you finance the business? The amount of financial information in the business plan depends on how much money you seek and the stage of your financing. The plan should include three elements:

● *The funding request*: State how much money you need, why you need it and what you will do with the funds. Don't try to keep the amount as small as possible – allow enough for contingencies

• *Financial statements*: If your company is already operating, include the latest audited accounts and comment on trends and fluctuations
• *Forecasts*: Use the information you have gathered on the market, product and costs and make realistic assumptions to build a scenario of the next several years for your business.

The financial forecasts should include profit and loss statements, cash flow and pro forma balance sheets for up to five years. The level of detail (monthly, quarterly or annual) should depend on the type of business. For example, seasonal businesses usually have high financing needs for specific periods of time, for example just before the snow for ski businesses. Your forecasts should show the peaks and troughs of your business. ■

☞ CASE STUDY

The Health and Safety Inspectorate (HSI)

'It's unsafe and it's not organized. We also expect to hear a reply from you or a personal visit might be nice . . . we think you should look very carefully at your standards of safety, otherwise you might find yourselves trying to explain why someone's son or daughter will not be coming home. Nobody wants that to happen, but it will sooner or later'.

This extract is from a letter sent in late 1992 to Peter Kite, Managing Director of OLL Ltd, the company that arranged the Lyme Bay canoeing trip on 22 March 1993 in which four school children drowned. Peter Kite was subsequently jailed for two years for manslaughter having been found guilty of gross negligence: his plea that he had delegated the responsibility for safety was rejected.

During the spring of 1996, Joanne Linder, Graham Dudlyke, George Parker, and Adriana Saenz were students on the MBA program at Imperial College Management School where they had joined forces to enter the European Business Plan Competition. They had varied backgrounds. Joanne was a qualified Company Secretary and associate of the Chartered Institute of Secretaries and Administrators. She had an international marketing and account management background with the large clients of a leasing subsidiary of ABN AMRO Bank. Graham worked in the treasury and corporate finance departments of a major international bank. George was an analytical chemist by training and formerly a college lecturer. He had spent the last 15 years as an officer in the military, reaching the rank of Commander Royal Navy. Adriana was a graduate physiologist. She had grown up in Bogota, Colombia where her family owned a number of businesses.

They formed the Health and Safety Inspectorate [UK] to '*supply the UK travel industry with a unique, comprehensive out sourcing facility for the health and safety assessment of overseas holiday facilities. By setting the industry standard, HSI [UK] provides cost effective protection against the threat to their competitiveness from current legislative changes.*'

The opportunity arose from two significant developments in English law.

● In 1993 the EEC's Package Travel Directorate became law, producing a class of business it called holiday 'Organizers' who were responsible to the consumer for any deficiency in the quality of the product sold. For the purpose of this legislation, 'Organizers' were any organization or individual who arranged and sold any two, or more, elements of a holiday, e.g. flight and hotel, car rental and hotel, etc. This effectively encompassed all tour operators and a large percentage of travel agents. The overall effect within the travel industry was to make such 'organizers' responsible for any health and safety fault in holiday locations such as faulty wiring, unsafe balconies, polluted swimming pools, unsafe food storage and preparation or inadequate fire prevention procedures.

● In March 1996 the Law Commission recommended a new crime of 'Corporate Killing'. Under these proposals it would be possible to bring criminal charges of gross negligence against a company[1] with the possibility of unlimited damages. Moreover, in such circumstances, insurance was only available in the case of a civil claim. This threat of legislative action from an injured party following an incident whilst on holiday clearly pointed to a need for travel companies to be able to show that they had taken 'reasonable precautions and due diligence' to ensure the safety of their customers.

Legal advice is that 'reasonable precautions and due diligence' firmly put the onus on organizers to 'take all due care' to prevent accidents happening in the first place. This can only be achieved through a program of formalized risk assessment and risk management – which in practical terms means physically inspecting holiday facilities and identifying potential danger.

Previously, some organizers carried out no health and safety inspections. Some employed experts in only one particular aspect of health and safety, such as fire prevention or structural integrity. Others were carried out either informally or formally by organizers during routine visits to re-negotiate contracts. The partners considered that this use of existing staff gave rise to the following drawbacks:

● Negotiators are not experts in health and safety risk assessment. The quality of their inspections would be, at best, variable. Moreover, such inspections might not reasonably be expected to provide the basis of a defence against negligence in court.

● The relationship that the holiday company staff had with the suppliers of hotel and travel facilities might not provide a conducive basis for an objective and impartial assessment.

● Negotiators were under considerable time pressures. Health and safety risk assessment might not be their priority.

The team talked to a number of executives in the industry, including representatives of the Tour Operators' Safety Committee, and confirmed that this was, indeed, the case and that it was generally accepted that the role of contracting and inspection must be split. Market research also confirmed the team's view that many tour operators now accepted that the cost of inspection would have to be absorbed, despite the very narrow margins within which they operated.

HSI (UK) concluded that they could fill this gap by providing a unique service to both the UK travel and travel insurance industries through the following products:

● Standards of health and safety, set to the industry best standard to accord with the Department of Health/Chartered Institute of Environmental Health (CIEH) guidelines.

[1] Previously it had only been possible to prosecute an individual for unlawful killing by negligence under English law.

● Inspections by qualified health and safety inspectors based upon these standards. Customers would receive a detailed report of all inspections. Inspectors would be qualified members of the CIEH, all of whom are trained in food control, health and safety at work, building structural and fire risk, and pollution and environmental protection. The team had satisfied themselves that there was significant over-capacity of inspectors in the domestic market.

● Recommendations as to necessary action to meet\shortfalls would be given. This would enable the client to take the necessary course of action.

They would target their market entry to the most popular destinations for outward bound travel – mainland Spain, the Balearics, the Canaries, Greece and the Greek Islands where over 60 per cent of UK package holidays were taken.

They concluded that there was no comparable, fully comprehanesive service available but that they probably had a small window of opportunity. Therefore, they determined their competitive strategy would be to:

● offer the first, fully comprehensive risk assessment service
● set the standard
● make personal contact with all prospective customers
● offer a first class product
● provide impeccable customer service
● initially target high yield resorts
● realize early economies of scale
● progressively reduce prices for repeat business
● thereby reduce switching costs
● develop customer loyalty
● hence, deter competitors.

Adopting a conservative entry strategy, their financial analysis showed break-even during the second year of operation. All they had to do was to win the internal competition and the European competition to validate their ideas.

Postscript

In June 1996, HSI represented Imperial College at the European Business Plan Competition and was narrowly beaten into runners-up spot. However, the level of enthusiasm showed by the judges and competitors alike, encouraged the team to pursue the idea commercially. In November 1996, the company was registered as Assurity Ltd., with three of the original team as founding directors. By March 1997, after a concentrated period of product development, the company was working with one of the top UK tour operators and finding the value of the many lessons learned on the Imperial MBA. ■

This case is an extract from the Business Plan presented by the HSI team at the European Business Plan Competition.

Time pressures 'can cloud the mind'

Daniel Muzyka and **Sue Birley** point to the huge time commitments that beginning a new venture involves.

It always takes longer than you think – isn't that always the case, almost a rule of nature? Yes, and as one experienced entrepreneur we know always says, 'take your initial estimate of how long it will take you to start the business, double it and add 50 per cent'.

Why is this so? As you would expect, it is a mixture of things, partly to do with process and partly to do with the entrepreneurial spirit. The 'trouble' is that entrepreneurial opportunities are usually captured by entrepreneurs who, by their very nature, are optimists. This optimism extends to the time taken to accomplish tasks – the problem is that the rest of the world is not as engaged with our ideas, does not accept the need for urgency and takes its own time.

Of course, there is a learning curve effect. The second time, you are sure to be much better at setting realistic timescales and priorities – assuming there is a second time. So find a surrogate – talk to those who have gone through this before you and check your expectations with them.

The consequences of getting the wrong time frame are clear. You and your team can become unduly frustrated at the wrong moments and abandon a perfectly viable opportunity. Even worse, you may accept a disadvantageous funding deal, buy a bad business or sign a lease on a poor location just because it was the path of least resistance. Time pressures can cloud the mind.

It can also be fatal financially. If your sequencing of costs and revenues is badly mis-timed, you can enter the 'Valley of Death' earlier, and stay in longer, than is sustainable. This is not to say that you have to get it absolutely right. Nobody does. But, as we have said earlier in *Mastering Enterprise*, many profitable businesses fail because they ran out of time (*see* Figure 1).

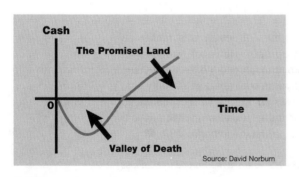

Figure 1

So here are a few of the common sources of delay in starting a business – as seen through the eyes of an impatient entrepreneur.

Customers

Most entrepreneurs assume that finding customers will be quick and easy. After all, they are offering a novel product with new value-added to the market. Why wouldn't potential customers switch their buying habits?

Unfortunately, and not unexpectedly, this is rarely the case. It takes time to identify the right customers – the supermarket buyer, the building specifier, the specialist niche consumer group. It takes time to communicate with them – their

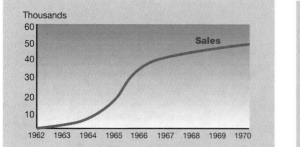

Figure 2: F International *the first eight years*

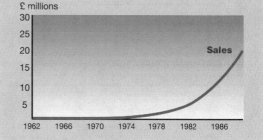

Figure 3: F International *the first 19 years*

diaries are likely to be much fuller than yours and they have priorities that may not include you. It takes time for them to try your product or service and time to decide that they will introduce it – maybe next year.

You can bootstrap this process by focussing on 'opinion leaders' early on and leveraging their enthusiasm into the rest of the market. However, examination of the growth path of most new ventures will show a long period of establishment and consolidation – often with only a few customers – before the venture finally takes off. Take, for example, the case of F International. The sales path for the first eight years looks strong and positive (*see* Figure 2) but put against the next 19 years it is almost horizontal (*see* Figure 3).

Suppliers and distributors

Getting the right suppliers and distributors is critical to success. Yet at the start the entrepreneur is in a position of relative weakness – he or she does not have a trading business, just a potential business. Moreover, you may want them to do some development work for you or arrange special terms for delivery or payment.

It will take time to find those prepared to talk and to negotiate a deal. You will probably have to meet many people in order to share your ideas and convince them of your intent. Incidentally, this applies not only to independent start-ups but also to existing businesses. A management buy-out, for example, is a new venture as far as suppliers are concerned. You are no longer a 'blue chip' company with a reliable payment record and you may find the 'terms of business' change accordingly.

Securing a location

For many businesses, certainly those in retailing, finding the right location is key. It can also be frustrating, demoralizing, time-consuming and expensive. Indeed, if you have never dealt in the commercial real estate market, we have one word for you – beware. This can be far worse than buying a house. For example, we know of one entrepreneurial team establishing a series of shops that took over one year to sign a deal on the first site. They then discovered it would be another six months before all the leasehold improvements could be put in place so that they could open their doors – and that was just a builder's estimate.

Regulations

Where do we start? Clearly you cannot avoid them and, depending on your industry, they can be legion. Even in the best circumstances where the rules are clear and the bureaucrats helpful, you can find that the relevant committees only

© FT Pictures

Which one would you go for? For many businesses, finding the correct location is the key

meet once a quarter, you have just missed the last one and there is a waiting list. That is assuming that you will need only one round.

Let it suffice for us to give you just one example of the creative problems posed by bureaucracy. One entrepreneur who was trying to start a food processing business in Germany was faced with two sets of codes from two different government departments. Each of the codes, while a bit ambiguous, seemed to suggest to the bureaucrats in charge that certification was required from the *other* department first in order for them to proceed. But neither was willing to contact the other – after all, it was not their problem. And there was no provision for inter-departmental contact without permission 'from above'.

How did the entrepreneur deal with this? At first, not well. Six months went by and nothing had happened. In the end, entrepreneurial creativity led him to invite each to lunch at the same time without the other knowing. He arranged an exchange of documents over lunch. The problem was solved, honor was preserved and the bureaucratic machine was undamaged.

Team development

On p. 167 Vicky Meakin and Peter Snaith talk about how to build a team for a growing business. We would simply add to this by stating the obvious – it takes not only time but also commitment and tolerance.

You need to attract the right people and keep them interested in the new challenges they will face almost every day. This can be particularly difficult in the early days when you are assembling the business.

It will take time to negotiate an acceptable agreement, particularly if there is equity involved, and then it may take months before they are ready to join you. Alternatively, you may find a critical person leaving the team half way through a negotiation for funding or just as you have landed your first major sale – and you do not have anyone else to take their place.

This is a subject all on its own. Even if you have a piece of technology that works on the laboratory bench, how do you know it will survive the ravages of the consumer world?

Technological developments

Take the example of a new type of catamaran that has passed all the laboratory simulations. Fine, but now you are going to have to produce in bulk and try it out at sea – not just once but many times (you need to know about longevity) and under different weather conditions (you need to know about safety and strength). These tests will almost certainly throw up more technological problems that you had not predicted – and you cannot plan for what you do not know.

During all this process of assembling the resources of your business you will be trying to work out how much money you need and how to raise it.

The search for money

As earlier parts of *Mastering Enterprise* have made clear, identifying potential funding sources, communicating with them, capturing their interest, helping them to pursue their due diligence, negotiating a deal and discussing the formal documents with lawyers is likely to take some time. Moreover, you are likely to be dealing with more than one source of funding.

So if you are looking for venture capital, it can easily take six months from the first meeting to the time when you finally receive a cheque. Of course you will hear of someone who raised their finance in a couple of weeks, but they will have forgotten to tell you that they had floated the idea with potential investors six months ago.

As any psychologist will tell you, you cannot 'burn your engines at the red line' constantly without a break. Yes, you can sustain extended periods of energetic engagement in pursuit of an idea, but most people cannot run continuously without some balance, some time to recharge both physically and emotionally and some time to see their family occasionally.

Energy and commitment

Take, for example, the end (or rather the beginning) of a management buy-out. The team has worked non-stop for six months or a year negotiating the deal and at the same time doing their 'day jobs' running the company. The deal is done, the relief is enormous, reaction sets in and you finally realize how exhausted you really are. Clearly you need a holiday. But that is not possible – the new venture needs your undivided attention.

Are we being over-dramatic? After all, we hear all the time of investment bankers who work non-stop, almost day and night, to close deals or of corporate executives almost sleeping on the factory floor to solve a production crisis. But these stories do not compare with the time and effort that is needed to get a new venture off the ground. The investment bankers have fixed requirements to meet, deal with a limited number of individuals in negotiations and, for the most part, have clear, known targets; executives have the resources of their corporation to help them. The entrepreneur is unlikely to have a rich relative to bail him or her out. The business is yours to manage – as is your health and energy.

Relationships

We know of no definitive studies of divorce rates or the break-up of relationships among entrepreneurs. But experience suggests that they are all too common. It may seem trite, and indeed perfectly obvious, to remind entrepreneurs that their families might like to see them some time, but as one venture capitalist we know has observed when asked why profitable businesses are offered for sale: 'The entrepreneur has decided to go home and introduce himself to his wife and children – if they are still there'.

Taking care of time

Are you discouraged by now? That was not our intention. All we are asking for is a dose of reality. So try to:

● establish a realistic time frame for all your plans. Try to work out where delays are likely to cause you the greatest problems and set up contingency plans

● set realistic expectations for the members of your team, and those you depend upon for emotional and financial support – and that includes both your management team and your family (who are also part of the team)

● think about, if you are intending to start a new venture, what can be done while you are still employed. Getting the core members of your team in place or thinking about your business plan will take time and effort but need not interfere with your job

● Think about the funds you need to support your basic lifestyle – you may have to think about personally 'downsizing'. You really do not want to have to worry about this while you are closing critical parts of a deal or working 80 hours a week getting the office or factory together.

In short, successful entrepreneurs are usually good time managers as well. That is how they manage to do 48 hours work in 24. ■

Negotiating the start-up obstacle course

Robert Johnson describes the difficulties encountered in starting a business and how to tackle them.

One of the difficulties in understanding start-ups is that there are few theories that one can derive from studying them. Without living it oneself, one can only examine anecdotal evidence of what the entrepreneur can expect when starting a business. Yet there has rarely been a successful start-up that has not encountered major difficulties along the way and a number of these problems are common to most start-ups.

By understanding what to expect, the entrepreneur can at least be better prepared to deal with what often seems to be an unending parade of crises that have to be resolved yesterday. Here, then, are the problems which I believe are most critical as well as most common to entrepreneurs in starting up a business.

Everything takes longer than planned

This is unquestionably the most pervasive problem as it underlies many of the others as well. Despite genuine attempts to 'be conservative' in their plans, entrepreneurs always underestimate how long it takes to get things done. (*See* p. 122.)

A common mistake is failing to understand fully the sales cycle for their product or service – in the first instance, the time it takes just to get to the real decision maker(s); then the time it takes to close the critical initial sales; and finally the time it takes to roll out sales and achieve more aggressive targets. Another common mistake is underestimating the time it will take to develop a new product and actually get it to market, often involving countless stages, tests and approval processes that can drag on endlessly.

Yet the problem is not limited to the big, obvious areas of risk in a new business, for even the smallest things take more time. Entrepreneurs don't often realize the time it will take them to set up an office, to get communications and IT equipment and then make it work properly, to establish sound operating procedures and many more seemingly mundane things.

Often the entrepreneur has come from a larger organization where such things were simply handled by someone else; now he or she has to do everything, from buying toner for the copier, to setting up the price sheet for their product line, from negotiating a supply agreement, to franking and posting the mail. The multitude of tasks, big and small, are never ending and simply take time.

Thus the entrepreneur must be very clear about what deadlines are most critical to meet and focus on achieving them, because many things will simply take a lot longer than expected.

Gaining market credibility is very difficult

Virtually every new venture starts out with little credibility. Even people with lots of experience and visibility in an industry will find their credibility tested when they set out on their own.

This problem is exacerbated when one has to educate the market on a revolutionary product or service. Changing buying behavior is one of the most difficult challenges any business faces, and it is even more so when the company is a new kid on the block.

Often there are false starts, dead-ends and adjustments before the company gets its marketing right and begins to gain the credibility so necessary to build the business. This is one reason why you often hear the advice to stick with products, technologies and markets that you already know well. Having the knowledge of, and a network in, an industry and then building on that network are important factors in bridging the credibility gap.

Forecasts are rarely accurate

In many new ventures one can project costs reasonably well; but trying to forecast sales can be exasperating – no one gets it right. When David Potter introduced the first Psion Organiser, there was no way to predict what initial sales would be. There were no comparable products, and it was difficult to

© FT Pictures

The pick of good timing: David Potter spawned a new industry with his Psion organizer

explain to people the benefits of a product that they did not know they might want or need. Fortunately, Potter's timing was right and a new industry was spawned; others have not been so fortunate.

Others have also encountered higher costs than expected, particularly when the venture has involved extensive product or systems development. The net result of such problems is that most new ventures run out of cash; and if there is one rule that entrepreneurs must heed, it is: 'don't run out of cash'.

Certainly profit and loss are important but in a start-up the key is to stay on top of your cashflow. Indeed, for the first four years of our company's life, we ran the business from a cashflow statement.

Increasing turnover (by itself) does not always solve the problem

Many entrepreneurs are good salespeople; and when things get tough, they do what they do best – sell more. This often helps, but there are some cautions.

Sometimes sales increase at the expense of margin, and often a business can never regain the higher margins once they have begun to fall. Prices are often set too low initially and margins can get squeezed. Sometimes the focus on turnover leads to relaxed financial disciplines and ultimately to credit or even cost control problems.

In my own information business, a premature sales push led us to lose focus on building the supply of our data, which resulted a year later in a lower level of information available to sell and thus even more pressure on sales.

The moral: protect your margins and keep your focus while building turnover (*see* p. 297).

Just as a new business encounters credibility problems in the marketplace, so will it find developing relationships with suppliers difficult. Sometimes just identifying suitable suppliers takes longer than you expect. **Supplier relationships are demanding**

Entrepreneurs are often surprised to find a supplier with whom he or she had regular dealings in their former company taking a tougher stance now that the entrepreneur is running a new business. It is not easy to establish credit-worthiness and securing favorable terms usually comes only with time. Likewise, ensuring quality and timely supply requires diligent oversight.

You will need good reasons why suppliers can benefit from having a relationship with your company. Be prepared to spend time on initiating and building relationships with key suppliers.

It is no secret that small businesses are often the victims of the credit payment policies of larger companies. But in many instances the real problem lies inside the new business itself. Credit control is often ad hoc and lax, pressures to build turnover lead to poorer quality customers and people find countless reasons not to push their customers to pay. Yet it need not be that way. Establish tight credit and collection methods from the start and you can help avoid unnecessary cash crises. **Getting paid is not always easy**

Growing businesses rarely have enough space to grow, yet they cannot afford to commit to excess space. Thus the entrepreneur finds herself or himself constantly struggling with how to plan and provide for space needs. It can lead to long-term commitments, involve requests for personal guarantees (which should be resisted) and tie up valuable cash. **Premises produce headaches**

The best solution is to be wary of long-term commitments early on and even pay a premium, if necessary, to retain flexibility.

The quality of the management team is crucial to the success of any business, yet few new ventures start with more than one or two people, let alone a complete team. Building and developing that team is very difficult. It is hard to find the right people (another reason why one's network in an industry is so important), and the process demands a lot of the entrepreneur's time. (*See* page 167.) **Building a good team is difficult and time-consuming**

One agonizing decision for many entrepreneurs involves whether to pay the fees and use a search firm. But for some key positions outside help is needed. Also, in the end not every person works out well, so the process begins again.

Despite the difficulties, this is one of the most important tasks that the entre-preneur must handle – it takes a real team to build a significant business. Do not compromise on key appointments. If it is taking longer than you want, persevere and go for the best people you can find. It will pay off at the end of the day.

Managing people is the biggest challenge

The entrepreneur finds him or herself selling to customers, negotiating with suppliers or subcontractors, working with an advertising agency, dealing with banks and investors, and doing a myriad of other things outside the company. Yet the toughest task – and indeed the most time-consuming (at least mentally) – is managing people. This is the true test of an entrepreneur in trying to build a significant company.

This is also a test of one's leadership – the ability to get others to buy into the entrepreneur's vision, to motivate them and sustain their commitment to the business idea and to get them to work together to achieve the goals set for the company. It involves leading and exerting authority while also learning to delegate and empower. It means welding together and moulding the team while also addressing conflict head on. It also involves painful decisions and lots of time spent talking with people.

The message is simple: be prepared to spend the time required on people issues and be prepared to make difficult people decisions.

There will be conflicts among partners and investors

Entrepreneurs often are so committed to their business idea that they see their company as a kind of family. So it can be devastating when conflict arises with one of their key partners.

Yet such conflicts inevitably occur along the way in a developing business, centered on such issues as whether people share the same vision and sense of purpose, whether key executives are growing with the business and bearing the load equally, whether individuals and investors share compatible exit goals and many other such matters.

These are not easy problems in the best of companies and it can be even more difficult for the entrepreneur who thinks of his team as a family with common goals. This is where communications among all parties is mandatory and where listening skills are critical. Don't wait until such conflicts occur to ensure that open and effective communications are part of your corporate culture.

The pressures on the entrepreneur are relentless

The entrepreneur often finds himself or herself immersed in every aspect of the business, often fire fighting at the expense of planning, feeling responsible for everything and everyone, and 'living the business' to the exclusion of nearly everything else. There is no question that the pressures are heavy and constant and decisions have to be made like a fighter pilot. I've even heard some successful entrepreneurs say that if they had known in advance what they were going to go through, they probably would not have done it. Yet many not only survive, they thrive in that environment.

I believe that one of the keys to survival and success is for the entrepreneur to find a way to achieve some sense of 'balance' in his or her life. That may sound odd, since everything discussed above suggests that such a goal is not achievable for an entrepreneur, but I think it is essential. The entrepreneur must maintain a 'real life', taking the time (difficult though it may be) to be with the family, to stay in touch with friends, to look after his or her health, to develop spiritually and to find other interests besides work that can help sustain him or her as an individual. If an entrepreneur can do this, then he or she will find it easier to deal with the other problems discussed above and hopefully will ultimately enjoy the fruits of success in a business venture. ■

Building a network for business co-operation

David Grayson outlines the roles for government in helping small business.

Business – especially small businesses – is inherently suspicious of government and is therefore wary of any business advice services provided by government. Whatever the objective quality of the advice, there will always be the suspicion that information given in confidence to a business adviser will somehow find its way into the hands of tax and regulatory authorities. Conversely, business support organizations that are clearly seen to be run by and for business are much more likely to win the confidence of small business clients.

Beyond sound and stable macro-economic policies and a reasonable regulatory framework for business, the most effective government contribution is not, therefore, direct provision of business information and support services. Rather it is to encourage business-led organizations to do so. This can still involve government in a number of roles:

● *Funder:* pump-priming and providing core funds for services that are desirable for improving business performance but which small businesses are unable to pay for – or certainly unable to cover the full cost. Specifically, funding services where there is market-failure.

● *Cajoler and catalyst*: to bring different organizations together and to provide a forum where they can agree on common standards and services. This may sometimes involve banging heads together or rewarding good collaboration between business organizations that are being asked to work together.

● *Champion*: to encourage quality and continuous improvement; encouraging benchmarking between business support organizations and establishing an authoritative accreditation and certification system to ensure quality – either through voluntary self-policing or statutory means.

● *Stimulator*: to help business organizations develop a long-term vision of how the external environment is changing, how this will affect small companies and, therefore, to help business support agencies respond both in terms of what they do and how they provide it.

Government also needs regularly to ask itself whether any direct assistance that it provides to business could be better provided through independent business support services either commercially or with the help of subsidies.

Additionally, government has its own unique channels – for example, embassies around the world – which can provide additional advice and support for businesses wanting to trade internationally.

The UK government's drive to establish a network of one-stop shops for small business support – the Business Links – has tried to adopt this approach and practice. The US has been doing something similar with the creation of a network of Manufacturing Extension Centers specifically designed to help small manufacturing businesses. In both cases, they are attempting to create local partnerships of existing publicly funded/subsidized support services under local business leadership. In the case of Business Links this has involved chambers of commerce, Training & Enterprise Councils, local enterprise agencies and local councils.

Business support services must involve entrepreneurs in these processes – especially at the local level where they are delivered to customers – if they are truly to be seen as business-led and government-backed and not vice-versa.

These one-stop shop initiatives have a number of aims:
- Raising the quality of service to small businesses.
- Bringing together a range of different organizations' services.
- Developing new services.
- Reaching more businesses.
- Changing the primary focus for publicly supported business development agencies (from an almost exclusive emphasis on the self-employed and micro-enterprises towards a greater balance, including a concentration on companies that have the aspiration and the potential to grow, recognizing these will include some start-ups).
- Proactively going out to find this new primary target audience.
- Reducing the duplication between agencies and thereby freeing up resources for new service development.
- Moving from producer-led to customer-focused activities.
- Hollowing out from government a range of services to business that were previously run by government.
- Anchoring business support more firmly into a coherent economic development strategy for a locality.

A key innovation has been the introduction of Personal Business Advisers (PBAs) in the UK Business Link system and 'Engineers' in the US Manufacturing Centers. Analogous to account managers in an advertising agency or a relationship manager in a corporate finance house, these are the gate-keepers to a range of help both from within the centers and from commercial services nationally and internationally. A recent census of the 500 PBAs now working in the 89 UK Business Links shows that 89 per cent of them have previously run their own business or worked in a small business. They bring a wide range of sectoral expertise to the network.

Video-conferencing

In the UK the government has quite consciously funded state-of-the-art information technology for Business Links because the fast-growing small businesses that it wants to attract know the value of fast communications and market intelligence. Business Links is offering video-conferencing facilities into some major UK embassies and consulates to help small companies make direct contact with customers and suppliers. This will become part of a set of integrated international trade services.

Government-subsidized business support services should not and cannot replace the market, however. They are there to help owner-managed businesses to make the transition to team-based organizations, to experience the added-value that competent external advisers can bring and to help start-ups/early-stage businesses that are not yet able to pay for such services commercially. Publicly supported services can also introduce small businesses to new forms of

☞ Business links

Wendy McCouaig and Steve Tillet both turned their business ideas into realities with the help of Business Link Kent.

Wendy's project was the result of a visit to the US where the buggies for hire in shopping malls caught her eye. She decided that it would be a good idea to introduce the buggy to large UK shopping centres. Wendy had a prototype KiddyKar buggy designed and built which was given the seal of approval by her 22-month-old son Donnie (pictured left) and by Thurrock

Lakeside which quickly placed the first order.

Steve (pictured right) needed finance to expand his racing seat manufacturing company, and he, like Wendy, turned to Business Link Kent for help. An adviser helped him draw up a three-year business plan and make a successful application for a business innovation grant. The grant, he said, enabled him to switch from making seats by hand to manufacturing them.

Reproduced with kind permission of Business Link Kent

support: for example, to help first-time and passive exporters, or to help them to understand the value of design. This is not picking winners – but if they have worked with a businessman or woman over an extended period, experienced business advisers are usually able to spot those with the aspiration and the potential to grow.

There is a strong argument that government-backed business support agencies should be charging for some of their services. First, because this will generate net extra resources that can be ploughed back into the development and extension of services. Second, and arguably at this stage even more important, charging is about credibility, demonstrating value and setting the right culture. There is growing evidence to show that small companies value much more those services for which they are paying. If business support services are to succeed, they must be run in a business-like way and operate commercially (albeit with a clear public purpose).

International support

National support services also need to provide international business support, and the characteristics of world-class business support are very similar to those of successful international companies.

Services must be customer-focused, entrepreneurial, forward-looking, open to change and improving continuously, networked to a wide variety of external partners, their help tailored to meet the needs of individual customers rather than being based on 'schemes' with pre-determined qualification criteria.

Achieving this can be measured against a number of benchmarks:

- Positive impacts on customers.
- The percentage of total budget that is generated from clients' fees.
- The quality of these earnings: is there a genuine increase in 'real' customer billings (not just recycling public grants).
- Percentage of the primary target audience that is regularly using the service.
- Numbers of clients who are repeat business.
- Introduction of new clients by existing clients.
- Numbers of two-way referrals with banks and management consultancies.
- Percentage increase in first-time exporters and in passive to active exporters.

There are a number of international examples that can be drawn on. The German Steinbeis Foundation focuses on sectoral expertise – especially for technology businesses – by connecting small companies to a range of sectoral technical expertise in education establishments and big company R&D centers; the US Manufacturing Extension Centers mobilize the expertise and resources of individual partner organizations; the New Zealand TRADENZ agency and the Singapore Enterprise Council are strong in integrated international trade services, helping small companies with market intelligence and so on; in continental Europe, the Danish Technological Institute and the Emilia Romagna district of northern Italy have promoted and supported networking in the small business sector by building business support services around clusters of small companies in particular sectors.

There are a number of future challenges that business support services face:

- Finding robust measures of the impact that they have on their clients.
- Reconciling the different timescales that politicians and media have for seeing results compared with the time that it really takes to change culture and practice.
- Accounting properly for public funds without shackling the entrepreneurial drive and enthusiasm of business-led local partnerships.
- Establishing credibility with clients as 'understanding the needs of businesses'.
- Achieving the right balance between bottom-up flexibility and responsiveness to genuine local market differences, with the economies of scale and assurance of minimum quality standards that a national business support 'brand' has to have.

There is now an exciting opportunity to build on the initial success of support services such as the UK's Business Links by, for example, working with big companies to develop the capacity of their small business suppliers, by getting groups of small businesses working together to achieve quality standards (perhaps to exploit a particular overseas market or to develop staff training programs together) and through supporting the commercialization of technological innovations, either in new small businesses or through helping innovators to find licensing opportunities and joint ventures.

In particular, business support services can play a key role in building an 'infrastructure for collaboration' between government, successful technology entrepreneurs, big business, universities and centers of technical expertise. ■

Catching the customers on the Web

The Internet will have a huge impact on the way business is done – especially for small and emerging companies. **Albert Angehrn** and **Jean-Louis Barsoux** explain the ramifications.

For all that has been written about the Internet, most managers remain confused regarding its likely strategic impact on their businesses. Our aim, in this article, is not to try to predict the likely technological evolution of the Internet but rather to provide managers with a generic framework (the ICDT model) for understanding the opportunities and threats generated by the Internet – and for developing a strategy to leverage these. The Internet, as this article will make clear, is of particular relevance to small companies and emerging businesses; entrepreneurs cannot afford to ignore it.

The Internet, and its related basic services, such as electronic mail and the World Wide Web, have created a new space in which to do business. This has given economic agents – whether individuals or companies – alternative channels for exchanging information, communicating, distributing different types of products and services, and initiating formal business transactions.

What to make of the Internet: the ICDT model

The ICDT model (*see* Figure 1) takes its name from the four 'virtual spaces' created by the Internet: a virtual Information space; a virtual Communication space; a virtual Distribution space; and a virtual Transaction space. The four spaces are treated separately because they correspond to different strategic objectives and require different types of investment, and organizational adjustments.

The virtual information space (VIS) is about visibility. It operates like a large billboard. It shows who's who, what's available, how much it costs and so on. It may offer flexible access that allows visitors to 'choose their own path' but it remains a one-way communication channel.

The virtual communication space (VCS) is about interaction. Like a café, it provides a 'space' for engaging in relationship building, exchange of ideas or opinions. The 'space' itself can range from a simple chat-line to a sophisticated 3D space in which individuals 'meet'. Members of the virtual community can communicate at high speed, low cost and bypass traditional physical and geographical constraints.

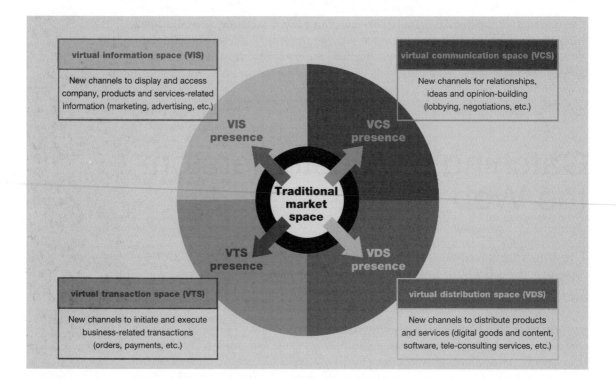

Figure 1: The four visual business spaces

The virtual distribution space (VDS) is about service delivery. As with the postal service, there are constraints on the types of items that can be delivered through this channel – it is only suitable for products and services that can be wholly or partly digitalized. Furthermore, the recipient takes 'something' away but payment itself happens elsewhere.

The virtual transaction space (VTS) is about trading. It is a bit like a stock exchange in that goods and services are not transferred in this space, only orders, commitments, invoices or transfers of payment.

Access to markets and resources

Information space

In terms of engaging with the environment, the VIS is the virtual space that has attracted the most attention – primarily because it affords instant global access, whether to potential customers or business partners.

For many companies, the Internet represents little more than a parallel way of diffusing standard information and their Web sites mirror the content, not to say the appeal, of their corporate literature. However, simply creating a Web site does little to stimulate interest. It establishes contact but if the aim is to connect with other economic agents then the information provided has to be pertinent.

Relevance can be enhanced by customizing the channel to user groups. For example, potential business partners may have very different company or product information needs from potential consumers.

But this is not a one-off effort. If a company wants people to return to the site, and to build up an on-going relationship, then it needs regularly to update the content of its pages. That requires dedicated personnel and investments in multimedia competencies. Moreover, there is a lot of information to extract from monitoring the flow of visits to the site. Companies that take the trouble to compile and analyze this information may find it a cheap way of understanding customer preferences.

Communication space

The VCS presence of most companies remains underdeveloped because businesses are still not sure what objectives it might serve. Part of the problem is that the interface with customers has traditionally been the responsibility of the marketing department, which is more used to broadcasting to than interacting with customers.

The VCS provides an opportunity to exchange information and opinions through e-mail, in on-line forum discussions, or more advanced interaction spaces. Discussions among visitors regarding their experiences with the product and ideas relating to its usage may have an unforeseen payoff for the company. Besides helping to differentiate the product, it may also yield unexpected insights on possible product adaptations or highlight untapped market segments. There is also a case for opening similar sites for corporate users – potential partners, suppliers or distributors from within the same industry – who might interact in closed user groups, discuss industry trends via on-line forums and formulate requests for meetings with company representatives.

Distribution space

Exploiting the VDS potential of the Internet is primarily aimed at cutting costs and lead times. Of course, software and publishing companies have been particularly quick to latch on to the possibilities of dispensing with intermediaries and delivering their products directly.

But the Internet can also be used to distribute to customers auxiliary services associated with 'physical' products such as cars. Instruction manuals, customer support and consulting services, product-related training and updates – including digital pictures and music – can all be provided over the Web in ways that 'augment' the value of the 'core' product.

What is more, the Internet creates the possibility of offering new value-adding services. Some companies have found that they can repackage the information they use to control their own processes and make this information available to customers as a service.

A typical example is the magazine or newspaper that gives outside access to its archives – initially designed to support its own journalists. Another example is the Federal Express service that allows customers to track their parcels on-line. This reduces the number of expensive calls to customer service representatives and has increased customer loyalty in a fiercely competitive market.

Transaction space

The objective here is clear: to engage in business-to-business or business-to-customer transactions such as ordering, invoicing and payment. This has both revenue-generation and cost-reduction potential in that it facilitates order processing and shortens lead times. The cost of an Internet transaction in banking, for example, is a fraction of the same transaction at a bank branch. Business-to-business transactions have benefited considerably from this

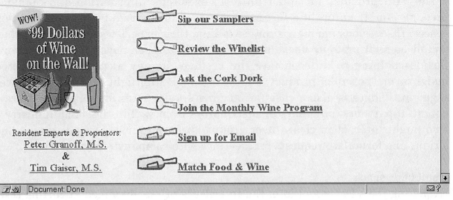

Figure 2: Virtual Vineyards is a Web-based wine and speciality food shop

channel. It allows companies to trigger automatic ordering, to invoice and make payments easily. This has been facilitated by Electronic Data Interchange (EDI) platforms, which provide a high level of security. In fact, many businesses are insisting that potential suppliers install EDI if they want to be considered.

Business-to-consumer transactions do not yet benefit from the same kind of security or reliability as offered by the EDI system. Currently, the huge potential for wide-reaching commercial activity with consumers is stifled by legal, security and reliability concerns.

Commercial activity so far has been limited to low-value purchases such as software, books, music and magazines. One such example is Virtual Vineyards, a Web-based wine and speciality food shop. Visitors can purchase directly from the company using an on-line form.

A more secure system is proposed by IBM which enables visitors to browse through a catalog of products via the Web and then place orders interactively via a secure credit card information form. Many companies are looking into ways of improving security so it is only a matter of time before on-line transactions explode. Once security can be guaranteed, a company will simply need to hook up its Internet site with its internal accounting system or other transaction-processing systems. This is an advanced type of application that will demand heavy investments.

Internal Web sites

Internal Web sites, known as Intranets, offer businesses most of the same functions as groupware at a lower price, and without the need to tie themselves in to a single groupware vendor. They make it easier for employees to access and share internal information. Although covered in detail in the original paper on which this article is based, they are not detailed here.

So far, the Internet has had limited impact on how most companies operate and its strategic impact has been weak. However, once it fulfils its potential, the cumulative influence of the Internet within the four virtual spaces may produce a different order of change altogether. The full exploitation of the communication and transaction spaces, in particular, may upset a lot of our basic strategic assumptions about how best to absorb, process and leverage information. This assertion is based on what remains a little documented phenomenon – the emergence, thanks to the Internet, of a new breed of business, the global start-up.

Changing the rules

The most embryonic start-up becomes a multinational company, at low cost, simply by virtue of setting up a Web site. As the joke says, 'the great thing about the Internet is that no one knows you're really a dog'. But many of these new entrants are not dogs at all. The Internet has done much more than magnify their visibility. It has also provided them with a low-cost distribution network, with a way of searching for business partners and of collecting critical information about distant markets and resources. The Internet does more than simply let new entrants compete on a par with established companies; it can sometimes give them the edge. Consider the challenge of accessing resources. The China Internet Company, backed by the Xinhua News Agency, has established a network of Internet sites for 40 industrial cities. This is accompanied by a complete catalog of Chinese laws relating to trade and export, a translation service and news. Given the paucity of a physical infrastructure for information about exports, the Internet will quickly become the key channel for companies wishing to do business with Chinese suppliers.

Similarly, where companies are offering a specialized product or service, the Internet serves to trawl for customers worldwide. It has the capacity to transform former niche markets into mass markets. Moreover, the low cost of distribution on the Internet makes it viable to serve whole new market segments. For example, on-line newspapers have created a new readership among expatriates living in remote locations who were previously neglected.

The Internet also allows small companies to conduct forms of market research that would previously have been prohibitively expensive even for big companies. As already mentioned this can be done by tracking the behavior and preferences of 'visitors' to Web sites. Furthermore, the Internet also allows companies to conduct cut-price surveys that are much more effective than phone or mail surveys in that they allow branching (that is, different questions based on different responses to previous questions).

While a virtual marketspace creates new business opportunities, at the same time, much of the conventional wisdom of business is threatened. For example, the size of a business will no longer be much indication of the scope of its geographical activities. The traditional concern with 'where to do business?' is superseded by the concept of 'how to do business?'

A well-established network of physical assets may no longer be of much use – indeed, it may even get in the way of speedy strategic reconfiguration. The key competencies embodied by a company will no longer relate to products but rather to processes and particularly the capacity to link up quickly and effectively with different types of network.

Of course it raises a new set of practical issues. How do you build up trust and commitment without face-to-face contact? How do you increase the motivation to share information where the outcome is uncertain? How do you anticipate the key networks and make the right learning connections?

Companies hoping to leverage the potential of the Internet will also have to create new roles or even whole functions: a scanning function to monitor and influence Internet opinion; a new service development function to think up new ways of creating value for customers; liaison roles to support networks of remote members; usage analysts to perform market research on Web; and archivists responsible for keeping track of content generated on the company's Web sites.

The winners will be those companies that organize themselves to capitalize on the Internet's capacity to increase sensitivity to resource and market opportunities worldwide and to share knowledge and experience internally. ∎

The bandwagon of corporate governance

David Norburn looks at the relevance – or otherwise – of the current debate on corporate governance, especially non-executive directors, to the growing business.

'Daddy, daddy, will I be like you when I grow up?' 'Of course, son. You'll start shaving, behave badly but soon you'll be responsible. You have to think of others – the stakeholders in the family. What you will need is a set of rules, of responsibilities. What you need is corporate governance.'

In parental eyes, how apt that the child should ape its elders; the entrepreneur managing the growing company seeking the acclaim of maturity, and governance the vestment. But what is governance and how applicable is it to the growing company? Is it necessary and, if so, when should it be adopted in the corporate life cycle?

Primarily, governance is the structural mechanism that attempts to ensure the long-term wealth of the business for the benefit of the shareholders. After all, the shareholders are the owners of the business. The question is, how should it be introduced? And what are the systems and procedures appropriate to make it happen?

Take the UK as an example. Following alleged directors' abuse – in cases such as BCCI and Maxwell – and concern over the large remuneration packages of a number of corporate managers, Sir Adrian Cadbury chaired the Committee on the Financial Aspects of Corporate Governance. The elements of his recommendations in 1992 were:

- the separation of the chairman and CEO roles
- full disclosure and criteria for the chairman's remuneration
- no service contract beyond three years without shareholder approval
- a separate audit committee staffed exclusively by non-executive directors (NXDs)
- a separate remuneration committee staffed with a majority of NXDs
- interim financial statements with full auditor discussion
- NXDs to have full paid access to independent advice.

Three years later the Greenbury Committee added:

- remuneration committees should be non-executive and independent
- remuneration committees should adopt a policy of full transparency on directors' pay packages
- share options should be phased over time and fully disclosed.

While the specific details of these recommendations are peculiar to the UK, the underlying theme is common in many countries and, on the surface, seems very sensible. Yet the debate is fierce.

Sir Arnold Weinstock, in his speech on retiring as chairman of the UK company GEC in 1996, commented: 'I don't like non-executives being set against executive directors as Cadbury seems to imply. It destroys the cohesion of the board. They should be supported by non-executives not held in suspicion by them'. In other words, Sir Arnold saw non-executive directors as boardroom policemen. Warming to his theme, he continued: 'One or two of the Greenbury provisions are a bit peculiar. They are used as an excuse to virtually persecute directors. Trust must exist in a democratic capitalist society between shareholders and the people who run their company'.

Interestingly, similar concerns were also expressed by a significant shareholder. The UK's largest pension fund, Mercury Asset Management, was quoted in *The Independent* newspaper in September 1996: 'We do not believe that blanket implementation of the various codes of practice is necessarily effective or desirable . . . the introduction of a code of best practice cannot of itself ensure that companies are managed with competence and integrity and each company needs to be analyzed on an individual basis'.

It is a fair question. After all, the guidelines are intended to protect the interests of the diverse shareholdings to be found in quoted companies. In the entrepreneurial business, control and sovereignty are much more tightly held.

What has this to do with owner-managed businesses?

The shareholders and the directors are almost always one and the same, certainly in the early days. Entrepreneurs as managers have an obvious dual interest in protecting shareholders' (their) interests while growing their wealth. External investors with a significant shareholding have the option of appointing a director to the board. So why should there be any discussion about corporate governance for this sector?

The answer is twofold:

- There is an increasing call for the growing business to appoint non-executive directors, primarily because it is felt that they will add skills not to be found within the firm. These include, for example, a different but complementary strategic perspective and guidance as to 'best practice' in managing the larger business. Moreover, they are seen as an important 'sounding board' and referee for the chief executive as he or she struggles with the problems of delegation and succession.

● As the growing company develops aspirations to become publicly quoted, those who consider the 'child' to have reached maturity require the adoption of 'grown-up' behavior. So stock exchange regulations in most countries will require some system of checks and balances on the activities of the executive managers – and these will often involve a view as to the appropriate constitution of the board and the balance between executive and non-executive directors.

Are NXDs really necessary?

There is a fundamental question about the type of person to be appointed – should they be 'truly independent' or not? – a debate still unresolved in the larger company arena.

Some feel that independence, which usually means someone who is not connected to the business or to the incumbent directors, is crucial if the monitoring role is to work; others feel that knowledge of the company or industry from another standpoint is an important new perspective.

Of course, the larger company can afford the luxury of both. But for the entrepreneurial company, this may not be relevant or affordable. Certainly, as the company grows, enters new markets and creates new structures, those who have experience elsewhere can be invaluable members of the team but on an incremental and individual basis.

Who should NXDs be?

Quite simply, in any organization, people, not structures and rules, make decisions. The development of strong corporate governance in the growing company should be based on animate skills not inanimate structural imposition. The first non-executive director is a very special person, requiring empathy, complementary skills and a clear understanding of the needs and motivations of the entrepreneurial business.

They are not easy to find and entrepreneurs should beware of ageing warriors from large organizations seeking their own corporate Valhalla of the trophy directorship, often proposed by commercial marriage brokers. After all, the past may not be relevant and there is a danger that these corporate executives may bring approaches that are inappropriate and culturally alien to the growing business.

The solution, as is often the case, can usually be found closer to home. All the research in the field of entrepreneurship reinforces personal networks, not structural groupings. At the end of the day, the owner(s) will only listen to, and pay for, advice and assistance that they respect and trust – and that usually comes from those they have known for some time.

However well intentioned, the bandwagon of corporate governance, laudably promoted by those concerned about directors' potential abuse of their position, is not a blanket solution for the growing company. The 'child' may well know best.

'Daddy, daddy, should I be like you when I grow up?' 'Don't be silly, son. Times have changed. What you need is speed and flexibility. I'm too old.' ■

A guide to surfing the social networks

Networking can help the individual and the businesss as a whole, say **Howard Aldrich** and **Amanda Brickman Elam**.

Importance of networking for entrepreneurs

New businesses are founded as a result of motivated entrepreneurs gaining access to resources and finding niches in opportunity structures. From the beginning, social networks are crucial assets for business owners struggling to make a place for themselves in competitive markets. Entrepreneurs try to build successful businesses by maximizing the opportunities they find and minimizing the obstacles they confront. Networking allows entrepreneurs to enlarge their span of action, gain access to resources and opportunities otherwise unavailable, and avoid obstacles.

In this article, we propose a framework for thinking about networks in a more systematic fashion. We offer an expanded vocabulary for describing your networks, emphasizing subtle but important distinctions between types of network relationships. By understanding the difference between types of ties, you will be better prepared to choose a networking strategy that fits your particular circumstances.

Network composition

Entrepreneurs are embedded in networks of social relationships. Some are personal, such as ties to family, friends, and neighbors, and others are business-related, such as ties to customers, vendors, and creditors. Social relations are, to varying extents, purposive: some arise because of accidental or unplanned encounters with individuals, some are created via organizational memberships, and others emerge as planned interactions for obtaining access to specific information. In this sense, then, all entrepreneurs construct networks of social relations in the process of obtaining resources for their firms.

A personal network consists of all those persons with whom an entrepreneur has direct relations – for example, partners, suppliers, customers, bankers, family and friends. The simplest kind of personal network includes people whom we meet on a face-to-face basis and from whom we obtain various services, including tangible goods, advice, information, and moral support.

Networking as an activity can be distinguished from normal business behavior by focusing on the nature of the transaction. So, for example, a single, brief, market-mediated transaction, such as buying a newspaper, usually involves two people who never expect to see each other again. We will describe such transactions as 'contacts', rather than network 'ties'. By contrast, taking a customer to lunch is contact between two people who may well expect to be starting a long-term relationship and, as such, the activity is a first step toward building a network tie. 'Ties', rather than 'contacts,' are the basis of 'networking'.

We can think more systematically about networking if we organize the types of relationships that make up a person's total set of relations into three embedded circles, according to the strength of the relationship – strong, weak, and

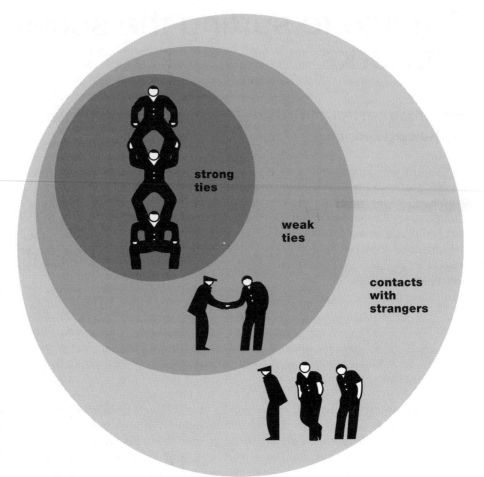

Figure 1: Framework of network relationships

inconsequential (dealing with complete strangers), as shown in Figure 1. The innermost circle represents strong ties, the middle circle includes weak ties, and the outermost circle covers contacts with strangers.

Strong ties

The most durable and reliable relationships in a personal network are strong ties. Strong ties are usually of long duration and are based on a principle of implicit reciprocity. In other words, they are long-term, two-way relationships, with something to be gained by both sides. Consequently, strong ties are typically more reliable than other ties and involve a strong degree of trust and emotional closeness. Individuals tend to make heavy investments in this type of relationship, requiring fairly frequent contact with the other person.

Because of the effort involved in creating and sustaining a strong tie, most people have only about five or six strong ties in their network. Ten strong ties would be very unusual, and twenty would be truly heroic! We rely on strong ties for advice, assistance, and support in all areas of our lives. An example of a strong tie would be a person you feel comfortable turning to for advice about an ethical dilemma you face at work, or perhaps asking someone to watch your children for you on short notice. An entrepreneur's strong tie network is usually composed of a majority of business associates, a few close friends, and one or two family members.

Strong ties are especially important for business owners, as they provide a means of avoiding the opportunism and uncertainty inherent in typical market-mediated transactions. In social situations where people expect to deal with each other over an extended period, strong ties yield three benefits: trust, predictability and voice. Trust is a crucial component of business dealings, as it tells us who we can count on in difficult situations, and it substantially enhances predictability in relations. Predictability refers to how the other party will behave if situations change. And, finally, voice means making your complaints known and negotiating over them, rather than silently sneaking away. Each of these benefits is enhanced in long-term relationships. Hence, strong ties carry substantial benefits for entrepreneurs who work in challenging environments where people expect to interact frequently over a long time span.

Weak ties
Whereas strong ties are based on trust, weak ties are superficial or casual and typically involve little emotional investment. Weak-tie relationships are typically of shorter duration and involve lower frequency of contact. They are also less reliable and more uncertain than strong ties and often fade into dormancy, only to be revived when assistance is required. As shown in Figure 1, they can be thought of as arm's-length relations, involving persons whose handshake we seek but whose full support we cannot count on.

Individuals have many more weak ties than strong ties. A quick look in your address book and business card collection can give an approximate count of your weak ties. Younger and more junior people typically have fifty to one hundred weak ties in their networks. By contrast, older, more senior people may easily have one hundred or more. Examples of weak ties include the relationships you may have with a customer or client, with a supplier or investor, and even with your family doctor.

In contrast to strong ties, weak ties are characterized by opportunism, uncertainty, and exit. Opportunism is inherent in typical market-like transactions, which are generally driven by self-interest and leave little or no room for trust. Uncertainty means you have difficulty in predicting the weak tie's actions. And, lastly, exit refers to the notion that, when you are faced with opportunism and uncertainty, it is probably easier to go elsewhere to complete a transaction involving a weak tie, rather than to negotiate for a better deal.

Weak ties do not carry the same secure benefits that strong ties do, but they do have a major benefit of their own, namely that of diversity. Relations with weak ties can expose entrepreneurs to channels of information not available through strong ties, as we will point out.

Contacts with strangers
A third type of network relationship can better be described as contacts, rather than ties. These types of network relations are entered into for pragmatic purposes and usually occur with strangers or individuals with whom no prior

relations have existed. Contacts with strangers are typically fleeting in duration and require little or no emotional involvement. An example of a contact with a stranger would be buying a piece of equipment from a person who advertised in a trade publication.

We have only a limited understanding of the relative value and importance of these pragmatic contacts with strangers. Arms-length, self-interested transactions are at the core of economic models of markets and, for that reason, are taken for granted. In fact, very little is known about how they are established, because their existence is simply assumed in economic models of how markets work.

Models of entrepreneurship and business life-cycles emphasize the context-dependent nature of the three types of relations we portray in Figure 1. For entrepreneurs, strong and weak ties may be more important than contacts with strangers for the mobilization of resources occurring in the early stages of business development. Later, when a newly founded business is on its feet, arms-length transactions and contacts with strangers assume more importance.

This framework helps to clarify the types of relationships found in personal networks. In reality, of course, the boundaries between categories are not so easily defined. The differences between strong ties and weak ties are the easiest to distinguish. Differences between weak ties (which may involve infrequent contacts with others who are barely known) and contacts with strangers (who are completely unknown) are a little more difficult to recognize. Consequently, most current research addresses strong ties, few studies touch on weak ties, and none really focus on contacts with strangers.

Effective networking

Effective networking is a challenge for most entrepreneurs, for whom time is a valuable resource. The foremost questions concern where to focus your energies, how to expand your network, and how to keep track of your ties. We offer three general suggestions on how to improve your networking: strengthen direct ties, cultivate diversity, and systematically plan and monitor your ties.

Strengthen direct ties

Networking with your weak ties to turn them into strong ones is a way of overcoming the weaknesses inherent in pure market-like transactions, of strengthening the resource base of your business, and expanding your circle of trust. Strong ties are important because they encourage the development of trust, predictability, and voice in network relations. These benefits help to mediate the risks inherent in building new businesses. However, time and resource constraints mean that you'll probably never have more than five to ten strong tie relations, and so you must pay strategic attention to weak ties.

Cultivate diversity

Diversity is crucial for entrepreneurs, as it provides access to critical information, such as potential markets, new business locations, innovations, sources of capital, and potential investors. There are two ways to cultivate diversity: use your strong ties or expand your weak ties. The first way is to cultivate strong ties with people who have ties to very different parts of the business environment in which you operate, opening up channels of information otherwise inaccessible. Entrepreneurs can leverage their direct relations by a judicious choice of strong ties who have access to diverse others – people quite unlike themselves.

A second way to gain access to new information is to expand your weak ties. While strong ties are clearly important, a network made up of all strong ties will be of limited value to an entrepreneur. The reason is straightforward. Because people tend toward emotional and personal balance in their strong ties, their inner circle tends to be fairly homogeneous. For example, according to research we have conducted, male business owners almost never have women in their strong tie circles. In homogeneous networks, information known to one person is rapidly diffused to others and interpreted in similar ways, and an entrepreneur gains little new information from talking to more than one strong tie.

By contrast, people are less concerned with balance in their large circle of weak ties. The persons with whom we have weak ties, such as casual acquaintances, are less likely to know each other than are those with whom we have strong ties, such as close friends. Heterogeneity is both more likely and more tolerated among a person's weak ties. Contacts with casual acquaintances, different from yourself, link you to diverse others, each of whom has a close circle of persons unknown to you. If these strangers have information, or resources, of value, then you can gain access to them indirectly through the diversity of your weak ties. (You could also accomplish the same goal by diversifying your strong ties, but that requires very intense and often unsettling maneuvering.) So, in essence, a large set of diverse ties may be better than a small set of overlapping ties because you achieve better access to critical information.

'Brokers' – people who facilitate links between persons who are not themselves directly connected – are central to the expansion of many personal networks. For example, venture capitalists often play broker roles because they bring together technical experts, management consultants and financial planners to supplement an entrepreneur's limited knowledge and experience. Some social settings facilitate the activities of brokers, such as bars and restaurants in Silicon Valley, California, which serve as central meeting points and support a complex pattern of social relationships stimulating high start-up rates. Finding and using brokers can help an entrepreneur cultivate diversity by expanding weak ties.

More systematically plan and monitor network ties

Personal networks which are of real value to an entrepreneur must include a balance of both strong and weak ties, that is, of strength and diversity. Effective entrepreneurs are usually to be found in positions that are connected to lots of diverse information sources, as well as in positions benefiting from a reliable set of strong ties. The challenge of effective networking is to find ways of more systematically organizing your personal networks to maximize the flow of resources that are so critical to business development after startup.

Effective networking involves three steps. The first is to collect the contact information about your network ties in one central repository. People organize information about their network ties in various ways. Some people compile it into one address book or business card file, while others keep bits and pieces of it tucked away in file drawers. Some people even go as far as setting up computer databases to track the information. Whatever you do, become more methodical in how your network information is categorized and organized.

The second step is to create a feedback loop for monitoring and pruning this collection of ties to keep information manageable and productive. This means reviewing your collection of ties at regular intervals. Your review will provide descriptive information on frequency of contact, results from past contacts, and other information on the state of the relation. Based on your review, you should trim those ties that are out-of-date or no longer useful.

The third step involves some strategic thinking. How balanced is your network? Is your network helpful in providing you with the resources you need? How can you improve your network? Do you need to devote more time to maintaining strong ties? Which of your weak ties is worth the effort of developing into a strong tie? Do you need to increase your weak ties or are you trying to keep up with too many?

Conclusion

The picture which we have drawn shows entrepreneurs embedded in a social context, channeled and facilitated, or constrained and inhibited, by their positions in social networks. Effective networks are crucial to business success because they increase your span of action, economize on time and other resources, and possibly help you to control an unstable business environment. Networks balanced between strength and diversity, strong and weak ties, are of the most real value to entrepreneurs. The challenge is to find ways of more systematically planning, monitoring, and pruning network information. ∎

5

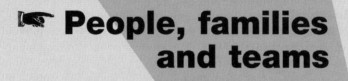

☞ **People, families and teams**

Contents

Contributors

Alden G. Lank is the Stephan Schmidheiny Professor of Family Enterprises at IMD in Lausanne, Switzerland. He is the founding executive director of the Family Business Network and its president and a member of its executive board.

Bill Snaith is a senior tutor at Durham University Business School working in the area of team-managed businesses.

Dennis W. N. Ng is a postgraduate student at Imperial College Management School.

Sue Cartwright is Senior Research Fellow in Organizational Psychology at the Manchester School of Management, University of Manchester Institute of Science and Technology.

Laura Kellogg is a consultant with Sibson & Company, a leading management consulting firm with ten locations worldwide, specializing in organizational effectiveness and remuneration. Her expertise includes organizational change and design, professional service firms, and sales force effectiveness.

Cary L. Cooper is Professor of Organizational Psychology at the Manchester School of Management, University of Manchester Institute of Science and Technology.

Vicky Meakin is a team-managed business tutor at Durham University Business School.

Introduction

Part 5 returns to people. But this time, we are looking at groups. First, we confront the family. It is trite but true that anyone who has both a family and a business inevitably has a family business and must confront and manage the tensions and choices which have to be made. One tension which is particularly difficult for most is the choice and timing of a successor – and this is so all over the world, as we see so clearly when we look at the 'bamboo network'. The second group of players we look at is the management team and our authors discuss the issues of selecting and building a 'goal scoring' team.

Making sure the dynasty does not become a Dallas

Alden Lank explains why so many family businesses tend to break up.

Many of the more than 300-plus delegates at the seventh world conference of the Family Business Network held in Edinburgh in September 1995 were astonished by what they were hearing. More than one speaker underlined the fact that only a small minority of family enterprises ever survives beyond the first generation in the hands of the founding family. Yet a significant number in the audience represented second and subsequent generations. What had gone wrong with all the others? Why had they been so fragile?

Studies on the longevity of family organizations made in several countries all come to the same conclusion. While it is impossible to make exact transnational comparisons (there are as many definitions of 'family enterprise' as there are researchers in the field), the general tendency is clear: between two-thirds and three-quarters of family businesses either die or are sold out of the founding family during the first generation's tenure. Only 5 per cent to 15 per cent continue into the third generation in the hands of the descendants. These figures compare unfavorably with the staying power of equivalent non-family controlled companies.

As family enterprises are a – if not *the* – major contributor to the economic and social well-being of all capitalist societies, this fragility is a cause for concern. What factors can explain the lack of longevity?

First of all, there can be little doubt that *family enterprises are the most*

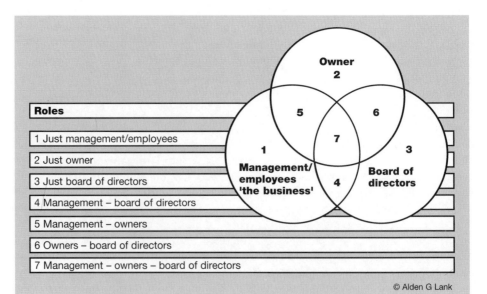

Figure 1: A typical corporation

Roles
1 Just management/employees
2 Just owner
3 Just board of directors
4 Management – board of directors
5 Management – owners
6 Owners – board of directors
7 Management – owners – board of directors

© Alden G Lank

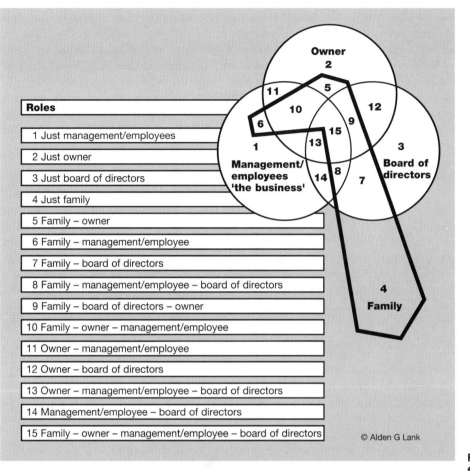

Roles

1 Just management/employees

2 Just owner

3 Just board of directors

4 Just family

5 Family – owner

6 Family – management/employee

7 Family – board of directors

8 Family – management/employee – board of directors

9 Family – board of directors – owner

10 Family – owner – management/employee

11 Owner – management/employee

12 Owner – board of directors

13 Owner – management/employee – board of directors

14 Management/employee – board of directors

15 Family – owner – management/employee – board of directors

© Alden G Lank

Figure 2: A typical family corporation

complex form of business organization. At first sight, this statement may seem preposterous. However, reflect on Figure 1. It depicts in highly simplified form a model of a typical (all but the smallest) corporation.

The chief executive officer (CEO), holding Role 7, is faced with managing all seven sets of roles in a synergistic manner in pursuit of the business's mission and objectives – no sinecure under the best of circumstances. Figure 2 adds but one dimension: family. Note that by so doing, the number of roles to be managed by the CEO in position 15 has more than doubled – a significant increase in complexity.

This conception of the family controlled corporation begins to explain some of the negative dynamics commonly associated with family organizations. Popular television series such as Dynasty and Dallas, for example, delight in highlighting the squabbles between and within generations. These conflicts are often attributed to 'personality differences'. Yet an analysis of Figure 2 shows that the basis of the differences may be related more to role than personality.

A good example is the important, frequently emotionally charged decision concerning the dividend pay-out ratio. A person sitting in Role 15, let us say as chairman of the board/CEO/owner/family, quite logically can have a very different opinion from the younger sister occupying Role 5, with no seat on the board and not being employed by the family's enterprise. In the former case, one could expect a strong desire to maximize re-investment of profits in the business, while the sister might like to see higher figures on her dividend cheque.

The inevitable overlapping of family with the three circles in Figure 2 leads to challenges which no totally publicly held corporation has to face. Here is one all-too-common scenario taken from a real family enterprise.

Georges, 64, is CEO, sole owner and member of the board. His son Jean, 31 and a bachelor, is vice president manufacturing and technology and likewise member of the board. Daughter, Marie, 34 and married with one son, Marcel, 12, is vice president sales and marketing and a board member.

Marie and Jean thoroughly detest each other and have been in sibling conflict since early childhood. Marie (as well as Jean) expects to be nominated CEO and take voting control whenever Georges decides to retire. Marcel is an outstanding student and already has shown entrepreneurial skills and an interest in the business. In his mother's mind, there is no doubt that he will replace her as head of the family organization when she steps down.

There is a board meeting scheduled for next Friday to decide on certain strategic investments which will start to impact the bottom line ten years from now. It is not far-fetched to suppose that the next board meeting will be hardly typical of what one could expect in a publicly held corporation. The family's emotional dynamics, in all probability, will either covertly or overtly rule their discussions on what, in theory, should be a purely rational business decision. Yes, family businesses are different.

Beyond the inherent enhanced complexity, what other factors explain the fragility of family companies? What causes them to leave the founding family's control or go bankrupt? There are two parts to the answer. First, they disappear for the same reasons as any corporation, including:

● opportunity to sell out at an attractive price (in a capitalistic economy this provokes no automatic opprobrium)
● inability to anticipate or adjust to changes in the market place
● insufficient investment in R&D
● inadequate control of costs
● lack of access to affordable capital
● other poor management practices.

However, not surprisingly, family enterprises also face certain challenges specific to themselves such as:

● failure to find capital for growth without diluting the family's equity (total ownership control being a sacrosanct principle for many families)
● inability to balance optimally the family's needs for liquidity and the business's need for cash
● poor estate planning and the inability of the next generation to pay inheritance taxes
● lack of willingness of the older generation to 'let go' of ownership and management power at an appropriate moment
● inability to attract and retain competent and motivated family successors
● unchecked sibling rivalries with no consensus on the chosen successor
● inability to attract and retain competent senior non-family professional managers

- unmanaged conflict between the cultures of the family, the board and the business.

The above list is striking for the predominance of factors related to *managing the process of ownership and management succession – the single most important reason for the fragility of family enterprises.*

What does research on the experience of long-lived, multi-generational family companies tell us about how to manage the inherent fragility of this most prevalent and oldest form of business organization?

Families that are aware of the special complexities of being managers and/or owners of their own company already have a head start. For example, being able to see that conflicts may stem from the differing perspectives of the various roles described in Figure 2, each of which may have a rational basis, could defuse a highly emotional situation.

The probability of maintaining a healthy and vigorous enterprise (as well as family) will also be enhanced if the owning family accepts the truth of the six following conflict-management propositions:

- Over time, conflict is inevitable in families and in family businesses
- Conflict can be healthy or unhealthy, functional or dysfunctional
- How conflict is managed is one of the key determinants of effective families and family businesses
- While there are several conflict management strategies, there is no panacea
- The goal in conflict management should be to maximize win-win situations for all parties and to arrive at the best decision, given the family's and the family business's mission, goals and objectives
- Pre-establishment of the 'rules of the game' can obviate many conflicts.

These propositions put conflict in perspective and remind us that conflict per se is not negative. In fact, a company or a family with no conflict has probably lost the ability to innovate and adjust to changing circumstances.

Figure 3 outlines three broad categories of options or strategies of conflict management. (I am defining conflict as a type of behavior which occurs when two or more parties are in opposition or in battle as a result of a perceived deprivation whose cause is attributed to the other party or parties.)

The first category (*Avoidance*) groups those approaches which attempt to avoid coming to grips with the grievances or issues separating the parties.

- *Ignorance* may be a simple reflection of the reality or a deliberate attempt to keep one's head in the sand

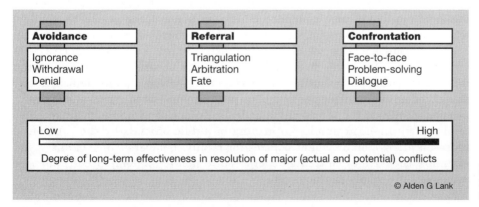

© Alden G Lank

Figure 3: Conflict management options

- *Withdrawal* implies a recognition of conflict as well as a decision to move back from the fray
- *Denial* permits fooling oneself and others (at least in the short term) into believing that a conflict does not exist, while knowing full well at the conscious or subconscious level that something is wrong in a relationship.

Avoidance mechanisms have limited long-term usefulness except in the most minor of cases.

Referral strategies basically place the responsibility for conflict management in someone else's hands.

- *Triangulation* is all too common in family businesses. Here a third party – often Mom – acts as a message carrier between the warring parties, for example sibling versus sibling, Dad versus daughter and so on. This strategy may keep the lid on the situation for a short period but it puts Mom into a highly unenviable position. In any case, once Mom is out of the picture (for example dies), one can expect a major explosion with few survivors
- *Fate* basically refers actual or incipient conflict to God or chance. The reasoning goes: 'Eventually this problem will go away. Why talk to Dad about succession? He will just get angry and evade seeking a solution. He's already 78 and can't last forever'. This line of thought explains why so many succession issues are resolved in family businesses by the lawyer and accountant while riding in the limousine en route to the cemetery to bury Dad.

Confrontation strategies acknowledge the existence of conflict and require the parties to work together to find a mutually beneficial solution. On occasion, an outside professional facilitator may be very useful in creating the conditions for positive *problem-solving dialogue.*

Experience shows that the earlier the confrontation the better. One highly successful first generation husband-wife team recently explained the two most important reasons for their success. 'As co-CEOs there must be absolute clarity in and outside the company concerning how roles are divided. And we do not allow anything to fester between us for more than four to 12 hours.' Families which allow four to 12 *years* of hurt and frustration to develop (a not uncommon phenomenon) may find that not even skilful confrontation will save them.

Source of wealth Increasingly, families in business are re-discovering the wisdom of the maxim: 'an ounce of prevention is worth a pound of cure'. In the context of conflict management, this means achieving consensus around the 'rules of the game' in regard to the family, its enterprise and the interface between the two before the issues in question become a problem. The labels given to the (preferably written) text vary from family protocol, strategy and mission to credo, philosophy and values.

No two families ever produce the same texts and there are huge disparities in the degree of detail and prescription. Typical topics include the roles of the different governance institutions (such as family assembly, family council, family shareholders' committee, board of directors and executive management), behavioral norms for the family and businesses (for example no washing of family dirty linen in public, no bribing of public officials by the company's representatives), employment policies for family members (rules of entry and exit, how they are to be treated compared to non-family employees) and who represents the family on the board.

Many of these manifestos specify the family's view on the business as its source of wealth (for example the current generation of owners acts as steward of the inherited capital for the next generation), guidelines for dividend policy, philanthropical objectives, the workings of the internal stock-market and so on.

As important as the final document is the process used to produce it. The very discussion of broad concerns such as 'what do we stand for as a family *and* as an owning family' bring the generations together around the fundamental raisons d'être of their familial relationship.

Once the 'rules of the game' are on paper, many potential conflicts will be defused on the basis of the criterion that 'the family has already decided that . . .' This does not mean that the key principles are engraved in stone. They can be revisited periodically by the family as circumstances change.

Earlier it was stated that the single most important cause of the fragility of the family business was the inability to manage the succession process. Let me conclude by focussing on management succession, making several recommendations to the outgoing (successee) and incoming (successor) generations in regard to management succession.

From the potential successor, I would ask for a careful analysis of the reasons for joining the family company. Is it because it is the only job available? Is it only because that is what your parents expect of you? Is it because you fear you will be disinherited if you decide to go elsewhere? Is it because you figure that the working hours would give you more time to play golf? If the answer is yes to any of these questions, it may be wiser for all concerned for you to look for another company.

Have you the required education for entering the business? Have you had experience outside the family enterprise? There are at least three good reasons for working elsewhere before joining the family's enterprise. First, it will give you an indication of your true market worth. Second, if you succeed, you will be able to enter the family enterprise, should you so desire, with a proven track record. Third, if you fail, there will be less negative fall-out for you and the family if it happens in someone else's company.

If you have met the above criteria for entry, are you active in designing the career path which will maximize your chances of being a valid candidate to replace the outgoing generation? Are you insisting on receiving objective feedback on your performance and opportunities for training and development? Are you sure that you are the most qualified candidate?

My recommendations to the successee are predicated on one primary conviction: the final choice must be made on the basis of who has manifested the most competence to lead the family's enterprise into the future. This may mean that your sentimental favorite, based on kinship, will have to give way to a non-family successor – difficult as this may be for you.

As the current leader of the organization, it is the successee who has the fundamental responsibility for managing the succession process. My advice would include the following:

● Never force the potential successor to enter or stay with the business against his/her will

● See that a career path is built which will provide the potential successor(s) with challenging assignments, diverse experiences, realistic objectives and standards, quality feedback on performance, opportunities for continuing education and training, appropriate rewards

- Manifest interest and concern
- Share your hopes and desires for the future (without expecting that the successor will automatically accept them)
- Involve others (be they family, board members or outsiders) in advising on the final choice and try to maximise consensus
- Announce your own intention of phasing out with the timing made explicit
- Stick to your intentions
- Ensure that you have a game plan for your retirement period.

There are, of course, many other recommendations which could be made to successees including, importantly, deciding on what their departure *style* will be. Here are some archetypes (originally formulated by Sommerfeld and Spence, *Family Business Review*, Vol 2 no.4, Winter 1989):

- *Monarch:* refuses to depart voluntarily and typically dies on the job
- *General:* agrees to depart but spends most of his time plotting to return to power
- *Ambassador:* gives up the CEO post, may stay on the board, represents the enterprise externally in industry associations and so on
- *Reborn Entrepreneur:* keeps contact with the company but starts a new, non-competitive venture
- *Hedonist:* cuts ties with the company and spends time doing things he or she never had time to do earlier – sports, hobbies and so on.

Unfortunately, there are too many Monarchs and Generals (particularly successees of the founding generation) and too few of the others.

Letting go can indeed be difficult, if not impossible. Yet this is the final test of greatness for the outgoing generation. If more of them could do the necessary planning for this critical transition and honor the established process, the inherent fragility of family companies would be transformed into increased robustness and health – to the advantage of both the family and its enterprise. ∎

Succession in the 'bamboo network'

Family businesses run by Overseas Chinese have been the engine of economic success in the Pacific Rim but, says **Dennis Ng**, succession problems could arise as Western and Chinese cultures clash.

An economic miracle

Over the past 30 years, many have studied the reasons for the success of the Pacific Rim economies. In particular, the Overseas Chinese's dominant participation in the development of these economies has been the subject of much

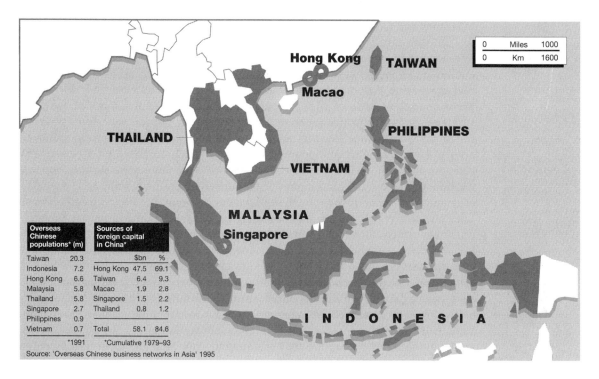

Overseas Chinese populations* (m)		Sources of foreign capital in China*		
			$bn	%
Taiwan	20.3	Hong Kong	47.5	69.1
Indonesia	7.2	Taiwan	6.4	9.3
Hong Kong	6.6	Macao	1.9	2.8
Malaysia	5.8	Singapore	1.5	2.2
Thailand	5.8	Thailand	0.8	1.2
Singapore	2.7			
Philippines	0.9			
Vietnam	0.7	Total	58.1	84.6
*1991		*Cumulative 1979–93		

Source: 'Overseas Chinese business networks in Asia' 1995

Figure 1: Overseas Chinese in South-East Asia

academic and media attention. The economic strength of the Overseas Chinese in this region is substantial. The 55 million Overseas Chinese control some US$2 trillion in cash or liquid assets. To put these figures in context, these 55 million people, taking into account their officially acknowledged power in the ASEAN economies, constitute 10 per cent of the region's population and around 70 per cent of the region's economy. The Overseas Chinese produces nine out of ten of the region's billionaires and around two-thirds of the retail industry. It is worth noting that the majority of their businesses are family businesses.

The main explanations for the economic success of the Overseas Chinese have always returned to one answer: culture. The reasoning was that there were other countries in similar circumstances but which did not enjoy the same economic miracle. Better management as an explanation would not hold as an argument as the quality of management is dependent on the quality of the people managed. Hence, culture must be the missing link. The Overseas Chinese's cultural makeup, with their emphasis on tradition and Confucian roots, served the Chinese family businesses well against a variety of economic policies implemented by the host governments, and provided the flexibility to be competitive in changing economic climates. With greater collectivism, centralized control and clear vertical order, the Overseas Chinese family businesses have managed to generate the coordination and control needed to stimulate massive growth as late comers to the world economy and capitalism.

Despite all the success achieved, the Overseas Chinese, often referred to as the 'bamboo network', due to their unique characteristics, are now being tested as they have never been before. The test will come from the passing of the founding generation of the businesses.

Succession and unaccompanied minors

Traditionally, due to the ingrained respect for authority, the succession process for Chinese family businesses has been less problematic than their western counterparts. Nevertheless, past experiences have shown that it does suffer from similar problems to western family businesses, such as successor incompetence and generation differences in opinions. To complicate the situation, due to the accumulated wealth of the Overseas Chinese, and the effects of western influence, many families have sent their children abroad to study at a very tender age, with some leaving home as early as the age of six. These children, often referred to as unaccompanied minors by psychologists (and airlines, who came up with the term), will be the successors of the Bamboo network, but will possess a different cultural makeup. The different cultural makeup is an extra consideration which previously did not pose any threat for the Overseas Chinese family business succession. The scramble for western qualifications is not only due to western influence and economic prosperity. In the past, the Asian economic climate has favored the opportunistic and dashing entrepreneurs, but the circumstances are changing, and there is now a greater need for organizational and management skills. Many Overseas Chinese parents hope that one day, their children will return to the family business with a western MBA. What is ironic is that the process of a western education may cause complications to the unaccompanied minors' succession of the family businesses, to the extent that succession may never take place due to cultural differences between the parents and the unaccompanied minors.

Cultural identities

The issue of a possible cultural gap arises because unaccompanied minors live at the juncture between two cultures. Their 'marginality', as identified by psychologists, gives them certain psychological properties. One of the main properties has been identified as 'double-consciousness': the simultaneous awareness of oneself as being a member and an alien of two or more cultures. Unaccompanied minors, being adolescents leaving home to study abroad in a different culture for an extended period of time, are 'marginal' people, and perhaps the effects are more exaggerated, since they leave home at an age when self-identity has barely had time to form. Their 'marginality' occurs because unaccompanied minors, while being influenced by western values during their time abroad, usually return to their families for holidays, and hence their Chinese values are reinforced during that period. This bombardment by two different cultures has implications on the unaccompanied minors' cultural identity.

The issue of cultural identity has been studied in America on Chinese-American adolescents. For unaccompanied minors, it is possible for more than one cultural identity to exist. A spectrum of identities has been identified by American psychologists studying Chinese unaccompanied minors, ranging from the individual who rejects all aspects of being Chinese in an anxiety to identify with a western culture (the so-called 'banana' type – yellow on the outside but white on the inside), to a radical individual who may espouse a new 'Asian' consciousness who rejects both Chinese and western cultures.

Five models can be used to show where marginal people arrive on the spectrum (*see* Figure 2). These are assimilation, acculturation, alternation, multi-culturalism and fusion. The first two models involve the individual acquiring a different culture. The two cultures form a hierarchical relationship with the newer culture dominating. The difference between the assimilation and acculturation models is that the acculturation process is an involuntary one, and that the individual, while being a competent participant of the dominating culture, will always be identified as a member of the minority culture. The first two models will result in the 'banana' end of the spectrum. The fusion model suggests a new form of culture being formed by fusing the existing and the new culture. The result is likely to be towards the new 'Asian' consciousness end of the spectrum. In the middle of the spectrum is the category of bicultural competence or biculturalism, achieved by the alternation or multiculturalism model. The alternation model suggests that an individual can alter his/her behavior accordingly to suit the cultural context. The alternation model suggests that it is possible for an individual to maintain a positive relationship with both cultures without having to choose between them. The multiculturalism model assumes that an individual can maintain his/her identity while developing another positive identity within the new culture.

'Banana' ----------------------------	Biculturalism -----------------------	New 'Asian'
from	from	from
assimilation / acculturation	alternation / multiculturalism	fusion

Figure 2: Spectrum of identities and coping models of unaccompanied minors

By definition, a person is considered culturally competent (for one culture) if he/she appreciates and internalizes the basic beliefs of a given culture. This implies the ability to accept a culture's basic worldview and act within the constraints of such a worldview. To be biculturally competent implies being culturally competent in two cultures simultaneously. Whether an un-accompanied minor is biculturally competent or not is vital for effective succession within the Overseas Chinese family businesses. I have found that virtually all of my research sample of Overseas Chinese unaccompanied minors who managed the succession process effectively are biculturally competent. The reason is that the 'banana' types suffer problems adapting back to their original culture, and hence usually do not return to their originating country, let alone their family businesses. The ones who adopt the fusion model usually refuse to return to the family businesses, and prefer to do their own thing. It has to be said that only a handful of unaccompanied minors adopt the fusion model. An intriguing finding is that there are discrepancies according to where the unaccompanied minor goes to study. An emerging pattern indicates that unaccompanied minors in the United States tend to be less biculturally competent than those who study in other countries. The Chinese culture, when encountering the American culture, appears to cause the most 'cultural confusion' among unaccompanied minors who are exposed to both cultures. Many unaccompanied minors who studied in the United States say that they feel 'too Chinese to be western, and too westernized to be Oriental.'

From the biculturally competent unaccompanied minors' point of view, by experiencing different cultures, they have become more aware of their own cultural makeup, and can consciously deal with any psychological dissonance which may occur. Biculturalism has provided these unaccompanied minors with

Bicultural competence

The Dragon Mural in Hong Kong's Tiger Balm Gardens: the economic success of the Overseas Chinese has always been attributed to culture

© Veronica Garbutt

an advantage in business too. By being aware of more than one culture, the unaccompanied minors can be more effective as managers and leaders of international businesses. Further, with Overseas Chinese family businesses growing in size and geographical influence, the traditional Chinese methods of conducting businesses require adaptations and change. Biculturally competent unaccompanied minors can draw on their experiences in both cultures to extract the benefits of western cultures and western management, while retaining the secrets of the Overseas Chinese economic culture.

Conclusion

It can therefore be argued that biculturalism is an important characteristic for Overseas Chinese unaccompanied minors to possess in the succession of family businesses. Further, as we already know, western cultures are not homogenous. Each western culture influences unaccompanied minors differently, with some cultures being more dominating than others. This has an effect on the unaccompanied minors' ability to become biculturally competent. In other words, when Overseas Chinese parents decide to send their children to different countries, they may have unconsciously already made the decision as to who will be the successor to their family business.

From my experience with Overseas Chinese family businesses, the most pressing problem currently faced by these businesses is succession. The scenario of a biculturally incompetent successor is almost always the case. The resulting conflict causes emotional distress among the family members, and in the worst cases, can threaten the very existence of the family firm. However, all is not lost: with effective open communication and mutual respect of the cultural makeup of all family members involved, there is no reason why the Overseas Chinese family businesses, with their brilliant track record in adapting to difficult circum-stances, should fail to cross the succession hurdle. It is possible for unaccompanied minors to become company majors, but they cannot do it alone. ■

Critical link between business and organization

Laura Kellogg explains the importance of managing the human dimension in start-up and high-growth companies.

In a rapidly growing entrepreneurial company, sustained success reflects how well the business and the organization are in concert. It is far too easy, during a phase of high growth, for a company to risk subordinating or ignoring organizational and human resource issues for short-term business challenges.

However, human resource management is not just the administration of remuneration, benefits and personnel issues: it encompasses the strategic management of human capital, which over time makes or breaks a business. Successful human resource management enables a seamless, explicit integration of business and organization. To achieve this integration, the entrepreneur must answer (in order) the following questions:

- *What is the company?* (mission and values statement)
- *Where does it want to go?* (goals)
- *How will the it get there?* (strategy)
- *What does it need for the journey?* (organizational capabilities)
- *How will it recognize the destination?* (vision of success).

Integrating the business and the organization, especially during rapid growth, requires flexibility and foresight. One broadly applicable approach, helping the entrepreneur identify how to manage human resources, is to depict how the company will grow through discrete strategic eras across key dimensions that characterize the business. That is, develop a series of snapshots, including the 'start-up', (current) high-growth phase and near to mid-term future. Next, map out the organizational capabilities required to support each era.

The kinds of dimensions on which to characterize the business might include:

- *business objective* (build brand awareness, commercialize technology)
- *competitive premise* (product excellence, creative solutions)
- *nature of customer relationship* (transaction-oriented, consultative)
- *investment priorities* (expand through acquisition, secure organizational capabilities)
- *role of management* (low involvement, goal-setting focus, high priests of culture).

Other relevant dimensions are: nature of business risk, role of technology, client portfolio and so on. Pick six to eight dimensions that best describe the company and define each at distinct points in time.

Making the critical link between business and organization entails characterizing the human resources requirements. Assess and define the company's need during each era for:

- *structure*: to support the business. In general, look from the outside-in and let customer-facing activities shape structure. Determine the balance between

© FT Pictures

formal and informal structures, the role(s) of teams and so on. How can the structure be flexible to support growth?

● *work and job design*: to get the work done. Determine what kind of job positions will be needed to do the work and how those jobs fit in the structure. How will growth impact what work needs to get done and when could scale dictate a different design of the work itself?

● *staffing*: to ensure that people have needed skills and competencies. Determine the profiles that fill the jobs. How different are profiles during the start-up and during high growth and when must generalists begin to specialize?

● *support systems*: for the staff, including performance management, training and development, and recognition and rewards. When does 'one size fits all' no longer suffice and what messages should systems reinforce for the near and longer term?

● *behaviors*: how the company's values manifest themselves in the internal work environment. How is risk taking viewed or what characteristics of the 'start-up' are critical (versus detrimental) for the future?

● *leadership and management style:* to have vision and to build and mobilize the organization to execute strategy. Will the founder be the right leader in one, three, six years?

One of the greatest challenges for a leader of a rapidly growing entrepreneurial company is managing that alignment between business and the people. Successful management of the human resource dimension means integrating business strategy and organizational capabilities to achieve company goals. ■

Putting together a goal-scoring team

Vicky Meakin and **Bill Snaith** explain the factors involved in assembling and developing a successful management team.

The creation of any new venture or enterprise will inevitably mean building a team to support the development and growth of the emerging business. What this means and how it can be successfully achieved is often somewhat elusive. The concept (*see* Figure 1) seems simple enough: recruit a group of people, bring them together, give them something to do and then sit back and wait for a successful outcome. However, this approach is simplistic and rarely achieves what is desired. So what goes wrong?

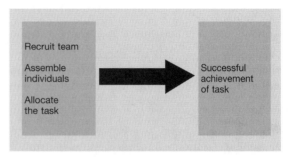

Figure 1

In answering this question, it is interesting to note that in a new enterprise many management teams are made up of individuals brought together on the basis of their past performance, skills and knowledge.

In effect, this is close to the well-known 'Peter principle' of being promoted to a level of incompetence. This does not mean that managers are not skilled or effective within their given functional area but that they perhaps lack the ability and enterprizing outlook needed to take account of the broader picture and to see where their knowledge and skills can assist others in achieving a common goal.

'Assist' is the key word here because individuals in an emerging team should be especially able to contribute in areas other than their own specialized knowledge or expertise.

In determining what goes wrong, it seems that there is often something missing, a void during which the direction and momentum of the team is lost. In order for a newly created team to be truly successful in facilitating and managing growth, it should possess a dynamic that ensures that direction is clearly established and that momentum is sustained.

Figure 2

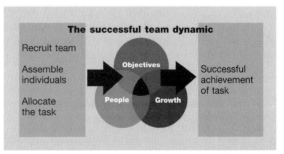

This dynamic, which we call the 'successful team dynamic', comprises three key factors: objectives, people and growth (*see* Figure 2). Combining and integrating each of these in the right way is likely to produce the best outcomes.

In a new venture, a management team is often brought together with little thought of the parameters, rationale and benefits of its existence beyond the broad aim of 'establishing and directing the business'. Yet, without a clear *raison d'être*, both the management team and enterprise can be doomed to fail. This is

Objectives: establishing the need for a team

why a newly formed management team can often best be defined as a group rather than a team.

A group is a collection of individuals who have their own area of specialism and often work in isolation on tasks that are part of achieving the group's overall objectives. A team, however, is a collection of individuals with a mixture of skills and knowledge that combine when working together to achieve the defined objectives. It is this mixture that enables the enterprising and innovative spirit of the team to develop. A team consists of people who are not only eligible to achieve the task (as they need to be in a group) but must also consist of people who are suitable in terms of their fit with the other team members.

People: combining eligibility and suitability

Figure 3 defines eligibility and suitability. Within a group, eligibility is the critical success factor because individual skills and expertise are vital in achieving overall group objectives. A team, however, requires a combination of eligibility and suitability within and between its members in order for objectives to be successfully achieved.

Eligibility	Suitability
Relevant qualifications	Aptitude to learn and contribute to the team
Relevance of experience	Versatility, a willingness in approach to team tasks
Evidence of successful achievements	Role fit with potential or existing team members

Figure 3

In choosing a group member, eligibility would be the prime consideration. In choosing a team member, eligibility *and* suitability must be considered. The newly formed business will require a great deal of innovative and creative thinking that only the right mix of people, personalities and skills will achieve.

In recognizing this distinction, it is important to be aware that a team will often be highly effective with members who may be less eligible but are more suitable. Suitability ensures the right people can work together. This is critical in achieving the successful team dynamic to develop the business.

Attributes and behaviors that need to be present in the team will be those consistent with directing and co-ordinating the combined efforts and contributions of all team members.

Within the newly formed venture, it will be particularly important for members to feel free in being enterprising. Carrying out management tasks will require the specialist knowledge and experience that 'eligibility' brings. But working through these tasks to achieve appropriate enterprizing decision-making will require suitability. Clearly then, bringing together the right people in an emerging team not only ensures that the tasks are achieved but that the team works well together and grows in confidence. This is important as it is likely to be reflected in improved business performance.

Having now established the need for a team and having clarified the need for both eligibility and suitability, the remaining key factor for achieving a successful team dynamic is the growth and development of the team.

Growth: developing the management team

Growth can be synonymous with development. Within this context, this means ensuring that information is shared and understood by all in the decision-making process. Opinions expressed should be listened to and all contributions welcomed.

For example, within a growing business venture a proposed sales strategy will obviously have an impact upon finance, production, marketing and so on. The successful management team will be able to understand and critically appraise the sales plan and so contribute to the formulation of an appropriate strategy.

In practical terms, this may mean the sales manager gaining a fuller understanding of the implications of his or her plan by talking with the production manager to appreciate and understand issues surrounding scheduling and lead times involved in meeting increased order volumes.

Individuals within the newly emerging management team need to be developed beyond their own specialist area so that they gain a fundamental appreciation of all aspects of the business and become able to make effective contributions that can influence decision-making. This does not mean they lose their specialism but rather that they can fully contribute to the decision-making process by demonstrating an understanding of business-wide implications.

This is not as easy as it may appear. Individuals within a newly formed business tend to find it hard to adapt and will inevitably stick to their strengths in order to protect their position and avoid making mistakes. Yet this is perhaps the very reason for limited growth of the team and the failure to realize business goals. Indeed, this becomes critical in achieving continuing success beyond the early stages of growth.

The successful team dynamic is about exploring risks with an underlying acceptance that team decisions may not always fully work out. But where they do not, they can be learned from. The effective management team will therefore share ownership and responsibility for developing strategy and for the results of their decision-making. This 'trusting' environment exemplifies the 'learning organization' and is consistent with true team growth and development.

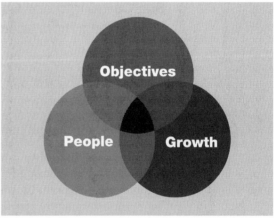

Figure 4

Even having identified and achieved all of the above, success is still not guaranteed. The remaining key to the successful team dynamic within a new venture is to maintain each key factor in synergy (*see* Figure 4). Each key factor should integrate to achieve synergy, which means that there is no clear linear progression through the three factors. Constantly monitoring how they interact with one another, in relation to early growth and development of the

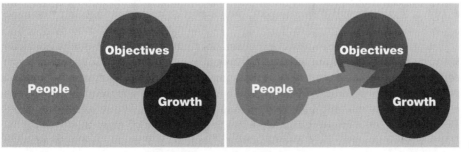

Figure 5

business goals, will identify imbalance and focus efforts on the appropriate factor.

When you have established and developed the team and are achieving success, the goal posts can move. One key factor may move out of alignment. For example, a team member may leave or an area of the business may undergo a surge of growth. In Figure 5, the key factor of people moves out of alignment and needs to be re-aligned by perhaps co-opting an additional member onto the team or placing an increased team focus on that specific business area. This re-alignment will eventually balance the team. ■

Distilling a strong team spirit

Teams do not always work as well as they can or should.
Sue Cartwright and **Cary Cooper** offer some suggestions on making them more effective.

Theoretically, teams should produce more ideas, make better-evaluated decisions and be more successful in implementing those decisions than individuals working alone.

So why is it that teams often spend excessive time (and money) only to come up with rather 'tired' designs and schemes, overly complicated systems and procedures, or unworkable solutions that never see the light of day or create more problems than they solve?

Working in teams ought to be energizing and provide an opportunity for individual members to broaden their professional knowledge and personal skills. Yet team meetings frequently become a forum to play games, a chance to assert individual superiority and put other people down. Despite their resources and initial dynamism, even top teams can run out of steam or become paralyzed by disagreements and an inability to reach a consensus.

Teams are perceived to have the advantage over individuals because they can draw on collective resources and expertise. This assumes that:
● there is, in fact, some expertise within the group – a selection issue
● that individuals will willingly pool their expertise and work together to pursue a common goal – a process issue.

If all the available resources in a team are to be utilized, it is important that team members feel comfortable about opening up and sharing information with each other. As this may mean admitting what you do not know as well as asserting what you do know, team members must not feel intimidated by others or consider that in being honest they may provide political advantage to others. This is still often a major stumbling block for the most able of teams.

It is part of the culture of business for individuals to compete with one another

– particularly in uncertain and ambiguous circumstances. In the case of cross-functional, international or very senior teams, there is bound to be a strong element of competition. After all, individuals will have succeeded and secured their membership to a 'top' team by rising through the organizational ranks, going it alone and standing out from the crowd.

To develop sufficient trust to be able to function effectively as an entrepreneurial team, team members need to spend time together to get to know each other. The England football team should, in theory, reflect the best individual footballing skills in the country. Yet it is frequently said that the England team underperforms because team members have little time to train together, to get to know each other, to be able to recognize each other's strengths and weaknesses, style of play and so on.

Pressure driven

The theory of group development as a four-stage process of 'forming, storming, norming and performing' is familiar to most managers. However, in practice, most teams are so driven by pressure to meet the project deadline and get on with the 'performing' as quickly as possible so that the relevance of process and relationship issues are overlooked.

Typically, the first signs of any potential dissent or interpersonal difficulties within the team are ignored or smoothed over by the majority rather than confronted. The team has not time 'to get bogged down' in issues that are perceived to detract from the task. But unless fully aired and resolved, grievances or bad feelings within a team invariably escalate into conflict or cause individuals to withdraw psychologically from the team.

For teams to work together, sufficient time needs to be set aside for building relationships. Ideally this should involve the team in social activities away from the workplace. Some organizations have returned to T-group type techniques as a means of improving team relationships. This involves getting together teams on a non-task driven basis to meet and explore work relationships without a specific business agenda. Others place a strong emphasis on activities, such as outdoor events, that help teams learn the value of co-operation. As organizations increasingly move towards the concept of 'virtual' teams, linked by technology, opportunities for face-to-face contact need to be created and are of great importance.

While most team-building initiatives focus on developing cohesiveness, this should not be at the expense of stifling challenge in a team. Constructive criticism and debate in teams is healthy and positive, provided members confine their criticism to the issues and behavior of others, rather than attacking their personality. Behavior can be changed; personality is more difficult. Therefore some training in conflict-resolution techniques and the giving and receiving of criticism is another important aspect of making teams work well.

Given the importance of the decision-making process in teams and of obtaining team members' commitment, it is clearly necessary to be able to assess participation and involvement within the group. In their book *Organizations and the Psychological Contract* (BPS Books, Leicester, UK) Makin, Cooper and Cox suggest a range of decision-making behaviors that can dictate team effectiveness (in ascending order of effectiveness):

Teams are perceived to have the advantage over individuals because they can draw on collective resources and expertise.

● *Apathy*: no one contributes to group discussion, not because they are in agreement but because they are totally disillusioned.

● *'Plops'*: a suggestion is made but totally ignored.

● *Dominance*: one particular individual dominates the meeting. This is often accompanied by apathy.

● *Pairing*: this is the simplest form of groups within a group. The psychological support offered by pairing is considerable.

● *Voting*: this is sometimes the only way to resolve disagreements. There are times, however, when it is appropriate and others when it is inappropriate.

● *False consensus*: if agreement cannot be reached, one way out of the impasse is to couch a decision in such broad terms that a number of interpretations are possible. A false consensus becomes apparent when the time comes for the decision to be implemented. Each side has a different understanding of what was agreed.

● *Consensus*: this is the most desirable conclusion. Genuine agreement leads to genuine commitment.

There are also practical steps that can be used to make teams work:

● Regularly changing the venue and seating arrangements at team meetings. Teams can get set into patterns of thinking – and interacting – if they always meet in the same room and sit in the same place. Changing seating arrangements also avoids cliques or pairings developing.

● Hold 'second-chance' meetings before a final decision is made so that the team has time to reflect rationally and come back on issues. This avoids the danger of making rash decisions that were carried more by enthusiasm or time pressure than sound judgment.

● Record minutes of team meetings with the name of the person required to take action alongside. This ensures that everyone is clear about what has been agreed and what they are required to do.

● Highly creative and energetic teams often come up with lots of ideas and actions but are poor at allocating the role of 'completer/finisher' to progress them, provide teams with regular feedback on their performance, and finally, Celebrate team successes. ■

⇝ CASE STUDY

Garibaldi goes to marketing school

*This is an edited version of a longer case study written by **Inger Boyett** of the University of Nottingham, and **Don Finlay** of Coventry University.*

The Garibaldi School, built in the 1960s in Mansfield, Nottinghamshire, on the edge of one of the UK's major coal fields, was designed to accommodate 1,100 pupils, aged 11 to 18. It is sited next to a large council estate close to a number of coal pits. There were 800 pupils at Garibaldi School in 1993, with a predicted rise to 1,000 over the next two years, and a teaching staff of 45.

In 1989, a new head teacher, Bob Salisbury, was appointed. Salisbury moved from a school in an affluent suburb on the outskirts of the city of Nottingham. 'The only thing I knew about this school before I moved here was that it had had two serious fires some 15 years before…the local saying was 'red sky at night, Garibaldi's alight'.'

On arrival at the school, Salisbury talked to parents, staff and children to find out about his new school. Very quickly, he discovered just how low the school's perceived image was. The consensus seemed to be that it was an 'ugly' kind of school, rough and not one that anyone would send their children to unless they had no other choice.

Surprisingly, though, Salisbury had been struck by the good atmosphere within the school. The youngsters were co-operative and pleasant and, despite the fact that it was clear that the staff were suffering problems of morale, they seemed talented and enthusiastic. 'This got me thinking[about] how an image of a school is created…and how that matched with what you actually found inside.'

Despite no previous experience, Salisbury recognized that he had a marketing challenge on his hands; not only did he need to change the school's external image to ensure that ideal numbers of pupils were attracted to it – to maximize per capita funding – he also had to look at revenue generation to resource many of the improvements he wanted to make. Following a meeting with staff, it was decided that Salisbury would approach a local industrialist to attempt to gain assistance.

The managing director of the local Mansfield Breweries, Ron Kirk, was a member of the school's governing body, and the majority decision was to approach him first. Kirk suggested that Salisbury should see Mansfield Breweries' marketing consultants, Miles Communication in Nottingham, to talk through possible marketing strategies. Kirk arranged for Miles Communication to talk Salisbury through the basic rules and strategies for marketing. 'It was quite honestly fascinating,' says Salisbury. 'A lot of things we now churn out are directly attributable to that first talk with the marketing company.'

Improved communications

A first stage was to set up improved communications with parents through newsletters and also a questionnaire sent to parents, local politicians, local industry and others. This enabled the school to produce an 18-point guide to improvements it could make and the school management team also developed a mission statement, three-year and five-year plans and strategies for implementation.

The three-year plan was achieved within the first 12 months, and the five-year plan within three years. But Salisbury was aware that, despite having met so many of the school's objectives, the process had to be continuous and many of the improvements they wanted to make required resource input that was not available through the normal budgets.

He approached a Derbyshire theme park – 'The American Adventure'. But with low ticket sales they had no money to offer. With his newly acquired marketing expertise, Salisbury asked how they marketed their product and how many visitors they had from Garibaldi's local area. The response provided Salisbury with an opportunity of proposing a deal.

'I said, well why don't you let us market North Nottinghamshire for you? Provide us with promotionally priced tickets, we sell them for you and take a cut of the profit.'

The theme park management agreed and within the first three months Garibaldi, utilizing a cheap advertising arrangement negotiated with the local newspaper, sold over £17,000-worth of tickets. Garibaldi's proceeds were used to buy a school minibus.

Marketing campaign

But Garibaldi's marketing campaign had proved so successful that it came to the notice of a larger competitor of 'The American Adventure' – Alton Towers in Staffordshire. Three businessmen arrived at the school one day and said that they wanted to talk to Salisbury about ticket sales. The offer they made was that if Garibaldi shifted loyalty from 'The American Adventure' to Alton Towers they would provide the school with a better deal – a better reduction on tickets, support for advertising and a better share in the profits.

Another excursion into the world of business involved making contact with British Thornton, a scientific and educational equipment manufacturer. Salisbury suggested that the company build showrooms at the Garibaldi School: a modern language center; a new science laboratory; and a new home economics room. Together they would form an East Midlands center where prospective buyers could see products not only displayed but also in use. Garibaldi staff would be available to discuss products and show visitors around.

Salisbury also suggested that the school would put up half of the refurbishment costs. In fact this came as a grant from the local TEC (Training and Enterprise Council – a government-funded body that aims to encourage education-business links) so the cost to the school was zero.

The deal was successful for both parties. British Thornton gained three relatively cheap showrooms and Garibaldi not only received improvements to three of its teaching areas but also a three per cent commission on any orders generated.

Garibadi's involvement with the local TEC was enhanced once the new language center was up and running by a link with a company called Applied Language Services. The company is now admistratively based at Garibaldi, a service offered by the school, and provides evening and weekend language courses for companies using school facilities.

Using the administrative skills available within the school has also provided the opportunity to provide further exhibition space to businesses, particularly those aimed at the educational market. One company, Trent Copyfax, has found that using Garibaldi for exhibitions is not only successful in providing a backdrop for its products but also administratively effortless since the school team takes over the exhibition organization, arrangements for refreshment, providing facilities and even marketing the exhibition to other schools.

In 1993, along with a number of other East Midlands-based organizations, including a printing company, a manufacturer of yachting equipment and an airport systems company, Garibaldi School entered and subsequently won a competition sponsored by the East Midlands Electricity Board to find the East Midlands Company of the Year. ■

Copies of the unabridged case can be obtained from the School of Management, University of Nottingham, Nottingham NG7 2RD.

6

☞ **Alternative perspectives**

Contents

Contributors

Max Boisot is Professor of Strategic Management at ESADE in Barcelona, Spain. From 1984 to 1989 he was dean and director of the first MBA program to be run in the People's Republic of China in Beijing.

Pedro Nueno is Bertran Foundation Professor of Entrepreneurial Management at IESE Business School, University of Navarra, Barcelona. He is also a member of the board of directors and chairman of the academic council of the China Europe International Business School in Shanghai.

Michael G. Scott is Professor of Entrepreneurial Studies in the Department of Management and Organization at the University of Stirling. His research interests include entrepreneurial career aspirations, small business failure, the impact of legislation and 'portfolio' entrepreneurs.

Akin Fadahunsi is a Ph.D. student at the University of Stirling.

Sarath Kodithuwakku is a Ph.D. student at the University of Stirling.

Gordon Redding is Poon Kam Kai Professor of Management Studies at the University of Hong Kong and was founding director of its business school. He is also a visiting professor at INSEAD.

Bert Twaalfhoven is Founder of the European Foundation for Enterprise Research.

Introduction

Part 6 roams the world. It is important to recognize that much of the literature in the field of entrepreneurship is from the USA and Europe and, therefore, based upon western values and cultures. Therefore, this part explores enterprise activities and the impact of national and religious culture in other communities – China, Japan, Korea, Sri Lanka, Nigeria, and the emerging countries of Eastern Europe.

A corporate culture in a world of global villages

As an introduction to a part devoted entirely to enterprise in an international context, **Max Boisot** examines the meaning of cultures and their implications for growing businesses.

The Buddhist and the broker

Imagine two characters, each faced with a communication task. The first is a Zen master concerned to impart to his disciples how to reach *satori*, or enlightenment. His knowledge is of the fuzzy and elusive kind, hard to codify, easy to misinterpret. It cannot easily be put into words and for that reason can only effectively be transmitted in face-to-face situations by force of example. It requires time, a high degree of trust and a sharing of values.

The second is a bond trader about to purchase commercial paper. He (or she) sits in front of a screen and enters his instructions on a machine. He transacts with a seller whom he has never met and who sits on the other side of the globe. His purchasing decision is readily codified as so many bonds at a given price. It registers as a small movement in the bond price that transmits worldwide in seconds.

If we are given to stereotyping, we can suppose that our Zen master lives in the ancient Japanese city of Kyoto and that our bond trader lives in New York, the heartland of American capitalism. Each inhabits a distinctive type of culture, shaped by the extent to which its critical knowledge can be structured and shared.

Culture as information flows

What our two, highly caricatured, examples bring out is that the extent to which we can codify our knowledge determines how far we can share with others. Numbers move faster and further than words, and words, in turn, transmit more readily than images or the atmosphere of a meeting. This relationship between the codification and diffusion of knowledge can be illustrated by means of a simple diagram (Figure 1) known as a 'culture space', or C-space.

Cultures are shaped by the structuring and sharing within groups of critical social knowledge. Four distinct types of culture are represented as points in the diagram. Their location is a function of the codification and diffusion properties of the information they draw on. Table 1 relates these properties to certain cultural features.

Of course, there are potentially as many types of culture as there are ways of grouping people together and these are often overlaid on each other. The culture of a street-corner gang, for example, is embedded in the wider urban culture; that of a corporate board in the culture of the enterprise; and so on.

Two types that increasingly preoccupy managers today are national culture and corporate culture. They are also interested in how they influence each other. Understanding this can be critical to a company's foreign operations. Many a Western enterprise operating in a highly codified manner, for example, has come to grief in countries whose culture is located in the lower regions of the C-space.

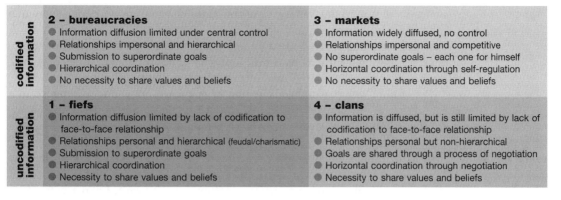

	2 – bureaucracies	3 – markets
codified information	● Information diffusion limited under central control ● Relationships impersonal and hierarchical ● Submission to superordinate goals ● Hierarchical coordination ● No necessity to share values and beliefs	● Information widely diffused, no control ● Relationships impersonal and competitive ● No superordinate goals – each one for himself ● Horizontal coordination through self-regulation ● No necessity to share values and beliefs
	1 – fiefs	**4 – clans**
uncodified information	● Information diffusion limited by lack of codification to face-to-face relationship ● Relationships personal and hierarchical (feudal/charismatic) ● Submission to superordinate goals ● Hierarchical coordination ● Necessity to share values and beliefs	● Information is diffused, but is still limited by lack of codification to face-to-face relationship ● Relationships personal but non-hierarchical ● Goals are shared through a process of negotiation ● Horizontal coordination through negotiation ● Necessity to share values and beliefs

The question is: who should do the adapting? The enterprise that wants to sell or the host country that wants to modernize?

Table 1: Transactions in the C-space

Do cultures converge?

The popular assumption is that globalization is moving us into a world in which the broker's culture will gradually eclipse that of the Zen master. Instantaneous communication is creating a global village, a world in which the word 'global' will count for more than the word 'village'.

But this is just another way of arguing that societal development and modernization gradually move cultures up the C-space and that, as they do so, they move them to the right, into a region of the space where information is highly codified and hence rapidly diffused. As Table 1 indicates, this region is characteristic of a market culture, one reason why globalization is associated by many with the development of a universal market order.

We have been here before. In post-medieval Europe, for example, development moved us away from a feudal order in fiefs and towards the embryonic bureaucracies of the absolutist states of the 18th century. A gradual decentralization towards a market order then took place from the 18th century onward, facilitated by the spread of literacy and education. Figure 2 traces this movement in the C-space.

It has always been assumed that development elsewhere will follow this course. Economic take-off requires a rule-based society and freedom to compete in open markets. Markets today have thus become a universal value even for countries such as China, still heavily located in the lower regions of the C-space.

An organization's corporate culture will follow a similar path in the C-space as it grows. It may start off as a highly personalized family business or entre-

Figure 1: The C-space
Figure 2: Cultural evolution in the C-space

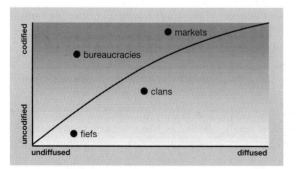

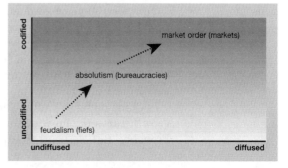

preneurial start-up in the fief region of the space but as it grows it gives way to a more impersonal bureaucratic order.

When the founding entrepreneur can no longer recognize the faces coming into work on Monday morning, then a different way of managing is required. As the enterprise continues to grow, some form of decentralization becomes necessary, leading not only to a greater codification of rules and procedures but also to a more extensive diffusion of information within the business. In many cases, internal markets are created – for capital, people, goods and so on.

Corporate versus national cultures

As the growing business moves up the C-space and to the right, it may internationalize its operations. It is then exhorted to 'think global but to act local'. Yet how realistic is this? Does it not create a potential clash between a corporate culture and a national one? Global managers will find it difficult to act local across more than at most one or two cultures. Local managers, in turn, will find thinking global quite a stretch.

Is it possible to act local without thinking local to some extent? Thinking local is not done in a day. It requires a lengthy accumulation of tacit knowledge, habits, values and beliefs that do not easily diffuse outside a given culture. Think how difficult it can be to understand the humour of a new culture even when its language has been mastered. In the absence of an ability to think local, acting local easily becomes an empty ritual, a behavior associated with day-trippers rather than long-term residents.

Alternatives to convergence

In the case of both national and corporate culture, growth and development have been assumed to entail a movement up the C-space and to the right – a convergence on a single cultural order. Moving up and across the C-space achieves important efficiencies, reducing both the costs and ambiguities of communicating and increasing the numbers that can participate in cultural exchanges. It also has its problems. With the loss of a tacit context comes a depersonalization of relationships, a loss of community and a general inability to cope with uncertainty.

Some cultures seem disinclined to move up the C-space. Sometimes there is a strong preference for keeping relationships personalized rather than impersonal. In others a lack of physical and institutional infrastructure makes it difficult to codify cultural exchanges in the upper regions of the C-space.

Consider the case of China (discussed in detail on p. 187). The Chinese leadership claims that the country is moving towards a market economy. The claim presupposes that the country is decentralizing on the back of well-codified institutional structures in the bureaucratic region of the C-space.

Yet, *pace* 50 years of a command economy, the country remains more feudal than bureaucratic. If it is decentralizing at all – and the evidence suggests that it is – it is doing so in the lower region of the C-space, from a fief-like order to a clan-like one. In clans, it is operating a kind of network capitalism, which, being based on *guanxi* (connections) and interpersonal trust, is far removed from a market order.

Is China doing so badly? The country has turned in one of the highest economic growth rates in the world since the early 1980s. Is the country modernizing? Probably. But contrary to expectations, it is doing so in the lower regions of the

C-space. Western managers operating on the assumption that modernizing cultures will all sooner or later converge on their way of doing things could thus be in for a rude shock.

Interestingly, when it comes to corporate cultures, Western managers that have moved their enterprises up the C-space are now trying to build their competence once more in its lower regions.

Cultures that seek to codify everything by reducing it to matters of procedures (bureaucracies) or price (markets) by degrees lose their capacity to deal with novelty and uncertainty. In large Western businesses this translates into a loss of entrepreneurship. Many large companies, following the example of 3M and ABB, are now seeking to restore an entrepreneurial culture by creating small businesses within large ones.

Here, recent development in information technology (IT) could help. The **The impact of IT** information revolution is taken by many to favor the culture of the broker. To some extent it does. By vastly increasing the data-processing and transmission capacities of organizations, whatever the level of codification, IT effectively pushes the diffusion curve to the right in the C-space (*see* Figure 3). The broker can thus extend his reach, as indicated by the horizontal arrow in the diagram, to a greater number of people.

Yet it turns out that IT also has something to offer the Zen Master. As the vertical arrow in Figure 3 suggests, a given population can now be reached at a lower level of codification than before: the fax replaces the telex and video-conferencing allows face-to-face meetings at a distance. Whether or not Zen masters avail themselves of these new technologies, they offer practising managers the prospect of building up highly personalized cultures independently of geographical distance.

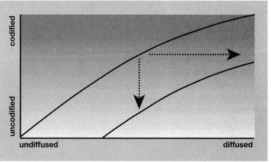

Figure 3: The impact of IT on the diffusion curve

The advent of high-bandwidth communication could thus restore an element of community to what is currently perceived as an increasingly impersonal market order. If cultural convergence there is to come about, therefore, it might well occur around the clan-like networks characteristic of Asian cultures rather than the impersonal market order that many Western observers take to be universal.

We have been moving in a small-is-beautiful direction for some time. Today companies are shrinking in size, more is being outsourced to a small network of partners and, in spite of those custodians of the market order, the Securities and Exchange Commission (SEC) and the Monopolies Commission, collaboration between companies now receives as much attention as competition.

It may be global in its reach, but it is the culture of the village that we should be attending to. The problem is that contrary to what Marshal McLuhan supposed when he coined the term, it is not a single global village that is being created by IT but literally tens of thousands of them. Operating within one village requires one kind of skill; operating across several requires another. If the right skill is lacking, conflict could result. There are therefore dangers as well as opportunities in a culture of global villages.

© FT Pictures

Zen and the art of communication: does IT have something to offer the Zen master?

Dangers because by bringing people closer together we lose the impersonality in relationships that often protects individuals from exposure to differences in values and norms. The great virtue of the market order is that it functions with only a minimum amount of adaptation to and alignment with local cultural requirements.

Opportunities because if the personalization of global relationships is skillfully managed it will teach managers to think locally but at a distance, thus effectively increasing the range of cultural environments that their enterprises are capable of adapting to.

To the extent that managers can chew gum and walk at the same time they must now learn to simultaneously think globally and locally. Acting locally is no longer enough.

Cultural adaptation versus cultural conformity

An effective corporate culture is a source of competitive advantage for a company if it achieves the right degree of fit with the range of environments in which it finds itself operating in.

The assumption that cultures converge on a market order is one that eliminates cultural variety in favor of consumer variety. It provides a greater choice of products – *sushi* bars in Manhattan, French restaurants in the Ginza – but a declining heterogeneity of the cultural environments in which to consume them. Managers then only have to adapt to a single universal culture – that of the market. How nice if it also happens to be one in which they grew up. The need for hard learning is thereby obviated.

Companies that believe in convergence on a universal market order may be less inclined to create a corporate culture capable of adapting to a range of different national cultures. Where an organization's products have a high technical content, this has not mattered much. Nuclear power stations and long-range airliners have until recently been perceived as 'culture-free' technical objects. No longer. Building power stations or aircraft tails in China has a nasty way of converting technical problems into cultural ones. On the other hand, organizations that believe that cultural differences will persist, that what distinguishes the French and the Italians is not about to disappear, may find it difficult to create a unified corporate culture that transcends national differences.

Such businesses need to bear in mind that to adapt is not to conform. An enterprise needs to maintain its cultural identity if it is to profit from it. Adapting a corporate culture to the multiple, divergent demands of multiple global villages may be the biggest challenge that international corporations face as they enter the new century. ■

The dragon breathes enterprising fire

Pedro Nueno looks at the changing economic face of China and how the reforms there can and will provide potential for the entrepreneur.

If the question is: are there entrepreneurs in China? The answer is yes. If the question is: are there foreign entrepreneurs in China? The answer is also yes. And plenty of them in both cases. Entrepreneurship is so rooted in human nature that unless it is strictly forbidden it emerges with strength. This is what is happening in China today.

Scholars have long debated whether some ethnic groups are more entrepreneurial than others. As the article on page 160 of Part 5 described, the fact that ethnic Chinese entrepreneurs control large portions of the economies of south-east Asia shows that some Chinese can be superb entrepreneurs. About 1 per cent of the population of the Philippines is ethnic Chinese yet they control 40 per cent of the economy. In Indonesia and Thailand, with 4 per cent and 10 per cent ethnic Chinese respectively, they control half of the domestic business

Super-entrepreneur Stanley Ho, with a net worth estimated at more than $2bn, appears to be in good standing with the senior levels of the Chinese authorities

© FT/Reuters

activity. In Malaysia about one-third of the population is ethnic Chinese but they control two-thirds of the economy. Hong Kong, Taiwan and Singapore have a majority of ethnic Chinese and they control practically the whole domestic wealth.

Entrepreneurs, as Harvard Business School's Howard Stevenson has said, are opportunity driven. They find out the resources they need once they have identified the opportunity (*see* Part 1). A network of contacts and trust is essential. Networking and trust are well-known characteristics of the Chinese culture. Many of the Chinese who left the People's Republic of China (PRC) and became famous entrepreneurs in south-east Asia kept their links with their communities on the mainland. Many have made their fortunes in activities related to the PRC in areas such as trade, finance and real estate.

Super-entrepreneurs such as Stanley Ho (with a net worth estimated at more than $2 bn) who has, among many businesses around the world, the exclusive franchise for the operation of the lucrative casinos of Macau, seem to be in good standing with the senior levels of the Chinese authorities. The Hong Kong tycoons associated in the Better Hong Kong Foundation to promote confidence in Hong Kong after the Chinese takeover in July 1997 combine their businesses in China with generous donations to charities on the mainland to establish good political relations through a demonstration of social responsibility.

These personalities are well known in China. Media networks carry information about them and they are idolized as role models. The Chinese authorities appear to let them play this function, using them as catalysts for the abundant entrepreneurial initiative in the PRC.

It is hardly surprising, therefore, that in December 1996 the first post-colonial chief executive of Hong Kong was announced as shipping magnate Tung Chee-hwa, appointed with the obvious blessing of Beijing.

Figure 1 shows who produces the industrial output in China. Since the start of economic reform in 1978, the output of state-owned enterprises (SOEs) has gone down to less than half and the trend continues. Collectively owned enterprises have doubled their industrial output, and individually owned enterprises have taken more than 10 per cent of industrial output, growing at more than 25 per cent a year. The 'other' column includes foreign enterprises.

Entrepreneurs in China: who are they?

It needs eight or more people to form a collectively owned enterprise and therefore this group ranges from co-operative-type enterprises to entities where in fact one member controls the company and the others are relatives or sleeping partners.

The bulk of foreign investment in China comes from Hong Kong, Taiwan and Singapore. Part of this investment is made by Chinese entrepreneurs who manage to establish companies abroad and invest back in the PRC.

Most Chinese entrepreneurs are former executives of SOEs who identify an opportunity while working for the state and have the contacts to transform that opportunity into a venture. In Japan, leaving a large company to start your own small business is not well received and you would not expect a lot of support from previous contacts (former employer, customers, suppliers, the financial community). In China this is not the case; entrepreneurship seems to be highly valued in Chinese society.

Entrepreneurs starting their own companies in China might have problems attracting employees, however. This is because SOEs normally supply housing, healthcare and pensions. Or at least that was the case until recently.

year	by the state	collectively	individually	other
1978	77.63	22.37	0.00	0.00
1979	78.47	21.53	0.00	0.00
1980	75.97	23.54	0.02	0.48
1981	74.76	24.62	0.04	0.58
1982	74.44	24.82	0.06	0.68
1983	73.35	25.74	0.12	0.78
1984	69.09	29.71	0.19	1.01
1985	64.86	32.08	1.85	1.21
1986	62.27	33.51	2.76	1.46
1987	59.73	34.62	3.64	2.02
1988	56.80	36.15	4.34	2.72
1989	56.06	35.69	4.80	3.44
1990	54.60	35.62	5.39	4.38
1991	52.94	35.70	5.70	5.66
1992	48.09	38.04	6.76	7.11
1993	43.13	38.36	8.35	10.16
1994	34.07	40.87	11.51	13.55

Source: Prof. Xiang Bing, CEIBS Working Paper No. 002, CEIBS, Shanghai.

Figure 1: Industrial gross output value by ownership type (% of enterprises owned)

1996 was the first year the SOE sector as a whole lost money. In the two or three years previously, roughly one-third of SOEs made money, one-third lost money and one-third broke even, managing an overall positive balance. In the seven years up to 1996, state sector losses multiplied by seven. These enormous shells – some partially empty – carry tremendous social obligations and this is one of the question marks over the reform of the Chinese economy.

As in Western countries, there is an important portion of marginal entrepreneurship made up of very small individual enterprises, sometimes run by senior citizens and most of them part of the parallel economy, engaged in elementary forms of trading in food, textiles, household and other consumer products. This sector is particularly difficult to quantify.

Some private Chinese companies are true success stories. Vanward Enterprises is a privately held fast-growing manufacturer of home appliances. The company produces 500,000 gas water heaters each year, employs 1,500 people (of whom ten per cent are engineers), operates 200 service centres in China and has overseas offices in Hong Kong and Singapore.

Vanward, owned by three brothers, carries out its own research and development and is expanding its product range to include microwave ovens, electric water heaters, electric rice cookers, electric heaters and so on. The company has ISO 9001 certification and has begun to export. Companies such as Vanward are the hidden champions of the Chinese economy.

Foreign entrepreneurs in China

Foreign entrepreneurs in China are mainly found in the service sector and their clientele is also primarily foreign. They are established in most cases as representative offices of 'mail box'-type companies based in Hong Kong. They provide advice on trade, finance, head-hunting, training, real estate, marketing, public relations, auditing, strategy and so on, and some employ over 100 people in China. In general, these enterprises must bill a foreign entity.

One can find highly qualified professionals who are fluent in Mandarin, knowledgeable about doing business in China and who benefit from the strong flows of foreign direct investments. While 'blue chip' companies tend to use the well-known global 'brands' for their service needs – and all the brands have a presence in China these days – there is room for entrepreneurs with industry or business connections abroad who can offer lower prices and a personalized treatment to smaller companies with smaller projects.

Access to capital

As in the West, most Chinese entrepreneurs start their ventures from their personal savings and those of members of their network of relatives and friends. In some instances the networks might include people in key positions in government or SOEs. If this is the case, a somewhat privileged access to funding might take place through longer-term financing of suppliers, shorter-term payment of receivables or even direct borrowing possibilities.

Other advantages of the network might also be used. Insider information or influence in land classification, for example, might be the contribution to a project of a well-connected entrepreneur who may then also find partners in Hong Kong or Taiwan willing to provide funding.

Well-run companies can make enough profits to finance their needs for working capital and investment. Banks are also sources of financing, and a successful manufacturer such as Vanward would not have the problems with a bank that its Western counterparts might have.

There is no doubt that there is a level of corruption in China. This is recognized by the authorities, publicly criticized and there are efforts to control it. While the situation in China is far from what can be found in Russia or some Latin American states, there is no doubt that some Chinese entrepreneurs benefit from access to easy government or SOE money.

Venture capital has recently been introduced in China with the creation of the Minsheng Bank. Related to the All China Federation of Industry and Commerce, this agency's aim is to provide financial support to entrepreneurs, particularly those with hi-tech projects.

The future of entrepreneurship in China

As China continues to reform its economy and more Chinese managers improve their management skills, as the weakening of the SOEs offer less protection to Chinese workers and as banks become more sensitive to the financing of healthy projects, the rapid growth of the private sector will open more and more opportunities for entrepreneurs in China.

Along the coastal provinces clusters of privately owned companies are emerging as suppliers or subcontractors to successful, larger privately owned companies, joint ventures or dynamic SOEs. But as economic reform makes progress and the market economy advances, unemployment in China will undoubtedly grow.

Entrepreneurs might benefit from this flexible labor market while at the same time providing a solution – probably the only possible solution – for millions of Chinese workers. ∎

Tackling adversity with diversity

Enterprise exists in every culture, not least in the so-called 'developing' countries, though it may be very different from the classic Western model. Two examples from Sri Lanka and Nigeria. By **Michael Scott**, **Akin Fadahunsi** and **Sarath Kodithuwakku**.

There is a myth that entrepreneurship is largely a phenomenon of developed, industrialized countries and that if only it could be transferred, together with western management practices, then problems of so-called 'underdevelopment' would be solved.

Yet the evidence is that entrepreneurship is a generalized social role found in all societies, merely varying as the context changes. If entrepreneurship is seen as the 'creative extraction of value from environments', then the elements we have been discussing in *Mastering Enterprise* – such as vision, opportunity spotting, risk and profit taking, resource mobilization and network development – may take a different (and sometimes invisible) form in different environments but are always present.

While international agencies seek to disseminate developed country models of best practice, there are equally interesting lessons to be learned from indigenous wealth-extracting methods.

The rich diversity of entrepreneurship is illustrated by the following two recent studies. These are part of a program of research into indigenous entrepreneurship in Africa and South Africa being developed by Dr Peter Rosa at the University of Stirling. The first, in Sri Lanka, shows how, in an apparently uniform and scarce environment, being entrepreneurial is a survivalist strategy through which 'winners' arise. The second, in Nigeria, demonstrates how wealth can be created by entrepreneurs through a parallel economic system.

Creating success in the Sri Lankan countryside

An intriguing question for students of enterprise is 'can we pick winners?' All the evidence is that we cannot and one reason is the large number of possible influences on success.

The Sri Lankan study set out to understand why, in a rural area, some people are more successful than others and what contribution entrepreneurial activity makes.

Studying wealthy farmers is not the same as studying entrepreneurs. Wealth might have come from previous generations through cultural and political effects or through access to better resources. Isolating the effects of enterprise from all the other political, resource and cultural factors is usually the major problem researchers face. Fortunately a kind of natural experiment was discovered in the shape of a land scheme.

During the 1980s the Sri Lankan government provided cleared land to new settlers – all similarly without wealth. With scarcely enough land to meet subsistence, few outside resources and little education, we might expect to find villagers in abject poverty. With a monoculture (rice paddy) and set ways of producing it, one might expect uniformity – and indeed to the Westerner all villagers look poor.

Yet there is an underlying diversity of activities that over a decade led to large inequalities of wealth. Economic activities include not only cultivation – rice paddy, cash crops – but also rice milling, hiring out of tractors and animals, village shopkeeping and money lending.

The agricultural cycle gives rise to shifting demands for labor and equipment. Middlemen are active at harvest, buying from farmers, who then engage in highly impulsive consumption – to the benefit of shopkeepers. This is followed by a demand for credit as farmers again need cash for fertilizers to start the next year. The task of the entrepreneur is to spot opportunities in this agricultural cycle of activities and match them with available or mobilized resources, resulting in capital accumulation and wealth creation.

How these processes operate in all their diversity can be illustrated in the following case study of a family with three adults and three school-age children. They cultivate nine acres and have a two-wheel tractor, a permanent building for storing paddy, four draught animals and a cow.

They start their cultivation early and they do as much of it using their own labor as possible to conserve cash. The tractor is hired-out for ploughing, winnowing and transport and they have a stand-by driver. They choose a planting method that is more risky in terms of yield but which needs less labor and is more effective in weed control. Savings are used to buy the fertilizer necessary for high-yield varieties.

By being early in the cycle, the family can subcontract its own labor to farmers who are falling behind. They do not sell all their produce at harvest but can store some until prices are higher. They also act as local collectors of rice for outside middlemen, with whom they have long-term trusting relationships.

The wife initiated the leasing of extra land, the profits of which help pay for the tractor, as well as providing cash for her money-lending activities. She appears to have earned about Rs 100,000 during the past eight years from an initial Rs 2,500 and has accumulated savings of about Rs 20,000 in her bank account.

Apart from paddy they also grow vegetables for their own use, and sell any surplus. Their cow has been leased to a fellow villager who feeds it and receives the milk while every other calf is given back to the family. Bulls are used to plough their paddy lands and also for transportation purposes. The bullock cart is leased to transport paddy and fire wood for the villagers involved in rice processing.

Entrepreneurial lessons

What can be derived from this case study? First, there is 'pluriactivity', that is the family are involved in many things – from farming, to trading, to leasing, to money lending. Just like a juggler with many balls in the air, entrepreneurs typically have more than one activity current at any one time.

Second, they combine various resources and it is the skill in accumulating and combining that enables them, thirdly, to activate new opportunities as they spot them.

Of course, pluriactivity itself leads to more chances of new opportunities being perceived. The capital accumulation process is itself a ratchet: profits reinvested (for example in a tractor) create more wealth for the next cycle.

All this implies rational thought (exactly when to plant, what varieties, at what rate to lend and so on) and hard work, accompanied by deferred gratification. (The family had the choice of building a new barn or a new house – they chose a barn in the expectation of building a larger house later). The development of key relationships is crucial and especially the reliance on interpersonal trust. Finally, the family makes use of information sources not to do what everybody else does but to seek more profitable windows in the market.

Building wealth through the Nigerian cross border trade

The previous case shows how entrepreneurship can be a survivalist strategy in constrained circumstances and the ways it can differentiate successful from less successful farmers. The following study shows how entrepreneurship can thrive even where it officially does not exist at all.

According to official statistics in Nigeria, most trade is carried out by governments or multinational companies. There appears to be little contribution from indigenous entrepreneurs, reinforcing a commonly held belief that Africa does not have enough entrepreneurs with the capability to move beyond survival into significant wealth accumulation.

This is linked to the difficulties indigenous entrepreneurs face in acquiring management and entrepreneurship skills appropriate for success in the formal sector, coupled with a tendency for bribery and corruption to cream off any added value.

The study indeed confirms the two major constraints on cross-border trade to be foreign exchange related problems (the non-exchangeability of the Naira through official channels) and harassment of traders.

Yet these very problems have been turned into entrepreneurial opportunities, and there exists a huge informal, or parallel, economy, transporting large volumes of goods and allowing considerable wealth to be accumulated by successful traders. There is, for example, an 'alternative' financial system based not on government sales of restricted foreign currency but on the activities of several thousand currency traders who are the real determinants of the Naira's exchange rate.

*All above board –
unofficial trading,
however, can be a
big spur for the
entrepreneur*

© FT Pictures

For most traders, the constant harassment is a way of life. For example, at border crossings there may be a dozen checkpoints (one army, one customs, the rest police), each of which imposes searches.

There are several strategies for evading harassment. Traders can simply pay up to lubricate the speed of transfer; they can use bush paths (but this risks robbery); goods can be concealed, mainly to avoid extortion rather than smuggling to avoid duties. But the most common method is to use specialist intermediaries, independent carriers called *kelebes* who operate from 'stations' a short distance from the border posts.

The *kelebes* carry the trader's bags or other containers while the trader casually walks across the border. Once over, a fee is paid to the *kelebe* (and any helpers he has subcontracted).

A high level of trust is needed for these transactions to be completed since the *kelebe* could easily make away with the goods, especially if the trader were detained. The reliance on trust is even more pronounced in the case of large-scale goods transported by lorry. Here the specialist intermediaries are drivers who undertake to get the goods across the border, using bribery to join armed convoys for example.

These are complicated procedures: the detailed mechanics of cross-border trade take years to learn and there is a system of apprenticeship as effective as any in the formal sector. The rewards can be substantial and successful traders have moved into a wide range of activities, from car and computer imports, to cotton processing on farms bought from trading profits and conglomerate businesses with assets of millions of Naira.

Entrepreneurial lessons

While there are many petty traders who simply establish well-tried routines and never innovate, the study identified others who were constantly looking for new profitable products – and 'pluriactivity' is again a feature.

The most successful entrepreneurs tend not to operate themselves but to subcontract the risk to others. This 'brokerage' role is a crucial aspect of entrepreneurship. Trust in relationships is paramount to the informal system. Just because there is a disregard of written rules (the official system) does not mean that well-observed rules do not exist.

Profit is extracted by several intermediaries at 'boundary exchanges' and the complexities of the trade require much learning-by-doing. Infrastructure chaos is paradoxically beneficial to traders because it keeps the multinationals out.

The official view may pessimistically be that harassment of traders adds costs to products, inevitably passed on to already poor consumers. Loss of revenue to government leads to higher taxes and more external borrowing from neo-colonial institutions. Bribery and corruption impoverish the traders, decreasing both motivation and wealth accumulation possibilities.

There is a different picture. The system would appear to produce entrepreneurial opportunities for far more people than would otherwise benefit from 'official' trading. Traders benefit by being able to reduce competition from less knowledgeable competitors because it takes so long to learn the system. An army of intermediaries also makes a living out of the system who would otherwise not have any utility under a more regulated system.

Conclusion

Entrepreneurship appears to thrive wherever one looks for it. It may not take familiar Western forms but the essentials of value extraction are always present, limited only by the ingenuity of the informal entrepreneurs themselves. ∎

Three styles of Asian capitalism

Gordon Redding compares and contrasts the entrepreneurial and organizational styles of Japan, Korea and the ethnic Chinese.

Not only are ways of doing business in Asia subtly different from those in the West but they are also different within the region itself in important ways. It is a region of immense variety, far more so than is Europe, and runs the gamut from an advanced democracy such as Japan to some of the world's worst totalitarian regimes, from the depths of poverty in Cambodia or the far west of China to the immensely wealthy Japan and the conspicuously spending rich of Hong Kong.

The 30 miraculously golden years just passed have seen the emergence of three powerful systems of business, each represented by a particular kind of organization: in Japan the large complex networked business, known as the *kaisha* or in its extended form the *keiretsu*; in South Korea the now internationalizing *chaebol*; elsewhere, in areas where business needs strong local knowledge and connections, the Chinese family business, that most unobtrusive and little-understood instrument of wealth creation and progress.

Each of these instruments for putting together the components of economic behavior has emerged as a distinct response to its surrounding circumstances. They are embedded in the cultures and development histories of their societies. They are not copies of Western forms and their behavior may not follow Western rules or ideals. In simple terms, they exist for different reasons.

Where the prime reason for existence and driving logic for the large American corporation is return to shareholders, that of the *kaisha* is to employ people. The *chaebol* has derived much of its dynamism from its contribution to the national development goals of Korea. The Chinese family business exists primarily to create and sustain family fortunes.

The outcome of these varying routes to modern capitalism is that the Japanese form is a large, professionally managed and very complex enterprise with wide ownership; the Korean is a huge family business run like a regiment; and the Chinese is a small family business networking to escape the limitations of its scale and doing so successfully.

These different kinds of organization compete on equal terms in world markets. In Asia today are some of the world's most competitive forms of enterprise, able to hammer each other in world markets on equal terms. In doing so, however, there is no logic which says that they have to all have the same book of rules.

Three questions remain especially hard to answer in observing this scene. Why are the Japanese and Koreans masters of the co-ordination of complexity on a huge scale in their organizations when the Chinese normally stay efficient with small-scale companies run on a personal basis?

Will the ethnic Chinese in the region now creating large organizations take them through the same managerial revolution which brought professional management and public ownership in the Western case or will their large companies remain dependent for strategy on a presiding genius and be thus unstable and vulnerable to the chances of succession, like China itself?

Will China find in its vast laboratory a new hybrid form of economy which takes from the success of the so-called Overseas Chinese and applies network and family capitalism to the task of finally modernizing an ancient and essentially imperial polity?

A subtext of this latter question is whether Hong Kong will be permitted to continue its demonstration of how to run a modern state of Chinese people under something other than autocracy. Was Machiavelli right in saying that the only sure way to take over a state used to governing itself is to ruin it, otherwise it will carp for ever about its lost freedoms and eventually undermine its new master?

Masters of large, masters of small

When a society develops a form of organization that is so common it becomes typical, it usually means that there is a shared heritage of influences which has shaped its modern organizations. These influences are historical and the more recent ones are those connected with the way a country modernizes itself, in particular the way it organizes access to capital and to human skill. Whether you get your capital from a market, from the government, from banks or from your

Masters of
complexity: *South
Korean economy has
roots deep in the
small business*

© FT Pictures

friends will make a big difference to how you go about using it and accounting for its use.

Capital from the market drives the frenzy of Anglo-Saxon companies to meet the quarterly expectations of a ravenous investing public, also incidentally directing investment rationally to fields of maximum return in the short run. For the Japanese, capital from the market is of less account than is capital from companies in the same group or from banks, and their interests are less in short-term gain than in the accumulation of long-term strength. Korean *chaebol* have a history of dependence for capital on government and of a consequent need to accommodate government guidance on strategy. Although Korea is now changing rapidly, such habits of mind are embedded and die hard. The end result in both cases is that it has been possible for each of these systems of capitalism to take the long perspectives needed to foster major corporations handling very complex industries.

Other features, older and deeper than modern policies, have helped to make it possible for large Japanese and Korean organizations to co-ordinate human skill, capital, technology, and market know-how to produce world-beating products such as the Lexus or to take a huge chunk of the world market in semiconductors. These extra features include societal norms supporting acceptance of authority and discipline, a sense of the importance of the organization in one's life and a consequent wish to belong to it, an association of individuals with the collective good of the group and intense competitiveness on behalf of the nation via the company.

Recently, attention has been drawn by Francis Fukuyama to another societal feature critical to economic efficiency. The notion of trust, what he calls the 'social virtues' or what others call social capital, has an important part to play in explaining why the Japanese and Koreans can handle very large-scale organizations efficiently and the Chinese cannot.

Trust has developed to a high level in a society when you can do business with strangers. In the West this happens when the society has built a fabric of commercial law and bodies such as free-standing professions like accountancy, and so on which serve to underwrite much risk and encourage exchange to grow more dense. In turn this raises the intensity with which resources are used and the resulting gains in productivity account for the transition from the pre-modern condition to the modern.

Although civil society in Japan is not a copy of that in the West, it nevertheless works similarly and the level of trust between strangers is both high and in constant use. The Korean case is different from the Japanese. The Korean economy is organized into great vertically structured units with roots deep into the small-business sector via subcontracting that serve to produce high levels of efficient linkage and modern levels of efficiency in the use of resources.

The Chinese family business specializes in small-scale efficiency, which at first glance is a contradiction. In Taiwan, Hong Kong (and increasingly South China) and throughout ASEAN (Association of South East Asian Nations) the 50m or so ethnic Chinese have perfected a formula for business which has turned them into formidable world players.

Their domains are OEM (original equipment manufacture) production, property, services, retailing, trading, and, in the region itself, capturing lucrative franchises in such fields as power, terminals, tunnels and gambling.

OEM's strength provides entry to the world business system. Here products go through faster and faster cycles and IT encourages smaller production runs and tighter delivery times to the world's boutiques, or to the assemblers and packagers of the latest bells and whistles on the latest toys, executive and other-wise.

It is in these circumstances that there are little businesses specializing in shirt collars and employing 30 people but linked to seven other little outfits specializing in buttons, fabric wholesaling, fabric dyeing or shirt-sewing. They receive an order involving a shipment of thousands of shirts to Los Angeles by next Tuesday and are able to say 'no problem'.

By letting others worry about brand-naming, distribution and market risk, as well as design, single companies can grow to manufacture the world market in GI Joe toys, 40 per cent of the US market in hair-dryers, huge proportions of the markets in cheap cameras, torches, photo albums, underwear, tennis racquets, as well as innumerable small components lying out of sight inside your average computer, washing machine or waffle iron.

This network capitalism of the ethnic Chinese in the region is designed to respond to markets which companies from advanced economies would say are disorderly, volatile and very difficult to cope with. Information is not openly available in the region about the right price to pay, whom to trust, what to expect of anyone, which official rules need navigating and how, who is credit worthy and for how much, how do you get paid and where are the necessary skills. This information is the province of the ethnic Chinese throughout many of the region's service and manufacturing industries.

The accumulating and holding of such knowledge is seen as strategic and the use of it is largely to pursue opportunity in the holes in such unlevel playing fields. This is often done by collaboration with other members of the net with whom capital, risk and more information come to be shared. This works as a response to uncertainty for the Chinese, for whom the meaning of danger includes opportunity.

The ethnic Chinese's secret has been the release of entrepreneurial talent and the building of systems of stable co-ordination of economic behavior to allow such talent to be fed with capital and efficiently controlled while at the same time escaping from the scale limitations which normally go with entrepreneurs. To connect these small businesses into world markets is no mean feat when it is done without bureaucracy. This is the achievement of Chinese capitalism so far in the last 30 years. But what happens next ? And will China be radically transformed in consequence ? ∎

Doing business in the 'Wild East'

The experience of entrepreneurial growth differs considerably across central and Eastern Europe. But **Bert Twaalfhoven** and **Daniel Muzyka** offer some broad guidance to the region and advice to indigenous and foreign entrepreneurs.

There is no easy way to describe the development of entrepreneurship in a whole region of the world nor is it easy to characterize the transition in central and eastern Europe; it is unprecedented in recorded human economic history. It is apparent, however, that this region of the world is experiencing both the best of times and the worst of times as the economic transition unfolds. The good news for entrepreneurs in the region is that opportunities abound.

The assumption at the time of the *Wende*, or fall of the Berlin Wall, was that the emergence of entrepreneurs and entrepreneurial business would represent one of the primary pillars in the economic reconstruction of central and eastern Europe. The other pillar was to be the remobilization and redesign of the vertically integrated state enterprises that existed under communism.

The informal economy, particularly in Russia, is very large and no one has exact figures. Early projections by the European Foundation for Entrepreneurship Research (EFER – a non-profit organization whose goals are to develop and support growth-oriented entrepreneurship in Europe and which has participated in many initiatives in eastern Europe, including the identification and training of key academics who would help develop a new generation of entrepreneurs) in preparation for a 1990 conference on entrepreneurial business in the region predicted an increase from 1m to 2m entrepreneurial businesses in

1989 to about 4m to 5m by the year 2000. The OECD currently estimates that by 1995 there were at least 12m entrepreneurial enterprises in the East. These businesses have become the primary engine for economic redevelopment in the former communist republics.

Why has entrepreneurial business taken such a center stage role? The answer is both positive and negative.

Almost everyone expected the large state combines to provide at least one of the pillars for reconstruction. These businesses accounted for most of the economic activity. To give you some comparisons, it is reported that significantly more than half the people in the US are employed in companies with fewer than 50 people; in the former East Germany, 11 per cent of the population was involved in such enterprises.

It proved very difficult to reconstruct these behemoths. 'Corporate culture', if we can use the term, as well as the asset base and the very nature of the products were all obstacles to effective economic performance. As we witnessed at an aerospace show in Moscow, one enterprise moved from manufacturing rockets to the construction of lawnmowers. Without requisite marketing skills, most of these activities were unsuccessful and the asset base proved to have little value. Finally, as operating entities they often proved too costly to operate, providing very low productivity and even lower quality. In the end, the economic value generated from the revitalization of the state-owned combines was less than expected.

While entrepreneurial activity in central and eastern Europe is adding value, there are a few cautionary notes. The entrepreneurial business that has emerged still only represents about a third of the number of small and medium enterprises in China. Furthermore, the 12m businesses in the area are a volatile lot. Central and eastern European entrepreneurs often witness very fast growth (for example 100 per cent to 200 per cent a year) but also experience very high death and restart rates.

Small and medium enterprises, created by a new generation of entrepreneurs, have not rescued the economy in its entirety. For example, unemployment in Poland, which was an artificial 1 per cent under the communist regime, is 17 per cent today. This represents the price of restructuring, which even very active entrepreneurial activity cannot erase.

Development

The nature of entrepreneurial activity in central and eastern Europe has gone through some distinctive phases. The first entrepreneurs were often operating arbitrage imbalances in existing resources and were finding opportunities at the borders, bringing cheaper goods from Russia to relatively richer countries in central Europe.

Furthermore, the transport and movement of commodities such as aluminum and petroleum gave some individuals and companies the ability to make significant amounts of quick cash, especially when coupled with massive fluctuations in currency. It is reported that by buying Russian commodities destined for transshipment in rapidly deflating roubles, Estonian entrepreneurs were able to realize massive gains selling these commodities on world markets in US dollars.

The evolution of entrepreneurial business next moved heavily to the importation of relatively higher-quality durable consumer goods from the West. This was coupled with increasing numbers of joint ventures with Western and Asian businesses to build on local assets, including cheap but knowledgeable labor, and growing consumer and industrial markets.

The evolution has continued with increasing numbers of 'home-grown' local businesses – some growing very rapidly – producing locally developed products and services, sometimes for export to world markets.

Is the state of entrepreneurship the same throughout central and eastern Europe? Have entrepreneurs and entrepreneurial business developed in parallel ways through the former communist republics? The answer is no. The reason is that it depends upon where you started.

We would summarize the primary conditions for the growth of entrepreneurial business in three factors: *infrastructure, resources* and *product-markets*.

The first, the infrastructure, includes legal systems, telecommunications, transportation and so on that all serve to support business. In some countries these were more developed than in others.

The second involves the availability of resources, especially from the financial sector. Throughout central and eastern Europe, the financial system has not responded fast enough to the needs of entrepreneurs and entrepreneurial business. While it was hoped that the system would play a key role in supporting growth business, the financial sector was not able to get off the ground rapidly enough to provide the kind of support required. Entrepreneurs were often left to their own sources of capital. In fact the financial sector did not really understand how to deal with individual entrepreneurs. It was used to asset-base financing and the concept of depreciation hardly existed. Assets were kept on the books at the purchase value.

The third is the existence and nature of product-markets. In some countries, a consumerist tradition existed with the distribution channels and spending capacity to back it. In others, individuals could barely afford staples and were less than excited about products they did not perceive as necessary.

Given the differences among countries in the area on these factors, it is no mystery that entrepreneurial activity is different in both level and type. Other factors that seem to have had an impact on the ability of the various countries to support and develop entrepreneurial business include such conditions as the length of time under communism, the long-standing cultural attitudes toward business and the prior existence of business relationships and networks.

Some countries were under communism only from 1945 while others, such as Russia, initiated it in 1917. The size and affluence of the cultural diaspora (for example the large Polish population in the US and Canada) was also a factor in the rapid development of new entrepreneurial business.

The following are some examples of the difference in development of entrepreneurial business.

Poland has been very successful and well served by the growth and development of new entrepreneurial businesses. Poles from outside the country were willing to further accelerate efforts started under the communist regime to liberalize business.

The Czech republic has been very successful in throwing off the weight of repressive state-owned enterprise in favor of a new small and medium-sized

Foreign enterprise in the Czech Republic: but the Czechs have quickly and successfully built their own world-class companies

© FT Pictures

business sector and significant numbers of growth businesses. Drawing on good education and historic parallels with German enterprise, German capital has found its way strongly into the Czech republic, making it a very successful country that is building some new world-class industrial companies.

Slovenia has also done very well in supporting new enterprise and permitting the development of entrepreneurial business. Entrepreneurship has a long tradition in the area, though it was previously limited by law. Strong traditional links with northern Italy, Austria and Germany that go back many years have also helped.

Group 1: Progressive	Group 2: Developing	Group 3: Embryonic
Czech Republic	Bulgaria	Albania
Hungary	Croatia	Armenia
Poland	Estonia	Belarus
Slovenia	Latvia	Georgia
	Lithuania	Kazakhstan
	Romania	Russia
	Slovakia	Serbia
		Ukraine
		Uzbekistan

Figure 1

These countries, along with Hungary, represent the more entrepreneurially progressive countries in central and eastern Europe. Two other groups of countries are shown in Figure 1.

Those in Group 3 are still struggling with the early stages of the development of entrepreneurial business. Even with these, however, the signs are clearly positive. Group 2 countries are exhibiting signs of improvement in the infrastructure, resource systems and product-markets required to support higher levels of entrepreneurial activity.

What all of this experience has shown is that there are multiple assets and liabilities in the economic landscape of central and eastern Europe after the *Wende*. There are significant natural resources, large numbers of well-trained technical people (including engineers and scientists – there are 12m engineers in Russia alone, for example) and in many cases, a significant desire for change. On the liability side, cultural attitudes and expectations, a poor infrastructure and a poorly organized and oriented financial system have all served to slow down the successful development of growth-oriented entrepreneurial business.

Entrepreneurs in central and eastern Europe have found many opportunities and many paths to entrepreneurship. Some have joint ventured with Western companies. Others have split off from large state-owned enterprises. Others have found opportunity in services that have not existed before in local markets. But there are two characteristics of the development of entrepreneurial activity on the part of local entrepreneurs that are different. **Nature of entrepreneurial activity**

First, entrepreneurs often develop a set of 'horizontal' activities. For example, one entrepreneur we know made money in currency dealing. With this money, he was able to set up a series of loan companies that evolved into giving loans primarily for real estate development. From this set of activities, he later evolved into the real estate investment and trading business. Having not found a good set of building contractors, he then moved into the real estate construction business.

Many entrepreneurs have moved horizontally across fields in this manner. For many this was unfortunate as they reached beyond fields where they had been competent as well as lucky into areas where serious personal weaknesses in their management skills led to disaster. For a few who possessed the right skills and orientation, this was a way towards developing serious wealth. Interestingly, this type of horizontal entrepreneurship is a phenomenon that exists today in Korea, Japan and the financial holding companies of Italy and Belgium. However, the modern world is increasingly demanding global specialization.

The second characteristic is related to the first. Entrepreneurs were usually managing a portfolio of activities at any one time. Along with the management responsibilities they accumulated from the horizontal expansion of activities, entrepreneurs also acquired what they instinctively saw as a portfolio of businesses with a varying risk profile. The wiser ones were willing to close down activities they found no longer profitable as local markets and opportunity evolved.

Given the varying nature of the environment in which they develop, entrepreneurs in this region face many different challenges. However, there are some common patterns we can discern from recent discussions with some successful growth entrepreneurs from around central and eastern Europe. **Recommendations to local entrepreneurs**

At a recent informal conference, entrepreneurs from the region cited several consistent operating weaknesses. The most profound involved the inherent lack of marketing and sales management skills. This weakness only served to emphasize the impact of 40 years of a communist system that found no value in such activities.

A second area of weakness was employees and management. They found their managers were often not willing to take real responsibility for business activities. They wanted the rewards from new activities but were unwilling to show significant initiative in pursuing these activities. This is particularly true of Russian-dominated countries where decision-making is hierarchical. They also found their employees less than totally reliable, having retained many bad habits from the old regime such as late arrival and early weekend departure.

While these attitudes are changing rapidly in some countries, entrepreneurs still found that they needed to manage the turnover of their employees because some were simply not able or willing to grow with them.

A third weakness they cited involved their business partners, suppliers and distributors. Due to a desire to make short-term gains in new deals and currency speculation, entrepreneurs have often found business partners to be less than totally trusting and trustworthy.

They also stated that two areas where they needed to develop skills, based on their own experiences, were in the nature and role of working capital and business finance in general. Financial planning – the setting and management of regular budgets – was an area of general weakness.

The weaknesses in resource allocation and gathering became even more important in the face of the lack of trust found in the banking sector. The scramble for money and the appropriate allocation of resources was a pressing problem that was further exacerbated by a need to find resources from among family and friends.

One successful entrepreneur at the conference, who was a former, privileged factory head in a state combine under the old regime, said that while there was success there was also significantly increased stress. He reported that his family did not understand why he could not, as company president, leave for the *dacha* on Friday morning and not engage in work all weekend. He noted that not only was business practice from the West becoming a reality but so were all of the side-effects.

Beyond dealing with these problems, we have a few suggestions for local entrepreneurs.

First, focus your business activities. Expanding into new, if related, enterprises may seem a reasonable idea and may be your best way to create new businesses. On the other hand, building a strong set of competencies and a business network is probably the surest way to succeed.

Second, be prepared to build barriers to further competitors coming into the business, especially in the face of extensive 'copy cat' competition. As one Hungarian entrepreneur noted, 'success attracts success; when someone finds a successful niche, they instantly have competition'.

Third, evolve with the customer – business is getting more sophisticated and so are the markets, distributors and customers. Underestimating the consuming public in the East on the basis of prevailing standards will limit long-term success.

In line with this, we would make a fourth recommendation: do not measure yourself solely against local competition but use the broad standard. New competitors lurk outside the borders of the countries of central and eastern Europe. One very successful software company from the area went so far as to set up an office in the most competitive environment for its business – Silicon Valley – as early as possible.

Recommendations to western entrepreneurs

Many entrepreneurs we have met, as well as larger western enterprises, have either moved into central and eastern Europe or are thinking of doing so. We have a few recommendations, based on the experience of others and the development of the market, to make to those who would like to enter the 'Wild East'. Our recommendations start with the need to heed the lessons we have just reviewed.

The first would be to not underestimate consumers. Some entrepreneurs have led the way into this region with substandard-quality products and services. They might find a temporary market but they soon find that, via imports, joint ventures or locally developed products, they have been displaced. Never underestimate your customer.

The second point is to move with understanding into your markets. Take a local partner. No matter how educated or perceptive you are, a local partner is always going to have a better perspective. Further, pay special attention to how other entrepreneurs, who may have parallel or similar ideas, have moved into the market. Learn from their successes and failures. Since there are few hard and fast rules in this situation, recent experience is a good teacher.

Third, we would suggest that you plan to over-invest in training. While management experience and employee attitudes and training are continually improving, significant levels of training are still in order. Training can be realized through the normal formal means but also through rotation into operations in the West. Some western enterprises suggest that without regular visits to western operations, people 'slip back' into bad habits.

Training itself must impact business skills, employee orientation and, in some cases, technical skills. The reality of training, however, is that in some countries, there is a high level of turnover. Trained employees find welcome homes in other developing enterprises.

Fourth, set realistic time frames for returns. This is not such a problem for western managers but it does appear to be a problem in some entrepreneurial initiatives due to prevalent growth rates in the East as well as the unrealistic expectations of local management. Some western entrepreneurs have found that their local management teams have fallen apart when ventures did not become ultimately successful in a year or two. Make sure everyone knows and shares how long it will take to 'make it'.

In the end, two practical messages from many western entrepreneurs and companies establishing entrepreneurial enterprises in this region are 'do not attempt everything yourself' and 'get western-styled auditors and accountants to ensure proper budgeting and control'.

You cannot afford to over-extend yourself by engaging in too many activities. Move one step at a time with the assurance that the results you are seeking are correct, reasonably planned and realized. ■

7

☞ **Managing growth**

Contents

Contributors

 **Neil C. Churchill** is Professor Emeritus of Entrepreneurship at INSEAD and formerly Paul T. Babson Professor of Entrepreneurship and director of the Center for Entrepreneurial Studies at Babson College, Massachusetts.

 **Jonathan Levie** is a research fellow at London Business School. His research interests focus on strategy and resource acquisition in young, growing companies.

 **Michael Hay** is Associate Professor of Strategic and International Management at London Business School and Director of the Foundation for Entrepreneurial Management.

 **Sandra Vandermerwe** is Professor of Marketing and International Services and Chair of Management at Imperial College Management School.

 **John W. Mullins** is Assistant Professor of Marketing at the University of Denver. His research interests include marketing strategy, risk and the factors that facilitate the growth of new products and new companies.

 **Bernard Taylor** is Professor of Business Policy at Henley Management College.

 **Fernando Bartolomé** is Professor of Management at the Instituto de Empresa in Madrid and Visiting Professor of Organizational Behavior at INSEAD. His research interests include individual and interpersonal behavior.

 **Hans A. Breuninger** is a Senior Consultant at Management Partner in Stuttgart.

Introduction

Part 7 explores the issue of growth. We begin by asking the important question 'Why grow?' It is important because the vast majority of new ventures clearly do not grow to any great extent – and part of this must be by choice. We then examine the various stages that an enterprise may go through as the company develops. In particular, we look at two key elements for success – appropriate marketing strategies for a growing venture, and the balance that the entrepreneur must strike between 'home and work'. We conclude by looking at the factors that define successful entrepreneurship.

Section 1
Early growth

To grow or not to grow

Sue Birley considers issues involved in the decision whether or not to grow a business.

Throughout this series, there is an implicit assumption that anyone who starts a business will also want to grow it. Yet we know that there are countless people who deliberately start what we choose to call life-styles ventures – those where self-employment or low employment is the primary aim. Despite this, we constantly hear politicians across the world using the immortal phrase 'if every small business would employ just one more person, our unemployment problems would be solved'. Suffice it to say, this is a little naive. Certainly, these same politicians do not appear to hear the silent response of 'Why should I?' This is a powerful question and one that is important to pose – and to understand – especially as we consider Parts 7 and 8 of *Mastering Enterprise*, which are dedicated to growing the entrepreneurial venture.

I will attempt to explain by referring to two analyses that I have conducted on behalf of the international accountancy firm Grant Thornton. The first study, 'People In Business' (1995 Grant Thornton, Melton Street, London), asked one simple question: 'What are your nightmares?' In the UK the five issues that most kept people awake at night were:

- If I introduce outside shareholders, how greedy will they be?
- All my wealth is in the business; what happens if it gets into trouble?
- Would outside shareholders change the way I run the business?
- How much is the business worth?
- Could the business do better for me?

Moreover, more than half were asking themselves: 'Do I really need to grow the business?' and 'How much would life change if I did grow the business?'

What is behind this? It is quite simple. A large number are, in effect, saying: 'The business is the source of my income, my wealth and my pension and I am worried that if I lose control it may unravel, leaving me with nothing . . . and, in any case, I started the business to be independent and in control of my own future, not to hand it over to others'.

How do we answer this? In two ways:

- We know that the majority of companies that fail are small and young. In other words, the larger, and thus more credible, the business the greater the chances of survival. This makes intuitive sense.

• Some 40 per cent of those who responded to the study were, in fact, relatively relaxed about these issues – and they were the ones who had taken the plunge, diluted and grown their business.

Clearly, therefore, whatever their final decision, growth is an issue that exercises all owner-managers. So, we decided to explore this further in the annual *European Business Survey* (Grant Thornton International and Business Strategies Ltd, ISBN 1 874378 09 6) of entrepreneurs in 17 countries across Europe by asking respondents: 'What personal goals matter to you when making business decisions?' The results are consistent with our first study. The relationship between growth and control are key.

However, this is still a simple view. We know that the sector is heterogeneous, that all owner-managers do not have the same set of goals and that goals may change as both they and the business age. Therefore, we looked for patterns and found four consistent themes. We called them:

• *The protectionists* who wanted to maintain their business at its current size thus protecting their investment.

• *The business oriented* who combined growth and control goals with a need both to protect their income and their investment.

• *The dynasts* who wanted to grow their business, protect their investment and pass it to the next generation.

• *The family businesses* who wanted to keep the business at the current size and pass it on to the next generation. ■

The six key phases of company growth

Neil Churchill describes the six phases of growth – and sometimes extinction – common to almost every company.

Entrepreneurship is widely recognized as an activity that creates value. This, in turn, is usually seen as starting a new venture – recognizing an opportunity, fashioning it to suit the entrepreneur, acquiring the resources to pursue it and then capturing the opportunity by creating a company.

However without discounting the importance of starting a business – for nothing occurs without the start – the value is really created as the enterprise grows, creates jobs, satisfies the needs of more and more customers and, in the process, makes money for the stockholders. All of which creates value for society. A growing company continues to create value if it spawns more and more new products or services, creates more jobs, pays more taxes and so on – that is, renews itself after each product cycle.

This article describes the different periods, phases or stages of growth most successful companies experience and the nature of the changes that occur. A

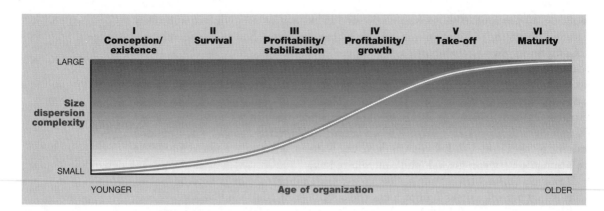

| I
Conception/
existence | II
Survival | III
Profitability/
stabilization | IV
Profitability/
growth | V
Take-off | VI
Maturity |

**Figure 1: Growth
stages**

second article, on p. 236, examines the problems most often encountered in these
stages and some solutions that have been successfully used. Finally, a third
article, divided into two parts on pp. 232 and 259, deals with one of these major
problems – cash – and why it is so important and how to manage it on a company
and product-market basis.

Each stage of growth has its own challenges and these challenges can be
approached in a number of ways.

One such framework was developed in the early 1980s and has been used ever
since by entrepreneurs and consultants. It was re-examined in 1994, updated
(five stages, one with two sub-stages, became six stages) and deemed by several
hundred owner/managers to be applicable in helping them assess what skills and
resources were needed both for the present and the future. Owners who can
assess the stage at which their companies are operating can use the framework
to understand better existing problems and anticipate further challenges.

The framework covers six stages of development (*see* Figure 1). Each stage is
characterized by an index of increasing size, complexity and/or dispersion and
described by five management factors: managerial style; organizational
structure; extent of formal systems; major strategic goals; and the owner's
involvement in the business.

**Stage I:
Conception/
existence**

In this stage the company has not really come into existence. This is because (a)
it is still somewhat conceptual, or (b) it has not solved the problem of obtaining
customers, or (c) it cannot deliver the product or service contracted for in the
necessary quantity or with the necessary quality. Some key questions are:

● Can we get enough customers, deliver our products and provide services well
enough to become a viable business?

● Can we expand from that one key customer to a much broader sales base?

● Can we develop the product from a pilot production process to a production
basis?

● Do we have enough money to cover the considerable cash demands of this
start-up phase?

The organization is a simple one; the owner does everything and directly
supervises subordinates, who in the main are of average competence. Systems
and formal planning are minimal to non-existent. The company's strategy is
simply to remain alive. The owner is the business, performs all the important

tasks and is the major supplier of energy, direction and, with relatives and friends, capital.

Companies in the conception/existence stage range from newly started restaurants and retail stores to high-technology manufacturers that have yet to stabilize either production or product quality.

Many such companies or products never gain sufficient customer acceptance to become viable. In these cases the owners close the business when the start-up capital runs out and, if they are lucky, sell the business for some of its asset value. In other cases the owners cannot accept the demands the business places on their time, finance and energy and they quit. The companies that remain in business become Stage II enterprises.

In reaching this stage the business has demonstrated that it is a workable **Stage II:**
business entity. It has enough customers and satisfies them sufficiently with its **Survival**
products or services to keep them. The key problem thus shifts from mere existence to the relationship between revenues and expenses. The main issues are as follows:
● *In the short run, can we generate enough cash to break even and to cover the repair or replacement of our capital assets as they wear out?*
● *Can we, at a minimum, generate enough cash flow to stay in business and to finance growth to a size that is sufficiently large, given our industry and market niche, to earn an economic return on our assets and labor?*

The organization is still simple. The company may have a limited number of employees supervised by a sales manager or a general foreman. Neither of them makes major decisions independently but instead carries out the rather well-defined orders of the owner.

Systems development is minimal. Formal planning is usually limited to cash forecasts and project plans. The major goal is still survival and the owner is still synonymous with the business.

In the survival stage the enterprise may grow in size and profitability and move on to Stage III. Or it may, as many companies do, remain at the survival stage for a long time.

These companies are often 'hobby'-type businesses where the owner enjoys, for example, skiing and so runs a ski shop and the non-economic aspects of the enterprise are positive. Also, these can be family businesses, such as small restaurants employing a number of extended family members.

In many cases these businesses become profitable and move to the next stage. In others the founders have chosen non-viable enterprises in an overcrowded industry (often the case), badly located or faulty in conception and they cannot, or refuse to, do what is needed to make them profitable. They operate these businesses until they die or retire and while some are sold or passed on to children who wish to change them, most just cease operating and drop out of sight.

In this stage the company has attained true economic health, has sufficient size **Stage III:**
and product-market penetration to ensure economic success and earns average or **Profitability and**
above-average profits. The company can stay at this stage indefinitely provided **stabilization**
environmental change does not destroy its market niche or ineffective management reduce its competitive abilities.

Organizationally, the company has, in many cases, grown large enough to require functional managers to take over certain duties performed by the owner. The managers should be competent but need not be of the highest calibre since their upward potential is limited by corporate goals.

Cash is plentiful and the main concern is to avoid a cash drain in prosperous periods to the detriment of the company's ability to withstand the inevitable rough times.

In addition, the first professional staff members come on board, usually a controller in the office and perhaps a production scheduler in the plant. Basic financial, marketing and production systems are in place. Planning in the form of operational budgets supports functional delegation.

The owner and, to a lesser extent, the company's managers should be monitoring a strategy essentially to maintain the status quo. As the business matures, it and the owner increasingly move apart, to some extent because of the presence of other managers.

Many companies continue for long periods in the stability stage. The product-market niche of some does not permit growth – this is the case for many service businesses in small or medium-sized slowly growing communities and for franchise holders with limited territories.

Other owners actually choose this route. If the company can continue to adapt to environmental changes, it can continue as is, be sold or merged at a profit or subsequently be stimulated into growth. For franchise holders this last option would necessitate the purchase of other franchises.

If the company cannot adapt to changing circumstances, as was the case with many automobile dealers in the late 1970s and early 1980s, it will either fold or drop back to a marginally surviving company.

Stage IV: Profitability and growth

In this stage the owner-manager consolidates the company and marshals resources for growth. He takes the cash and the established borrowing power of the company and puts it to risk to finance growth.

The important tasks include making sure that the business stays profitable so that it will not out-run its basic source of cash, to hire – a bit in advance – and develop managers of a higher quality than those needed to run a stable company. They will have to address the tasks of attaining a higher level of activity and managing it successfully once there.

Better systems are needed and attention should be given to forthcoming needs. Operational planning is delegated and strategic planning is shared with the key managers. The owner continues as the owner-manager and is active in all phases of the company's affairs.

If it is successful, the growth company may make a commitment to a higher growth rate and transition to Stage V – the take-off stage. Indeed, Stage IV is often a first attempt at growing, say regionally, before making a total commitment to growth. If a Stage IV company is unsuccessful, the cause may be detected in time for the company to shift to Stage III. If not, Stage II may be possible prior to bankruptcy or a distress sale.

Stage V: Take off

In this stage the key problem is determining means to achieve rapid growth and how to finance it when it occurs. The most important problems that then follow are delegation, cash management and cost control.

Delegation

Can the owner delegate responsibility to others to improve the managerial effectiveness of a fast-growing and increasingly complex enterprise? Further, will there be true delegation, with controls on performance and a willingness to see mistakes made, or will it be abdication, as is so often the case?

Cash

Will there be enough cash from operations and savings to satisfy the great demands growth brings? If not, where and how can additional financing be obtained? Will the owner tolerate a high debt-equity ratio or a dilution of owner's equity?

Cost control

Rapid growth can bring such demands on managers and at such a frantic pace that things begin to 'slip though the cracks' as time is spent hiring and training new people, and dealing with new and larger problems. Further, as growth can cover normal signals, there may be inadequate warnings to alert the overworked management to what is going wrong.

The organization is decentralized and, at least in part, divisionalized – usually either in sales or production. The key managers must be sufficiently competent to handle a growing and complex business environment. Systems, strained by growth, are becoming more refined and extensive. A considerable amount of planning is being done that deeply involves all key managers. While the managerial staff has grown considerably, the company is still dominated by both the owner-manager's presence and ownership control.

This is a pivotal period in a company's life. If the owner rises to the challenge of a growing company, both financially and managerially, it can become a big business. If not, it can usually be sold – at a profit – provided the owner recognizes his or her limitations soon enough.

Too often, those who bring the business through the previous stages are unsuccessful in Stage V, either because they try to grow too fast and run out of cash (the owner falls victim to the omnipotence syndrome) or are unable to delegate effectively (the omniscience syndrome).

It is of course possible for the company to traverse this high-growth stage without the original management. It is not uncommon for the entrepreneur who founded the company and brought it to success to be replaced either voluntarily or involuntarily by the company's investors or creditors.

If the company fails to make the big time, it may be able to retrench and continue as a successful and substantial company in a state of equilibrium. It may drop back to Stage IV or, if the problems are too extensive, it may drop all the way back to the survival stage or even fail.

The greatest concerns of a company entering this stage are, first, to consolidate **Stage VI:**
and control the financial gains brought on by rapid growth and, second, to retain **Mature**
the advantages of small size including flexibility of response and the entrepreneurial spirit.

The corporation must expand the management force fast enough to eliminate the inefficiencies that growth can produce and professionalize the company by use of such tools as budgets, management by objectives and standard cost systems – and do this without stifling its entrepreneurial qualities.

A company in Stage VI has the staff and financial resources to engage in detailed operational and strategic planning. The management is decentralized, adequately staffed and experienced. And systems are extensive and well developed. The owner and the business are quite separate, both financially and operationally.

The company has now arrived. It has the advantages of size, financial resources and managerial talent. If it can preserve its entrepreneurial spirit, it will be a formidable force in the market. If not, it may enter a seventh stage of sorts: ossification.

Ossification is characterized by a lack of innovative decision-making and the avoidance of risks. It seems most common in large corporations whose sizeable market share, buying power and financial resources keep them viable until there is a major change in the environment.

Unfortunately for these businesses, it is usually their rapidly growing competitors that notice the environmental change first.

Conclusion

The findings of the various studies involved in the development of the six-stage model strongly suggest that the levels of chief executive leadership/management skills, management team functioning and organizational culture are related to the financial performance of organizations.

Specific skills such as vision, communications, leadership, delegating and performance facilitation are positively related to company performance. Chief executives and management teams who rate low in these skills have lower company financial performance than those who rated higher in the same areas.

Further, maintaining these skills as the organization grows can be challenging. In many companies, the higher the rate of sales growth the lower is the level of the organizational culture factors mentioned above that relate to profitability. To maintain or improve profit margins, management must focus on those elements that apparently become more difficult to execute often or well as the company grows.

The changing nature of managerial challenge becomes apparent when one examines Figure 2. In the early stages the owner's ability to delegate is on the bottom of the scale since there are few if any employees to delegate to, but it becomes critical later as the company grows.

In contrast, the owner's ability to do the job in these early stages gives life to the business. Small businesses are built on the owner's talents: the ability to sell, produce, invent or whatever. This factor is thus of the highest importance.

As the company grows, other people enter sales, production or engineering and they first support and then even supplant the owner's skills – thus reducing the importance of this factor.

At the same time the owner must spend less time doing and more time managing. He or she must increase the amount of work done through other people, which means delegating. The inability of many founders to let go of doing and to begin managing and delegating explains the demise of many businesses in Stage IV.

The owner contemplating a growth strategy must understand the change in personal activities such a decision entails and examine the managerial needs depicted in Figure 2. Similarly, an entrepreneur contemplating starting a

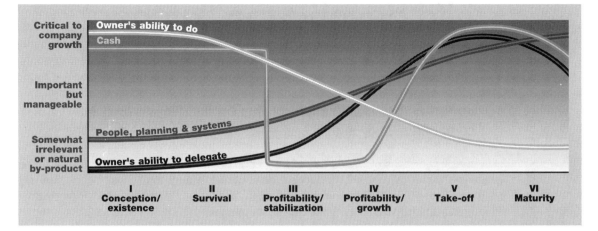

Figure 2:
Management
factors and stages

business should recognize the need to do all the selling, manufacturing or engineering from the beginning, along with managing cash and planning the business's course – requirements that take much energy and commitment.

The importance of cash changes as the business changes. It is an extremely important resource at the start, becomes easily manageable at the success stage and is a main concern again if the organization begins to grow. As growth slows at the end of Stage V or in Stage VI, cash becomes a manageable factor again. Companies in Stage IV need to recognize the financial needs and risks entailed in a move to Stage V.

The issues of people, planning and systems gradually increase in importance as the company progresses from slow initial growth to rapid growth. These resources must be acquired somewhat in advance of the growth stage so that they are in place when needed.

A company's development stage determines the managerial factors that must be dealt with. Its plans help determine which factors will eventually have to be faced. Knowing its development stage and future plans enables managers, consultants and investors to make more informed choices and to prepare themselves and their companies for later challenges.

While each enterprise is unique in many ways, all face similar problems and all are subject to great changes. That may well be why being an owner is so much fun and such a challenge. ∎

Life beyond the 'kitchen' culture

Jonathan Levie and **Michael Hay** explain why so few young companies enjoy significant growth and offer some solutions.

Every year tens of thousands of new enterprises are founded. Very few of these grow significantly; yet those that do contribute disproportionately to exports, employment and growth of the economy. Why do so few young companies grow in a meaningful way, and what can be done about it? This article addresses these questions.

The dilemmas of growth

Entrepreneurs are regularly faced with dilemmas of growth. For example, consider the case of a young business with one successful though increasingly uncompetitive product. New product development costs money and since young companies usually have little in the way of retained earnings, outside equity is often the only option. The requirement to generate a return for the new shareholders almost certainly means that the company must grow in size and scope. Should the entrepreneur accept a dilution of ownership in return for the funds?

Let's assume our company successfully develops its second major product. Some time later, it gets a large order from a multinational. The order represents 50 per cent of its present annual capacity, which is already 80 per cent filled. Should the entrepreneur accept the order?

This may not be an easy decision. Further outside finance may be needed to fund the necessary expansion in fixed and current assets (in this case, debt may be an option). In addition, the increase in size of the organization may require the entrepreneur to change the way the business is run, effectively reducing his or her direct control of day-to-day operations.

The issues that created dilemmas of growth for our hypothetical entrepreneur were intense competition and static markets, increased organizational complexity and greater reliance on external resource providers. According to survey research conducted at London Business School[1], most owner/managers resolve these issues by treating them as barriers to growth rather than as agents for change.

We compared the results of three UK-wide surveys of small and medium-sized private companies conducted in 1992, 1994 and 1995 and found that perceptions of barriers to growth changed little with the economic cycle.

The most commonly cited major *external* barrier to growth was a market characterized by intense competition and lack of growth. Relatively few respondents included lack of access to finance, labor or equipment as major barriers. Two main *internal* barriers to growth recurred in all three surveys: management capability to handle growth and owner/managers' reluctance to cede perceived control in return for growth finance (either equity or debt).

A common strategy for living with these perceived barriers is to identify and hold some small protected market niche and practise financial and managerial self-sufficiency. However, low barriers to entry to the industry (in printing, for example) or market or technological instability (in software, for example) reduces the feasibility of such a strategy.

If management is unable or unwilling to grow out of its present strategic position of weakness, then competition will intensify over time as more capable (or simply more resource-rich) competitors enter its domain.

Respondents in the survey may not have fully appreciated this link between internal and external barriers. Those who recognized internal barriers as very important tended to come from low-growth businesses. Yet when asked to weight the relative importance of internal versus external barriers to growth, respondents tended to give greater weight to the external barriers.

In our view, the first barrier to be overcome is the control barrier. This is the perception that to gain the resources needed for the organization to grow and thereby survive, the entrepreneur must surrender control of the company – to new shareholders, to bankers and to others in the organization.

The control barrier

Many owner/managers refuse to grow their companies because they associate growth with loss of control. We argue that this association is based on an inappropriate model of management and that, if this is recognized, focus can then shift to the more real barrier of management capability for growth.

Our main point is that by thinking in terms of control – rather than use – of assets, the entrepreneur is using old models of capitalism that equate ownership with control and old models of administrative thinking that see control as the only form of management. Research in the US has shown that high-growth companies make greater use of external resources than low-growth companies. In other words, the agenda of management in high-growth businesses is not control or ownership but use of assets. This conceptual difference is not just about renting rather than owning. It is fundamentally about how to manage assets.

Recent research in the US reveals that chief executives of higher-growth companies put greater emphasis on developing an organizational culture that motivates employees and on creating and communicating a vision for the organization's future. This motivation and communication is transmitted both within the business and to the owners of external resources. Successful motivation and communication by chief executives (as measured by their staff) was associated with higher sales and higher returns on investment.

The research found, however, that during rapid growth, these important behaviors often came under intense pressure and profitability declined. A major reason may well be that chief executives were just too busy fire fighting at operational level or immersed in the new challenges that growth brings (such as communicating with new stakeholders) to fulfil the crucial role of motivator and communicator to the organization and its other resource providers.

Let us describe what growth is like for unprepared organizations. A frequent complaint of both entrepreneurs and of their staff is that the culture of the company becomes colder as the organization grows.

Inside the organization

As one Danish entrepreneur put it, the culture of the very young company is like that of the family kitchen – warm, intimate, where problems are shared and solutions sought informally, and where there is a clear sense of togetherness.

Then, as more and more strangers enter and the kitchen expands to accommodate them, it becomes more of an impersonal institution. The entrepreneur complains that he or she doesn't know everyone's name anymore. Staff who were there from the early days complain that relations with the entrepreneur are not what they were.

This estrangement results in misunderstandings, resentment and jealousy of the '9-to-5' newcomers and of the staff appointees who have privileged access to the entrepreneur. Employee comments on the entrepreneur such as 'he's changed', 'she is more remote', 'he only cares about making more money now' are typical.

As relationships become more distant, performance measurement becomes more formal. Long-serving employees get passed over for promotion and personnel problems fester. The threat of unionization looms. The entrepreneur cannot understand the change in atmosphere in the organization and looks back wistfully on the kitchen culture of yesterday.

These problems stem from a failure to communicate the changes that are taking place in the organization – and in the role of the entrepreneur. Frequently, rapid growth means that the entrepreneur will be devoting more time to managing external resources, such as major foreign customers, merchant banks, corporate shareholders, the media and the stock market. This tends to take up much more of entrepreneurs' time – away from the company – than they expected. All their staff see of this is that they are not available the way they used to be.

To make matters worse, the entrepreneur's former colleagues are now supposed to report to new functional managers, often recruited from larger organizations. These new managers tend to change the information flows inside the organization from a web to multiple vertical funnels because this is how they were trained. Large-company systems and structures, however, may actually impede growth in a smaller organization, whose strength comes from the rapid and focused combination of cross-functional skills.

Faced with this scenario of the future, it is no wonder that so many owner/managers of young businesses are reluctant to grow. Is there an alternative to this unhappy path of corporate evolution? The answer is yes.

Turning barriers to growth into agents for change

First, the entrepreneur has to be conscious of his or her critical role as principal communicator of the changes that are and will be taking place, both in the company and in the role of the entrepreneur within it. Organizations undergoing change need a strong figurehead. Research shows that the chief executive's efforts on this dimension are critical.

Second, one structural solution, used successfully by many successful entrepreneurial organizations, is to replicate, rather than replace, the old kitchen culture. This can be done by superimposing on the emerging functional structure, a mosaic of project-focused, inter-functional teams. Canny entrepreneurs bring advisers, customers and suppliers in as team members where appropriate. These teams are formed in response to specific needs and disbanded when the project is complete.

Leader of teams

The entrepreneur's role in team management, as with the original team he or she brought together in the kitchen, garage or rented premises, is to recruit, motivate, envision, resource and reward the teams.

Conceptually, the multiple teams can be managed in the same way as the first team. (For example, reward systems still need to be based on collective results. In many start-ups, the entrepreneur will share some equity with the initial team. Significantly, our 1995 survey results suggested that businesses with employee share ownership schemes tended to have faster growth over the previous five-year period than companies with other incentives such as performance or profit-related pay.) There is one important difference, however, between then and now. This time, the entrepreneur will not be able to lead the team because there is not one team but many.

The transition from team leader to leader of teams can be extremely difficult for an entrepreneur, who became successful by doing, not by getting things done through others. Some entrepreneurs eventually realize that they are just not enjoying the new role and sell out or bring in outside management.

Research suggests, however, that bringing in new management is not necessarily the solution. The solution is to match the form of management to the phase of evolution of the organization. A young company undergoing rapid growth still needs entrepreneurial management. The role of the entrepreneur in a rapidly growing young business, however, is subtly different from that of the entrepreneur at start-up, as we have attempted to show.

External resource providers

The fear of loss of control to people inside the organization is an innate fear of entrepreneurs. Much more explicit is the fear of loss of control to outsiders, particularly financial resource providers such as bankers, venture capitalists and private equity investors (business angels).

This fear is valid but only if the relationship with these resource providers is poorly developed. Failure to build and maintain close relationships of trust and mutual benefit with these resource providers can result in loaded legal agreements, persistent demands for time-consuming but trivial data and unexpected withdrawal of resources just when they are most needed.

As with relationships inside the company, this is a communication issue. We have seen examples where a history of good communications maintained share prices during profit downturns, kept a bank manager calm as the company teetered on the brink of insolvency and maintained the loyalty of customers during a product quality crisis.

Of course, some resource providers may not respond to the need of the young organization for long-term relationships of trust and mutual benefit. The path of growth is not smooth, and the entrepreneur will, at some stage, need to rely on those external resource providers to keep their nerve. If a relationship does not look like it will withstand difficult times, it is best to seek out a new partner. After all, resource providers should be agents for change not barriers to growth. ■

[1]Hay, M. and Khamshad, K., (1994). 'Small firm growth: intentions, implementation and impediments'. *Business Strategy Review* 5(3):49–68.

The Quest For Growth: A Survey of UK Private Companies, (1994) London Business School/Binder Hamlyn.

The 1996 Pulse Survey: Survival of the Fittest (1996) London Business School/Arthur Andersen/Binder Hamlyn, 1996. (Free copies of a summary of this report are available from Arthur Andersen – please call Lorraine Hilder on ++44 171 489 6075.)

⊷ CASE STUDY

Abilene Caterpillar

This case was written by Neil C. Churchill, Professor of Entrepreneurship at INSEAD. It is intended to be used as a basis for discussion rather than to illustrate either effective or ineffective handling of an administrative situation.

Stan Treanor took over the family's Caterpillar dealership in 1976 when sales were $23m and equity was $3m. During the following six years, business was very good with sales increasing to $119m and equity to $20m – due strictly to earnings. Then in 1982, the market for oil collapsed and, since the company's main source of revenue was engines for drilling rigs, sales plummeted to $23m. As Stan put it, 'That didn't take any six years so I had to learn very quickly to manage on the downside'.

In the fall of 1981, Boone Pickens, the oil speculator, gave a talk at Abilene Christian University and mentioned that he could buy oil companies for their reserves cheaper than he could drill for them. At present day prices, Pickens said that if he drilled, he could only get back eighty cents on the dollar. This impressed Stan for, if everyone believed that, they wouldn't be doing any more drilling. As Stan recalled: 'This waved a red flag. And I started making some changes in the credit department. But since I didn't know what was going to happen – neither how far down things would go and how fast they would fall – I thought I should begin to trim the sails so I wouldn't capsize when the storm came. I didn't want to stop ordering inventory because if I was wrong, I would lose sales and incur opportunity costs. I just wanted to trim the sails and survive whatever storm would arise.'

Stan began with receivables and almost immediately told his accounts receivable manager to tighten up on credit and collect all the account balances that were either getting large or were slow in collection. This was difficult for her because, as Stan stated:
'She was really nice and could handle customers wonderfully in an upside market because the customers loved her, but on the downside market she just couldn't get tough enough. I worked with her but she just couldn't do it. It got to where I would tell her that, 'If you don't get such and such a day's receivables down by such and such a date you're terminated'. But she just couldn't do it. I had to replace her and I did so with a guy who loved playing in that environment. He was probably the greatest credit manager I could have had and he did a great job. He rescued the company, but he became the victim since I later had to terminate him. I don't know what else I could have done; he had made so many customers mad at him and the Sales Department hated him although they understood why it was necessary that he did what he did after we'd got everything collected. But when we began to build relationships, we just couldn't do with him. It wouldn't work so I had to get someone else. You go through a constructive destruction process; after we finished that we had to rebuild. It's sad but I don't know of any other way we could have done it.'

Since Abilene had a practice of 'carrying the paper' itself on customer sales rather than financing customers' purchases with the banks, the second thing Stan did was to sell them off to a finance company.

He sold all $15m of these notes to CIT on a 'non-recourse' basis at a price calculated on a 16 per cent interest rate. As Abilene had charged some 21 per cent or 22 per cent interest when the notes were issued, as it had been a period of very high interest rates, Abilene made a profit on the transaction. As Stan put it, 'What I want to do is get rid of all those notes because if I had to start repossessing those tractors, then I'd have a bunch of used inventory in a downmarket and I didn't want that exposure. Making a profit was just a delightful bonus.'

At the time of Picken's speech, Abilene had 500 drilling engines in inventory and in noncancellable orders that totalled about $30m. Stan felt that these were too many and started to sell the engines and the rights to the orders to fellow dealers. They all thought he was crazy, as did Caterpillar, but he sold most of them for what they cost him and the rest at a variety of discounts. All during this period, Stan was still ordering items that were needed since the company kept selling and servicing equipment right throughout the decline.

Stan's philosophy was, 'If an item isn't creating enough value, liquidate it and do it quickly because the loss is already there whether you want to recognize it on the books or not'. He closed down facilities, laid off people, and sold telephones, disks, fork-lift trucks, everything that he felt couldn't create value. He did it quickly and before others realized what was happening stating, 'I think it really saved us, because the people that waited really got little if anything for their assets'.

Since Stan had no idea as to either how fast or how far the business would contract, he was concerned as to how he would deal with the employees. He considered putting everyone on half-hours or on four-day weeks; whether he should cut wages or whether he should lay off 25 per cent or so at the start and more if things kept going down. He also realized that when he got down to the bottom, it would be very competitive and the companies that survived would be those who were the most efficient with the most productive people.

Stan had productivity rates that Caterpillar sent out to every one of its dealers. These contained information on the performance of each department for each Caterpillar dealer in the United States. This information included overall average productivity rates as well as the productivity rates of the best 25 per cent of the dealers and the worst 25 per cent of the dealers for each department. As an example, the average number of dollars each person would sell in the Parts Department was $400,000 per person per year, in the Sales Department, $1.5 m per person per year, and so on. What fascinated Stan, and got him thinking, was the difference between the performance of the top and bottom 25 per cent of the dealers in almost every department. Stan saw it this way: 'What I saw was that the difference between the departmental performance of the best 25 per cent of the dealers and the bottom 25 per cent was three to one. For example, in the Parts Department, if average was $400,000, for everyone, the 24 dealers in the top 25 per cent category would average about $600,000 per person per year and the lower end $200,000. This three to one average difference from top to bottom, or 50 per cent from the average to either extreme, was present in almost every department. It was almost unbelievable.'

Stan decided that he would use the productivity rates to downsize his company. For each one of his departments, he set them slightly below those of the top 25 per cent dealers. In Parts, for example, instead of $600,000 he used $550,000. He then projected a three-month moving average of sales, annualized it, and divided it by the productivity figures. This produced the number of people that he should have in that department. He made the same calculation for each department, gave the managers the calculations and instructed them to lay-off the least productive people as they contracted towards the targets.

The result in the Service Department was a 30 per cent profit after allocated expenses but before interest and taxes where the average Caterpillar dealer's was typically 15 per cent and in the Parts Department, Abilene was at 12 per cent and the average of the other dealers was 9 per cent. As Stan put it, 'We actually ended making more profit, after the contraction, in the Parts and Service Departments than we did before, when things were good. It was just phenomenal'. But he continued: 'Terminating all those people, was very difficult. But if you are going to survive, you are going to have to be the most effective producer in a buyer's market. In a seller's market you don't have to worry about efficiency; you're worrying about opportunity profits but when the market goes down you've got to be worrying about efficiencies, costs and profits.

'It was hard to lay off people we had worked with for years, but when the house is on fire, you jump, you really have to move quickly. I tried to communicate with the people and with few exceptions, they understood and were not hostile. I had many employees who came up to me later on the street and said, 'Look, Stan, you don't remember but I used to work for you and I know you're going through a hard time and if things get turned around I'd like to come back and work for you, and we understand why you had to do it'. It's more how you lay-off people. If you just send them a pink slip through the mail, that's pretty bad, but if you sit down and talk to them about the situation and why we have to deal and communicate, they understand.'

The financial statements before and after the contraction showed a reduction in assets, equities and sales of 75 per cent. Stan took the $56m that he received from the collection of receivable and the sale of inventory and assets and paid $22m to the banks, $15m to his vendors and retired $19m in stock.

During this period of decline, Abilene Caterpillar took a number of write-offs but continued to make profits on operations. Overall it had negative profits of 0.3 per cent on sales the first year, in the second year, a profit of 2.3 per cent after tax, and in the third year, with the recession still continuing, they were out of the woods with a profit of 3.5 per cent of sales.

Stan explained: 'The hardest thing for me was to recognize emotionally and intellectually that our growth just couldn't go on. How many times do you hear all the big companies saying things like, 'Our purpose in Caterpillar is to grow in the future as much as we have in the past'. And while they were saying that, they lost $3bn! You have got to recognize that growth cannot be the purpose of an organization. The purpose is to serve society's needs. Thus, if society's needs contract in the area that you're managing, you need to contract the resources. ∎

Copyright © INSEAD 1995

The above case is an abridged version. Copies of the complete case may be obtained from the European Case Clearing House, telephone (+44) 01234 750903; fax (+44) 01234 751125; E-mail ECCH@cranfield.ac.uk.

A marketing mission for success

Sandra Vandermerwe explains the power of customer focus.

Be they new, old, large or small, modern businesses can only succeed by being enterprising. Yet being enterprising without focusing efforts, energy and resources on customers does not lead to sustainable growth.

Driving and sustaining growth means getting bigger by getting better at identifying and articulating customer opportunities and turning these into commercial success stories that others cannot easily copy. It means going beyond just putting more innovative products and services on the market – quicker, faster, cheaper – to developing deep and life-long relationships with customers in chosen markets by giving them exactly what they want when, where and how they want it.

The true marketing mindset is proactive

The true marketing mindset involves having the imagination to perceive a world others do not immediately see. As all the classic entrepreneurs – such as the oft-quoted Bill Gates and Richard Branson – have shown, being proactive means having the courage to anticipate rather than just respond to customers and thereby actually creating and becoming the future.

Being proactive means recognizing that customers do not really know what they want, as the marketing text books would have had us believe in the past,

'Big machines don't need to think for customers, small chips can do the job'

© FT Pictures

and that therefore customers must often be led and educated. In any event, say the great entrepreneurs, customers cannot be expected to verbalize a future they have not yet experienced. (Most people thought Andrew Grove of semiconductor manufacturer Intel was crazy in the 1980s when he said that 'big machines don't need to think for customers, small chips can do the job'.)

However, being enterprising means more than just 'seeing' things differently or seeing different things. It involves knowing how to articulate imaginative ideas into language and concepts that others can and want to understand and make actionable. The marketing mindset becomes a way of thinking, an organizing logic around which all decisions throughout the business are made about what to do (and what not to do), who does what, how, when, where and how well.

One cardinal rule that holds for business of any size is that a conscious decision must be made about whom to serve so as to position the enterprise against competitors. Though market segmentation is not new, it is amazing how it still lacks the attention it needs. Getting people to see that there are different customer segments can be the single most important decision made at start-up or renewal. The questions are:

Being all things to some people

- What market segments are/could be out there?
- Which are likely to be the growth markets of the future?
- Are these accessible to us? Do we have to create them?
- What kind of competition is in/likely to get in there?
- Where can we succeed quickly to demonstrate our capabilities and build a reputation?

Enterprising through a marketing mindset means working at market segment opportunities on three levels:

- Creating innovative products and services for *existing* markets.
- Creating, and making solid, opportunities in *emerging* markets.
- Building opportunities for *imagined* markets – out there potentially but yet to be created.

Defining new 'market spaces'

Businesses take off or renew themselves because they operate in all of the above three categories with a view to growing the business or growing where the action is, instead of fighting for a larger share of a shrinking or profit-diminishing pie.

Entrepreneurs do not rely on historical indicators of success such as market share, especially at the initial stages of a venture or a re-form. As they start up or renew they look to building enough expertise (critical mass) to get the base they need to expand rather than to make and move more and more of the same thing (economies of scale).

They are aware that when market share is used as the signal for success, the danger often comes from outside the industry. (Rank Xerox, for example, was looking at its high copier market share in the 1980s but, while it was telling customers to make one and photocopy the rest, the real competition – Hewlett Packard – was saying to customers: 'Who needs a photocopier? Make as many as you want from our laser printers'.)

Marketing mindsets push for the long-term value of customers and demand investment up-front whatever that takes. The aim is to maximize 'share of spend' in markets and to grow and develop them rather than just meet this week's budget and sales quota.

Instead of confining thinking to product/service categories within narrowly defined industry categories, the marketing mindset deliberately looks for opportunities to add value in new 'market spaces', explicitly expressing in language what customers do/should do/could do to get the results they want rather than just what products/services can do.

Missions are defined by creatively framing them in a descriptor, or descriptive phrase, such as 'document management' (Xerox growth mission) or 'delivering global logistic management' (growth mission for Federal Express) rather than 'copiers' or 'courier services'. These missions serve to creatively focus energy and fix resources.

Operating in the 'customer's activity cycle'

It is in the 'market space' where the real opportunities are to be found for imaginatively adding value. So the enterprising business understands and articulates activities in the 'customer activity cycle' (CAC) and pushes to provide a total experience rather than provide just bits and pieces. Opportunities are 'seen' because the critical value-adding activities customers go through are identified and then the enterprise works backwards to ask:

- What are the opportunities for adding value?
- Who does what?
- What do we have to be good at in order to provide these for customers – now and in the future?

After Richard Branson discovered that what business travellers to Hong Kong wanted most of all was to buy a suit there but that they had no time, he decided to introduce an in-flight tailoring service for any Hong Kong-bound passenger who wanted a suit made in a hurry. The customer is measured on board and the details are sent by fax to a Hong Kong factory that then makes the suit during the customer's visit and delivers it to the returning flight. If you track Branson's strategy, all his thinking follows the same logic. The entrepreneur takes advantage of the discontinuities or value gaps caused by complacent organizations and industries who are boxed into their own so called 'core offering'.

The 'market spaces' in the existing, emerging and imagined markets determine activities, not vice versa.

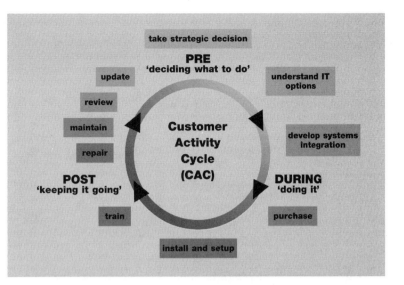

Entrepreneurs and/or their partners do, and become best at doing, whatever is needed to provide customers with a total experience in these 'market spaces' and it is by getting continuously involved in these activities that they grow.

Figure 1: 'Value gaps' in the Customer Activity Cycle: IBM customer (simplified)

While IBM was thinking products instead of customer activities (*see* Figure 1) it gave enterprising companies – which have subsequently grown as big as IBM – the gap they needed. By the time a consulting company such as Andersen Consulting had been with a corporate client for months or a software house such as Microsoft had been working on a customer's systems and then training the staff – the best IBM could hope for was to win on price and specification.

Maintenance and repair had become routine and reactive at the old IBM, enabling 'lean, keen and mean' third-party operators to fill the gap. Without a relationship base to review and update decisions, staying in the customer activity for the next cycle became increasingly impossible.

Today we see a very different IBM, intent on delivering computer-centric 'global networking capabilities' where the PC is likely to be incidental. Growth is coming from enterprising entities such as IBM UK, which create, provide and support value-added services through the CAC (such as in Figure 2) with the object of taking both their corporate customers and themselves into a new world order.

Individualizing offerings

The marketing mindset thinks about customers as individuals. The worst that could happen is to lose and have to replace a good customer, which costs time, energy and money. Innovations revolve around creatively using resources, information and technology to cater to the unique needs of these individuals, moving and growing with them, adapting offerings along the way.

For example, women have long had trouble finding jeans to fit them and suit their own particular shape. Levi Strauss now individualizes its jeans in the US. A sales assistant takes the measurements, which are entered into a computer, and three weeks later the customer receives the personalized jeans for an extra $10.

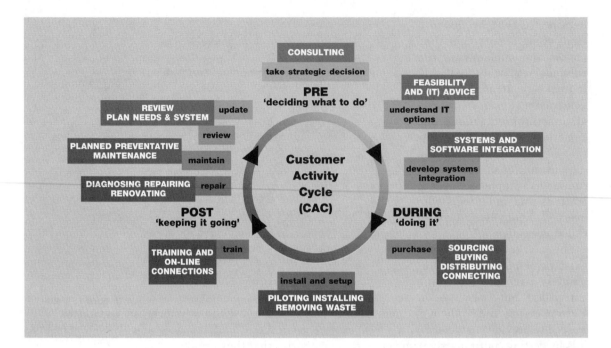

Figure 2: 'Value adds' in the CAC: new IBM (simplified)

Corporate Clothing Consultants, run by three entrepreneurs in South Africa (*see* Case study on p. 245), is different from traditional suppliers of uniforms that offer a set 'menu' of items from which the client has to choose. CCC's mission is 'total wardrobe performance' and though it creates a consistent identity worldwide for clients, it nonetheless caters to each end-user. Through its data base, direct technology and face-to-face contact, CCC knows end-user needs ranging from job to climate, size to circumstances (for example maternity), tastes to allergies. Each person gets his or her own box containing details of the possible clothing combinations and a toll-free help line they can call for assistance, be it 'creating the look' or simple clothes care.

Becoming one with the customer

Being proactive means more than just doing things 'for' customers when asked. It means doing things 'with' customers, being able to anticipate because the business is at one with customers, involved in their daily lives and having an integrated view of them.

Customers become a visible and physical part of day-to-day activities. Innovation becomes a way of life rather than a discrete activity. Oticon, the Danish electronic hearing aid manufacturer run by entrepreneur Lars Kolind, brings the deaf into head office. Clinics have been created there where customers come and talk and are examined and helped by people from product development, engineering and servicing departments.

Entrepreneurs often project themselves as the customer and make their employees go out and 'be' the customer rather than rely on statistics. Coloplast (which sells urine bags, catheters and so on) serves the European paraplegic market with 'continent management' during each stage of the CAC – during the accident period, the rehabilitation time and when customers have to manage a new normal active life. Coloplast uses a paraplegic salesforce in Italy because it says only they know how the customer feels at each critical point. Employees go to sports and other events and participate with customers to see how products work.

Instead of simply spending money on broadcasting their virtues, enterprising businesses are constantly pushing ahead, encouraging dialogue with customers in order to test and validate their ideas. They establish a permanent presence in their lives, either face to face or electronically, and engage through forums and special events. They build 'listening systems' based on customer activities.

Microsoft, for example, goes out and watches customers in their homes and offices. They 'see' how customers prepare, say, a mailing list and base innovations on these observations rather than asking them for improved word processor attributes.

Integrating activities to form new 'competitive spaces'

Enterprising businesses join forces within and without their boundaries to form single value-adding competitive spaces – communities aligned to the CAC that are interdependent and are consciously made so as to get both synergies and synchronization.

The reason they reshape industries is not just because they invent new technologies; it is because they redefine boundaries as they shape themselves and their partners around customers' activities. They know that customers respond holistically and want integrated solutions – and that they couldn't care less how companies are organized, who reports to whom or who owns what.

So enterprising businesses do not waste resources restructuring. It is more important for them to know how to bring the correct people together to form one value-creating and delivery system than to put people into neat categories. Instead of looking to head office, the employees in enterprising businesses look to each other to solve customer problems. If not all the skills needed to provide one integrated experience are to be found in one unit/business line/country, they put them together.

Price Waterhouse, which has been renewing itself to become a flexible entity for worldwide service delivery, sees this as a huge part of its recent successful growth. It makes sure clients know the team they will get and that they know these people know how to work as a team.

Using the economics differently

The marketing mindset is interested in the long-term profitability of customers rather than the profit of just single products/services/countries. What it wants to know is what it can get from customers – present and future – over their lifetime if it provides value better than anyone else. The entrepreneurial business asks:

- What will this take?
- What will this cost?
- What will we lose if we don't do it?
- What will that cost?

Not only do they quantify the value of customers to themselves but they also know and understand the value of themselves to customers. They use new economics to achieve this rather than just competing on price and specification. For example, CCC researches the whole world and knows the cost to global customers of every possible combination to each and every possible destination in all countries in which the client operates – including duty, freight delivery and so on – and it makes this part of its tender.

Conclusion   Modern businesses must use a marketing mindset if they are to succeed. Whereas in the past start-up and small businesses did this fairly instinctively now they must put more conscious effort into understanding, articulating and communicating the marketing mindset as the dominant logic to focus decisions and fix resources. Traditional businesses need actively to allow and encourage people to use their instinct and creativity to identify and interpret customer opportunities and find innovative ways to interact and give customers what they want. The goal is the same: to take the enterprise into a future yet to be defined which they themselves will create. Risky? It depends on how you define risk . . . ■

•❖ CASE STUDY

Cash flows and the operating cash cycle

*In this first of a two-part case study, **Neil Churchill** and **John Mullins** provide a model for determining the rate of growth a company can sustain from its own cash resources.*

Doing business takes cash. Doing business, profitably, produces cash. The problem is that the cash usually goes out before it comes in.

When the business is growing, even more cash goes out before it comes in. Often when you are growing fast, the cash going out continues to exceed the cash coming in and you are forced to raise additional capital through loans and equity offerings.

We have all heard stories about a company that was growing at a rate of 20 per cent or 25 per cent a year and develops a new product or method of distribution. It suddenly finds itself growing at 50 per cent or 100 per cent a year. The owners are euphoric over their success, delighted with their profits but dumbfounded when they find themselves out of cash and stopped dead in their tracks. Why does this happen?

Their cash required for growth in the next period exceeded the cash produced by the current period's sales. As this two-part article will demonstrate, when you exceed the rate of growth your past sales and normal credit terms can finance – your maximum internally financiable rate of growth or MIFROG – you need additional capital, a need you must plan for in advance.

This article shows entrepreneurs how to examine cash inflows and outflows and use them to determine cash needs for growth. It provides the tools needed to answer two critical questions for growing companies: how fast can we grow without the need for external financing beyond normal working capital sources and how can we use asset management and operations management to increase the internally financiable rate of growth?

This rate of self-financiable growth, or MIFROG, is applicable to a company, to a product or product line, to a market segment (such as Germany or the US) or distribution channels such as direct sales to consumers or through distributors. We now examine the key components of MIFROG: the operating cash cycle (OCC) and the amounts and duration of the cash flows within it.

Every business has an operating cash cycle (*see* Figure 1). Companies invest cash in materials or merchandise, engage in various marketing and operating activities and then deliver and invoice for their product or service. Unfortunately, they must then wait until some time later to collect the accounts receivable and put the cash to use once more. The length of the operating cycle determines the rapidity with which cash is used. The shorter the cycle, everything else being equal, the faster you can redeploy your cash and the faster you can grow from internal sources.

The operating cash cycle

Let's look at the operating cash cycle for a hypothetical retailing or distribution company, the M&C Company as described in Figure 2. This company holds its inventory for 80 days before it sells it. Its customers then wait 90 days before they pay their invoices. Thus M&C has a total cash-to-cash operating cycle of 170 days.

But not all the cash it puts out is tied up for the whole OCC as we will see in the following section. Within the OCC, cash is tied up for longer or shorter durations depending on the timing of the outflows. Working back from the end of the cycle (bottom of Figure 2), M&C ties up cash in accounts receivable for 90 days, as described above. Prior to that it ties up cash in inventories for 80 days.

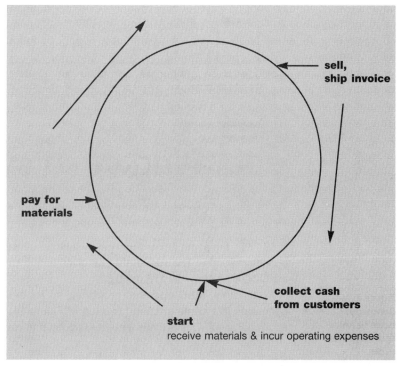

Figure 1: The operating cash cycle

However, its suppliers provide it with 30 days' trade credit, so its inventory cash is outstanding for only 50 days. Thus, M&C's total investment in working capital totals 140 days – the 90 days of accounts receivable plus the 80 days of inventory offset by the 30 days of trade credit – shown by the first shaded area in Figure 2.

Besides inventory and trade accounts receivable, M&C uses cash for everyday operating expenses. In the absence of accrued expenses or other credit, these expenses, such as weekly payroll, selling expenses, weekly utility bills and the like, occur all through the 170 days of the operating cash cycle. This is shown as an even flow in the shaded portion of the chart at the bottom of Figure 2.

We can calculate the amount of cash employed in the operating cycle by looking at M&C's cash flows in Figure 3. Thus to produce a dollar of sales we need $0.60 of cash for inventory (which becomes cost of goods sold) and $0.35 for operating expenses. Since the inventory / accounts receivable is not tied up for the whole OCC but only for 140 days, the cash employed for cost of goods sold is $0.60 x 140/170 days or $0.494. For a dollar of sales we also need $0.35 of cash for administrative and operating expenses. Since this cash is spent evenly over the period, the total of each expenditure multiplied by its days outstanding is $29.75.

When this is divided by the days in the OCC, the 'average' operating cash outstanding

Figure 2: M&C Company: Cash flows in and operating cash cycle

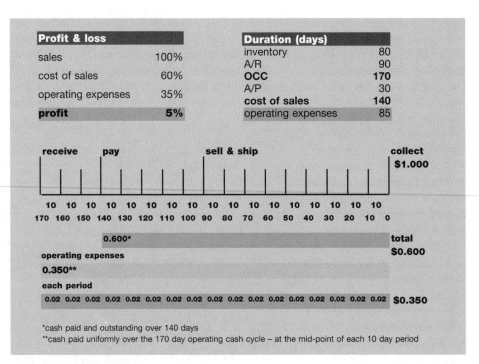

is $0.175 – the same amount you get by taking a simple average over the period, $0.35 x 85/170 or $0.175. The sum of the two gives us the cash employed per dollar of sales in the OCC – $0.494 + $0.175 or $0.669.

Fortunately, M&C operates profitably, so for every dollar of sales it produces, it generates five cents of cash (See top of Figure 2), which it can reinvest to produce additional sales. This is the last number we need to calculate the MIFROG over the OCC.

Figure 3: M&C Company: Cash flows in and operating cash cycle

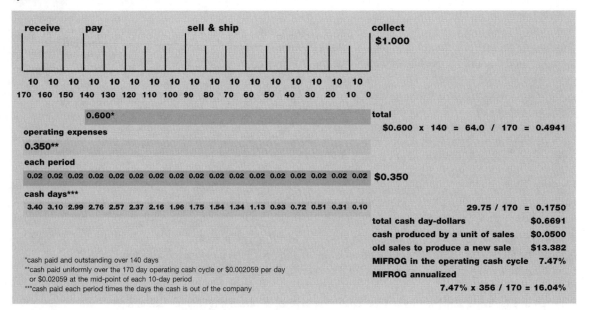

As shown in Figure 3, M&C needs to invest $0.6691 over the operating cash cycle in order to generate one dollar of sales in that cycle. Part of this amount comes from current operations as $0.05 per dollar of sales. Thus M&C needs $0.6691/$0.05 or $13.38 of sales in a past cycle to fund $1 of sales in a new cycle. This gives the company a rate of growth of 'new divided by old' of $1 divided by $13.38. This is a MIFROG of 7.47 per cent over M&C's 170-day operating cash cycle. ∎

MIFROG over an operating cash cycle

This article concludes on p. 259.

Section 2
Long-term growth

Breaking down the wall, scaling the ladder

Neil Churchill looks at some of the potential problems – and their solutions – that companies face as they enter long-term growth.

As stated in *The six key phases of company growth* (Part 7, Section 1, p. 213), value is created when businesses start but much more value is created when enterprises grow. A growing company creates jobs, develops and disseminates innovative products that satisfy the needs of more and more customers and, in the process, makes money for the stockholders and creates value for society. However, growth brings challenges that are often new to the founding entrepreneurs, who are not always prepared to handle them well.

This article examines the dynamics of growth, the demands it makes, the challenges and changes it brings, and suggests some ways of dealing with these demands and capturing the opportunities growth can bring. It does so under seven headings: the wall; the flow; the force; the links; the ladder; the reality; and the harvest.

The wall: delegation

As a company grows it becomes larger and more complex. Additional people must be hired, often possessing an increasing variety of skills that, collectively, go considerably beyond those possessed by the entrepreneur.

To do their jobs effectively, these people need both information and 'intellectual space'. The owner-manager must change from a personal, hands-on style of managing people to one of coaching and managing managers. Delegation of authority is particularly difficult for founding entrepreneurs for two reasons.

First, these entrepreneurs have closely managed their companies through lean times and find it extremely hard not to interfere when they see a worker doing something wrong and wasting resources. They want to jump in and fix the problem rather than holding back and dealing with the problem through the worker's manager.

Second, they have a tendency to believe that all the managers they hire have the same information, motivation and drive that they themselves possess. Thus they have a tendency to turn a whole task over to a manager without having a meeting of the minds as to what is to be accomplished and what milestones are to be attained and when. In essence they abdicate authority rather then delegate it.

This 'wall' of delegation seems universal. I was once talking to the director of a Scottish economic development agency and commented that when American companies get to around 40 to 50 employees they 'hit the wall', in the sense that marathon runners do, and either learn to delegate or drop back and fail to grow. He commented that this occurred in Scotland, too, but at around 25 employees. He posited that the difference was due to the fact that his market was smaller and that Scottish companies had to export earlier than in the US. This increased the complexity of their business and they had to start delegating earlier.

The basic keys to delegation are four: delegate responsibility; agree upon the objectives to be attained; grant others the authority to take the actions needed to achieve the objectives; and collect and monitor information on how things are progressing.

There is a fifth key in an entrepreneurial company that lives upon innovation. This is, first to measure progress towards the agreed-upon goals – not the methods – utilized to get there and, second, evaluate this progress not just to see if the goal has been reached but what has been learned that may cause a re-examination of the objectives in the light of enhanced knowledge.

These, and other steps (which will be covered later in articles on the entrepreneurial corporation) must be taken if you want the company to continue to innovate by growing without bureaucratization, a process that is likely to 'blow out the entrepreneurial flame' that formed the base of the company's success.

Everyone knows that starting a business requires cash but not everyone realizes **The flow: cash** that growing a business also takes cash. The two-part article on cash flow that began in Part 7, Section 1, p. 232 and concludes on p. 259 explains how profitable operations produce a cash flow that can be used for growing the business. It also shows how rapid rates of growth can outrun this cash flow and require additional capital if growth is to be maintained. It further looks at the role of operations management and asset management in improving this cash flow and a company's MIFROG (Maximum Internally Financiable Rate of Growth).

Beyond growth, cash must be managed strategically. Entrepreneurship involves innovation and innovation entails a certain amount of uncertainty. An unresolved problem such as Problem A in Figure 1 can block any awareness of even larger problems down the road. Thus entrepreneurial managers follow the strategy of venture capitalists and disburse cash incrementally in order to gain additional understanding of the situation before committing all the finance required.

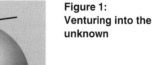

**Figure 1:
Venturing into the
unknown**

They spend a modest amount of money to acquire knowledge of a venture situation and then use this knowledge to re-examine the situation and then either stop the project and 'cut their losses' or go ahead and spend more to gain additional insight into the potential of the project. This is currently being called an 'options approach' to capital allocation. To the extent that time and competition permit, this slow approach to a new opportunity husbands scarce resources.

The force:
leadership

The entrepreneurial company moves by focusing on innovation. The spark-plug for this at the outset is the entrepreneur. As the company grows, other people join in, a hierarchy develops and personal face-to-face contact is supplemented, if not supplanted, by more formal means of communication.

Without constant reinforcement of the company's goals, sub-goals develop and people begin to work towards different ends. The entrepreneur must recognize the need to communicate his or her passion, commitment and vision to everyone in the company – to get them to 'sign-up' and achieve personal satisfaction in furthering the organization's goals.

A recent study* found that the chief executives of high-growth companies ranked forming and communicating vision the third most important skill just after financial management and motivating others, whereas their counterparts in low-growth companies ranked it number seven.

The links:
networks
instead of staff

Start-ups and growing businesses are usually both undercapitalized and chronically short of cash. Instead of having all the resources they need to bring people and skills inside the business, entrepreneurs use 'networks' of people who can help them out on an as-needed basis.

Some of these people are paid for their part-time services such as lawyers, accountants, consulting specialists and the like. Others in the network are not paid but jointly share with one another information on technical problems, market trends, suppliers, customers and which specialists to use for what and when.

Networks even involve competitors. Entrepreneurs who compete with each other for customers, technical breakthroughs and market share co-operate together when faced by a common 'enemy' such as a big company or an industry-wide technical or market problem. One watering-hole in Silicon Valley was known for this networking where entrepreneurs, faced with technical problems, would get solutions from competitors – albeit with information six months behind where the competitor was at the time.

A particularly important use of networks is to obtain a mentor or adviser or even an advisory board for the owner-manager. The problems facing entrepreneurs in a growing business may be new to them but they are not unique in the world. Having a mentor or an adviser who 'has been where you are going' is an invaluable asset for an entrepreneur.

Such an adviser, or board of advisers, can warn about problems on the horizon, help craft solutions to problems and, since the job at the top is a lonely one, be

*('Stages of small business growth revisited, insights into growth path and leadership/management skills in low- and high-growth companies', (1994) Eggers, J. H., Leahy, K. T. and Churchill, N. C., *Frontiers of Entrepreneurship Research*, Babson College, Wellesley, Massachusetts, USA)

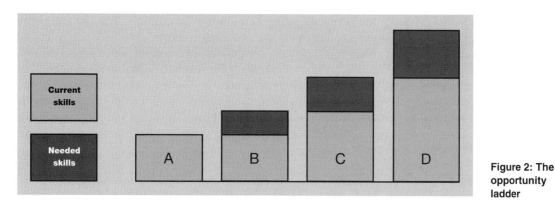

Figure 2: The
opportunity
ladder

someone an entrepreneur can confide in and 'bounce ideas off'. Further, they, like
all the nodes in the network, come quite inexpensively.

The focus of growth for entrepreneurial companies is recognizing opportunities **The ladder of**
and crafting them to fit the business in order to be able to seize and exploit them. **opportunity**
A truly entrepreneurial company is always on the lookout for new opportunities,
particularly if they are a little bigger than what can currently be handled. The
true entrepreneur finds the opportunity first and then marshals the resources to
be able to exploit it.

This is represented in Figure 2 by the shaded and unshaded portions of
'opportunity' boxes. The business currently has a resource-capability represented
by unshaded Box A. The entrepreneur sees an opportunity that requires the
resources of Box B, which exceed its current capability by the shaded area. If the
company is successful in capturing this opportunity, it then has the skills
represented by the unshaded area of Box C. If it finds and captures an
opportunity the size of this whole box, it then develops more resources and can
again look for bigger opportunities and so on.

What is important is that the successful capture and exploitation of a new
opportunity can help the organization climb the opportunity ladder. An
opportunity the size of Box D would probably never be available to a business the
size of A but, by seizing and exploiting bigger and bigger opportunities, the
organization is able to 'play in a new athletic field' and grow and prosper.

The important thing for the entrepreneur to realize is that an opportunity
should not just be evaluated on its financial return to the company but where, if
successfully captured, it will lead the business by increasing its financial
resources, its capabilities, its credibility and its reputation. The important
question is: 'How does this opportunity help me climb the opportunity ladder?'

Companies may last for many decades but entrepreneurs do not. As owner- **The reality:**
managers grow older their personal goals change. While they might risk all they **the biological**
had at age 28 on a good opportunity, since they possessed little and had both **imperative**
time and energy to make it back again, at age 60 they are much less inclined to
take such a risk and be forced to live those 80-hour work weeks all over again.

As the goals of the owner-manager change, so do those of the business. And
with this change in goals so must there be a change in strategy. This strategy

change is one of the reasons family succession is so difficult. The goals of those entering into management are often quite different from those who are phasing out and conflict, often unresolvable, ensues. When successful succession occurs, it is wonderful, but it must be carefully planned for. When it does not work, someone else has an acquisition opportunity.

The reality: the organizational imperative

As organizations grow larger their methods of operation change. One such change is the process of dynamically developing the strategies needed to achieve the company's vision and attain the company's goals.

At the start the company goals are simple and clear: first survive, then make a profit and finally grow. Initially, the strategy is set by the founding entrepreneurs where it flowers in their minds at unpredictable times – when they awaken at 3am, while they are driving, or looking in the bathroom mirror. It is also communicated to others in the company in a quite informal and personal manner.

As the company grows in size and complexity so does its strategy; and the process of developing and modifying it needs to become more formal. With increased complexity and with delegation, this formulation and reformulation becomes a joint process with other members of the management team since they now possess knowledge that the owner-manager does not have and which is critical to the company's strategy.

These more formal and complex organizational processes, structure and controls that emerge with growth produce a middle management to facilitate operations. Unfortunately, this middle management can easily begin to 'march to their own drummer' and a bureaucracy results. This bureaucracy has been termed the 'enemy of entrepreneurship' by a past chief executive of one of the most entrepreneurial, large companies in the US. Only the leadership and constant attention of the owner-manager can provide the 'force' necessary to prevent the rise of bureaucracy.

Harvest: exiting the organization

The final stage of the owner-manager in the company is when he or she chooses to exit or to reduce the level of their activities in the company. The obvious choices are family succession, sale to others or going public through an initial placement offering. (These issues will be covered in depth in Part 10.)

A sale of the company can occur in a number of ways. First, and most commonly, to one or more members of the family through management succession. If this is not desirable, the second most common way is to management via a management buy-out or a management buy-in or sale to an outside organization. (To be covered in Part 8.) Thousands of businesses in Europe, founded after the Second World War, are currently involved in one of the above processes.

Two other harvest strategies also exist. One, often overlooked, is for the owner-manager to shrink the company into a more manageable size and to focus it on the activities that are at the core of the business's profitability. This can make the business more valuable and easier to manage, giving the owner-manager time to make a choice of selling it at higher value or putting it on 'auto-pilot' and withdrawing totally or in part pending a final disposal of the business. This strategy is far more desirable to the other alternative of liquidating the business by disposing of its assets.

As Sue Birley pointed out earlier in this part (p. 212), not every owner-manager wants to grow. One owner-manager said to me at the end of the first three-week unit of a nine-week owner-presidents program at Harvard Business School: 'Neil, I am not coming back to Unit II. I like this program and have learned a lot but everyone here wants to grow. I own two ski lodges, one at Aspen, Colorado, and one at Snowbird, Utah, and I like to ski. I don't want to grow'. While we know the exhilaration of growth, we have seen its problems and the demands it makes. Who can fault him for choosing as he did? ■ **In closing**

Secrets of the 'supergrowth' league

Bernard Taylor describes the lessons learned from a 15-year study of 'middle-sized' companies in the UK, Germany and the US.

This article summarizes the conclusions of a 15-year study of 200 high-growth medium-size companies over the period 1979–80 to 1994–95. This involved 15 researchers in the UK and two in Germany interviewing chief executives and writing around 100 case studies. The research was supported by grants from Price Waterhouse and the Anglo-German Foundation. The German research study was carried out by Professor Dietger Hahn and Dr Ulrich Grüb of the University of Giessen Institut für Unternehmensplanung. The resulting book (*Supergrowth companies: entrepreneurs in action* (1996) John Harrison and Bernard Taylor, Butterworth-Heinemann, Oxford) is the first longitudinal study of UK high-growth medium-size companies.

We defined 'medium-size' in 1980 as companies with a turnover of £10m–£100m and in 1990 we raised the benchmark to £20m–£200m. To justify the label 'high growth', we required that companies should have grown by at least 20 per cent per year over a five-year period.

We included all kinds of independent companies, whether privately or publicly owned, on the London Stock Exchange or one of the mini-markets but excluded two sectors – property and financial services, where some of the profits are made by deals rather than by regular trading, as well as companies in turnaround and recovery and those that had grown mainly by acquisition.

We had 176 companies in the original sample and found that on average they had grown by around 40 per cent a year over five years from, say, £10m–£100m to £50m–£500m in sales and from £1m–£10m to £5m–£50m in profits.

These 'supergrowth' companies are the vanguard of UK business. They succeed because they innovate. They break new ground, open up new markets, launch new types of products and services, introduce new forms of organization and more cost-effective ways of operating. **Why study high-growth medium-size companies?**

They create wealth and jobs. The 200 companies that we analysed probably generated 50,000 – 100,000 jobs and £3bn–£4bn of capital over a 10-year period. The supergrowth companies are the unsung heroes of industry. The impact they have on the national economy and on local communities is quite out of proportion to their numbers. While large companies, banks and government departments are closing operations and shedding thousands of jobs, these companies are setting up new businesses and taking on new people.

The importance of this mid-size, high-growth sector was recognized in the US in the early 1980s by the establishment of the American Business Conference (ABC), which brought together the leaders of mid-size companies that had grown at least 15 per cent annually for the past five years.

Mid-size is a relative term that varies with the size of the market. The Americans define mid-size as $25m – $1bn turnover – about 15,000 companies in the US, less than 1 per cent of all businesses. McKinsey researchers found that in a five-year period, from 1978–83, these mid-size companies had increased their workforce on average by 10 per cent a year while over the same period the Fortune 500 had lost three million jobs.

Researchers in Germany, too, have discovered the importance of *Mittelstand* companies. They found that the more successful companies had kept their businesses simple and uncomplicated with narrow product ranges, target customer groups and a few preferred suppliers.

The lessons

A major benefit to be gained from studying high-growth, mid-size companies is that they can provide examples of best practice for other entrepreneurs who wish to grow their companies.

Lesson No. 1: Find a market niche you can defend

Successful medium-size businesses do not confront established brands in their key markets. Instead they invent new products and services and open up new market segments. They also create barriers to entry in the form of patents, distribution licences or supply agreements with large customers.

Alan J. Brazier of Vax International invented Vax, a vacuum cleaner that would not just clean but also wash and dry carpets and floors. After years of frustration he established his own factory, put together the funds for a television advertising campaign and in two years, from 1985–87, established Vax as the number one cleaner in its segment with a market share of 67 per cent. When Hoover launched a similar product, Brazier took it to court for infringing his patents and won a seven-figure settlement.

Lesson No. 2: Compete in areas that require speed, flexibility and customer service

In our study, the leaders of UK supergrowth companies cited 'flexibility to adapt to changing customer needs' as the most important factor in their success.

Also, when asked to compare their companies' performance with their competitors, they thought their companies' main competitive advantages were in 'customer service' and 'management organization' – this usually referring to a 'star-shaped' organization composed of a small central team and an array of business unit teams that could communicate easily and take decisions quickly.

Lesson No. 3: Diversify into related products and adjacent markets

After establishing a position in a niche market, the supergrowth company's second priority is to diversify quickly into related market niches in order not to become over-dependent on one product, one customer or the economy of a small region.

Peter J. Wood, an 'intrapreneur' who operates within the Royal Bank of Scotland, pioneered the telephone selling of motor insurance policies in UK and his company, Direct Line Insurance, quickly became the market leader, selling over 2 million motor policies a year. By 1994 the business was making £110m profit on gross premiums of £685m. In ten years his staff had grown from a nucleus of 30 people to 3,000 in 1994. But competitors were not idle. Wood knew that they would attack his core business and he moved quickly to offer the same target customer group a range of related financial services in household insurance, mortgages and home banking.

As Lord Weinstock is reported to have said, 'A niche becomes a grave'. Having established a new product in a market niche, the entrepreneur is quickly surrounded by competitors offering similar products, often at a cheaper price. The only answer is to keep innovating.

Lesson No. 4: Leave the industry before the window of opportunity closes

Supergrowth companies thrive as new industries merge and grow. At the embryo stage, they succeed by introducing new products and services, opening up new channels of distribution, pioneering novel production methods and experimenting with innovative management approaches. During the growth phase they expand geographically from regional to national and later to international coverage. They offer a wider product range and serve different customer groups.

The embryo and growth phases may take five to 10 years. For the medium-size company, these times are exciting and highly profitable. But, in due course, industries mature, innovations are copied, large international competitors arrive and, in the UK and the US where there is an active market in companies, medium-size companies are quickly acquired, merged and consolidated into major groups.

When the industry begins to consolidate, the leader of an emerging business has to decide whether he or she wants the company to become a major player – which usually means losing control of the business – or to sell the company and possibly start a different business.

Charles M. Fisher, the chairman and chief executive of Sharpe & Fisher, is a UK family businessman who saw that his industry was consolidating and moved out just in time. Founded in 1912, Sharpe & Fisher was a builder's merchant based in Cheltenham but by the 1980s its star business was its DIY store operation Sandfords, which accounted for almost half of the group's profits. Charles Fisher and his management team examined the prospects for Sandfords and decided that as a family business they would not be able to compete with the buying power and the marketing strengths of fast-growing national multiples such as B&Q and Texas. They sold Sandfords at its peak for £40m to Ladbroke's Texas chain.

Since then, from 1991–95, the company under Charles Fisher has used the *money to expand its original chain of builder's merchants from 6 to 23 by acquiring private companies at recession-reduced prices. The chain is concentrated in a band between Sussex and Wales. Despite the severe recession in the construction industry, profits have more than doubled, and earnings per share have increased five-fold.**

The international dimension

Comparisons with supergrowth companies outside the UK are very revealing. Most UK supergrowth companies are publicly owned and professionally managed – most of their founders are 'professional entrepreneurs', managers trained in large companies such as Ford, IBM and ICI. They are mostly selling services, which means that some find it difficult to trade overseas. When they do, they like to acquire a company in the same niche or, like Body Shop and Kwik Fit, they sell through franchises.

The companies usually have a limited life because they are acquired by large companies. They are not often supported by government loans though some have used bank loans, often to their cost. They usually, sensibly, rely on retained earnings and equity capital. With rare exceptions they do not expect technological support from universities, and they find that large UK companies, except for some retail multiples such as Marks & Spencer, do not yet understand the Japanese idea of customer-supplier partnerships.

German mid-size companies are more often family owned and family managed. They are well integrated into their communities, funded by the regional banks and are sponsors of local activities such as football teams. They frequently work closely with universities and research institutes. A large proportion of them are in manufacturing and have long-term relationships with major customers such as Siemens Nixdorf, BMW and Daimler-Benz. Many of these companies are big exporters and they normally sell through agents around the world.

US supergrowth companies grow much bigger than their UK counterparts and they stay independent longer. They also have more funds available. Their home market is bigger than the European Union and they can tap into huge technological resources in the major universities and the defence industries. There are also many more supergrowth companies in the US, partly because 'entrepreneurship and small business' is a favorite course in most American business schools.

However, in each country these mid-size, high-growth companies are a powerful force for innovation and growth, attracting investment, introducing new technologies, opening up new markets, and creating wealth and employment. They succeed by identifying, and often creating, a new market niche, responding imaginatively to customers' requirements, expanding quickly into related product-markets and innovating continually. ∎

* 'Small quoted companies', *The Director*, April 1996.

⬩♦ CASE STUDY

Corporate Clothing Consultants (CCC)

*This case is extracted and edited from a fuller version written by **Sandra Vandermerwe** and **Sue Birley**, both of Imperial College Management School.*

Greta Abrahamson, Chris Levine and Archie Leggatt were entrepreneurs in South Africa. Greta and Chris were leading couturiers, dressing wealthy, sophisticated women and, as such, were keen rivals. Archie owned and ran the premier fashion design school in the country, supplying designers to major fashion houses across the world. Yet in mid-1988, their lives changed completely when they were approached individually by South African Airways (SAA) and asked to design company uniforms to match the new SAA corporate identity.

© Courtesy of South African Airways

The proposition was deceptively simple – the reality was very different. They had to clothe pilots, air hostesses, technicians and ground staff all over the world, a total of 12,500 employees. But that was not all. In the changing political climate, they were told that the corporate identity program was considered vitally important to the country. They would be paid a minimum fee and given free international travel. In short, they were being asked to work for 'god and country'. How could they refuse? Suffice it to say, they could not and so Corporate Clothing Consultants (CCC) was born as a part-time activity.

By the end of 1996, the company had more than 100 employees, 52 subcontract manufacturers and had clothed many of the major companies in South Africa, including SA Telcom, Nedbank, Fedex, Boland Bank and ESCOM, the South African electricity company. They had also expanded into the global market in 1996 by winning a competitive tender to clothe the employees of TNT, a major international courier. So what was the secret of this success story?

'None of us could afford to refuse and we all knew it. To be left out would have been infinitely worse than whatever had to be done.'

The opportunity

Like all successful entrepreneurs, they recognized the moment and seized the opportunity. Moreover, they used their first contract to learn about the business, to develop a clear understanding of customer needs and to develop creative ways of capturing customer interest. They believed that they should be projecting an image of quality and service while at the same time making people feel good about themselves. This was not easy.

Getting the clothes to individuals, each of whom was a different size and shape and had different tastes and needs depending upon climate and job, was complex and had to be managed with precision.

The partners CCC was an unlikely combination. Three very successful, energetic, creative people, all with very different personalities, their own clear view of the fashion business and their own ways of working – and yet it worked. The reasons are simple:
● In fashion terms they found that they were on the same wavelength. For example, in preparation for the SAA deal, they had each designed clothes of similar style and quality. As a result, trust was added to professional respect.
● They were all perfectionists, believed in attention to detail and were constantly innovating, using every new job as an opportunity to hone and enhance their service.
● Having begun, they were hungry for success – growth was the only option.

> *'In fact, we designed for each other, not SAA.'*

The service Most of the competition had a range of 40 standard trousers and blazers from which the client chose and to which the suppliers added a corporate logo. CCC was very different. It produced a new design, including the cloth, for each client. Indeed, by 1996, the concept had evolved well beyond the original design service requested by SAA to providing the client with not only design but also buying, manufacturing, warehousing, pest control, delivery and insurance.

This meant looking carefully at the users of the product and adding value for them. They designed styles that gave the staff maximum choice. They gave the client a quality image in the marketplace and employees individual service, offering a telephone hot line and consultants to help them get results out of the clothes in the most effective way.

Managing growth Clearly, they had a good feel for the market and for customer needs – but so do many aspiring entrepreneurs. However, not all manage to deliver their promises, particularly at such a rate. What are the managerial lessons for this case?

Like most entrepreneurial teams, they have evolved a way of making decisions that has no written rules – except that they talk all the time. They use their networks and are constantly on the look out for new leads. They also understand their own limitations. For example, they do not have the level of technical ability to control the details of stock movements and costs. So they hired a professional.

> *'We set about learning what the employees need and want, and then we translate it into clothes which management also likes.'*

They go to great lengths to give customers what they want, even if it means going outside the traditional business. To do this, they constantly talk to their clients, both the senior management and also, perhaps more importantly, they constantly involve employees – who have to wear their clothes – at all stages of the process.

> *'People often find the three of us quite intimidating. They assume that we are judging them by what they are wearing but then the funny combination amuses them, they relax, get to know us and find we are really quite nice.'*

Any successful new venture is based upon the skills, passions and credibility of the founders. Employees rarely have these to the same degree and the trick for any entrepreneur in growing a venture is to know which activities to delegate and which to hold close. Greta, Chris and Archie built the credibility of CCC on their own personal reputations and abilities as designers. This was the one activity they were not ready to delegate – and it paid off. Potential clients were always surprised, and pleased, to see at least one, and often all three, turning up to do presentations and to talk to employees.

They have built critical mass through careful development of a large network of suppliers and are equally careful about relations with them. They know that they are attractive to these suppliers because their orders are not seasonal, as with retailers, but they do not trade on this. Indeed, they are considerate of suppliers' cash needs and always pay on time. Last, but not least, they enjoy themselves. And their challenge? To maintain all this in the future. ■

'We don't want a quick fix. We know it will take time and investment.'

Home and work – a volatile mixture

The pressures that private and professional life exert are great and their interaction often stressful – most of all for the entrepreneur. **Fernando Bartolomé** examines the issues.

Most people would like to succeed at work and in their private lives. We have a relatively standard way of thinking about what that means: to have a good job and advance in one's professional career while having a good marriage and a good relationship with one's children.

Some may define success – in particlar, success in private life – differently. Some men and women today may say that success doesn't necessarily mean marriage or having children. However, these are the exceptions among the people I work with: mostly successful executives in large multinational corporations.

The model of professional and private life success for these people fits the conventional model. The only change that I perceive is that while only a few years ago the conventional model of private life success for male executives was to have a traditional family with a stay home wife, the proportion of people for whom the ideal is a dual career family is increasing slowly. But this increase is mostly among women, not men. Indeed, if one listens carefully to men who also say that their ideal is a dual career family, one discovers that they are 'closet traditionalists' and would be much happier if they found a traditional wife.

How difficult is it?

Is it easy to have it all? No. It is extremely difficult and it is becoming increasingly so. There are several reasons for this:

● Work demands are increasing. Organizations are trying to do more with less. Personnel reductions, particularly among middle management, are pervasive.

● Work stress is increasing. The main source of stress is not only work demands but uncertainty and insecurity. In the past, excellent performance was almost a guarantee of a secure job. Today outsourcing and globalization puts even the job of the excellent performer in jeopardy. This stress is multiplied by the frequent lack of transparency from the top of organizations about their strategic personnel decisions. When people feel highly stressed at work, it is very difficult for them to pay attention to their private lives.

● The relationship between the genders is changing. We live in a brave new world where men and women expect more out of their relationship and are struggling to get new definitions of what a good relationship is. Our parents' model has become obsolete. We have to reinvent what a good relationship between a man and a woman in the 90s means. These experiments are risky and stressful.

● Our standards of what it means to have a good relationship with our children have been raised. The definition of what being a good mother means has remained quite stable. But the definition of what being a good father means has changed substantially.

● Both men and women would like to have it all. Many women today are unwilling to 'sacrifice it all' for their families.

Women feel the problem most intensely

After a period when they tried to be 'superwomen' and have it all, many women reached the conclusion that this was impossible and gave up some aspect of their lives. Some chose not to marry. Many decided not to have children or have less. Many postponed having children until later in their lives. Some of them had them. Many did not.

Furthermore, research shows that even in dual career families women are still doing about 70 to 80 per cent of domestic 'jobs' in private life. Even very 'liberated' women tend to feel more responsible for the quality of private life and particularly for the well being of their children than men do.

In my research on these issues I have found that when I ask executives how should men and women in an ideal world divide between themselves the job of taking care of their children when they are between 0 and 5 years old, the average response is that the ideal division should be 70 per cent for the mother and 30 per cent for the father. Many women share that view. When I ask them how much did each parent actually do, the average man does about 20 per cent of the job.

What can be done?

The problem is difficult but not impossible to deal with. There are no perfect solutions but there are some ideas that may help.

First we should put things in perspective and avoid clichés and easy answers. Let's debunk a few clichés.

'*The main problem is time.*' Not true. In my research I find consistently that executives devote only 50 per cent of their waking hours to work. And this is true even if they work long hours.

For example:

1 Week =	168	hours		
Average weekly sleep	49	hours		
Total waking hours	119	hours		
Daily Average Commute	1	hour		
Daily Average Time at Work	10	hours	× 5 =	55 hours
Average work hours during the weekend	4	hours		4
Total working hours				59

59/119 = approx. 50%

Executives are often startled when they make this calculation. They can't believe the numbers. But they are accurate. Note that the percentage of waking hours devoted to work would decrease substantially if we included holidays and vacation time in our calculations. Time is indeed an issue. But not *the* main issue.

'*The main problem is my boss.*' That may be true in some cases but it is often an excuse. Many executives who say this have never discussed with their bosses how to protect their private lives. Women are better than men at doing this. However, even women may find difficulty negotiating about these issues with their bosses and therefore avoid doing it.

What the individual can do

- Stop blaming others. Stop blaming the organization, the boss, incompetent subordinates, demanding clients etc.
- Start analyzing what one could do without asking for anybody's permission to improve the situation. Learn to manage one's time better. Learn to prioritize. Learn to delegate. Learn to cut unnecessary activities such as meetings.

Some of these things one may do alone. Some may need co-operating with others. A lot of time and energy can be saved this way.

In my work with executives I often ask them the following question: 'How many hours would you save a week without your results deteriorating?' Average response = 6 hours.

My next question should be obvious: 'Why aren't you saving those hours?' The typical response is to blame stress, the boss, clients etc. But I am convinced that the problem lies elsewhere and it is called lack of passion.

Develop private life passion

For many men and some women, taking care of their private lives is more *duty* than passion. 'I ought to attend the PTA meeting' or 'I have to pick up the children at school' or 'I have to take them to the doctor'. There is indeed a lot of duty that needs to be taken care of. Some of it can be delegated to others: day care centers, babysitters, school, vacation camps. A lot cannot be delegated. And there is much that *should not* be delegated.

For example, we may be tempted to delegate the more painful or uncomfortable activities, but this may be totally wrong. This is often a problem for men. A child cries in the middle of the night, and a man may tell his wife: 'Why don't you take care of him? You are much better at it.' In some cases the woman herself may volunteer, 'I'll do it.' It is very easy to feel grateful and go back to sleep. Easy yes. But also maybe stupid.

Learn to recognize opportunities

Taking care of a sick child is both a pain and an opportunity. An opportunity to discover more deeply your love for your child, to communicate your love to your children through your actions, and to learn maybe to become a better partner.

Avoid the mañana syndrome: seize the day

I work with people of different ages. When we discuss this topic, the older they are, the sadder they feel. Because they can't go back.

A few weeks ago, I was conducting a session on this topic. A young executive was paying a lot of attention and looked very sad. During the coffee break I asked him what was going on. He answered, 'You got me a bit late. One of my children is already eight years old. But the other is three. With that one there is still a lot I can do.'

His sadness was right and natural. There are a few essential things he has missed and can't recover. There are only a few years when you can hold a baby in your arms. And they happen only once. 'Carpe diem!'

Develop a sense of priorities

I often ask executives to prioritize three areas of their lives – Children, Couple, Self. I ask them what is the right order. Many say Children, Couple, Self. But the right order is the opposite: Self, Couple, Children. Some women find that idea troubling and difficult. But, if one thinks about it, it is logical and evident. You can't take care of anybody if you don't take care of yourself. You can't have a healthy relationship with anybody if you have a lousy relationship with yourself. The best way of taking care of your children is to take care of your marriage. If you destroy your marriage you will hurt your children. The best way to take care of your children is to take care of your spouse and give them a great example of what it means to love and respect another human being.

Prioritizing doesn't mean that one thing is more important or has more value than the other. All may be equally important. But it does mean that one has a sense of how each aspect of one's life relates to each other and what is the best way of achieving a positive synergy.

Beyond the individual

The responsibility starts with the individual but doesn't end there. To protect the quality and stability of private life and particularly to protect families, society as a whole has an important role to play. I will suggest here briefly some of the elements of this societal contribution:

● *The crucial role of a healthy economy.* Unemployment, underemployment, job insecurity, poorly paid jobs are the most serious threats to the well-being and stability of families.

● *The importance of social justice.* A better distribution of income, a more just society, and a better distribution of work, if the economy doesn't produce enough employment, are important contributing factors to creating the economic and social conditions where families can thrive.

● *A decline of materialism and consumerism.* At the deepest level, materialism conflicts with something that I would call 'relationism'. When we hectically seek material wealth and possessions, when we try to achieve happiness by buying the best car, the latest record, the ideal Caribbean vacation etc., we may pay too much attention to things and too little to people and relationships. Things do not bring us together. Corny as it may sound, love does. And it requires valuing people more than things.

Cultural changes in our conception of male and female roles

The quality of private life and particularly the quality of family life will improve when men and women feel equally responsible for the quality of their private lives and when they have an equal degree of passion for it. Today still a woman suffers more when she has to leave her children in a day care center than a man does under similar circumstances.

Women today would like to have a more fulfilling professional life *but* without risking the quality of their private lives. The first wave of feminism fought under the banner of 'women's liberation' and often interpreted that liberation as jettisoning female roles and functions that they believed themselves to have been brainwashed to assume. The second wave of feminism is ready to assume the existence of deeply rooted feminine impulses, such as nurturing, to value them and to integrate them into a richer ideal of what being a woman means.

Unfortunately, men have not yet achieved an equal transformation. Very few wanted to be liberated from their traditional roles. It was actually the feminists that suggested to men that they should desire to be liberated of their traditional roles as money earners and sole providers of economic security. There were few men fighting women to defend their right to feed a baby or get up in the middle of the night to nurse a sick child.

But today, forced in part by their wives, slowly but surely some men are starting to discover the value of these aspects of their lives and are proposing for the first time in history a new, much richer definition of the 'fathering' role.

Structural changes

The term 'family friendly policies' is now widely used at State and Company level. The more advanced a society, the more varied are the tools that it offers people to help take care of both work and family. But laws and policies are often ahead of practice. Laws are easier to change than people. When a society, for example, offers family-friendly solutions to men and women, women use them much more often than men. A recent report illustrates this very well.

In the Netherlands in 1994, 36.4 per cent of the labor force had half-time jobs. However, while 65 per cent of the women had chosen this option, only 16 per cent of men did. The reasons for this are many, including the differential pay between men and women. But, certainly, the willingness of women to sacrifice professional success in favor of paying attention to family needs plays an important role – as does the unwillingness of many men to accept similar kinds of sacrifice.

☞ Special problems for the entrepreneur

Some characteristic facts about entrepreneurs are: they are never nine to five people; the working day is never long enough for them; they tend to dominate their companies and impose their personality on others. They impose their rules and demand that others work as hard and as many hours as they do; the somewhat artificial separation between professional and private life does not really exist for them from a psychological point of view.

The clichés – 'he is married to his company', 'the company is his baby', or, in some cultures, 'the company is his mistress', are psychologically extremely accurate. I have met executives in large corporations who are passionate about their jobs. But entrepreneurs' passion is different. In their case, their company is an extension of themselves. One could assume that so are their children. But they are not.

Why may this be so? I'd like to propose several psychological hypotheses that make sense to me. First, children are the result of a brief act of conception. A company, on the other hand, represents the fruition of a complex, prolonged and extremely involving act of creation. There is a second hypothesis that intrigues me. Most entrepreneurs are men. Their children are the result of a joint act of creation, and in that venture it is the mother who plays the most crucial, involved creative role. A child 'belongs' much more to the mother than to the father. (As the saying goes, one can be sure of who his mother is. As to his father, there is never any certainty). In creating a firm, on the other hand, the entrepreneur is both father and mother – he is even the midwife. The company is his baby in a way his children are not and it provides him with the most unique opportunity to project himself. This leads to an extremely strong narcissistic involvement. Thus, when things go well, the gratification is huge. When they go wrong, the entrepreneur cannot think about anything else.

An interesting research question would be to ask if women entrepreneurs are as deeply interested in their firms as men are. Obviously a woman's involvement in creating a child is much more complex and profound. Certainly our society expects her to become more involved in the nurturing of her children. A Freudian psychologist would hypothesize that this cathexis, this investment of emotional energy on her children would diminish the energy available for investment in work. This makes sense, but is it so? What do women entrepreneurs feel more passionate about: their companies or their children? Anecdotal evidence seems to indicate that women entrepreneurs are also more emotionally invested in their companies than in their children.

Another factor that may contribute to entrepreneurs' extraordinary degree of involvement in their organizations is the fact that most of them are self-taught. Most do not start with the tools of the educated MBA. Or, if they have them, they quickly learn that many of those tools do not work very well in the quirky world of the entrepreneurial concern. Additionally, many entrepreneurs also discover that the tools and approaches that experts propose to them – specially about how to handle people – are useless because they are 'designed' for managers and do not fit the entrepreneurial personality.

At the core of the entrepreneur's motivation there is the desire to express himself and control his destiny, to be himself, to be his own boss, to create his own child. That impulse runs against following the advice of others. As a consequence, the self-taught entrepreneur often finds himself with his hands, heart and mind full of the simultaneous jobs of learning, nurturing and growing his firm. This leaves him with very little time and almost no energy to nurture his family.

☞ Special problems for the family business

Family firms are not easy places in which to work. They are difficult for family members but also for non-family employees. Creating a family firm means accepting one of the highest risks a person may take in life, because it involves mixing at the deepest level professional and private life and, consequently, risking failure in both. Many family firms are Greek tragedies in progress or just waiting to happen. The main victims are the family members, but everybody, including non-family employees, is profoundly affected when things go wrong. Even under normal circumstances the life of the non-family employee can be particularly stressful. S/he has to deal not only with functional business problems but also with all the complex psychological problems involved in working in a family firm.

In his classical article 'Real Work' – *Harvard Business Review* (January-February 1989) Abraham Zaleznik established a distinction between 'real work' and 'psychopolitics' in organizations. And he argued for the need to focus on real work and avoid the dysfunctional distractions of psychopolitics. In the family firm psychopolitical problems are magnified to an extraordinary degree, and the organization may die or suffer enormous damage unless its members are able to recognize these problems and deal with them effectively.

Conclusion

Entrepreneurs are rarely highly introspective people fascinated by psychological problems. This does not mean that they may not be psychologically intuitive and skillful under normal circumstances. But when important emotional or relational problems develop in their firms they rarely have the analytical tools or the necessary skills to handle them.

Those who are healthy or wise enough may realize that they need help and be willing to ask for it. If they are lucky, they may find a competent expert to help them, but, unfortunately, these wiser entrepreneurs are rare.

Being oriented towards action and control, top executives in general, and entrepreneurs in particular, are highly reluctant to depend on others and ask for help. Some are reluctantly willing to ask for technical help with finance or production problems. Asking for psychological help is much more difficult for them. They are, understandably, afraid of opening that Pandora's box.

And, yet, these men and women who decide one day to create their own firms or to get involved in the complex adventure of building a family firm, should be warned from the start that one day they are likely to need help in dealing with the specially difficult human problems which are typical of these firms. They also need to be aware that failure to ask for help may lead to massive failure in both their professional and private lives. ∎

The fertility decline in most European countries is a deeply worrying trend. Whether this trend is due to increasing selfishness and materialism or to economic insecurity and whether it may be reversible are fascinating questions. But the trend itself is extremely dangerous.

Some worrying facts

Hopeful signs exist. There are, for example, indications that in Scandinavian countries the fertility rate is again climbing.

Some hopeful signs

When one visits families or watches them in their homes or in the streets, we discover with pleasure that men are much more deeply involved in raising their children today than they were only a few years ago.

Companies which have introduced family friendly policies report excellent results in reducing employee turnover and increasing productivity.

The road is long. There are forces that will help and others that will hinder progress. But the effort to help men and women in our society to fulfil themselves at work and to excel in their private lives is worth continuing.

The future

It would be wrong, however, to expect others – the State, the company I work for, my boss – to take care of this issue for me. At the end it is each individual who has to assume the main responsibility to achieve his/her own goals as a human being and to be consistent with the values he/she professes to have. ∎

Re-inventing Germany's *Mittelstand*

Daniel Muzyka and **Hans Breuninger** report how some of Germany's famed *Mittelstand* companies are rediscovering the spirit of entrepreneurialism.

West Germany's economic landscape is populated by *Mittelstand* companies, businesses that belong in the small and medium-sized sector. Three-quarters are family owned and a large percentage are manufacturing-based. Many *Mittelstand* companies started their existence around the turn of the last century while others were founded after the Second World War. There can be no doubt that since the war, *Mittelstand* companies have been a major engine for German industrial growth and played a substantial part in the economic boom that took place in the 1950s and 1960s.

They have succeeded in capturing opportunities on a regular basis, not only within Germany but also in the European Community and on a wider global scale. The label 'Made in West Germany' came to stand for first-class technology, high-quality craftsmanship and was recognized world-wide. In the 1990s, the *Mittelstand* share of world markets was between 70 and 90 per cent. It was often enough to guarantee a good share of export markets without a great marketing and sales effort and contributed largely to the famous German trade surplus.

Although within recent years in Germany *Mittelstand* companies still represent DM50bn in exports, many of these companies have begun to show signs of 'age': outdated organizational structures; outdated management models; slow and costly product development processes; lack of innovation; little creation of value-added. Another difficulty is that the new generation no longer appears to care for the family heirloom and even wants to divest itself of it. The Institut für Mittelstandsforschung in Bonn estimates that by the year 2000, some 300,000 family owned *Mittelstand* companies will be looking for new owners.

We believe that the key question for these companies is how to become entrepreneurial again in their business processes – how to regain and maintain their capacity to identify and capture opportunity in a flexible and continuous way.

The first phase of our study involved the selection of a series of companies that appeared to have been successful in changing, at least to a degree, to a more entrepreneurial, successful, value-creating organization. What we observed is that many of the changes that had seemingly taken place within the organizations over the last five to ten years had come about by way of a major entrepreneurial transformation.

We wanted to understand the nature of this transformation and the models to which they have been transforming. We were interested in researching two major questions:

● What is the nature of the opportunity-driven, self-sustaining management model evolving within German *Mittelstand* companies?

● What is the nature of the transformation that was required from traditional *Mittelstand* management practices so that this new management model could be implemented?

Our intention was to get as large a cross-section of the German industrial sample as possible while including the service sector. We finally decided on the following companies: MHZ (Mechanischer Hachtelzug) (windows and furnishings); Kolb & Schüle AG (textiles); Binder Vacuum Technic (vacuum cleaners); Golding GmbH (costume and fine jewellery); Trinkaus & Burkhardt (private bank).* All are typical *Mittelstand* companies that are also active in the international markets, exporting their goods or services. With the support of these companies, we developed research cases to understand and chart the development and transformation processes they had undergone. Interviews were arranged with executives and management. The questions asked tried to explore the state of the companies concerned before the changes occurred and what happened afterwards; what triggered those changes and who and what was the major force driving them.

Our research resulted in 12 basic findings, which will be discussed below under four basic themes:

● *Performance focus*: performance/operational goals
● *Strategic orientation*: opportunity orientation, growth and renewal imperative, value innovation
● *Organizational system*: networking systems, transformational approach, pan-technical orientation, information architecture
● *Operational system*: rationalized value chain, extended supply chain, balanced growth and profit measurement.

In attempting to become more entrepreneurial and innovative, the companies had to make adjustments in objectives, structure, processes and behavior. Creating self-sustaining organizations required re-engineering and re-orienting multiple elements in the business systems, including issues across all functions.

The performance focus

A first observation about these companies was the pervasive understanding of the need for an overall strong performance. This was accomplished, in part, by improving the perspective and the goals of the organization. Performance at an organizational, team and individual level became the name of the game in these companies. All three were fairly evident and shared. A further accomplishment was a more open communication of the actual company performance. These organizations have opened accountability for, and increased the profile and awareness of, overall organizational performance. Performance information is more obvious than it has been historically.

The second point involved the question of 'who knows about the goals in the organization and what they are?' In these innovative organizations virtually everyone had understood not only the goals for their own organizational unit but also the goals for the whole of the company. Management had recognized that if people do not know where they are going they will choose any road.

Strategic orientation

The strategic orientation of these companies proved slightly different from the traditional enterprise in the following aspects.

Traditional companies worry about resources, about assets, the balance sheet, and the organizational funds. The strategic orientation in the companies in our sample was directed largely toward identifying and capturing opportunity. The selection of opportunity was clearly based on the skills and abilities of the organizations as well as on the realization that opportunity would lead the organization in required new directions.

This more active search for opportunities was combined with a growth imperative; growth became a central strategic theme. However, this did not have to mean growth for the sake of growth. In the case of the researched organizations, there was a focus on growth with the primary intent to ensure a major renewal of product lines and business.

One of the most striking observations from the study was the focus on value innovation within the organizations. Traditionally, many of the companies had produced and sold products based on their expertise and technology (that is, 'if we believe it is better, then the market should accept it as better because it incorporates our improved technology').

The companies all appeared to have an iterative model of creating and introducing new products and services that involved the search for a combination of real customer need and the skills and abilities the company could bring to bear in order to create value for both parties. Innovation became ultimately a value-based, not technologically based process.

One of the consequences was that this drove the development of products through successive contacts with the customer before product introduction. This also prompted the companies to seek out market niches and to grow through the exploitation of successive niche opportunities. The companies were re-oriented to the pursuit of market-based opportunities. They acquired a more pervasive understanding of a need to capture opportunity for both renewal and growth and a more public awareness (within the companies) of the need to focus on opportunity at all levels.

The organizational system

Another finding was that communication and knowledge transfer appear to be much more networked in recent years in these companies, creating a 'networked' architecture and its processes in the organization. One of the great enemies of innovation in European companies today is the existence of the so-called 'silo problem' where information and decisions must go up the organization, go over and hopefully come back down again so that a problem can be solved. The companies researched seemed to have found a partial solution. They work in teams, in project groups and new problems or challenges are worked on horizontally across the whole company.

While networking, systems of networks and so on are fashionable concepts, the question remains whether they are an efficient way to communicate and operate in organizations. We found that while they may not be 100 per cent efficient, in each of these organizations it could be seen that teams consisting of people from different functions were able to work together and to process innovations.

The leadership in these organizations worked aggressively to improve communication and knowledge transfer. In some cases, developers or product managers, who rarely, if ever, saw a customer, were sent out to conduct market research with end-users. The main improvement, though, was in creating new business products and services through a co-operative, pan-technical approach.

No longer could individuals be simply secure in, or proud of, their technical knowledge; they had to apply it with others to create value.

The notion of change was also embedded in these organizations: change as the status quo. Most of these organizations had gone through a recent transformation, trying to move the organization from one style of management to another. Typically, at the outset of a transformation the present model is defined and a future one is portrayed. Between the two there is often an amorphous mass, defined as transformation or a corporate change process.

The companies in our sample proceeded differently. They took the mass in the middle, where everything was still unsolved, and taught people how everyone of them could play a part in the change process. Therefore, it never became a question of 'earlier/later' or 'before/after' but of companies that continued to innovate, that continuously renewed themselves and that constantly profited from this mass.

Based on their competence and expertise gained, they pursued the change process, which was often driven around the opportunity being pursued at a particular time. In the end, transformation on a fluid (as required but unplanned) basis became a way of life. Any impact on personnel seemed to have been minimized by circumventing job cuts and focusing on re-orienting and re-training people.

In several cases, the organizations in our research displayed an approach to developing opportunity and innovating products that was significantly more 'cross technology' and cross-functional (or cross skills) than can be found in other companies of their size. They exercised a 'pan-technological' approach and found new opportunities in mapping several skills and technologies together with customer needs. A lot of the products and product ideas that these companies have developed have come from the sharing of technical knowledge – not from better solutions for a technology.

A fundamental support of the performance of these organizations came, however, from an increased knowledge and a better management information architecture within the organization. (It should be said that the information architecture not only included hardware-based solutions but also better organizational processes to collect, analyze and disseminate knowledge.)

Information in these organizations is widely available. There is an open information architecture that permits the companies to collect, disseminate and leverage information in a competitive fashion.

This also had an impact on the nature of control. The broad availability of information on performance and reaction to market situations made operational control more subtle. Because of greater visibility and transparency, individuals were prone to control their own actions.

Information literally created power for these organizations. In some cases, it made them the equal of much larger competing organizations. In most cases, the availability of 'facts', rather than of opinions or beliefs, helped them to improve decision-making, to act more quickly and enhance cross-technical/cross-functional co-operation.

The organizations had taken broad steps to rationalize their value chain in focusing on those activities that were the key to future growth potential and **Operational system**

© FT Pictures

Bayer's training workshop in 1901: Bayer became a giant company but the medium-sized 'Mittelstand' sector has been the engine of the German economy

return. They had retreated from a need to supervise all value-added steps. Instead they exercised only a nominal control over quality or technology.

This did not require downsizing but meant a review of their value chains and a greater refocusing on activities that would provide them with future growth potential and, for the most part, maximum return. In many cases, they abandoned the concept of producing everything in-house. This led to higher economic returns. They actively addressed the question 'where do we add value?' and focused operations on the areas that were identified.

In order to open up the value chain, even in terms of medium-sized players, the companies established strong supplier relationships, especially across borders. They sought out cost- and value-effective partners outside Germany while retaining either major value-added processes nationally or the possibility and capacity to undertake them in Germany if necessary.

Despite their size, the companies tried to achieve lower levels of cost by moving at least some of the production out of high cost areas, that is Germany, and found similar production quality elsewhere if they provided appropriate controls. In many cases, this followed actively sought information and contacts with suppliers throughout the world.

The organizations measured their operational performance with a more balanced view of success. They tended to measure both the efficiency of operations (the traditional measure) and the effectiveness of operations (can they achieve challenging goals?).

Even if they were worried about 'enjoying profits at the expense of growth', it was interesting to see that these organizations seemingly measured their operational performance by actively balancing growth and profitability. It left them with asking themselves whether they were sacrificing growth or renewal possibilities for the sake of short-term profit.

The conclusions to be drawn are that German *Mittelstand* companies must be smarter and more adaptive to capture the opportunities. 'More of the same' – better or improved technology, harder work within the same organizational structures and so on – will not suffice.

Part of the adaptation may be a recognition that significant parts of production cannot be economically undertaken within Germany. Lower cost of transportation, differential national development of skills and significantly lower labor costs have had their impact. For many middle companies to be active players tomorrow, they may have to decide whether 'Made in Germany' is still an economic viability.

However, these companies have also made the point that active co-ordination, key development and utilization of core technologies, and active discovery of opportunities can add up to creating a significant value-added role for German companies. ∎

*A full version of this article, 'The Secret of New Growth in Old German *Mittelstand* Companies' by Daniel F. Muzyka, Hans A. Breuninger and Gerda Rossell, was published in the *European Journal of Management* in April 1997. Telephone 01865 201529. Fax 01865 251960.

✪ CASE STUDY

Unlocking the door to self-finance

*In the second part of a two-part case study **Neil Churchill** and **John Mullins** explain how the MIFROG model can be used to compare performance and forecast cash needs.*

The first part of this article, which appeared on p.232, dealt with cash inflows and outflows over the operating cash cycle. But while the growth rate in an operating cycle is important, most managers think in terms of growth per year. Annualizing the MIFROG (the maximum internally financiable rate of growth) for different products or markets, or comparing MIFROGs for different companies, requires a common time period for the analysis.

It is apparent that if M&C, the fictitious company being used as an example, can grow at 7.47 per cent in 170 days, it should grow more in 365 days. Thus we multiply the MIFROG in a single cycle by the length of the year divided by 170 days. This gives us an annual MIFROG of 16.04 per cent. This means that if M&C grows at a rate slower than 16.04 per cent, the company will produce more cash from sales than its growth requires. On the other hand, if M&C grows faster than its MIFROG, it will need to raise cash from external sources. Thus the MIFROG rate provides a tool for forecasting cash needs.

The levers that control the cash for growth

We can see from the M&C example that the factors that influence the MIFROG are, first, the amount of cash it takes to produce a unit of sales, second, the duration of each of these cash flows and, third, the amount of cash the resulting unit of sales brings to the company.

Profit & loss:	Present situation	With profit improvement	With shortened durations	Duration & profit impr.
sales	100.0%	100.0%	100.0%	100.0%
cost of sales	60.0%	59.0%	60.0%	59.0%
operating expenses	35.0%	34.5%	35.0%	34.5%
profit	**5.0%**	**6.5%**	**5.0%**	**6.5%**

Duration (days):				
inventory	80	80	76	76
A/R	90	90	84	84
OCC	**170**	**170**	**160**	**160**
A/P	30	30	30	30
OCC	**140**	**140**	**130**	**130**
operating expenses	85	85	80	80

Operating cash cycle for self-financeable growth				
cost of sales	$0.600 x 140/170 = $0.494	$0.590 x 140/170 = $0.486	$0.600 x 130/160 = $0.488	$0.590 x 130/160 = $0.479
operations	$0.350 x 85/170 = $0.175	$0.345 x 85/170 = $0.173	$0.350 x 80/160 = $0.175	$0.345 x 80/160 = $0.173
cash-days consumed	**$0.669**	**$0.658**	**$0.663**	**$0.652**
cash produced	$0.050	$0.065	$0.050	$0.065
old sales needed to produce a new sale	$13.382	$10.129	$13.250	$10.029
OCC SFG	7.47%	9.87%	7.55%	9.97%
Annualized SFG	7.47% x 365/170 = **16.04%**	9.87% x 365/170 = **21.20%**	7.55% x 365/160 = **17.22%**	9.97% x 365/160 = **22.75%**

Figure 1: M&C Company; levers to control cash available for growth

If management can decrease the amount of cash needed, decrease the duration that the cash remains out or increase the cash produced by a unit of sales, the MIFROG increases. These actions are illustrated in Figure 1 along with the original situation, an annualized MIFROG of 16.04 per cent.

Lever 1: decrease the amount of cash required
Let us assume that management can decrease the cost of goods sold by one percentage point and the cost of operations by half a percentage point as shown in Figure 1. The cash required to finance a sale decreases from $0.669 to $0.658, a savings of $0.011 in each operating cash cycle (OCC). If the cash generated by the sale had remained the same – $0.05 – due to an equal price decrease, *old sales needed to produce a new sale* would have been $13.16, the OCC self-financed MIFROG rate would have risen to 7.60 per cent, and the annual MIFROG to 16.32 per cent. Not a large increase. Fortunately for the company this did not happen. It left its prices the same and cash increased to $0.065 per dollar of sales.

Lever 2: increase the amount of cash produced
With sales producing $0.065 cash per dollar, the company only needs $10.129 of *old sales* to produce a dollar of *new sales* (Figure 1), the OCC self-financed MIFROG rate rises to 9.87 per cent and the annual MIFROG to 21.2 per cent. While the $0.015 increase in *cash produced* amounts to 30 per cent, the *cash required* is only $0.011 or only 1.64 per cent. Note the power of the profit margin. This is why software companies, once their products are developed, can grow so fast. They charge $150 to $300 for a

product whose cost of sales is less than $20. If the company had just raised its prices by $0.015 and left the cash requirements alone, it would have had an OCC SFG rate of 9.72 per cent and an annualized SFG of 20.86 per cent – an almost identical result.

Lever 3: decrease the duration of the cash flows

The third lever is shown in the last two tables in Figure 1 and is applied to both the initial and the improved cash consumed scenarios. Four days (5 per cent) are taken off the inventory holding period and six days (6.67 per cent) taken off the accounts receivable collection period.

The result is an OCC of 160 days instead of 170 days, which produces increased OCC and annualized MIFROG rates of 7.55 per cent and 17.22 per cent respectively for the 'present profit' situation and 9.97 per cent and 22.75 per cent for the 'improved profit' situation, since there is nothing to prevent management from pulling all three levers at the same time. This is an increase of over 40 per cent in the company's growth rate without external capital.

We have, until now, considered only a simplified situation in which the OCC **MIFROG and** encompasses all the cash flows necessary to finance a dollar of sales. However, most **multi-period** companies have to add physical capacity from time to time, spend money on R&D due to **cash flows** market or technological trends or react to competition that may require increased marketing programs that span multiple periods. Cash needed for such investments, be they for plant and equipment, R&D or other multi-period purposes, must be planned for.

Where multi-period cash flows exist, two changes must be made. The first involves the cash produced by a sale. The second involves apportioning the cash required to buy the capital equipment, to finance the marketing programs or support R&D over the OCCs benefiting from these expenditures.

Let's change the M&C Company into a manufacturing company by adding some machinery and equipment in the amount of $60,000 per $100,000 dollars of sales and separating cost of sales into materials and labor (*see* Figure 2). If this equipment has a 10-year life, then its cash component must be included in the required cash calculation. This is $0.06 per year or $.0279 in the OCC of 170 days. Adding this to the cash consumed by operations we get a total of $0.6853 that must be produced by sales in an OCC and a MIFROG of 7.30 per cent which annualizes to a MIFROG of 15.67 per cent.

The formula

The calculation of the MIFROG can be put into a formula as shown in Figure 3.

Calculations, comments and caveats

The cash components and their lengths

The length of the OCC is that of the longest cash component required to produce a unit of sales. In the examples above we have talked only of two such flows within the OCC: cost of goods sold and operating expenses.

There can be others extending over different periods such as pre-payment of television advertising 'spots', letters of credit in advance of inventory delivery and the like. The OCC is the longest of all the cycles.

Profit & loss		**Duration (days)**	
sales	100%	inventory	80
material cost of goods sold	40%	A/R	90
labor cost of goods sold	20%	**OCC**	**170**
operating expenses	35%	A/P	30
cash operating expenses	95%	**cost of sales**	**140**
profit excluding depreciation	**5%**	operating expenses	85

Capital equipment	
present capital equipment per $100,000 of sales	$60,000
present capital equipment per $1 of sales	$0.60
depreciable (and expected) life	10 years
depreciation per sales dollar per year	$0.060
depreciation per sales dollar per OCC	$0.0279

Operating cash cycle for self-financeable growth	
material cost of sales	$0.400 x 140/170 = $0.3294
labor cost of sales	$0.200 x @ = $0.1529
operations	$0.350 x 85/170 = $0.1750
cash replacement of fixed assets	$0.06 x 85/170 = $0.0279
cash required in an operating cycle	**$0.6853**
cash produced	$0.0500
old sales needed to produce a new sale	$0.685 / $0.050 = $13.706
OCC SFG	7.30%
Annualized SFG	**7.30% x 365/170 = 15.67%**

@ Labor costs are incurred equally over the first 80 days of work. If each 10 day period's costs are multiplied by the days remaining to cash collection, in the same manner as operating expense was calculated in Figure 3 in the first part of this article (p. 234), and the total then divided by 170 days, the resulting average cash flow out for manufacturing labor is $0.15294.

Figure 2: M&C manufacturing

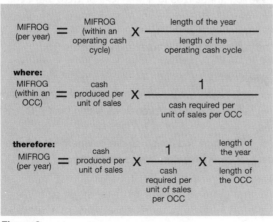

Figure 3

Consider the example where there are four cash component flows as follows:

Letter of credit for materials to be shipped to company	45 days
Inventory after receipt	50 days
Account receivable	60 days
Prepaid TV advertising	90 days

In this example, the longest cash-to-cash flow is that of cost of sales. It is the sum of the letter of credit, the inventory, and the accounts receivable – 45 + 50 + 60, or 155 days since the TV advertising was paid 90 days before the show that produced the accounts receivable and the letter of credit went out 95 days before the sales were made.

If, however, the advertising expense had to be paid 120 days in advance, then the OCC would be the sum of the 120 days of advertising and the accounts receivable of 60 days producing a 180 day OCC.

Given the 90-day pre-payment of advertising, the days outstanding of each cash flow is as follows:

Letter of credit cash	155 days
Inventory cash over the letter of credit payment	110 days
Prepaid advertising	150 days
Administrative expenses	155/2 days

Comments

The MIFROG rate is a powerful tool for bringing together operating management considerations that usually focus on the profit and loss statement and financial management considerations, which in turn focus on the balance sheet. MIFROG can be calculated for subsidiaries, product lines and product/market segments. It can be based on past averages or on planned, future performance. Thus it can provide unique insights into the consequences of management decisions.

Caveats

MIFROG is, however, based upon aggregated cash flows grouped together over different periods of time. It is close, but not always the same as the steady-state growth based upon a set of complex interacting factors. For situations where an exact number is needed, a spreadsheet approach is usually more accurate. MIFROG provides understanding for managing; the spreadsheet provides the accuracy needed to show a cash plan to a financial source. Both should be well-worn tools in your planning kit. ■

8

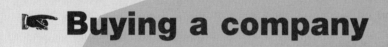 **Buying a company**

Contents

Contributors

Mike Wright is Professor of Financial Studies, Director of the Center for Management Buy-out Research (CMBOR) at the University of Nottingham and Director of Zeton Ltd. His research interests include management buy-outs, venture capital, privatization and entrepreneurship.

Ken Robbie is Senior Research Fellow at CMBOR, University of Nottingham. His research interests include management buy-ins, venture capital and entrepreneurship.

Robert Smith is Chief Executive of Deutsche Morgan Grenfell Asset Management.

Michael Hay is Associate Professor of Strategic and International Management at London Business School and Director of the Foundation for Entrepreneurial Management.

Robert M. Johnson is a lecturer in entrepreneurship at London Business School. Previously he was a successful entrepreneur in both the US and UK.

Patrick Dunne is responsible for 3i's MBI and Independent Director Programs. In the past five years he has probably been best known for pioneering the BIMBO concept in the UK. He is the author of *Running Board Meetings*, to be published in April 1997 by Kogan Page.

Michael Ullman is an entrepreneur, businessman and Visiting Lecturer in Entrepreneurship at INSEAD, Fontainebleau.

Introduction

Part 8 examines a different route to ownership – that of buying a
company. We look at the growing phenomena of the management
buyout and the management buy-in, and explore the costs, rewards and
risks from the perspective of both management and other investors. We
ask what is especially attractive about this form of investment from the
perspective of the investor and what are the criteria that they apply when
deciding to invest. Having bought the business, we look at the issues
that face the new owners as they attempt to turn the company round.

Entrepreneurial spirit propels buy-outs

Mike Wright and **Ken Robbie** provide an introduction to the worlds of MBOs, MBIs and BIMBOs.

Since 1980 buy-outs have developed into an extremely important facet of industrial organization. There are some 1,000 buy-outs a year in Europe, with 600 of those in the UK where they account for over half the number of take-over transactions (*see* Figures 1, 2 and 3).

Buy-out opportunities come in several forms. The majority are management buy-outs (MBOs) and involve the acquisition by incumbent management of the business where they are employed. Typically the purchase price is met by a small amount of their own funds (3.2 per cent on average) and the rest from a mix of venture capital and bank debt. Management buy-ins (MBIs) are a similar form of transaction but differ in that the entrepreneurs leading the transaction come from outside the company. The BIMBO is a hybrid form involving both existing and new management.

The late 1990s also saw the developments of IBOs (investor buy-outs) where venture capital groups initiate and lead transactions, with management playing a marginal role. Other variants include MEBOs, where management and employees both provide equity as in many of the more recent buy-outs of UK bus companies such as GM Buses North and GM Buses South.

Buy-outs are commonly but erroneously portrayed as short-lived, highly leveraged transactions (LBOs) led by leveraged buy-out associations that are little more than a disguised form of asset stripping. This view typically associates the gains from buy-outs as emanating from financial engineering rather than anything to do with entrepreneurship.

Even in the US, which is usually associated with mega-LBO deals, there are large numbers of more modestly sized and less highly geared management buy-outs. Although UK and European buy-outs do involve high leverage in their financial structures and a high emphasis on cash flow generation, they also demonstrate significant entrepreneurial actions.

Figure 1: Number of UK buy-outs and buy-ins

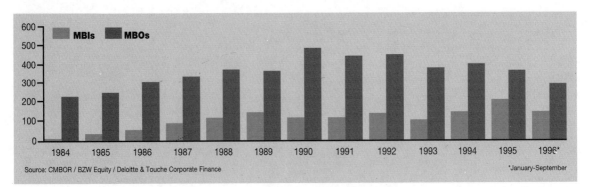

Source: CMBOR / BZW Equity / Deloitte & Touche Corporate Finance

*January-September

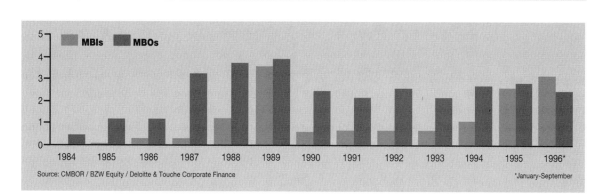

Source: CMBOR / BZW Equity / Deloitte & Touche Corporate Finance

*January-September

Direct equity ownership has given a significant impetus to the development of entrepreneurship, which fits in with the increasing recognition that entrepreneurship can involve the purchase of an existing company as well as the creation of a new one. Moreover, entrepreneurial actions can involve both major restructuring of existing operations as well as the development of innovations.

The leading individuals in MBOs and MBIs display similar characteriztics to those of entrepreneurs generally. From our research, the incentive of having equity in the business is the single most important motivating factor for management at the time of the transaction.

Moreover, managers attribute the most important reasons for improvements in post buy-out performance to their increased control in running the business, their direct equity ownership and the opportunity to develop their own strategy.

Crucially, this stimulus to entrepreneurial action by managers is bolstered by the monitoring and control devices exercised by venture capitalists and banks through detailed reporting requirements, board representation and the operation of debt covenants as well as the commitment to service outside sources of funds.

In buy-outs that arise on divestments from larger groups and from the privatization of state enterprises in particular, such mechanisms are held to reduce agency costs problems arising from the divorce between ownership and control in the former parents.

What characterizes the development of buy-outs over the last 15 years is the adaptability of the concept and the diversity of situations to which it may be applied. This is seen in the patterns of development of large and small deals,

Figure 2: Value of UK buy-outs and buy-ins

Figure 3: MBOs and MBIs as percentage of takeover activity

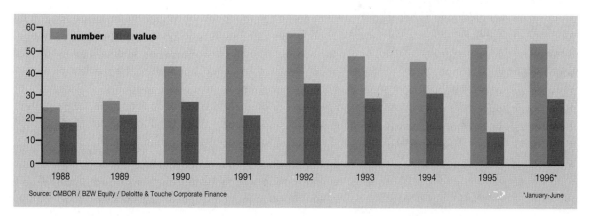

Source: CMBOR / BZW Equity / Deloitte & Touche Corporate Finance

*January-June

differences between buy-outs and buy-ins, and changes in the sources of transactions.

Sources of buy-outs

Internationally, the two most common sources of buy-out opportunities are divestments of parts of larger groups and family companies facing succession problems.

Corporate groups may seek to sell subsidiaries as part of a planned strategic disposal program or more forced reorganization in the face of parental financial problems. Public companies have, however, increasingly sought to dispose of subsidiaries through an auction process, partly in order to satisfy shareholder pressure for value maximization.

Though divisional management may still need to be involved in the disposal process, concerns that managers may in the past have acquired companies at highly advantageous prices mean that is it no longer common for them to be the preferred bidder, especially for larger deals.

For larger disposals, several venture capital companies may be bidding against each other to complete an IBO. Increased competitive conditions are placing pressures on venture capitalists to identify investments that can generate attractive enough returns for the fund providers. In order to reduce the potential risks involved, venture capitalists either retain existing management to run the company with an equity stake or, as in a buy-in, bring in experienced management to do so.

Privately held companies have become an increasingly important source of buy-outs in recent years. In 1986 only a fifth of buy-outs in the UK came from this source; a decade later, privately held family companies accounted for a record two-fifths of the market with the actual annual number of deals completed being two-and-a-half times greater (*see* Figure 4).

Figure 4: Sources of management buy-outs

While private deals are smaller on average than divestment buy-outs, recent years have seen large transactions such as The Sweater Shop. Driving this development has been the greater recognition by family vendors of the viability of such deals, their attractiveness for maintaining the independent identity of their business, tax implications and greater attention by intermediaries and financiers to this segment of the market.

The growing influence of second-time and serial entrepreneurs and the need for fixed-life venture capital funds to recycle investee companies will help to bolster the number of buy-outs and buy-ins involving private companies.

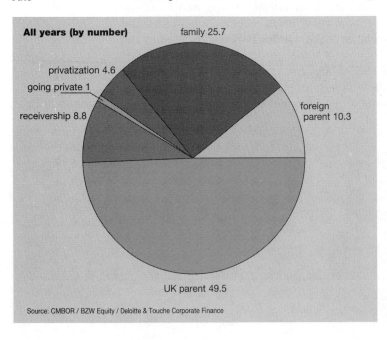

All years (by number)

family 25.7
privatization 4.6
going private 1
receivership 8.8
foreign parent 10.3
UK parent 49.5

Source: CMBOR / BZW Equity / Deloitte & Touche Corporate Finance

In recessionary periods buy-outs can play a major part in restructuring failed or **Enhance** failing businesses and, in an environment of generally weakened corporate **performance** performance, often represent the only viable purchasers when parents wish to dispose of subsidiaries. But such transactions need to be viable in a market economy. Increasingly, they involve profitable subsidiaries of failed groups where managers may have been prevented from undertaking entrepreneurial acts because of the financial constraints imposed by the failing parent.

Buy-outs are one of the most common forms of privatization, offering opportunities for enhancing the performance of parts of the public sector, widening employee ownership and giving managers and employees incentives to make best use of their expertise in particular sectors. By 1996 there had been over 200 such deals, more than four times the number of flotations of privatized companies.

Despite traditional management buy-outs coming under pressure from vendors, especially for larger divestment deals, buy-outs initiated by internal management will continue to remain attractive for smaller disposals as they are a cost-effective way for vendors to realize attractive prices for businesses where individual management may be particularly important for the stability of the business.

There are important notes of caution for any management wishing to initiate an opportunity to buy-out. Great care is needed in the early stages to ensure that confidential information is not disclosed to outside parties (advisers and prospective financiers) without the vendor's permission. Failure to negotiate this initial hurdle is likely to lead not only to the failure of the buy-out to get off the ground but also the instant dismissal of the management. Professional advisers have an important role to play in these circumstances in placing a buffer between management and the vendor.

It is also important for management to ask themselves searching questions about their commitment and ability to complete a buy-out and subsequently make it work. Do managers genuinely want to trade the (increasingly relative) security and demands of a larger organization for the very different demands of a buy-out? Will good line managers and divisional directors make the successful transition into good owner-managers? Advisers and prospective financiers will also want to obtain positive answers to these questions.

Most studies of post buy-out performance changes have concerned the short term **Wealth creation** after the transaction and generally confirm substantial improvements in profitability, cash flow and productivity measures between one year prior to buy-out and two or three years subsequent to it. Improvements in working capital management, particularly credit management, and productivity are important sources of improved performance.

Although experience in the US LBO market has indicated that much of the gain in buy-out transactions may be a result of downsizing, other US research, as well as our own UK research, points to the importance of innovative behavior by management teams. Significant increases in new product development are found to occur post buy-out, especially in smaller venture-backed transactions, which the entrepreneurs concerned consider would not otherwise have happened.

Our UK study showed that asset sales were generally low and were typically offset by new capital investment, particularly in plant and equipment. Our recent research shows that over years three to five after the change in ownership, buy-outs on average perform significantly better than comparable non-buy-outs.

The performance of management buy-ins has, however, been generally less strong, though they have typically involved more extensive restructuring. Coming from outside with less detailed knowledge of the business, it has often proved more difficult than expected for management and investors to achieve enhanced short-term profitability.

Often, for this reason, pure management buy-ins are replaced by hybrid buy-in/management buy-outs (BIMBOs) that combine the advantages of insiders' skills and knowledge and the outsider's entrepreneurial dynamism.

Exits, rates of return and millionaires

There is considerable debate about whether buy-outs are a long or short term form of organization.

Research in both the US and Europe shows that buy-outs have a heterogeneous life cycle – some last only a short time while others retain the buy-out form for long periods. While about half of larger buy-outs are sold or floated within four years, the majority last well in excess of seven years.

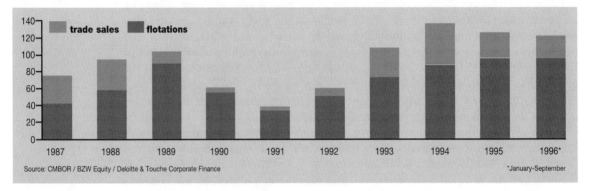

Source: CMBOR / BZW Equity / Deloitte & Touche Corporate Finance
*January-September

Figure 5: UK buy-out and buy-in exits

The principal factors influencing the longevity of a buy-out relate to the objectives and needs of the parties involved – owner-managers, financiers and the company itself. The extent and form of exit from buy-outs and buy-ins will always be influenced, at least to some degree, by the cyclical nature of stock and take-over market conditions.

There are also clear pressures leading to exit by means of a secondary buy-out or buy-in involving either a new set of managers from outside or the secondary layer from inside the company. In some cases these may involve inter-institutional deals and be motivated by circumstances where the first buy-out was backed by a venture capital company relying on a closed-end fund that needs to exit within a limited life span.

This exit route tends to involve relatively small companies in very specific niche markets, which may therefore not be attractive to strategic buyers or be feasible candidates for a stock market flotation. In some markets, such as France, secondary deals involving inter-institutional sales may be important means of making an exit for the institutions where incumbent management have significant majority ownership and wish to remain independent.

☞ The secondary buy-out

In 1986 ATS Technirent, a Berkshire-based computer equipment rental company, was sold to its management in a £3.5m buy-out from Micro Business Systems. The transaction was led by 3i with CVC Capital Partners and Kleinwort Benson Development Capital also participating.

ATS had been set up in 1981 by the now-defunct PC distribution business MBS. The first two years of the buy-out proved to be extremely difficult, and in October 1988 the MD was replaced by Bob Sutcliffe, the Finance Director. During this period, however, an important relationship had been established with Sun Microsystems and a new Sales and Marketing Director appointed. As a result of these early troubles, the company made a large write-off of the value of its rental stock in 1987, effectively preventing the prospect for paying future dividends.

Initially specializing in the rental of test and emulation equipment in the electronics industry, following the first buy-out, it was reshaped into a highly successful short-term workstation rental business. The company at the time of the second buy-out had 500 workstations and 400 PCs, with customers ranging from financial institutions to software developers.

By 1993 the company had increased its turnover to £8.6m (compared with £2.8m in 1987), with pretax profits of £2.2m (£0.1m in 1987), a workforce of 50 and was growing rapidly. Following an unsolicited trade offer to buy the company, management and the venture capital backer decided to reject the first offer and to pursue other offers. Management were made aware of the need for an exit, given the closed-end nature of one of the venture backers' funds. Bob Sutcliffe felt that early attempts to stage a second management buy-out were aggressively discouraged despite the goodwill displayed by the management team. After using intermediaries to find a buyer, it became apparent that the venture capital backers could not get the valuation they wanted from a trade sale. Management were then told that if they could raise the agreed finance, the venture capital backers were prepared to exit through a second buy-out. With a substantial uplift in the value of the business an IRR in the mid-1930s was achieved.

Advised by Deloitte & Touche Corporate Finance, Bob Sutcliffe, the Managing Director and Dave Shearer, Sales Director, virtually doubled their holding in the company to 25.5 per cent in a £11.2m transaction led by BancBoston Capital. Management also had a returns-based ratchet which could significantly increase their share holding. 3i retained their shareholding and

NatWest Ventures also became shareholders.

While the first buy-out had clearly demonstrated Bob Sutcliffe's ability to identify new markets and exploit them profitably, the second buy-out also involved management's awareness of both organic and acquisition growth opportunities as well as the venture capital backers' preparedness to fund major developments. BancBoston Capital (whose interest in the company had been increased through the relationship with Sun, one of their US clients) recognized the need for making money available for strategic acquisitions. As part of ATS's 'buy and build' strategy, the company acquired Show Presentation Services, a leading provider of audio-visual presentation equipment to production houses in the corporate market, in September 1995. The £7.3m transaction involving both additional venture capital and bank facilities increased group turnover by £4.6m. During 1996 this acquisition's premises have been doubled in size, employment has increased by ten and profits have risen from £1.75m to £2.2m.

Further major developments in 1996 have included the purchase in November of another company, Hire IT, a PC rental company with 20 employees. The first European office has been opened in Munich in close liaison with Sun. ATS Technirent itself has moved into new premises to allow for both the larger group size and the new controls which are required. Associated with the latter a new Group Finance Director had been appointed at the end of 1995 to strengthen the management team.

At the time of the second buy-out, ATS had just started two important new developments – the renting of medical equipment and video-conferencing rental for events and trials. While initial growth was expected to come from these, they have taken longer to take off than expected. In contrast the Sun rental growth rate has been twice original expectations.

The first two years of the second buy-out have seen considerable development of the company and high and profitable growth. Management have found the industry knowledge of the lead venture capital firm particularly helpful. Inevitably the first half of 1997 is likely to involve consolidation of acquisitions, but an IPO of the company is possible during 1998. With rental now established as a means of outsourcing ownership of technology, Bob Sutcliffe is confident that the ATS Technirent group is well positioned to work closely and successfully with major corporates in this field in the years ahead. ■

Buy-out and especially buy-in entrepreneurs may not simply be 'one-shot' wonders who have taken advantage of a promising opportunity that has been presented to them. As the market further matures, an increasing number of entrepreneurs who have bought out or bought into companies are exiting and seeking to become involved in further deals, adding to the growing phenomenon of serial entrepreneurs.

Large numbers of buy-out entrepreneurs have become millionaires on the flotation of companies that they have previously bought out. In 1994 and 1995 the 78 buy-outs and buy-ins that floated created 130 millionaires from the 303 executive directors in post. Though there is some concern that flotations occur at the peak of the gains from buy-outs, those which have come to market tend on average to generate greater performance relative to the market. The Center for Management Buy-out Research's Index of buy-out stock prices showed a 134 per cent increase between the end of 1990 and the end of September 1996 compared with increases in the FTSE All Share and the Hoare Govett Small Companies Indexes of 88 per cent each over the same period.

Financing and structuring

Among key factors in the long-term success of individual buy-outs and buy-ins have been the initial pricing of the transaction and the financing structure.

Prices are influenced both by economic conditions and by the desire by sellers to maximize the sale price and avoid accusations by shareholders that assets have been sold too cheaply to insiders. A number of mechanisms, such as auctions, earn-outs, retained equity stakes and other non-embarrassment clauses, have been developed to deal with these issues.

The result, however, is the potential danger that, for investors and management, prices may become too high. It is thus necessary for management to keep clear in their minds during the negotiation stage that it may be better to walk away from a deal that is too highly priced rather than be carried away with misplaced enthusiasm to buy, whatever the cost.

Figure 6: Buy-out and buy-in deal structure

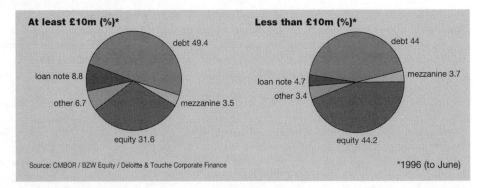

Buy-outs will typically be financed by a mixture of senior secured debt and a range of equity and quasi-equity instruments (*see* Figure 6). For larger buy-outs, especially when auctions and buoyant conditions mean that prices well in excess of the security value of assets have to be paid, subordinated (mezzanine) debt may be used.

Quasi-equity instruments, such as cumulative convertible participating preferred ordinary shares, are important both in ensuring the venture capitalist

☞ A buy-out followed by a buy-in

Brian Small and Simon Mallalieu, who completed the buy-in of LPK Upholstery in late 1995, both had experience of the buy-out market as they had been members of the team which had bought Kosset Carpets from the receivers of Coloroll in 1990. When Coloroll, which had bought Kosset in 1988, collapsed with debts of £400m in June 1990, the Kosset management approached the receivers to buy it. Although the acquisition value was £9.9m, total financing amounted to £15.6m. Small was Finance Director and Mallalieu Sales and Marketing Director.

At the time of the buy-out, Kosset was breaking even at the operating profit level after a two-year turnround from substantial losses.

Following the buy-out, Kosset acquired Crossley, Coloroll's other main carpet manufacturer for £5m; its Axminster manufacturing capacity was moved from Kidderminster to Bradford, making Kosset the largest single-site carpet manufacturer in the UK.

Despite the pressures of sharp raw material price increases following the invasion of Kuwait and the collapse of the company's largest customer, Lowndes Queensway, the company quickly returned to substantial operating profitability. Branding, a new pricing policy and a revised range of designs and products which were sold successfully to small independent retailers, played important parts in this progress. The famous Kosset cat, the company's logo which had been killed under the Coloroll management, was restored and, despite the recession, management resisted the temptation to move down market. The need to service the financial structure emphasized concentration on cash flow management. The need for control over manufacturing costs demanded particular commitment from the workforce. With union co-operation long established, working practices were modernized and a flexible and multi-skilled workforce created.

In 1993 and with the prospect of inevitable rationalization of the carpet industry, the company was sold to Shaw Industries Inc. of Georgia, who had been looking for acquisitions in the UK. Phildrew Ventures, the venture capital backer, had spread their investment in the company over three tranches. This investment, which totalled £8m, increased to over £15m, producing an Internal Rate of Return of 40 per cent.

Following the trade sale, the two entrepreneurs sought another opportunity. After two years on several projects, they were able to announce on 1 November 1995 that they had completed the management buy-in of LPK Upholstery, a privately owned Midlands furniture group specializing in upholstered furniture.

LPK Upholstery had been founded in 1979 and had developed into a £21m turnover group which includes the Dudley-based LPK Upholstery business and the Joynson Holland showwood furniture operation with manufacturing at High Wycombe.

The buy-in involved £6.8m of institutional equity arranged by BZW Private Equity and bank finance from Barclays. The equity backers, who also include Kleinwort Benson Development Capital, had been impressed by the two entrepreneurs when they had been first approached, and their successful track record in being involved throughout Kosset's turnround and buy-out period was an important consideration. Additionally they felt that LPK was a quality business, with a strong market position, excellent facilities and a reasonable size in home furnishings, a sector in which the two were experienced.

Mallalieu and Small were capable of giving the company new focus and impetus and taking growth opportunities which might not have been possible under the previous owners who left immediately after the sale. After an initial period of examining the company in detail with the ambitious and experienced management team they inherited, a series of actions have been taken which have helped turnover and profitability in the first year of the buy-in to grow substantially in line with the original plan.

Middle management has been strengthened, the product portfolio has been altered with new models introduced, the existing sites have been added to and reconfigured to increase capacity. There has been considerable investment in people, systems and distribution. Over the next year further major product developments are planned. Sales now exceed £25m and employment has risen from 350 to 400.

In the longer term the two entrepreneurs, who both have experience in much larger and quoted companies, intend to grow LPK, both organically and by acquisition, and take advantage of market opportunities as they arise. Their objective is flotation, with the intention of using this as a springboard for the development of a larger home furnishings group. ■

obtains a regular dividend and in putting pressure on managers to perform and/or seek to realize an investment in a timely fashion.

Venture capital backers will typically be looking for an IRR (internal rate of return) on their investment in the upper 20s per annum – slightly more for MBIs but less for large transactions. Bank lenders will be putting more emphasis on cash flow aspects and less on asset backing than in most corporate finance transactions.

This range of financial instruments enables buy-outs to be financed in sectors beyond those involving the classic LBO case, that is those which are mature with stable cash flow and low investment needs, and includes those with significant investment requirements and in technological sectors. For example, in the UK six per cent of the buy-out market involves companies in computing-related and electronics communications systems sectors.

Where there are differences in the valuation placed on a business by managers and institutions, the transaction may use an equity ratchet with management's equity stake varying depending on the achievement of performance targets.

Set over a specific period of time, these instruments are a mechanism for helping ensure that financiers' target exit horizons are achieved. However, setting the precise terms of equity ratchets is problematical, with disagreements between venture capitalists and management over the point at which they are triggered being quite common.

Monitoring and restructuring

In general, relationships established between management and venture capitalists appear to be an important basis for creating the flexibility required for effective monitoring. This emphasizes the need for managers buying out to take great care in selecting their venture capital partner.

While larger buy-out candidates do seem to make more use of advisers in choosing between a number of potential financiers, this is less true at the smaller end of the market. It is necessary to remember both that there is a need to select a financier with whom management can establish a successful working relationship and that there is something of an inherent conflict between the interests of managers and financiers, since, for example, a greater equity share for managers means a lower share for institutions. These issues need to be addressed carefully at the time of the deal, with the experience of managers' advisers providing the means to ensure that their interests are properly addressed.

Covenants attached to the provision of debt also involve close monitoring relationships between banks and their buy-out clients and they should be dealt with as problems rather than signals to put the company into receivership.

When problems arise, difficulties can emerge in restructuring smaller deals where management are important majority shareholders and in buy-outs with syndicated finance. While consensus between institutions and management is important in taking rectifying action, this may be difficult. The more recent trend towards smaller syndicates with members with compatible objectives has gone some way to addressing the problems of delay and obtaining agreement about the nature and extent of restructuring that have arisen in larger syndications.

Increasing competition for deals and increasing entry prices at times of market buoyancy underlines the need for management and venture capitalists to have clear objectives as to the direction of the buy-out or buy-in. The need for outside investors to help management to add value through strategic development assumes greater significance in such circumstances over any benefits from financial engineering.

Particular problems arise with management buy-ins, which show a significantly higher failure rate than buy-outs. Despite considerably greater investor monitoring than is found in buy-outs, there may be major difficulties with due diligence at the time of the transaction, with consequent difficulties in effecting turnaround strategies.

The cost of due diligence in relation to transaction value in smaller buy-ins, time constraints in negotiations, as well as real problems in identifying information often mean that it is not carried out effectively. Institutions and intermediaries have become much more aware of the potential risks in MBIs and are paying great attention to the screening and matching of both entrepreneurs and target companies through dedicated programs (*see* the article by Robert Johnson on p. 290, *Innovative funding for first-timers*). ∎

Rewards and risks on the MBO road

Robert Smith explains how a buy-out works and how success can result in substantial rewards.

Traditionally, most management buy-outs (MBOs) occur because a parent company wants to get rid of a particular subsidiary or, in the case of a private company, because an entrepreneur who has built up his or her own business has no-one within the family to succeed him or her and so they turn to second-line management to buy the business.

However, this situation has started to change as the MBO market matures. Increasingly there are in effect bands of 'nomadic' managers who spot a potential turnaround situation and want to go in if the parent can be persuaded to sell. These are more and more supported by small 'boutiques' of two or three people – usually from an investment banking background – who find buy-out opportunities and also find the management to put in. Usually they work up the transaction so that by the time they come to an investment bank such as Morgan Grenfell they have a business plan, an agreement with the parent company, a price and they are actually telling us on what terms we should shape our investment.

But to go back to the traditional scenario of a manager considering a buy-out. Generally he or she will have talked to an accountant who specializes in MBOS. They will then eventually come along and talk to an investment bank like us.

We then take up the negotiations with the parent company or the entrepreneur, though sometimes they already have the glimmerings of a deal. We then sit down and, hopefully, say 'OK we think this can work and it looks as if it would stand this much debt and this much equity'. The next stages then take in a study of the business plan and due diligence, processes that have been described earlier in *Mastering Enterprise*.

Another new development in the MBO market is that while everyone gets an accounting report there is a real move to getting a consultant's report – which will look at particular aspects of the company such as the likely movement of market prices or the costs of environmental issues.

In the old days buy-outs used to be done in a couple of weeks. One that took two or three months was the exception; now they are the exception for the opposite reason. Buy-outs have become a very long process, often six or nine months, and a lot of it is to do with banks negotiating covenants with the vendor.

Usually the managers faced with an MBO opportunity have little idea of all that is involved. They may never even have spoken to their own high-street bank manager, certainly never met an investment banker. The idea of equity, ratchets and preference shares is far removed from their experience.

Incidentally, though, while they may have no idea what is going on at the beginning and they can often get the feeling that things are getting out of their control as their advisers seem to be doing all the talking, they learn very quickly. Within two weeks they usually know everything.

Given incentive   They are also worried about putting up money. However, generally speaking, the actual amount of money that managers put up is not important. Let's say we are dealing with a £100m buy-out. In effect we say to the management team: 'you can have 10 per cent virtually for nothing'. That 10 per cent is itself almost an arbitrary figure. Five per cent may seem too small; 20 per cent too big. Yet if the deal goes through and we exit at a good price then there will be large amounts of money available for everyone. If there is a performance ratchet in place, the managers can end up with a 20 per cent or 30 per cent share. But to go back to the original 10 per cent. This is given to managers virtually for nothing because the principle is from each according to their ability. So, for example, if we know a manager has done buy-outs before and is worth several million pounds we might not be too keen on his just putting up £10,000.

But assume a typical £100m MBO with £50m of equity. The management team would probably be asked to put up £500,000, say £100,000 or so each. For that they will receive 10 per cent of the equity. Really they should get 1 per cent because the investment bank has put up 99 per cent of the money. But the bank cannot do it without the management. They make the widgets and they have to be given an incentive.

The problem with this from the bank's point of view is that, if we do even moderately well, the bank gets its money back but the managers make 10 times their money. Fortunately or unfortunately you cannot do anything about that because managers simply would not do a deal on the basis of 1 per cent. So, unless managers are really disastrous, they are going to make some cash out of an MBO.

They can make a lot of cash. To go back to the example. If we double the equity and the company is now worth £100m – and it should double – generally you are not doing particularly well if your portfolio doesn't more than double over three to five years. Managers now have, as of right, 10 per cent of the equity, worth £10m, for the £500,000 they put up.

However, the ratchet might be operating at that level so they might actually get £15m or £20m. If that £50m becomes £150m you would be getting hugely more than £15m. As the bank has trebled its money, the managers would be getting £30m or £40m.

Where, then, is the downside, the risk, for managers? Well an MBO is very, very hard work and sometimes things fail to work out. It's high pressure and high risk and banks can rightly be very tough when they are investing sums as large as £50m. Generally they take a very hands-on approach to the management. For example, we almost always change the finance director. We always put in an independent non-executive chairman. One of us always goes on the board. If a year or 18 months into the process things are not happening then we have to do something about it. You can't just say 'gosh, we made a mistake; we'll write off £50m'.

Managers can also get worn out during the process. You get 'deal fatigue' where people will agree to almost anything just to get the deal done and that's where you make mistakes. ■

A management team to lure investors

What are investors looking for in an MBO/MBI? **Daniel Muzyka**, **Michael Hay** and **Sue Birley** sum up the priorities for those wishing to buy into a business.

Management buy-outs (MBOs) are an important part of the entrepreneurship picture worldwide, but especially in Europe. Among other things, in Europe there is a large base of existing businesses, significant amounts of corporate restructuring and a very large inter-generational wealth transfer in the form of businesses, many created after the Second World War.

All of this creates a set of opportunities that may be exploited as a base for entrepreneurial ambitions by existing managers (MBOs), external entrepreneurs wishing to buy into the business (management buy-ins or MBIs) or some combination of the above.

The major question posed by many wishing to undertake a buy-out is 'what are the investors looking for?' – in essence, what do we have to look like to be an attractive and credible investment opportunity? Two questions related to whether the business is an attractive investment are: 'Would someone back me

1 Leadership capability of management team	**management team factor**
2 Track record of management team	**management team factor**
3 Sustained share competitive position	**strategic-competitive factor**
4 Track record of team leader	**management team factor**
5 Completeness and balance within management team	**management team f.**
6 Complete business data	**deal factor**
7 Leadership capability of team leader	**management team factor**
8 Ease of cash-out	**financial factor**
9 Organizational/adminstrative capabilities of team	**management competence f.**
10 Expected rate of return	**financial factor**
11 Recognized industry expertise in management team	**management team f.**
12 Degree of product-market understanding	**product-market factor**
13 Marketing-sales capabilities of team	**management competence factor**
14 Process/production capabilities of team	**management competence factor**
15 Price/earnings ratio	**financial factor**
16 Major capital expenditure	**financial factor**
17 Financial/accounting capabilities of team	**management competence factor**
18 Clarity of method of exit	**deal factor**
19 Market growth and attractiveness	**product-market factor**
20 Business meets fund constraints	**fund factor**
21 Relative experience of investors in industry	**fund factor**
22 Ability of investors to influence nature of business	**fund factor**
23 Apparent method of exit	**deal factor**
24 Nature and degrees of competition	**strategic-competitive factor**
25 Seasonality of product-market	**product-market factor**
26 Working capital	**financial factor**
27 Current market share of business	**product-market factor**
28 Sensitivity to economic cycles	**product-market factor**
29 Ability to syndicate deal	**deal factor**
30 Time to payback	**financial factor**
31 Sale of assets	**financial factor**
32 Market size	**product-market factor**
33 Business and product fit with fund portfolio	**fund factor**
34 Location of business relative to fund	**fund factor**
35 Number and nature of co-investors in deal	**deal factor**

Figure 1: Ranking of general opportunity criteria

1 Ability to inspire others to action	**people skills**
2 Ability to build and maintain an effective management team	**people skills**
3 Ability to instigate, implement and manage change	**people skills**
4 Ability to manage a business in a crisis situation	**people skills**
5 Ability to maintain an overall strategic perspective	**business skills**
6 Leadership capabilities in product-marketplace	**business skills**
7 Perseverance in pursuit of achievement	**leadership style**
8 Ability to drive important decisions past objections	**leadership style**
9 Ability to take and manage risks	**business skills**
10 Ability to articulate vision	**vision and values**
11 Ability to articulate and persuade others of views	**people skills**
12 Creativity in defining solutions to problems	**decision process**
13 Ability to resolve business conflicts	**business skills**
14 Ability to share thinking with team	**people skills**
15 Degree to which the individual is action-oriented	**leadership style**
16 Ability to frame problems	**decision process**
17 Ability to select and focus on appropriate details	**decision process**
18 Ability to manage, learn from and move on from failures	**personal skills**
19 Strong professional career	**personal skills**
20 Confidence in own abilities and mission	**vision and values**
21 Ability to manage with incomplete information	**decision process**
22 Ability to resolve interpersonal conflicts	**people skills**
23 Ability to convey a sense of values	**vision and values**
24 An open decision-making style	**leadership style**
25 Listening skills	**personal skills**
26 A deductive analytical style	**decision process**
27 Ability to stick to decision once taken	**leadership style**
28 An inductive analytical style	**decision process**
29 Financial and accounting capabilities, skills and orientation	**business skills**
30 Ability to achieve consensus with his team	**people skills**
31 Ability to be consistent in decision-making	**leadership style**
32 Degree to which leader is directly involved in teamwork	**leadership style**
33 Technical leadership capabilities in area of interest	**business skills**
34 Orientation toward direct control of tasks	**leadership style**
35 Adminstrative capabilities	**business skills**

Figure 2: Ranking of leadership criteria

as managing director of a buy-out/buy-in?' and 'Would our management team be viewed as a good bet to exploit the value in a potential buy-out/buy-in?' These questions are related to what investors are looking for in a buyout/buy-in management team.

We undertook to address these questions in a study with the support and cooperation of BDO Stoy Hayward, the UK accountants. In the process we surveyed approximately 60 management buy-out investors. This provided us with some useful insights into what they look for in a busines opportunity, the leader of a management buy-out/buy-in team and the management team in general. The research first explored the factors they look at and, through various means, managed to capture the relative ranking of importance of each of the factors.

Overall business factors

The factors that buy-out/buy-in investors look at when evaluating opportunities are, with a few small exceptions, largely the same as those which venture capitalists consider (*see* Figure 1 and Part 3, page 82). The findings from the study suggest that the relative importance of the various factors is also similar.

Looking for the right management team

Management team factors reign supreme on the list of opportunity evaluation factors. The relative set of competencies of the team is also very important. The relative skills and capabilities of management to continue properly to manage the business on a free-standing basis combined with their ability to build and capture new value in the business appears to be a key interest of potential investors.

In terms of strategic competitive factors that MBO/MBI investors look at in evaluating an opportunity, the one that they appear to look at most closely is the ability of the business to sustain its existing competitive position after the buy-out or buy-in.

Financial and product-market related factors are only moderately important. This may seem surprising but the logic appears sound: if the business does not have a good management team, what good are the projected returns?

The ability to implement is prized over the ability to analyze and conceptualize what could be done. Of the financial factors that are seen as relatively most important, on average the ease of cashing out and the expected rate of return are the most highly regarded.

Fund and deal factors (the potential investment's relationship to the fund and factors related to the specific deal and deal structure) are of limited relative importance. This is not to suggest that they are totally unimportant but that when they are compared to other factors they take on relatively less importance. What it does say, though, is that buy-out/buy-in investors who see a deal with a good management team, even if it is not physically next door or among their most desired industries for investment, are likely to take notice and invest.

Stronger expectations of a business track record

The one factor related to the specific deal that does stand out, however, is the completeness of business data. MBO/MBI investors, unlike their venture capital counterparts, do have the luxury in these circumstances of looking at the track record of the business.

A business deal that is presented to them with a complete record is more likely to be prized than one without. This tends to reduce the basic uncertainty surrounding the possibility of returns and gives the investors the ability to focus on the magnitude and nature of the hidden value in the business. The message to the business team is clear: put together as clear and concise a story regarding the business as possible.

Expectation of a short investment horizon

As you might expect, investors in management buy-outs are not looking at the same long-run sorts of investments as venture capitalists. They see value in existing operations and seek to invest in realizing the value, be it through repositioning the business, restructuring the operations and/or the leveraging of new product opportunities. However, they wish this repositioning to take place in a two to three year time frame.

The very long-run value creation is left to the management team with the hope that several years of investment and partnership will sufficiently help to create and communicate the value in such a way that they may realize a good return on their investment.

This shorter time horizon is also partially reflected in the increased sensitivity of MBO/MBI investors to the relative seasonality of a business. If one measures

© Allsport

High scorers?
Investors have an
eye for the right team

exit times in a few years rather than the five to seven year horizon of a venture capitalist, then seasonality can have an impact on exiting.

Furthermore, the time horizon may also be affecting the moderate importance attached to the clarity around the method of investor exit when looking at an opportunity. This is not something a long-term venture capitalist would be concerned about.

One of the issues we explored that is related to the nature of the returns was the relative role of asset sales. Was a business more desirable if, in the process of exposing the basic value of the business, there were assets that could be sold off? The answer to this question is fairly straightforward: there is little general interest in the sale of assets. This particular factor ended up 31 out of 35.

Leadership criteria

With regard to the criteria that they look for in the leader of a management buy-out/buy-in team, the answer from investors is both clear and consistent with their investment horizon and interests. The factors they look for and evaluate in a leader are more related to their basic motivational skills than the nature of their decision-making process (*see* Figure 2).

Investors are looking for someone who can build and maintain a highly motivated management team dedicated to realizing economic value through action and change. In essence they are looking for someone who will quickly articulate and drive the necessary changes past objections as well as mobilize people to undertake the necessary actions in order to induce required change.

They are also realistic in looking for someone who can manage the changes they undertake. With change comes some form of crisis and investors prize crisis management skills very highly.

It is suspected that due to their horizons they are less interested in the leader's abilities to manage long-term values or to build long-run consensus.

Furthermore, they are not looking for leaders who build their portfolio of skills strongly upon their administrative abilities. Also tied to this is the little relative value they attach to specific management styles. In fact, comparatively little attention appears to be paid to the nature of the leadership style exhibited.

What the experience of the buy-out/buy-in investors suggests is that would-be MBO/MBI entrepreneurs may wish to take an inventory of their management style and to reconceptualize their role as a business leader. The leadership style they may have as managing director of a business within a holding company or larger corporation may not be appropriate. The leadership abilities that can bring success in a corporate context (for example, building a management team in a corporate division, building a consensus around the direction of the business, and satisfying the informational and political needs within the corporate hierarchy) may not be suitable in the buy-out/buy-in context.

Nature of the management team

We also explored the characteristics MBO/MBI investors look at in evaluating management teams. These characteristics were then ranked by these investors through our research (*see* Figure 3).

The picture that emerges is a concern on the part of investors that the potential management team has the ability to manage their business-related conflicts and reach decisions in an expeditious manner. Trust within the team is something that is relatively highly regarded by potential investors as is a previous track record as a team.

Other characteristics that are important are overall commitment to a single set of goals, balance and motivation within the team, and a general understanding and appreciation of investor needs. The ability to manage interpersonal conflict is also prized.

How they achieve these elements is something that is of less concern to potential investors. Again, the shorter-run horizon may be making itself clear in the relatively moderate weight attached to such factors as team spirit, trust of lower levels of management, collective sense of ownership, group creativity and the like.

From this research with potential investors there appears to be no consensus on, or relative importance attached to, the demographics of the team (team size, age and so on). While balance is prized, the need to augment or change the team is not something of ultimate importance to investors. Nor, for that matter, is the relative long-run consistency, fit and underlying motivation of team members. As long as they are committed to the buy-out/buy-in for the initial period, the long-run motivations are set aside.

Reflecting the logic of venture capitalists, MBO/MBI investors make it clear both through their comments and the surveys we conducted that personal financial commitment was

Figure 3: Ranking of team criteria

#	Criterion	Category
1	Effectiveness of group decision-making	team decision-making
2	Ability of team to lead the organization	team and the firm
3	Previous profitable track record	team effectiveness
4	Success in managing business-related conflicts	team effectiveness
5	Trust within team	intra-team relations
6	Commitment to group goals	intra-team relations
7	Ability to manage interpersonal conflicts	team effectiveness
8	Balance in team skills	demography
9	Level of collective motivation	team effectiveness
10	Team understanding of/commitment to investor's needs	team and the investor
11	Respect for team by lower management levels	team and the firm
12	Personal financial commitment	team and the investor
13	Group creativity in decision-making	team decision-making
14	Attainment of cross-functional solutions	team decision-making
15	Collective sense of ownership	intra-team relations
16	Team's trust of lower managment levels	team and the firm
17	Consistency in analytical approach	team decision-making
18	Fit between team and investors	team and the investor
19	Team spirit	intra-team relations
20	Personal interaction/communication	intra-team relations
21	Commonality of/desire for group goals	intra-team relations
22	Need to augment team size/change team composition	demography
23	Consistency in team (group) behavior	intra-team relations
24	Career improvement motivation	team and the firm
25	Size of team equity	team and the investor
26	Team size	demography
27	Age of team members	demography
28	Commonality in age of team	demography

important but that the absolute amount of such commitment is less important. The investors have the required money, they just want to know that depending on their means the team has enough commitment and therefore motivation in the deal to lead them to maximize their performance.

In summary, the ultimate team is one that is able to articulate and act on what needs to be done. The ability to deliver in the shorter run is a matter of major concern for investors.

The bottom line   If you have a business you believe has relatively clear potential for value creation, given the right team and a change of ownership, do not hesitate to contact a buy-out/buy-in investor. Money is clearly available and they are interested. The business need not be in any particular sector or necessarily geographically close to potential investors. No particular industry or other business characteristics are important beyond the competence of the proposed management team and a basically sound business. The bottom line is that a good bottom line will yield investors. ■

✦ CASE STUDY

The React Group

*Written by Professor **Daniel Muzyka** and Entrepreneur-in-Residence **Michael Ullmann**, both of INSEAD, this edited case was developed to describe a particular business situation rather than to illustrate either effective or ineffective handling of a particular situation. The development of this case was funded through the generosity of the International Alumni Fund of INSEAD. This case is disguised.*

Robert Andrews, President of the React Group, a conglomerate of 15 companies in the clothes manufacturing business, is meeting with his Vice President of Finance, Jim Woodward. They are reviewing the current cash position of the group as of 1 September 1989 and are faced with some difficult decisions.

A cash shortage they had predicted nine months before was now scheduled to occur earlier than expected. Given the rigorous covenants and aggressive repayment schedule associated with the debt from the leveraged buy-out (LBO), combined with certain unexpected operating problems, the React Group would be unable to meet its next scheduled payment on its senior debt obligations due on 15 November 1989. Management will have to begin to make some difficult choices, including 'rationing' cash to meet payments to suppliers.

Andrews decides that a meeting of the banking syndicate must be called and that negotiations to reschedule the company's debt must be undertaken in earnest to avoid default. By the end of the day, Andrews had contacted and scheduled meetings for the next week with the lead bank in the syndicate (Norton Simon), the React Group's lead venture capitalist (Roper Capital), the company's solicitors (Nelson Walters) and the corporate accountants (Raymond Jones) regarding the impending cash problems.

The React Group, one of a growing number of management buy-outs in the UK, was formed from the clothing division of the Gartner Ltd, a company which had recently been taken over by an aggressive, successful and well-publicized conglomerate, Multicorp. Multicorp, having acquired Gartner for its home furnishings business, had been willing to consider the sale of the clothing business.

The React Group was a diversified clothing business which both manufactured and imported the whole spectrum of clothing from children's to adult wear. Customers for various companies in the conglomerate included Marks and Spencer, the large British clothing retailer. In addition, several of the divisions of the React Group made various well-known branded lines, including athletic clothing such as swimwear. There were many seasonal businesses, but various of the businesses peaked during different seasons.

Many of the businesses were relatively small, located throughout the UK and Ireland. Clothes were also imported from the Far East through a successful importing operation. The businesses all shared a common focus on the design and marketing of clothing.

The early days of the new management's reign were busy. The businesses had deteriorated markedly due to a softness in the UK economy and a lack of sufficient management attention. As a result, the agreement to take over the company, signed on 28 July 1989, preceded two disastrous operating months for the business.

A new financial director and management accountants were added, who brought in control systems that provided management with a significant capacity to monitor the financial status of each of the group's 15 companies. Central cash control and reporting was instituted.

In line with Robert Andrews' beliefs about the clothing trade, the new entity proved much more responsive in its reincarnation. A new image was forged and the 'React Group' – a group of companies that would react more quickly to market and customer needs – was formed. A corporate communications organization was chosen to build and communicate this new image.

The new management also replaced many of the top managers of the company. Seven of the 15 major heads of businesses were replaced. In addition, weak parts of the overall enterprise were cut and several companies were sold almost immediately.

After the financial director came on-board in November, several issues became apparent. First, certain contingent liabilities in the range of £6m were uncovered, primarily in the import business. Most budgets proved to be quite near to the business plan of eight months before but the larger contingent liabilities relating to the foreign exchange cover and to letters of credit of the import business were eating up 60 per cent (as opposed to 20 per cent) of the agreed overdraft. It also became clear that there would be a lack of required cash in the first quarter of 1990 unless trading improved.

Discussions with Norton Simon indicated that it felt no need to tell the rest of the syndicate about the likely cash shortfall in 1990. Norton Simon indicated that this cash shortfall was only projected, outside of the published budget time scale and all debt payments were current.

Andrews realized that he had yet another daunting task ahead of him. Cash flow projections would simply not cover the debt repayments and the operating needs of the business. Projections suggested that by mid-November, the business would have a cash short-fall of at least 10m.

Discussions with individuals at Norton Simon and other professionals suggested that they appreciated management coming to them so early and that something probably could be worked out. Having only been able to run the business for six months, and at the point when he was just feeling comfortable, Robert Andrews did not want to 'foul the deal'.

Another, more pressing issue was confronting him, however. New bankruptcy laws, for which there was little precedent, had an ominous tone which appeared to imply the management at React. Management was personally responsible for amounts owed to unsecured creditors after it was known by management that sufficient cash was not available to meet them. This was referred to as 'wrongful trading'. The liability could run into the millions of pounds since suppliers to the React Group were paid on the order of £1m per week.

The 15 November deadline passed relatively uneventfully.

Andrews recalls: 'As we expected, we just didn't have the cash. We went into technical default. And we began a new round of negotiations. Of course we got the formal letters from the lead bank for the syndicate noting that we were in technical default. However, none of the banks, including the lead bank, wanted to call the loan. The negotiations continued. We had the feeling that all of this could be worked out and that people would act reasonably – there was enough interest around to continue to make this deal work. We were, however, operating with very little cash'.

At this point, the search for additional capital began in earnest. To make the business viable and protect the interest of the unsecured creditors, it was quite necessary to seek additional funds and/or to reschedule the existing debt. Two significant funds, Zeon and European Ventures Unlimited (EVU), appeared to be interested.

Management also attempted to become more creative. Andrews and his team began looking at alternative deals, including bringing in a trade buyer to provide an equity infusion. As part of this analysis, it also considered selling off bits of the business. With the assistance of strategy consultants (London Strategy Consultants), they ran literally scores of economic models.

During this period the banks discussed various options but were fundamentally unwilling to make any new commitments. There was a real reluctance on the part of any of the existing players to inject 'new money'. Combined with the fact that Roper was being unhelpful and Norton Simon was sending various signals but was unable to actually achieve a solution to the problem, the negotiations dragged on until December.

Finally, in December, some options were beginning to emerge. However, the options were conditional upon the agreement of various parties in order to execute them. Zeon was very excited about the possibility of providing an equity infusion based upon an increase in the scale of the React Group around the strategic core businesses. It was unwilling to put in the cash required at that time for a simple downsizing and preferred that EVU come into the deal with it.

Norton Simon suggested that management should work more closely with EVU. However, EVU made strong suggestions that management should sell off several of the core businesses, including those supplying Marks and Spencer (an account management felt was important and profitable) while reducing the business to strictly branded businesses. In addition, EVU noted that if Norton Simon and React Group management wanted their continued advice, they would have to commit themselves to paying £200,000 in fees to EVU if the deal did not go through and would have to pay an additional £300,000, under any circumstances, for a full audit of the business by an auditor specified by EVU.

Management did not agree with the approach of EVU. However, they determined that for purposes of their fiduciary responsibility to the unsecured creditors, it would be necessary to allow EVU to continue to work with all parties, even to the point of having themselves removed as part of the deal. EVU'S accountants were employed to undertake another long form audit of the React Group businesses – an audit which took into January of 1990 to complete. The audit indicated that the businesses were generally valuable and viable with proper financing.

By this time, management had decided that even if their percentage of the business was cut in half, it was still better to take the deal. In these circumstances management cannot legally refuse any deal that keeps the company alive. Management also identified an option by which certain 'non-strategic' businesses could be sold for approximately £12m, providing much of the cash needed in the short term. The banks, however, would still have to 'roll-up' some interest and reschedule some of the debt in order to make the business viable. This would 'clean up' the balance sheet, a requirement in these increasingly conservative times. So, by the end of the year, negotiations with the banks were in a critical stage.

All of the negotiations continued but a critical juncture had been reached. On 2 January, Robert Andrews and his associates had met with their legal counsel who made it clear that they were now at the point of having to act – the unsecured creditors were now clearly at risk with negotiations deadlocked and no written offers on the table and no apparent resolution in sight.

The attorneys also pointed out to Andrews and his associates that despite the goodwill of the venture capitalists in evaluating the businesses, no written commitments had been forthcoming. As a result of the statements and the position of the venture capitalists, the syndicate banks all went into further heavy discussions.

During the first week in January, all of the parties who had been put onto the field kept jockeying for position. Unbeknownst to the management of the React Group, various parties to the deal were meeting separately to plot independent courses of action not involving management. Roper had put together a new management team. Norton Simon phoned the management of React and said that Merchants (an investment banking group brought in to advise management) and Roper were going to present the new management team to the syndicate. This was to occur on a Friday 14 January.

However, the new management team did not even make it past the first screen and was rejected by the syndicate. Robert Andrews and his associates went back to a meeting of the syndicate banks with their position. There could be disposal of peripheral businesses but they felt that the unsecured creditors would be best served by the ongoing operation of the company and the maintenance of the key strategic businesses. Management of the team would have to be provided with cash to run the strategic core businesses while selling off about £12m in 'non-essential' businesses (including concessions from the debt providers) and the debt providers would have to 'share the pain' by providing concessions which would attract new equity into the business.

At this point, Norton Simon asked EVU to make a final presentation and made representations to the syndicate that EVU was willing to 'do the deal' if only they could wait a few days. EVU, after first agreeing to make a bid for the business and then deciding not to bid, finally decided to present a deal on January 27. The bank syndicate members met along with management and the existing venture capitalists to hear EVU'S presentation, which turned out in Andrew's words to be 'truly unrealistic'. Norton Simon and the banks were quite 'upset' at the presentation. After EVU had completed their presentation, they were asked to leave along with management.

The decision was finally in the hands of the banks – management had no other options and no time to structure any. Their conclusion was simple. Robert Andrews says: 'After hearing that EVU had no reasonable deal to offer, the bankers simply said "enough is enough". They indicated they would provide no further financing and that management should reach its own conclusions'.

On the evening of 26 January, Andrews called in the receivers who had been waiting in the wings for the last few weeks. Discussion of what should be done and what were management's rights and responsibilities ensued. At that moment, Robert Andrews and his management team ceased to have effective control of the React Group.

Robert Andrews offers many reasons for the failure of the React Group: the buy-in nature of the deal; the amount paid for the company; the position of the banks; the nature of the venture capital industry; and the role and nature of advisors.

Andrews notes that subsequent to the failure of the React Group, many deals in the City have fallen, leaving banks with an image problem. He believes that there is a different psychology among the banks today – they are more likely to attempt to make a deal to keep the business together: 'They can get more if they put them in administration rather than into receivership. The motivation is economic as well as creating an image of responsibility'.

In the end the React Group was parcelled up and sold off. Though the final report of the receivers has not been filed, early indications are that the banking group did not realize the 80 pence on the pound that they expected from the sale of assets.

Robert Andrews received several offers of executive positions despite the well publicized failure of his business. He subsequently accepted a senior executive position with a Paris-based textile enterprise. ■

Innovative funding for first-timers

Robert Johnson explains 'funded search' – a way in which young entrepreneurs can find others to pay to set them up in business.

Kirk Dodson is a very talented young entrepreneurial individual with a few years' work experience and nearing completion of his MBA. He tells you that his aim is to run his own business and asks you for advice on how best to reach that goal. What do you tell him?

Most people would strongly advise Kirk to get more industry experience, including managerial experience, preferably in charge of a small company or a division of a larger company. Then, say the wise counsellors, he will be in a position to run his own business. Certainly that is appropriate advice for many people but for some (like Kirk) there is another alternative – buying their own business right away. Rubbish, you say. How can anyone with little industry experience, no real managerial experience and little capital (indeed still in debt from financing an MBA) be serious about buying and running a business?

It is not so far-fetched as it sounds. An increasing number of graduating or recent MBAs have found that there is a quicker and more rewarding path for getting into business for themselves – using a 'funded search' to find and buy a business to run. In a funded search an entrepreneur raises a search fund (say £100,000) from a group of individual investors (say ten individuals investing £10,000 each) to pay the expenses of the search and a nominal salary during the search period (say eighteen to twenty-four months). Working full time, the entrepreneur researches target industries and searches for a company to acquire.

Once a company has been identified and a deal negotiated with the seller, the search fund investors have the option – but not the obligation – to invest *pro rata* in the acquisition. If an investor chooses not to invest then his original investment rolls over into the acquisition on the same basis as the new investment funds. As part of the deal, the entrepreneur (now the CEO) receives equity in the company – usually a combination of shares at completion of the acquisition and additional shares based on performance.

There are a number of key factors necessary to make a funded search work.

First and foremost, the young entrepreneur must have the commitment and the talent to run a business. From the investors' point of view this is the real risk in the deal – can this person actually run a company? The criteria for a target acquisition must take this into account, which means that the searcher must find a stable business that does not have a lot of inherent risk in it. This may mean a 'boring' business but sometimes boring businesses turn out to be fun businesses and even highly profitable when properly managed.

Has the concept worked? I am aware of 18 people in the US and two in the UK who have raised search funds; all are either now running their own companies or are currently searching. Two of the US entrepreneurs have sold their companies, producing generous returns for their investors.

What must the young entrepreneur bring to the table? Enthusiasm, commitment, persistence and the ability to run a business – now. What does the investor buy in the search fund? Essentially, an option; then, the opportunity to be involved with a bright young entrepreneur in what may be his or her first big winner. ■

Bimbos and Bingos boost buy-ins

Patrick Dunne looks at the growth of management buy-ins in the UK and what it takes in financial and personal terms to make a successful deal.

Management buy-ins (MBIs) have grown in the UK to the point where there are now just under 200 a year, about half the number of Management buy-outs (MBOs). In continental Europe the MBI is at an early stage of development and there are, for example, perhaps only 20 a year in Germany compared with 50 MBOs.

Awareness of what an MBI entails is low among owners of companies and managers on the continent. However, the characteristics and particularly the motivations of these owners and managers might suggest significant growth ahead. The views I will be expressing here are based on some 450 UK and 50 continental European MBIs that 3i backed up to the end of 1996.

What is an MBI?

An MBI involves a manager or team of managers from outside a particular company, together with their financial backers, purchasing equity control of it. In the process, the manager becomes executive chairman, chief executive, managing director, Geschäftführer or président directeur général – in other words the boss – and gains a significant equity stake.

The 1990s have also seen the emergence of two powerful variants of the MBI – the BIMBO and the BINGO. In a BIMBO the MBI team joins forces with managers within the business enabling them to obtain equity through a partial MBO. Hence the hybrid name. BIMBOs possess several advantages over a conventional MBI and these are described later. In a BINGO a sizeable (more than 25 per cent of the total funding) amount of growth capital is raised in addition to that used to buy the business. This cash is then used for a major growth project such as a new factory or other significant capital expenditure.

Who carries out management buy-ins?

Contrary to popular belief, buy-in managers are not super-hero financial wizards swooping in on ailing companies, rapidly transforming them and then selling them on. The people who do these buy-ins in the UK, France, Germany and Italy seem to be remarkably similar in profile and all want to grow the company. There are essentially two main types: the break-out manager and the second-time entrepreneur.

The break-out manager

Figure 1: MBI manager functional background

An early to mid-40s frustrated divisional chief executive within a larger corporation with five or more years experience as a chief executive. They have no particularly dominant functional background before they became CEO, though more have been in sales and marketing than any other single function before becoming CEO.

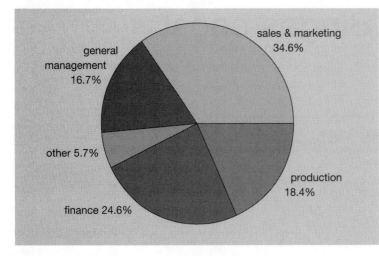

general management 16.7%

sales & marketing 34.6%

other 5.7%

production 18.4%

finance 24.6%

Break-out managers typically invest £100,000 in the UK and £200,000-plus in France and Germany. This will be the greater part of their net worth. Their motivations may be one but usually several of the following:

● To gain independence and control over their own destiny.

● To make significant capital thereby gaining financial independence.

● To escape frustration with their current position – career

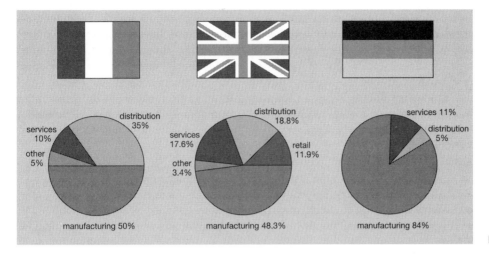

Figure 2: Sector

progression may be blocked or perhaps more senior roles appear unfulfilling or bureaucratic.

● An MBO is not possible because the business they run is not for sale at a feasible price.

● They may have a former colleague or friend who has done an MBO and consider themselves at least as able.

● They consider a start-up too risky and are more comfortable building on a business that already has critical mass.

● They could be a corporate victim, having been taken over, delayered or downsized.

Break-out managers face a number of common dangers. They may not be a suitable manager for the companies typically available. Many of the most successful larger corporations are run along functional lines and do not prepare people well for running independent companies. Trying to look for a target while still being in employment in the full-steam ahead or stop 1990s can be another difficulty. For many the real trigger is a takeover of the company they run.

☞ Boss Chop Factor

Highly successful 45-year-old Joe Starr, is managing director of a company within a large group. He arrives home with some excellent news for his wife Ann.

'Hi, got some great news.'

'Oh no we're not moving again are we; we've only just settled here.'

'No, no this time we stay but I get to run the whole division. They have decided to retire Stan (his current boss) early and have given his job to me. Twenty per cent more cash, a sweet option deal and a new Mercedes S Class.'

'That's great, well done. Let's celebrate and go out.'

Later that evening, over a meal and champagne, Ann turns to Joe and says:

'Why did they retire Stan?'

'Well, I guess they thought he had run out steam and decided he should make way for a younger man, give me a chance to really prove myself.'

'How old is Stan?'

'Fifty.'

'Aha. So I guess that gives you five years max.'

Joe is suddenly quiet. He's never really had to think about this before. It's a somewhat terrifying prospect – perhaps he should do something to get control over his own future?

In France and in Germany the fear of failure is a very important deterrent. As there have been fewer MBOs the envy motivation is lower. Status in the local community is more important than in the UK and therefore a senior position with a larger group might be more attractive despite lower wealth. One fascinating trend across Europe that has emerged during the 1990s is what I call the 'Boss Chop Factor'. This is encapsulated in the domestic scene outlined in the box on the previous page, which could just as easily be taking place in Paris, Düsseldorf, Barcelona or Turin.

Second-time entrepreneur

This type of buy-in manager has the following characteristics:

- Slightly older than the break out manager, late 40s or early 50s.
- Already successful through an earlier buy-out, start-up or even buy-in.
- Has sold out and has no intention of giving up business or indeed working for anyone else.
- Tends to invest the same as a break-out manager despite having considerably greater wealth.
- May want to take a chairman's role and not be as totally consumed as in previous ventures.

The relatively high numbers of MBOs in the UK over the last ten years have provided a growing pool of second-timers. Lower numbers of MBOs across the continent, combined with the fact that owners of companies tend to hang on longer, means that the pool of second-time CEOs is likely to be smaller. However the tradition of the wealthy local worthy backing a friend or former employee is much stronger, which ought to mean that there is a good supply of investing chairmen.

What else motivates them? They may be bored or frustrated or lack any real purpose if business has always been their life. Some may have a strong desire to prove it wasn't luck the first time.

Potential dangers for this group are that, of course, they may have been lucky the first time – the industry or general economic cycle may have been kind. More commonly, they may have burned themselves out or lost some of their sharpness

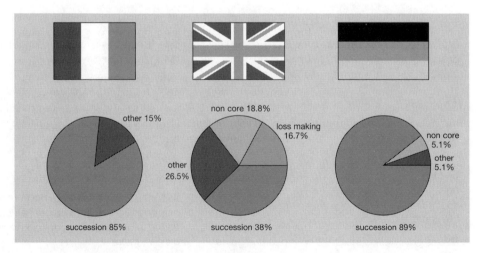

Figure 3: Reason sold

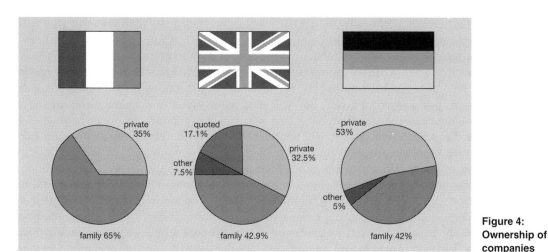

Figure 4:
Ownership of
companies

through becoming wealthy. Despite the dangers, second-time entrepreneurs are often the most attractive from an investor's perspective.

How do buy-in managers make money?

The entrepreneurs' aim is fundamentally to make the business they buy worth more than the price they paid for it. Their equity is also geared up. Every pound, franc or lira they put in will normally buy more of the equity than their financial backers who put in their money, as in an MBO, in the form of base equity, redeemable stock and debt. If successful, the investors get some of their money back along the way and the rest on eventual sale. It is sensible to have lower levels of debt in an MBI because of the higher risks involved in a new team who despite their no doubt excellent record may not fit when they get there.

What sort of businesses are bought by buy-in managers?

The heartland of MBIs, as shown in the charts, are the private and family companies, the European *Mittelstand* of £5m to £100m-turnover businesses. Ironically, most MBI managers spend most of their time hunting among the non-core subsidiaries of the large groups.

That there are succession issues in thousands of German *Mittelstand* companies is well documented and evident (*see* page 254). However, despite these companies making theoretically wonderful MBI targets, they are not so easy to achieve. Vendors tend to leave selling until they are in their seventies.

In terms of a preferred buyer for their life's work, the order seems to go something like this: a friend, a friend of their banker, another client of their banker, then someone in their own image but a bit younger. All of whom will have to come up with the figure that the most wacky Far Eastern overpayer came up with at the company's peak. Sadly, the business may have languished and need significant investment capital, hence causing further pricing pressure. So doing a sensible deal can be tricky.

For larger corporate vendors there has been an increasing tendency in the UK and in France for the vendor to want to deal directly with the institutional backer and not to want to receive approaches from managers directly. 'We want to talk to the money', they say. This is one reason why the UK market has returned to something of a feeding frenzy as M & A (mergers and acquisitions) directors and merchant banks send their truck loads of prospectuses out to backers.

BIMBOs: why so good?

The hybrid MBI/MBO, or BIMBO, which combines the objectivity of the MBI manager with the continuity of people within the business, often has significant advantages over a pure MBI:

● **More reliable information** Managers within the business will usually respond to the MBI managers' invitation to join in the equity and be more open than perhaps otherwise. They will also be involved in preparing the business plan for moving forward.

● **Less acquisitional drift** It is normal for any company going through a sale process to lose momentum. The good managers are out looking for jobs just in case. The vendors are dreaming of the cash that's about to arrive. An inordinate amount of time is spent showing people around, assisting due diligence and in adviser meetings. In MBOs, this is known to occur to a much lesser degree because the people within have a strong incentive to make sure it is in the best shape possible when they take over. A BIMBO goes a long way to achieving this.

● **Better motivation** Incumbent management's equity provides greater motivation. Discussions over who gets what slice of the cake may also result in a more tightly knit team from the start and less fractious behavior during a critical time.

● **Competitive edge** A BIMBO sends a clear signal to the vendor about the MBI managers' approach. Vendors particularly concerned about what happens to their employees when the company is sold will regard this favorably.

Of course there is a danger in BIMBOs and that is that the manager involves the wrong people in the equity and thus removing them later may be more cumbersome. My view is that the benefits of the approach far outweigh this risk.

Conclusion

Managers embarking upon the MBI route are making a clear statement in their belief in their own abilities as a managing director. There is no doubt that the MBI has now become an established way for managers to gain independence in the UK and it is becoming more prevalent in continental Europe.

Risks can be mitigated and opportunities created through the BIMBO route. The individuals that lead these MBIs are exceptional managers and growing numbers of MBO and MBI realizations have produced a pool of potential second-time entrepreneurs.

MBIs are fundamentally about growth. The only real way to fulfil the MBI manager's dream and to make money for investors is through genuine growth in the business. Many are now also raising significant growth capital in addition to acquisition funding at the time of their MBI. ■

Routes to a successful turnaround

Michael Ullman provides advice for those who want to transform a failed company.

Taking over a company that has already failed may not be every entrepreneur's ideal but the opportunities for successful turnaround are significant, the potential profits large, and the process not as difficult as many assume and potentially at least as exciting as beginning a start-up business from scratch.

Just how many companies are revitalized in this way is hard to ascertain since turnarounds like this are not always very visible. However, estimates suggest that in the UK alone many thousands of companies that go into receivership do not disappear at all but are reincarnated. In some sectors, notably the small retail sector, the amount of this 'churning' is considerable.

Why companies get into trouble

Companies that get into trouble usually do not have very good financial accounting and financial reporting. Trouble sneaks up on them and, as it does so, management starts thinking that the problem is the top line – their sales; they very rarely start thinking how they can cut costs or increase margins – the keys to a successful turnaround. In trying to increase sales they invariably drop their margins, further compounding the problem.

Another truth about failing companies is that the failure is almost always the fault of the current management. That is why businesses have to go into receivership – so that the management can be changed. If you take over a company and fail to root out the current management, the chances are that you will end up losing a great deal of money.

Because of this management failure, the external environment in which a company is operating usually has very little to do with the causes of failure. This is why a turnaround can be relatively simple to achieve. In normal circumstance you can take over a failing business and have it breaking even in a month – give it penicillin and the patient responds. The above applies mainly to the manufacturing sector. Service companies are slightly more difficult. Margins there are much more affected by the market, and the external environment does have an impact – but the general concepts outlined below are still of use.

How to bring about a turnaround

The keys to a successful turnaround are raising prices and reducing turnover. When companies set prices they tend to be either cost-plus or competition-based; but how many businesses go bust because they overprice their product compared with those that have underpriced it?

One of the universal lessons about turning companies round, apart from the rather obvious thing of putting in appropriate financial reporting and controls, is that when you get there, if you fire the management and reduce the sales, you will be astonished at the results.

This is because the former management was probably running round like headless chickens chasing sales at the expense of margin. Furthermore, they tend to mess up the manufacturing process by making it more complicated and less economic. The management takes on production runs that the factory manager, if he had any control, would never allow. The knock-on effects in terms of product proliferation and distribution costs just go on and on compounding the losses.

Successful turnarounds generally involve very little change other than a refocusing of the business. A lot of manufacturing businesses, even though they are run by people with a marketing background, are very unfocused. In one business we took over we dropped 25 per cent of the turnover. Instead we concentrated on existing core customers, just going back to basics, making sure the product quality was where it ought to be so that customers would repeat-buy the product. You can't fool customers all the time, though there is a naïve assumption that you can, and, if you do actually give them the right quality, the results can be amazing. In that business, sales were up 30 per cent on the core lines.

The main aspect to improving margins is taking out costs. That does not mean firing half the workforce – though it will probably mean losing the directors and any redundant staff. It is much more involved with sensible trading. For example, companies in trouble tend to spread their supplier base – they take on more suppliers – because they are not paying them, which leads to even more inefficiencies.

If you do get in trouble, and if you have the financial systems in place, then you'll know you are in trouble. What you need to do is go to your core suppliers and admit that you are not going to be able to pay them quite as promptly as you agreed. But you also say that you will pay them the difference it costs them not to collect the money from you. In other words, you get extended credit and pay them interest costs.

The alternative of spreading the supplier base means you get poor service and poor prices – which increases costs. When we took over one business we had a meeting of major customers. On an annual turnover of £5m, we reckoned we had identified cost savings of ten per cent in the first five days. A lot of that came from suppliers being reassured that they were going to be paid and having proper trading terms.

The importance of management

New management is a vital ingredient in a turnaround and it is important to work with people you know. You should not recruit strangers for this sort of operation. You need to know how people react and whether you can work with them – but be aware that this can be a limiting factor in looking at businesses.

There are criteria for choosing the managers you put in, but if you are taking over failing businesses, you tend to be buying them from receivers so you have a very short time-frame to originate a plan. You have to be able to get the resources in terms of replacement managers together quickly. But it still holds true that no one should take over a failing business without having a management team ready to go in.

Remember, too, that the existing second-tier managers, who are normally quite competent people, have usually been extremely fed up with the way the business has been run so that giving them the opportunity to set things right is normally a very liberating experience and you get lots of co-operation. In other words you can just take the top layer off and bring up the rest – a ploy successfully carried out by Hanson for years.

Rewarding the new management appropriately is very important but, contrary to a lot of current thinking, many managers are not very equity minded. Handing over equity can be a two-edged sword for the entrepreneur. For example, in one company I reorganized in the 1980s, the managers were, with some difficulty, persuaded to buy a stake. At the first opportunity they wanted to sell out, gaining about £500,000 each. Although I was the majority shareholder I was obliged to sell the company, which was a shame because we sold it too early.

Rewards should be much more geared to profit sharing and the like. Most people work for fairly instant rewards – money, status and motor cars. One has to be aware of what it is that motivates people and not just assume it is equity. I know of one sales director who made the owner of his company immensely rich; his undying loyalty was 'bought' when he doubled sales one year and the owner gave him a gold Rolex watch. That rather trivial incident taught me more than any theory of executive remuneration.

Finding and assessing companies worthy of turnaround

Finding companies suitable for turnaround is, on the surface, very easy. After all, the major business press such as the *Financial Times* devote sections to advertising companies for sale every week.

You can also approach those likely to be in the know such as accountants, venture capitalists and bankers. However, you can get unstuck this way and waste a lot of time. The best thing to do is to concentrate on an industry that you know and work your network. After the first successful turnaround you will find that they come to you.

There are enormous opportunities in what we might call 'dumb' industries – ones that are not fashionable or high profile and where management talent is not greatly evident. One example is the packaging industry. People say no one can make money in packaging but, of course, you can; it's often just a question of putting in the most up-to-date equipment. As a rule of thumb, failing companies most suitable for turnaround have a minimum turnover of about £5m, are involved in manufacturing and employ between 50 to 300 people.

Assessing the viability of turning round a business usually involves touring the factory with the management team you hope to install to see what improvements can be made in terms of cost-reduction. This does not apply to buying a well-run business, where you have to pay a premium. In many ways, the worse-run a business is the more attractive it is. You can see all sorts of ways of improving things as you go around the factory and usually they are fairly obvious and can be done quickly.

However, there are some caveats. One of the many things that companies in difficulty cut back on is maintenance and investment. You should be very careful with a highly mechanized business because it may look fine superficially. But if the insides are falling apart it could cost you a fortune. You can make an offer to take over a business that is conditional on getting things working but this can be difficult if you are buying from a receiver.

Indeed, dealing with receivers is generally very difficult, certainly in the UK. There are few – if any – ground rules because receivers are unusually free of any

*Sparking recovery:
most companies
suitable for turnround
are in manufacturing*

form of control or restriction. They can do exactly what they like. It has been known, for example, for receivers not to accept the highest bid they are offered and if you have made one higher than the one they accept there is nothing you can do about it.

A lot of the time you are also playing blind man's bluff on price so you need to have quite a margin of safety. You take on a lot of liability and the receiver will give you no assurances on assets. You don't know who's going to start claiming goods. You don't know who the other bidders are or even if there are any other bidders.

It is possible to buy just the assets of a business but if you do so without the liabilities that make it an on-going concern then that is almost like a start-up. You may have got a lot of equipment cheap but it's very hard work. You really do need both assets and liabilities. Even if suppliers have lost money with the previous owners you can usually negotiate terms.

However, to do that, you need working capital and that is something people can underestimate. That's why it is always a good idea to involve active partners, including venture capitalists and banks, in a turnaround deal, sharing the risks and rewards equally with them. Venture capitalists in particular can also be a useful source of financial and management discipline.

When the turnaround is complete and the once failing company is back on a healthy road, what happens then? In general, most entrepreneurs involved in turnarounds are looking for an exit. Few are prepared to devote their time exclusively to running the business. In the great majority of cases, turnarounds take place so that the company can be sold on. ∎

◆◇ CASE STUDY

Harley-Davidson

This is an edited version of a longer case study written by **Richard Schoenberg**,
Imperial College Management School.

Harley-Davidson had been owned by the industrial and leisure conglomerate AMF between 1969 and 1981. AMF's early strategy had been to expand production substantially, although the resulting rise in sales had been accompanied by a marked deterioration in product quality.

Since 1973, however, conditions in Harley's market had become far more competitive as overall motorcycle sales declined and Japanese manufacturers entered the heavyweight segment of the market where Harley-Davidson had previously been dominant. Although Harley-Davidson had remained profitable, its share of the US heavyweight motorcycle market fell from 99 per cent in 1972 to 30 per cent in 1981.

Uncomfortable with AMF, 13 members of Harley-Davidson's then management purchased the company from AMF in spring 1981 for approximately $80m. The majority of the new owners were keen motorcyclists and celebrated the independence of the company by organizing a mass 'Freedom Ride' to proclaim their vision of 'providing motorcycles by the people for the people'.

Early actions

The early 1980s were not easy for the newly independent Harley-Davidson. The world economic situation was worsening and motorcycle markets continued to decline. Harley-Davidson responded aggressively to bring its capacity into line with demand and to reduce its costs. In autumn 1981 the York assembly plant was cut back to one shift from two and 200 clerical jobs were cut. The following spring 1,600 of the remaining 3,800 employees were laid off. The company reported operating losses of $15m for 1982 on a turnover of $210m. Annual production of motorcycles fell 25 per cent to 30,000. Reports began to appear in the press that America's oldest motorcycle manufacturer was close to bankruptcy.

In November 1982 Harley-Davidson filed a petition with the US International Trade Commission (ITC) requesting protection from alleged unfair foreign competition – in essence alleged 'dumping' by Japanese manufacturers. It further argued that protection would give it breathing space to improve production efficiency and develop more competitive products. The ITC upheld the case and imposed additional import tariffs on Japanese-manufactured machines over 700cc for a five-year period.

Production improvements

Even before the ITC hearings the buy-out team had begun implementing production changes. A major step was the introduction of a 'materials as needed' (MAN) inventory system where parts were delivered to the assembly line 'just in time'. Action was also taken to reduce machine tool set-up times. In addition, Harley-Davidson began to view suppliers as 'partners in profit', awarding long-term contracts to those that consistently met stringent quality and delivery requirements. The assembly line was reorganized into a

series of 'work cells' and employee involvement was further encouraged through a new pay scheme. The combined benefits of these changes was significant. The company's 1987 annual report boasted that since 1981 manufacturing had achieved a 50 per cent improvement in productivity, a 68 per cent reduction in scrap and major improvements in product quality.

Research and product development

The buy-out team also moved quickly to enhance research and development capability, raising expenditure to five per cent of sales. A major pay-off was the introduction in 1984 of a new engine, for which much of the early design work is said to have been undertaken during AMF's ownership.

The new 'Evolution' engine was soon fitted to all but the Sportster models and showed marked improvements in reliability, performance and maintenance. Product development has continued but in incremental rather than radical steps.

Customers

Harley-Davidson's product has to be viewed in context. The main attraction of the motorcycles is not as a means of transport but rather in terms of 'image, charisma and style'. In the mid-1980s Harley-Davidson began actively marketing this style to young professionals while being careful not to alienate its traditional customer base of blue-collar workers.

The company made great efforts to involve purchasers with the culture associated with its products. Each motorcycle purchased came with a year's automatic membership of the Harley Owners Group (HOG), renewable thereafter for a small fee. Members received regular publications informing them of both club and product news as well as invitations to local HOG 'chapter' events such as bike runs, dealer open evenings and pub meetings. Each chapter was sponsored by the local Harley-Davidson dealer.

In addition to local chapter events there were larger national HOG rallies. The presence and active participation of top company executives was always a feature of these gatherings. HOG was first established in 1983 and membership grew by about 30 per cent annually. By 1994 there were 250,000 HOG members in 800 chapters worldwide.

Parts and accessories

Riders of Harley-Davidsons had long been in the habit of customizing their machines and in 1986 the company responded to this by considerably expanding its parts and accessories range in three separate brands, each marketed via its own lavish brochure.

Licensing

The mid-1980s also saw moves into the licensing of the Harley-Davidson brand names and trademarks. A 'MotorClothes' line was introduced featuring tough but stylish motorcycle leathers through to children's socks, all manufactured under licence. MotorClothes were sold exclusively though dealers, thereby both increasing dealer revenue and attracting new customers into the showrooms. In other cases the name alone was licensed: Harley-Davidson hi-fi's, a Harley-Davidson cafe in New York City and even a range of men's toiletries. Not only did the licensing bring in additional revenue it also further promoted the brand name and image.

Dealerships

Harley-Davidson also made considerable efforts to build strong relationships with its direct customers, motorcycle dealers, and to assist them in improving their own performance.

In 1987 a 'Designer Store' program was launched under which dealers were encouraged to redesign their showrooms to provide an improved shopping environment with near equal emphasis on displays of accessories and MotorClothes as on the bikes themselves.

Financial performance

The initial turnaround was largely complete by 1986. Not only had profitability been restored but turnover, profits and market share were all beginning to show steady increases. The opportunity was taken to float the company in June 1986 with a public offering of 2m shares at $11 a share together with $70m of 12.5 per cent unsecured subordinate loan notes.

The year 1986 also saw the company diversify away from its reliance on motorcycles. Holiday Ramblers Corp, a manufacturer of premium motor homes and travel trailers, was acquired for $157m. Holiday Rambler was run as an autonomous operation post-acquisition with separate management from the motorcycle business.

In a further demonstration of the company's growing strength the buy-out team went to the US government in March 1987 to request that tariff protection against imported Japanese motorcycles be lifted one year before it was due to expire. It was the first company in US history to take such action.

The company's share of the US heavyweight motorcycle market continued to rise steadily from 31 per cent in 1986 to 55 per cent by 1989 despite the fact that the overall motorcycle market was declining by almost ten per cent a year over the same period.

The early 1990s saw a revival of growth worldwide in motorcycle registrations and Harley-Davidson maintained its share comfortably in all major markets. At the end of 1993 it held 58 per cent of the US, 10 per cent of the European and 21 per cent of the Japanese/Australian heavyweight motorcycle markets.

This success was reflected in the tremendous loyalty of Harley-Davidson customers. A staggering 96 per cent of Harley owners claimed they intended to buy another — a figure thought to be one of the highest loyalty levels of any industry. This loyalty was also illustrated by the attendance of 100,000 people at a 'reunion party' in Milwaukee organized by Harley-Davidson to mark its 90th anniversary. Harley riders spent more than $10m on food, goods and services in Milwaukee during the reunion and raised over $1m in sponsorship for the muscular dystrophy association – a charity heavily supported by Harley-Davidson. ■

☞ Entrepreneurship in
the organization

Contents

Contributors

Neil C. Churchill is Professor Emeritus of Entrepreneurship at INSEAD and formerly Paul T. Babson Professor of Entrepreneurship and Director of the Center for Entrepreneurial Studies at Babson College, Massachusetts.

Kingsley Manning is Founder and Managing Director of Newchurch & Company and Visiting Professor at the Imperial College Management School.

Ian MacMillan is the George W. Taylor Professor of Entrepreneurial Studies at the Wharton School of the University of Pennsylvania and Executive Director of the Wharton School's Entrepreneurial Center.

Sandra Vandermerwe is Professor of Marketing and International Services at Imperial College Management School.

Zenas Block is Clinical Professor of Management at the Stern School of Business, New York University, and adjunct professor at Rensselaer Polytechnic Institute.

Introduction

Part 9 looks the ways in which large organizations in both the public and private sectors have attempted to introduce entrepreneurship. Two types of strategy are examined. The first is concerned to change the whole style of the organization from bureaucratic to entrepreneurial; and the second is concerned to develop new business through some form of corporate venturing activity. To illustrate these perspectives, we present two case studies of successful venturing.

The evolution of entrepreneurship in large organizations

Daniel Muzyka and **Neil Churchill** look at how large organizations can be more effective at capturing opportunity.

Large organizations have strived over the years to promote additional entrepreneurial activity and to capture more opportunities than their normal product development systems seem to permit. This has provided generations of entrepreneurship experts with food for thought. However, the evidence is strong that nothing leads to failure like success. Even the most successful companies were unable to identify and capture as many opportunities as quickly as entrepreneurs could 'in the wild'. This would seem to be good news for scholars and researchers as additional work is obviously in order.

Under the ubiquitous Taylor model of industrial organization, formulated nearly a century ago, the logic was to capture and systematize business activity in the form of clear, well-defined processes. Research and development were responsible for discovery, marketing was responsible for bringing discovery to the customer, production had its strictly-defined role, and so on. Functional control was key. And as for new business development, it was to be centralized, systematic, and efficient, and therefore less risky. Significant research has been dedicated to improving both the efficiency and effectiveness of internal product development processes.

Executives in larger organizations have begun to realize that it is not always possible to rely solely on a process for future business evolution. The door must be left open to innovation and opportunities that come from other sources and along other paths. Successive generations of ideas have emerged as to how best to do this. Some companies placed certain activities in separate organizational units – called 'skunk works' after Lockheed Aircraft's famous unit (which originated aircraft from the U-2 to the current Stealth fighter). Their purpose was to take responsibility for developing and testing ideas that might otherwise be missed and to boost the set of ideas and product/service options available to take to market.

During the 1970s, a new generation of organizationally separate units with innovation and opportunity development responsibilities evolved. Some companies (Exxon, for example) set up separate new venture or corporate venturing subsidiaries and business units. These units were responsible for developing opportunities which were usually, but not exclusively, outside the current product or technology offering of the company. Some of these corporate ventures (IBM's PC division, for example) created significant economic value. Many were not so successful.

During the 1980s, the idea of developing and supporting entrepreneurs within the main organization ('intrapreneurship') became more in vogue. Many companies now had a basic strategy and organizational system incorporating innovation processes. However, they held a door open to the efforts of individuals and teams working on innovations and that spun off from the company's main product portfolio. In the end, capturing these opportunities led to additional growth and renewal of the organization.

Each of these elements – the normal product development process, corporate venturing, and individual entrepreneurial activity – became part of the puzzle. Each appears to lead to opportunity capture by larger organizations. The questions today are: (1) how can we make these elements integrate better? and (2) how can we improve our models of management to permit organizations to be even more effective at capturing opportunity? With shorter and increasingly irregular product life cycles, these questions need to be addressed.

Today, managers and management researchers are turning back to the basics. We are all looking for a more self-renewing model, organizations that can update their portfolio of activities more fluidly. And while this is going on, entrepreneurs operating within the economy are continuing to find significant support and access to resources, even for large projects. Corporations that wish to have a significant future can no longer depend upon the failure of entrepreneurs to initiate their own businesses. They themselves must deliver by becoming entrepreneurial corporations. ■

Stimuli and stumbling blocks in a new venture

Ian MacMillan and **Zenas Block** outline ways of identifying, evaluating and selecting opportunities for corporate venturing.

Not all ideas are opportunities and many opportunities are not right for all companies. When a company provides overall direction and focus designed to improve the fit between its vision, strategy and goals and the ideas generated, it increases both the number of acceptable ideas and the efficiency of the selection process.

Opportunities can be found within a business itself, in the industries and markets it serves, and in the external environment. Most viable opportunities spring from problems, needs and change – for example a tamper-proof lock developed in response to a rise in the crime rate or new cancer treatment drugs developed from monoclonal antibodies as an outcome of major changes in biotechnology. **Sources of opportunity**

Internal sources

Internal sources of opportunity may be found in every aspect of a business. Examples include the need for, or the possibility of, reducing rejects in a manufacturing process, improving overall quality, supplying better service or replacing a raw material.

Identifying an organization's special competencies can also become the basis for creating a new business or improving its competitive position. What skills does the organization have that are outstanding and unequivocally excellent? Here are two examples:

● Japanese carmakers had to manufacture more reliable cars to penetrate foreign markets where their service network was inadequate. They elected to build cars that required less servicing rather than try to improve the service network. Their outstanding competence was the ability to manufacture high-quality products at low cost.

As this strategy hinged on the reliability of components, they taught their suppliers how to manufacture extremely dependable components. The success of this approach immediately became evident in the reliability of the cars produced.

● General Electric in the US, unable to obtain suitable materials from the plastics industry, created its own special plastics for use in its electrical products. After developing this special competence, GE decided to aggressively enter the engineered plastics market. This is now one of GE's major businesses, producing an operating profit of $1bn in 1991.

The great advantage of basing new ventures on internal sources of opportunity is familiarity with the identified resource. The great disadvantage is that there may not be any worthwhile opportunity to which that resource can be applied.

Although the odds of achieving success with technological innovations are small, such innovations have produced the really big hits, creating whole new industries. This was the case with semiconductors and biotechnology and will surely be the case with superconductivity. Businesses created this way tend to continue for many years, an example being DuPont and nylon.

Industry and market changes

Changes in a given industry or market are a major source of new opportunities, as Peter Drucker, the management theorist, has pointed out, and are probably the best source of opportunities with a high probability of success.

There are many examples of ventures generated by industry or market change. As pension fund administrators become a larger factor in the stock market, the need for solid research increased. The highly successful US firm of Donaldson, Lufkin, & Jenrette was formed in response to this opportunity. The growth of department stores was accompanied by a trend toward stocking only the better-moving items and reducing the inventory of speciality items, such as blue jeans and other product lines. As speciality items became unavailable, speciality retail stores, the fastest-growing business sector of the 1980s, were born. Examples include toy chains, athletic shoe chains and the Gap stores, which originally specialized in jeans and then, in response to the changing demographics of the 1990s, adjusted their product line to achieve renewed growth.

Wal-Mart is certainly the most successful instance of a business formed in response to industry and market developments. When Wal-Mart started, discount stores were mainly in larger cities and high-quality national brands were sold at high retail in smaller cities. Clerks in department stores often responded, 'We're out of it but we'll order it for you' to product requests. Sam Walton saw this gap and filled it with the fastest-growing retail chain in history, which kept prices low, provided better service, maintained high inventories of stock and utilized leading-edge information systems.

The needs and wants of the existing market are the most reliable sources of good opportunities in the short run. But the ability to foresee and meet future needs is the source of long-term opportunity and competitive advantage.

The external environment

Threats and opportunities produced by the external environment can be excellent sources of venturable ideas. Changing demographics, lifestyles, perceptions and values, government regulations and tax laws, as well as social problems such as crime and drug abuse, all create problems and the need for solutions.

Opportunities that buck environmental forces will face a difficult obstacle while opportunities linked to environmental forces will rise, like ships with a rising tide. Consider the explosive growth of fitness centres, low-calorie, low-fat, low-cholesterol foods; and the flood of services and products related to lifestyle changes and perceptions regarding health and exercise.

Paradoxically, though, this trend has been paralleled by the success of ultrarich Lady Godiva chocolates and premium ice creams, which runs directly counter to environmental factors. One explanation offered is that the calories consumed are a reward for the exercise and dieting that presumably preceded them. Another is that, for some, indulgence is and will always be present.

Drucker argues that the process of opportunity identification can be systemized and that opportunities can be found by monitoring seven basic sources: demographic changes, new knowledge, incongruities (gaps between reality and expectations), industry or market structure, unexpected successes or failures, process needs and changes in perception.

An incongruity is seen in the success of the steel industry's minimills, which defied the principles of economy of scale and have led to significant changes in the steel industry. Another incongruity involved the practice of building increasingly large vessels for trans-oceanic shipping to reduce costs. In fact, capital costs were actually higher and both pilferage and idle time in dock were greater. This incongruity led to containerized ships and shipping, drastically reducing loading time and labor costs and providing increased security.

An example of an unexpected failure was Ford's Edsel automobile. Prior to that failure, automotive marketing segments had been conceived of in terms of income demographics. Its experience with the Edsel led Ford to re-examine its marketing approach and move to the concept of lifestyle marketing segments, a key factor in the great success of the Mustang.

Federal Express unexpectedly saw an increase in shipments of high-priced, low-weight computer components. Upon investigation, FedEx learned that this unexpected success was attributable to companies using its service to keep their inventory levels down, which opened up new and previously overlooked market possibilities.

Process needs refer to interruptions or bottlenecks in a process. The Polaroid

Winning wheels; Ford switched its marketing strategy to score a success with the Mustang.

Land Camera filled a process need – eliminating the delay between capturing a moment and finding out whether the moment had been captured. According to legend, it was Land's daughter who asked him, 'Why do we have to wait?' The question led Edwin Land to invent the Land Camera and Polaroid film.

Many factors can trigger a flow of ideas, with change and problems being the best sources. Information and a resulting awareness of developments both within a company and industry and in the world at large are essential to the process. Training, education, exposure to information available at trade shows and conventions, publications such as trade and professional journals, and information sharing are powerful stimulants.

Evaluating and selecting opportunities

Deciding to pursue a new business opportunity should only be done after it is determined that the opportunity itself is both valid and right for the company and that the company has a business strategy and plan to which it is prepared to commit itself.

A number of questions must be answered and then a preliminary judgement made as to whether the proposal merits proceeding to the next step – concept testing or feasibility study.

Is the opportunity consistent with the organization's strategy?

It is not always possible to make a decision regarding strategic fit at an early stage of evaluation if size and profit potential are part of the strategic objectives. But if, at face value, an opportunity is inconsistent with a company's strategy, then it should be passed up. We are not suggesting that the venture must fit current capabilities but rather strategic objectives. In order to succeed, many companies must diversify to some extent – penetrate new industries, gain new knowledge and enter new markets – and if strategic fit meant perfect fit with today's competency and knowledge, such companies would be doomed to inevitable decline.

But what about opportunities that seem too good to pass up? What about a business proposition that looks attractive but involves entering a new industry that the company has rejected as a strategic objective?

In this case, a spin-off may be desirable. The venture may begin with full funding and majority ownership by the parent but, as the spin-off succeeds, the parent's ownership may be greatly reduced. This is not uncommon in Japan, where the parent organization may end up a minority investor. In fact, 17.5 per cent of the largest Japanese companies are spin-offs. Examples include Toyota Motor Corporation (spun off from Toyota Auto Loom Works) and Yamaha Motors (spun off from Yamaha Musical Instruments.)

To determine strategic consistency, the business concept must be scrutinized. The initial concept should indicate the product/service to be provided, the market segment targets, customers to be targeted, a guesstimate of market size, and the venture's potential value to the organization.

Aside from economic benefits, a venture can offer less tangible benefits, such as serving a defensive function, enhancing a company's reputation or providing a learning opportunity. In some cases, a company may start a new venture simply to study a business to determine whether and how to enter on a larger scale.

The following questions should be asked about any new-business concept.

What factors produce the opportunity?

By answering this question, a company can estimate how long those factors are likely to last. For example, a drop in interest rates might provide an opportunity for a new venture related to the building industry. How long rates are expected to stay low will affect the decision as to whether to enter the new venture, as well as how quickly to enter and exit. In contrast, environmental legislation is here to stay and as a source of opportunity can be regarded as fairly durable.

What are the character, size and nature of the market?

At what stage of its life-cycle is the market: not yet in existence, just emerging, static, growing, exploding or declining? Who are the players? What is known about present and potential competitors? What is the current and potential size of the market? What about pricing practices? Quality levels? Margins? What will this venture contribute in terms of value to the customer and with what competitive insulation?

The venture capital industry is a useful source of information about opportunity evaluation. Academic researchers have identified the following characteristics associated with successful ventures:

● Rather than identifying a market in general terms, successful ventures identify the true market in very specific terms, including a well-defined notion of the actual customer population to whom the value added by the proposed new product or service is clear.

● A market size between $10m and $100m is more likely to yield success than a very small or very large market. (This finding may not apply to corporate ventures by large organizations although it is quite appropriate for smaller businesses with limited available capital. For some corporations, even markets having a potential size of $100m are uninteresting.)

● Market growth rates between 30 per cent and 60 per cent are most favorable.

● Competitive insulation through patent protection or unique technologies involving products or services that cannot otherwise be provided with equal quality or satisfaction is a major success factor.

● Successful ventures tend to achieve a market share of at least 20 per cent.

To identify the factors necessary for a proposed new venture's success, a company has to ask, how must this function differ in the new business as opposed to our present businesses in order for the venture to succeed? Here are some obvious examples:

● A manufacturer of consumer goods moving into industrial markets. Direct selling must be done by people who understand their customers' business and can develop strong relationships with them.

● A manufacturer moving into retailing. The company must understand such issues as managing inventories, providing security to protect against theft, recruiting and training salespeople who are congenial, knowledgeable and helpful to customers, and selecting business locations.

● A manufacturer, retailer or distributor entering a new industry. The organization must develop knowledge of customer needs and wants, major competitors, supplier sources, technology, usage patterns and problems.

When analyzing required success factors, a company must also understand the relative importance of the various functions involved (such as marketing, manufacturing, finance, human resources and R&D).

For example, in the retail business, merchandising (what to buy, how to price, how to promote) and information systems are critical; in commodity businesses, buying and trading reign. If a company is considering, say, a venture in which the marketing function is primary, it can be disastrous to initiate the venture under a manager whose skills lie mainly in the area of technology management.

An organization seeking clues to the factors required for the success of a proposed new business should study leading companies in the target industry and identify what accounts for their outstanding track record.

Is the opportunity worth the effort?

To determine feasibility and potential value, an organization must analyze each opportunity's economic potential, asking itself what the upside gain and downside loss could be. For guidelines, we turn once again to the venture capital industry, in which the economic characteristics of successful ventures reportedly include the following:

● a break-even time of less than 36 months
● stable gross margins of 20 per cent to 50 per cent
● after-tax profit potential of 10 per cent to 15 per cent
● multiple rather than one-shot investments
● low asset intensity
● differentiation on the basis of product rather than price.

A few of these attributes are obviously inapplicable to many corporate ventures. A required break-even time of 36 months is not feasible in the case of ventures that are based on new technology, that have a high potential or that involve new or emerging markets.

Low asset intensity is undesirable if the corporation's economic power is to be used to erect entry barriers to competition. New industries are not created with low asset intensity (for example, semiconductors, biotechnology) nor can new entrants to a field, such as the automotive industry, be competitive without heavy investment in manufacturing facilities.

Some additional factors that venturing corporations should consider include:

- impact on overall corporate performance during the venture's early period – profits, ROI, cash flow
- impact on existing customers and business
- potential impact on total sales, profit, positioning and the value of company stock
- impact on the company's overall competitive advantage.

Is the opportunity feasible?

The ideal opportunity is one for which an organization already possesses precisely the mix of special competencies needed to provide the success factors and where the strategic fit is clear. But if the company lacks the means to provide the required success factors, it can also assemble the necessary competencies through alliances, joint ventures and so forth.

One universally required success factor is knowledge and experience in the proposed industry (except for cases in which the industry itself is entirely new). Unless an organization has or can employ knowledgeable people or can acquire a foothold firm enough to provide that knowledge and experience, the opportunity should be dropped or delayed until the company can learn something about the business through a small-scale entry or an acquisition. ■

Copyright Ian MacMillan and Zenas Block 1997

This article was adapted from a chapter in *Corporate Venturing: Creating New Businesses Within the Firm* (Harvard Business School Press, 1995).

A new order in the public sector

Kingsley Manning chronicles the rise of enterprise in the public sector and sets out some of the implications.

In the last 20 years the public sector in virtually all industrialized nations has changed dramatically. Long-held assumptions about the role and functioning of the public sector have been jettisoned to be replaced by ideas largely taken from private-sector business performance measures, strategy and business planning, management information and the entrepreneur.

With similarities and differences from their private-sector cousins, the entrepreneur in the public sector – the social entrepreneur – is increasingly becoming a key figure in shaping the future of a major part of the economy.

In the UK it is widely assumed that the changes in the public sector witnessed during the 1980s and 1990s are a local phenomenon, a product of Thatcherite ideology. In fact such a view is highly parochial; governments of all political persuasions, in every continent, are confronting in a similar fashion their burgeoning public sectors.

In most industrialized nations, the great post-war settlement, establishing the state as a central plank of the economy and the monopoly supplier of 'public' services, had begun to crack by the 1980s. The public sector had become stereotyped by institutionalized pay inflation, ineffective management, poor service quality and industrial strife. At the same time the consumer's expectations of the public sector, fuelled for some by increasing wealth and for others – the old, the sick and the poor – by increasing needs, continued to rise and to be disappointed.

The traditional public-sector model – strong planning, input measurement, rigorous administration, robust hierarchies and central control – appeared to have failed, to have outlived its time. By comparison, the business paradigm, with its emphasis on output measurement, decentralization, strategy and respon- siveness, appeared to offer a positive and demonstrably successful alternative.

Great swathes of the public sector with commercial characteristics, tradition- ally known as the 'commanding heights of the economy' or as natural monopolies, were therefore sold off to enthusiastic populations, who in theory already owned them. This is a process that is still going on today, witness the recent sale of Germany's Deutsche Telecom, with the positive political benefit of producing large revenues to support a range of political goals.

However, the sale of the protocommercial elements of the public sector – airlines, utilities, mines – leaves large tracts of the public sector, such as education, health, welfare, local and central government services, for which there is no private-sector model or where the private-sector alternative is politically unacceptable. In these areas governments have sought to introduce the structure of business and the dynamics of the market while largely sustaining public funding and control of the service. This has led to the development of a new type of organization – the social business, an organization delivering services of benefit to the community but operating in a business-like manner.

The UK, with its executive agencies in central government, health trusts in the national health service, local management of schools, capitation funding of universities and purchaser/provider splits in local government, has been at the forefront of these developments but is by no means unique. Similar developments have been taking place from Australia to Spain, from India to Poland. Much of this vast part of the economy, in the UK some 35 per cent of GDP, is now in the hands of social businesses, with varying degrees of autonomy from, though primarily funded by, government.

Explicit performance measures, distinct separate identities, exposure to some form of market mechanism and the presence of general management structures all characterize these organizations, as does the presence of the entrepreneur. Combine some autonomy with the possibility of explicit success or failure and even the beginnings of a management structure, and entrepreneurial activity results.

In the first instance that activity may be injected into the public-sector organization by importing managers from the private sector. Unconstrained by the cultural norms of the vocationally orientated public sector, these managers see opportunities for the organization and themselves and respond accordingly.

In so doing they establish role models for indigenous managers and professionals, who may have spent all their careers within the public sector, triggering off both changes in their behavior and a thirst for appropriate education and training. This process reaches its logical, institutional conclusion with the establishment of formal educational programs such as the UK civil service's MBA program at Imperial College Management School.

So a process of transformation occurs. The public sector takes on the characteristics of a business, introduces generic management principles and creates the framework for entrepreneurial activity. The progenitor of that activity, the social entrepreneur, may be a career manager but is just as likely to be firstly a 'professional' – a headteacher, a clinician, a borough engineer, a university academic. For these individuals the new order within the public sector provides not just an opportunity to administer the status quo but to bring about radical change, creating success for their own organization and themselves. Many take up the opportunity with the fervent zeal of a convert.

The opportunities for expressing that entrepreneurial enthusiasm – from rebuilding the sixth form, to achieving university status, to building a new hospital, to bidding for the Olympics – all go far beyond the current management task. The individuals have a vision of the service they want to deliver and the organization they need to build. These individuals are acting beyond the bounds of their managerial roles, they are acting as entrepreneurs.

Social wealth

However, they differ in one very important aspect from their private-sector counterparts. For the social entrepreneur the rewards do not include personal wealth-creation. Crucially concerned with increasing societal wealth – better healthcare, better education, better welfare services – the social entrepreneur's own financial return is likely to be modest, though public-sector salaries are not as mean as they once were.

Even so, there are rewards for the social entrepreneur and they can be considerable. Personal recognition, professional rewards, enhanced influence, status within the local if not the national community, all contribute to a significant sense of self worth. Such rewards are reinforced by the nature of the social businesses. By comparison to most private businesses, a social business is usually both large and important, occupying a position of predominance within its local economy and community.

With the downsizing and dispersal of manufacturing, the hospital, the local municipality, the school may well be a community's largest local employers. Success or failure for the private-sector entrepreneur will usually touch few lives outside the immediate family and staff; in the average social business, success or failure will both be public and affect the lives of many. Therein lies one of the critical areas of risk for the public-sector entrepreneur. Operating in the public domain, often in a substantial organization staffed largely by vocational professionals, adds greatly to the risks.

Failure, both personal and organizational, can come, as in the private sector, from errors in conception and implementation and from unforeseen changes in the competitive marketplace. But it may also arise from factors usually unknown in the private sector – from the exercise of self-interest on the part of the vocational professionals, from direct political interference, with both a small and large P, and from the expression of public disquiet, so eagerly picked up by the ever-interested local press and media.

Being a social entrepreneur is therefore a risky occupation with perhaps the added perversity that past success is no protection, indeed may only enhance future vulnerability.

Leadership skills The skills of the social entrepreneur are therefore both the same and different from those of the traditional entrepreneur. Both need vision, energy, determination and self-confidence. But the successful social entrepreneur requires other, perhaps rarer, attributes. These include the ability to act in a public and political forum, to engage and motivate an often doubting staff. Above all, the social entrepreneur has to master the transformation of an existing organization.

Achieving his or her goals, building the vision, within the public sector invariably means changing what is already there. In the public sector, cash limited and resource constrained, there is no green field, no debt-raising exercises, no diverting acquisitions; the future has always to be built on the foundations of the past. This requires leadership skills that even the most successful private entrepreneur might find difficult to muster.

Not surprisingly, the creation of the social entrepreneur sits uneasily within a public-sector framework that has taken centuries to evolve. The established assumptions of political control, public accountability and the role of the civil servant, fit awkwardly with the basic premise of the entrepreneurial manager.

For politicians and civil servants alike, there is an overwhelming temptation to paradigm hop, choosing to recognize devolved authority, all too often in the context of political convenience. Having let loose the social entrepreneur, having backed heavily the social business as a way out of the public-sector conundrum and having willingly accepted the credit for success when it has come, politicians have yet to come to terms with the implications and limitations for their own role.

The public sector not only consumes today's wealth but lays foundations for tomorrow's success. Future economic and cultural prosperity are dependent on how well we invest today in education, health, and the physical and social infrastructure. It is not only the amount we choose to spend in these areas but also how well those investment decisions are made and implemented.

Over the last 20 years, with little debate and considerable consensus, the manager, the social entrepreneur, has been placed at the nexus of that process. For those individuals it is doubtful that there can be a more demanding role but the stakes for the rest of us are also considerable.

It may have taken 500 years for the entrepreneur to come from the Rialto to the public hospital and the secondary school but the outcome of the experiment will be with us within the next decade. If successful, the social entrepreneur will have helped crack one of the great riddles of the late 20th century – how to deliver the public services that we all want and at a price we can afford; an entrepreneurial gamble in which we are all interested investors. ■

The boss as a force for change

Wherever we work we are all entrepreneurs now.
Sandra Vandermerwe and **Sue Birley** report on their research into how corporate executives act like enterprising leaders.

Once upon a time, the world was clearly divided between entrepreneurs and corporate executives, between the public and the private sectors. No longer. Now we expect civil servants to behave in a 'business-like' fashion, entrepreneurs to create large organizations and bureaucratic managers to behave entrepreneurially. They all must be competitive for customers. Clearly, we believe that 'nurture' can transcend 'nature', that we can change behavior to fit changing circumstances, that the entrepreneurial bug can be caught at any age. Witness, for example, the civil servants and corporate executives, notably in the UK, who have abandoned the apparent safety of employment to become owners through the mechanism of a management buy-out.

But they are the tip of a very large iceberg. Corporations and governments throughout the world are seeking a new type of corporate leader – not the manager of stability or the professional bureaucrat but one who approaches problems creatively and entrepreneurially and who thrives on the management of change.

What is it like for those chosen to make these transformations happen? What are the issues they have to deal with, and what are the factors they think necessary for success? To find out we asked executives from major organizations such as Baxter, BT, Ciba Geigy, Citibank, IBM, ICI, Jiffy Packaging, NatWest, Northumbrian Water, Price Waterhouse, Singapore Airlines and Zurich Insurance who had been (or are) involved in a radical 'customer transformation' to tell us about their experiences.

Selection of leaders

Our respondents were very clear why they had been selected for such projects. Some felt they had been chosen for their selling and influencing skills, some for their networking and co-ordination skills and some for attributes such as enthusiasm, energy, courage or patience – all of which contribute to the entrepreneurial character. The conspicuous absence of traditional skills, such as planning or cost-consciousness, is interesting.

Team selection

They were also clear on their selection of their team. They wanted people who were focused and self-drivers, self-starters, self motivated, self confident with a strong sense of urgency – in short, corporate entrepreneurs. (While they did require technical skills, functional background was rarely mentioned.) It seems that these change agents can come from anywhere in the organization provided they are prepared to take the risks associated with making new things happen.

'I have made it work if I have changed minds, not because I have increased sales by x per cent.'

Success factors   All reported that their projects had been wholly or partially successful, and they measured this by the level of acceptance of both the project and the process by their colleagues in the business and by their customers. They accept that they have to deliver bottom-line results but are also concerned about capabilities for growing the organization. They claim the two can only happen simultaneously by making the transformational process work.

The breakthrough   We asked about breakthrough events. When did they first feel that it was working? The biggest impact came from the 'buy-in', or acceptance, of senior management. This was demonstrated through clearer direction, more effective support, demands to do more on the project or to extend it. All were process based, reflecting a growing acceptance of change. Involvement and buy-in from customers was mentioned by 30 per cent of respondents and a special event, a meeting or forum in which a radical shift in thinking took place, by some 25 per cent as a catalyst for change.

The blockers   More than half our respondents were plagued by things such as corporate politics, the wrong people in place, suspicion, cynicism and members of the team hiding problems. Some top managers were reluctant to get involved 'until they began to see results'. There was also a tendency to short-termism, incrementalism and conflicting priorities. Trouble arose from poor communication and arrogance.

Reflections   We also asked if they would do anything differently a second time round. Again, the responses were concerned with the process. They would have involved more people earlier from various parts of the organization and would have 'engaged' top management more visibly. It is clear from this that the role of senior management is critical to the success of customer transformation – at least in the eyes of those asked to take on the task. This is not surprising. We find the same result when we examine corporate venturing strategies. Therefore, we asked about the role their boss played in the process.

'I am the boss!'
'He gave us space to change ourselves.'

The boss   As expected, the focus of responses was on active involvement. They were used to remove organizational road blocks, to 'get the rest of the organization off our backs' and 'sold the idea up the line'. They managed political and cultural tensions, insisted that the project was high priority and stuck to it and created an environment of trust. Some were more passive, simply 'allowed it to happen' while a few felt that their boss had been a negative influence who 'bowed too much to internal politics' or was an arbitrator in conflict situations rather than a leader of change.

On a personal level, the 'good' bosses – no matter the level – were seen as sounding boards and coaches, always there to give moral support.

All of our respondents had been involved in major customer transformation within their organization and so we asked them to sit back and reflect, to tell us what they felt had been the most important challenges to achieve a customer focus to date and how they felt this would change over the next decade. The answers, shown in Figure 1 speak for themselves.

Critical attributes for the future

It all points to a need to be proactive, not reactive, and to have imagination – a word that appeared frequently as critical in driving customer-based transformations. This was combined with creativity and an ability to recognize, interpret and evaluate new market opportunities and turn them into actionable projects. To do this, these entrepreneurs – for that is what is being described – need good communication skills, vision (the ability to encapsulate customer needs conceptually) and the ability to persuade their colleagues 'to get out of their boxes', see the big picture and act accordingly.

'True progress involves tenacity and patience'

People are being asked to both 'think and do' – to operate on two levels – strategically and operationally. They need to be able to disseminate and sell their ideas internally up, sideways and down as well as into the market. This requires a certain type of personality. In their eyes, they must be flexible – listening and learning from what they hear – trustworthy, open, resilient, tough, enthusiastic and extrovert, with integrity, honesty and honor – plus a sense of

Up to now	For the future
The marketplace	
● Adapt to market needs;	● Evolve and develop needs with customers;
● Understand customer needs;	● Anticipate customer needs;
● Superior products;	● Specific customer offerings;
● Instigate innovations (quality);	● Manage innovations faster (innovate);
● Build relationship with customer;	● Make customers partners;
● Know competitors' products;	● Know how competitors tick;
● Good market data.	● Dialog with the market.
Organizational style	
● Reduce bureaucracy/politics;	● People working in teams, mutually trusting and respecting one another;
● Manage enterprise-wide for cohesive offering;	● Manage trans-enterprise with partners;
● Get things done.	● Manage complex projects.
Systems	
● Good budgeting;	● Good feedback mechanism;
● Ensure information technology works.	● Understand impact of and harness emerging technology.
People	
● Get people to work well;	● Mobilize people's energy and drive;
● Train and control staff;	● Develop leaders, renew human capital;
● Compensate staff;	● Reward and involve staff in success;
● Stop internal strife;	● Fight the correct competition as one united front;
● Select the right people.	● Get the correct skill mix.

Figure 1

© FT Pictures

Sir Colin Marshall, Chairman of British Airways and Chairman of the Confederation of British Industry, 'never lost sight of the vision'. He is pictured, left, with other business leaders at a meeting last year.

humor. Furthermore, they must be patient. Consistency in pursuit of their goals is essential.

> *'I so admired Colin Marshall from British Airways who never lost sight of the vision and never got dismayed by the gap between what he wanted the company to be and where it really was'*

Where have we heard all this before? In the entrepreneurship literature. No longer do we see these people as impatient, determined, misfits. Now they are seen as integral to making change happen within organizations.

The new entrepreneurial organization

Leaders of, in their eyes, successful customer transformations have told us that to make it work, organizations must:
- develop new, proactive and process skills – this may entail pulling in more creative people from outside. It definitely means letting people go with their instincts and feelings
- encourage experimentation and reward success as defined by how customer-competitive it makes (or is likely to make) the corporation. This also involves managing failures successfully
- learn how to work on twin tracks – do what needs doing better now and, simultaneously, new things that may take longer
- unlock the enterprise within, defining risk differently and having 'venturesome' people making key resource decisions
- develop new leadership skills with a new set of language and tools to reflect not the entrepreneurial or management world of yesterday but what is needed today and in the future.

Most of all we need coaches at the top of modern organizations who will let corporate entrepreneurs 'own their ventures' and get on and make them work.

The corporation's responsibility is to support and reward this in new and innovative ways.

Question. Can existing top management take on this new role? Or will the new role require new top management? ■

A copy of the full paper on which this article is based will be published in Long Range Planning in June 1997.

KAO Corporation

*This edited case was originally prepared by Professor **Shuichi Matsuda** of Waseda University's Entrepreneurship Research Unit (WERU), Tokyo.*

KAO was founded in June 1887 by Tomiro Nagase, as Nagase Shoten, an imported fancy goods wholesaler. The company operated under the slogan, 'A clean nation is a prosperous nation'. In the 20th century, KAO caught up with and in many segments surpassed the major domestic competitors, Shiseido and Lion, to gain the leading position in the Japanese toiletry industry.

The company has continued to grow by expanding into personal care products and household products, with aggressive entry into foreign markets as well as overcoming declining growth in the mature domestic toiletries market.

The group's management is based on three fundamental principles:

**Management
style of KAO**

● Maintain a consumer-oriented spirit.
● All individuals have equal value.
● Combine abilities and goals to maximize effectiveness.

These principles drive KAO's three main managerial practices: total system management, group management, and R&D career focus.

Total System Management enables every function of the corporation to work together effectively. KAO's total system management practice makes its venturing system unique. All functions, such as R&D, operations, marketing and sales activities, are put under the charge of a single manager in a single venture framework. This manager is completely responsible for the direction of R&D and how the product should be introduced into the consumer market.

KAO also utilizes Total Creative Revolution (TCR) to raise quality. The TCR program is designed to encourage creativity and combine personal objectives with commitment to the organization.

Group management combines all employees into a single, large group for each major product area. This system allows more effective management practices and more timely information-sharing. This single group concept creates an environment in which employees are encouraged to find and apply their own particular abilities toward better job performance.

Group management depends significantly upon making frequent personnel transfers, based upon individuals' requests. This practice constantly expands an individual's personal expertise and at the same time brings these new ideas to bear in different areas. The strategy also increases the number of employees with multi-functional abilities who understand the functions of many areas of the organization. This practice is particularly important for continued growth.

R&D career focus

KAO focuses primarily on identifying seeds, such as new technologies, rather than on consumer needs, and over 60 per cent of the marketing staff has worked in R&D. The basic R&D or technological research perspective is reflected in the career paths of senior managers. As of 1993, four out of five senior managers had career experience in R&D. This means that researchers and engineers must develop their ideas in great detail before presenting them to senior managers. This seeds-oriented approach, with its R&D career focus, also gives true scientific innovators a more satisfying work environment.

Systems and practices to promote successful corporate venturing

KAO's basic strategy is to create simple and flexible organization structures that allow for the efficient development of new products, and that at the same time give greater autonomy to individual activities.

Full internal vertical integration

With a seeds-oriented R&D approach, KAO develops about 70 to 80 prospective substances every year, of which four or five are selected for the next stage of chemical analysis. In this stage, key properties of the new substances are identified and developed to maximize their effectiveness. The various derivatives are then developed into key materials which will be further developed and marketed in several areas.

By vertically integrating the entire process, from creating and evaluating new materials and producing raw materials to designing final products, as well as undertaking marketing and sales, KAO can develop more creative products with greater efficiency. This vertically integrated R&D approach is one of KAO's most crucial practices.

Twice each year, all KAO's top managers gather to discuss key R&D strategies. During the conference, approved ideas receive the authorization necessary to push them into the product development stage. In addition, long-term strategies for creating products which will be worth the challenge are identified.

A quarterly convention, attended by top management and those who head areas, such as sales and operation, introduces ideas under development in R&D divisions to all others in the organization. Furthermore, each week, top managers meet to decide whether or not certain new business or product ideas are worth further development. If approved, an idea is presented to the Management Committee, which reaches a final decision within two weeks.

When a new project gains approval, its proposer becomes project leader and all necessary specialists are selected. Yet all project team members hold other responsibilities concurrently. KAO managers believe that the success of any project depends heavily upon selecting the most qualified individuals, and top managers therefore supervise the project leader's staff selections to the project. Reports on the project's progress are made every two months to the Idea Evaluation Committee. If a project is decreed non-viable at any stage during the venturing process, the Committee immediately halts its further development and redeploys the staff.

Exploiting existing corporate resources to start the floppy disk business

Until 1981, KAO had only produced and sold surfactant, a raw material used to produce floppy disks, but had no intention of developing the actual disks. Since no one thought that a leader in the toiletry industry like KAO would consider developing floppy disk products, Tetsuga Imamura – a researcher at KAO's Tochigi Laboratories charged with considering the feasibility of manufacturing floppy disks – had a great advantage: his customers in the floppy disk industry were generous in sharing key information. Imamura also sent a researcher with the highest level of R&D in this field for further study at leading universities. KAO's R&D teams learned that surface activity control, a fundamental technology used for producing quality soap, was highly useful in the development of floppy disks. KAO's main product lines were already based upon this technology and its highly competitive surfactant technology gave it an additional advantage.

After much discussion in 1984, KAO executives made the final decision to manufacture floppy disks. They knew that one must have sufficient resources available when entering into risky new business. At the time when KAO made this decision, its core business had been continually achieving a double-digit growth rate both in sales and earnings.

Global strategies to expand the floppy disk business

A commercial floppy disk manufacturing facility was constructed in 1985 at the Tochigi plant, and a Floppy Disk Division was created with Imamura as manager. In 1986, KAO became the thirteenth manufacturer to introduce floppy disks into the Japanese market.

Imamura responded to this unexpected setback by changing the focus from the domestic market to targeting the North American market, where users would evaluate quality and price without such preconceived notions. KAO constructed its first plant in Canada, and this market shift soon proved to be extremely lucrative. In 1986 demand for the floppydisk products was 500m units in the US, 100m in Europe and 45m in Japan.

KAO continued to market its floppy disk products mainly to computer manufacturers and computer software firms as OEM supplier in Japan, while focusing its efforts on targeting the North American market. KAO's strategies for international growth were:
- to concentrate floppy disk production and sales in the North American market
- to ship floppy disk products to south-east Asia from Japan
- to acquire existing corporations in order to utilize effectively existing human resources and to increase production capacity
- to focus on the OEM market and supply products to most international computer manufacturers and software firms
- to boost production of the 3.5-inch floppy before demand dictated it, with the foresight that demand for high-density, smaller floppy disks would soon increase rapidly
- to begin an international business for duplicating information recorded on 5-inch floppy disks
- to increase the familiarity of the KAO brand worldwide
- to have centralized R&D in Japan.

Soon after production in foreign markets began, the US and Europe drastically curtailed floppy disk imports. However, KAO remained almost wholly unaffected. By channeling production through corporations which it had acquired in North America, KAO could act as a domestic manufacturer. In 1986, KAO acquired Didac of Canada and in 1987, it merged two existing companies in Spain and began manufacture. KAO acquired the plant and head office of Centennial Technology in 1988.

KAO's successful execution of these international growth strategies catapulted it to the top rank. KAO products gained credibility through competitive pricing and quality, and KAO is now the world's largest supplier of floppy disk products in terms of OEM. The company also holds the position of third-largest supplier in the international floppy disk market.

Risk management after entry decision

Financing the project proved more challenging than KAO had expected. The most serious problem was the sudden, sharp reduction of market prices. In 1984 a 3.5-inch flexible disk cost one thousand yen. But by 1986, when KAO began floppy disk production, the cost was 250 yen, and just over 100 yen by 1992. KAO had forecast that the market price would be lowered by 20 per cent each year, yet actual price dropped by 50 per cent. If, at the beginning of the venture, KAO market economists had estimated such a lowered price level, management may well have turned the project down. In 1989, because of these financial concerns, top management met to reconsider whether or not to continue the venture. Imamura was asked to submit a feasibility study of the business to determine ultimate cost and whether or not KAO could afford it.

After reviewing the initial business plan, he took the following measures to reduce total cost and increase sales volume:

● Greatly increased production at the Canadian Didac plant, since its manufacturing costs were calculated to be about half that at Tochigi.

● Updated the plant with highly productive, labor-saving equipment to produce high-quality floppy disks at lowered costs.

● Manufactured ten major raw materials and parts within the firm – a policy based on KAO's vertical integration concept. This improvement in productivity reduced variable cost.

An international floppy disk business headquarters was established in Massachusetts. In order to speed up the decision-making process by integrating top management with innovators, Vice-President Sasaki was temporarily transferred to the new headquarters.

KAO was fortunate to have become one of the world's leading floppy disk suppliers using only 10 per cent of its cash flow. Had the funds required to become a leader been much greater, KAO would have had insufficient funds to collect key information or to select the best direction for developing new products.

Contribution of floppy disk business to further venturing efforts

The technologies and knowledge which KAO gained from undertaking the floppy disk venture have contributed greatly toward R&D for the production of new materials and products. In 1990, KAO launched magnetic tapes for DAT (digital audio tape), including back-up tapes, as DAT manufacturers started marketing their products under unified specifications and standards. KAO views the production of back-up tapes as a promising undertaking since DAT would be used for storing computer data.

The total international demand for floppy disks was estimated to reach 3.3 bn units in 1993, and projected trends vary for each type of floppy disk. But KAO researchers believed that floppy disk products had a limited storage capacity and therefore pursued R&D in the area of optical storage disks such as CD-ROM.

Contribution of the floppy disk business to existing business

In the long run, the floppy disk business was expected to benefit KAO's core business in the following ways:

● since KAO's floppy disk products increased international market familiarity with the KAO brand name, the company could more easily introduce its toiletry products to foreign markets.

● the floppy disk business experience enabled KAO to train well-qualified staff with international business experience within a short time period.

● the development process of the floppy disk business stimulated further R&D, engineering, and technological innovation within the organization.

What KAO learned from its experience in the floppy disk business will be applied to the development of strategies for further globalization and diversification as it plans for the twenty-first century.

When top management decided to enter the floppy disk business, it drew up a business plan. Ten years later, when Vice-President Sasaki reviewed the plan, he discovered that only one of the original objectives, sales performance, had been achieved as originally planned. It was KAO's policy of frequently evaluating the progress of various ventures, and making necessary changes to increase efficiency and quality, that led to its success. ■

Most of the information for this study has been compiled from interviews with several managers, in particular: Executive Vice President Sumiaki Sasaki, who has maintained total charge of this project from the beginning; Executive General Manager of R&D Division Tetsuya Imamura; General Manager of Floppy Disk Business Center Izumi Miyazawa; and General Manager of Personnel Department Masatoshi Kitahara. In addition, the company's historical records, recorded speeches by Chairman Yoshio Maruta, and various related materials, such as that from periodicals, papers, financial reports, and Nikkei's financial data, were used to complete this study. The author would like to acknowledge the editorial assistance of Shelley Rossell.

Fostering the entrepreneurial spirit

Daniel Muzyka and **Neil Churchill** advise on how to maintain the process of innovation in a growing business.

One of the perennial questions posed by executives in companies of all sizes is: 'How do I grow?' In larger organizations the question may be: 'How do I get more growth out of my organization?' or 'How do we regain our earlier spirit for growth?', while executives in entrepreneurial activities ask: 'How do I preserve entrepreneurial activity as I grow?' These questions are all concerned with maintaining or increasing entrepreneurial activity within an organization. They have always been pressing but are even more so today. The reasons are clear. Many companies have been downsizing for more than five years, re-engineering 'inefficiencies' and 'slack' out of the system, and focusing their operations. As a result, many have failed to retain an adequate capacity to innovate and capture new opportunity.

So what is entrepreneurial activity? In the first article in *Mastering Enterprise*, we defined entrepreneurship as a process that can take place in many different types of organizations, even government.

The process comprises building a vision of an opportunity, fashioning it to fit the company and the market, marshalling resources to capture it, and then capturing the value in the opportunity by building the business. The essence of entrepreneurship is the identification and economic capture of market value, based on matching an innovation with a need. In this context, the questions above can be distilled into one: how do I build and preserve room for individuals and teams to engage in the entrepreneurial process within my organization?

We are not saying that corporations, as they grow, fail to put into place systematic processes for developing innovations and new products and businesses. We are suggesting, however, that this is not enough: they also need to provide the continued capacity and option for individuals and teams throughout the organization to identify and develop opportunities. These people need to find a hearing for their ideas and have the support required at least to try to develop them. Merging ability, motivation and means for identifying new opportunities make a company truly entrepreneurial.

An entrepreneurial corporation must support entrepreneurial behavior[*] and have a certain orientation, competitive logic, drivers, processes and tools that contribute to building and reinforcing entrepreneurial behavior and an entrepreneurial attitude. Over the past 12 years, we have researched entrepreneurial corporations in many industries and of many sizes – corporations that appear to maintain high levels of value-creating business development, innovation and entrepreneurship over the long-term. This article outlines some of the common elements.

Orientation

One basic orientation in organizations that have remained entrepreneurial over a long period is the pursuit of new business opportunities that produce value for their customers and, in the process, for themselves. One of the elements in organizations that have remained entrepreneurial over the long run is a basic orientation. Individuals throughout the organizations know there is a continuous search for opportunity. While the business may not grow every year, constant orientation toward growth and renewing the business produces a steady stream of new opportunities. This also recognizes the fact that corporations are unlikely to get entrepreneurial activity if they do not ask for it.

Such organizations are very demanding in terms of performance. In fact, performance is frequently evaluated in terms of the level of opportunity pursuit and innovation achieved. Several organizations we have studied demand that x per cent of their total turnover should come from products introduced within the last y years. This may not drive absolute growth but it is the sort of measure that ensures continuous new product and business development.

Competitive logic

Combined with this orientation toward growth and renewal is a basic competitive logic which we saw in medium-to-large entrepreneurial companies. The company's overriding competitive strategy is to create profit by continuously developing and introducing high value-added products (*see* Figure 1). Innovation is continuous and directed at creating value.

These companies are rarely low cost, low margin competitors. They introduce products that create value for customers, capture the value through value pricing and benefit from high gross margins in the process. These

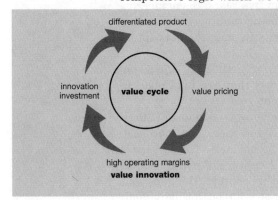

Figure 1: Competitive logic

[*]*See Manfred Kets de Vries' and Howard Stevenson's articles in Part 1 for a definition of entrepreneurial behavior.*

comparatively high gross margins are then sunk back into further innovation and entrepreneurial activity aimed at generating an even larger set of value-added products.

Two distinctive forces drive them to pursue opportunities. The first is useful tension in the organization (we call it organizational traction because it ensures continuous movement) and the second is an active 'action-learning' cycle.

Drivers

Organizational traction (*see* Figure 2), consists of a number of countervailing forces that operate in all the long-term entrepreneurial organizations we have studied. On one side are the consolidating forces – the recognition of what has been done well, clarification and sharing of knowledge, and focusing on successful activities.

Figure 2: Organizational traction *Countervailing forces*

On the other side are forces of progression – a continuous challenge for higher levels of performance, the search for new types of innovation and opportunity, accessibility of resources needed for innovation, and a focus on building and sharing for the greater good.

consolidation	dimension	progression
gratification	organizational commitment	challenge
reinforcement	continuous innovation	search
attribution	performance allocation	collectivity
termination	resource deployment	accessibility

With constructive management of these countervailing forces, an organization can build a culture that incorporates a sense of satisfaction and continuous commitment to new opportunity.

The action-learning process that characterizes many entrepreneurial corporations is a regular assessment of options, actions, and evaluation, combined with the active development and maintenance of knowledge (*see* Figure 3).

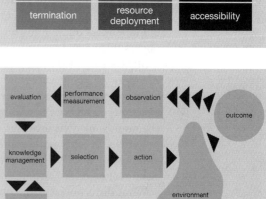

It can be difficult initially to distinguish significant differences in management style between entrepreneurial organizations and more classic organizations. One of the differences that becomes more apparent is that managers find ways to communicate, test and reflect on their activities more frequently.

In entrepreneurial corporations there is significant and active analysis and retention of lessons learned. This knowledge base is augmented through active innovation and experimentation. An important part of the constant emphasis on knowledge acquisition is the identification of distinctive skills and competencies and the search for new ways to leverage and evolve these competencies in pursuit of new economic opportunity.

Figure 3: Management decision process

Managers in these organizations may not always adopt the 'normal' solution to a problem if they believe that, with a little change, the problem may be avoided in future or made less significant through a little investment in the time and effort required to experiment with new problem-solving techniques. The same applies to their approach to underlying product technology.

Architecture

The search for new 'value innovations' is a very open process requiring a very open organizational architecture. What does this mean? The answer lies in the opportunity matrix shown in Figure 4. Corporations tend to focus innovation on certain types of opportunity (nature of opportunity) that arise from certain sources and associated processes (source of innovation).

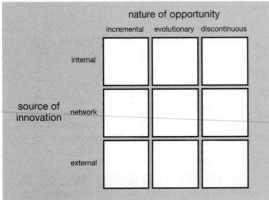

Figure 4: Sources and nature of opportunity
The opportunity matrix

The first dimension of the matrix shows that opportunity comes in several 'flavors'. The least dramatic are incremental opportunities. These represent small adjustments to existing products and services. On the next level up are evolutionary product line improvements – the next generation of products. The final and most dramatic type of opportunity is the discontinuous – referred to as 'blockbusters' in the drug business.

The other dimension of the matrix is the 'source of opportunity'. This source of an opportunity may be in the internal product development process. At the other end of the spectrum, an opportunity may originate from a customer or from entirely outside the organization.

The interim possibility is that an idea originates through the business network of individuals outside the direct line of those involved with new product or business opportunity development or from a supplier, distributor or alliance partner.

Most successful organizations focus on different combinations in the matrix; never neglecting incremental and evolutionary developments on successful existing products but searching for the high-value discontinuous ones. For example, some big drug companies are focused on opportunities that arise mostly through their own internal development process and will prove to be significant products in the marketplace. Other companies interview their customers extensively about what they would like in the next edition of their product – the next evolution.

What differentiates the entrepreneurial corporations we have seen is that they can cite products or businesses developed through all of the combinations. There are processes and paths through the organization for opportunities of any magnitude that originate from any source. This architectural openness is vitally linked to the pursuit of opportunity and entrepreneurial behavior in the organization.

Processes

Several processes generally support a company's entrepreneurial and innovative activities. Each of the entrepreneurial corporations we have observed has had a high level of communication and networking activity. The corporate cultures within these organizations were almost academic in nature, with individuals competing to share and build ideas. One managing director noted that his organization 'communicated perhaps very inefficiently, but obsessively and effectively'. In another successful, middle-sized company, top management had gone so far as actively to train people how to ask questions in order to refine communications further.

Extensive networking, combined with dynamic teaming were common traits of all of the organizations we have observed. No matter what the organizational structure, the organizations worked formally and informally to ensure active networking.

Internal clubs, interest groups and ad hoc cross-functional teams all contributed to networking and knowledge development. No matter what the organizational form, individuals would work persistently throughout their careers to develop personal networks.

As for resource allocation, these entrepreneurial organizations had worked persistently to ensure resource slack was distributed throughout the organization and was available to support new initiatives. Distributed slack takes many forms – individuals who are not 110 per cent booked, venture funds within the organization and informal 'slush' funds. These organizations were also skilled at the art of incremental investment and evaluation. They 'bet' on initiatives, watched patiently, but would re-evaluate performance, always asking the question: 'Should we terminate now?' The point is not that these companies are awash in money, but that they carefully manage their funding to make sure it is applied properly.

A few key beliefs and behavioral norms permeate the entrepreneurial organizations we have seen. First, the recognition that to venture is sometimes to fail and individuals are allowed to fail without compromising their membership in the organization. One company manager noted: 'If you are not failing you are not trying, and without trying, you won't get new opportunity'. The second, which is closely related, is the management of risk. Calculated risk is supported and encouraged. Personal and organizational mechanisms are in place to limit risks. They do not prevent risk taking, but limit overall losses from risky opportunities. The organizations actively help individuals to manage failure and ensure that small failures are learned from before they become large problems. **Beliefs**

The other pervasive beliefs include:
- organization structure is flexible and designed to serve opportunity and strategy
- corporate strategy and direction are emergent and created through the choice and pursuit of opportunities
- individuals seek value through membership in organizations which can be realized by recognition and creation of a sense of community.

All of these are underpinned by a fundamental belief in decentralized decision-making; letting those with the best perspective on a particular opportunity attempt to develop it.

Building and maintaining more extensive opportunity-focused entrepreneurial activity is not a simple proposition. There is no magic pill that will provide a solution. Nor will re-engineering, restructuring, or regularly turning over the management do the job. All of these acts tend to destroy an organization's delicate knowledge and network fabric. **How to (re)create entrepreneurship**

Why do so many initially entrepreneurial organizations lose the capacity to fully identify and pursue available opportunities? First, many successful growth companies fall victim to a focus on the resources they have created. Second, they tend to focus too much on the businesses that made them successful, at the cost of sustaining the organizational processes that played an equally important part. Thirdly, they try in vain to preserve what they have by establishing excessive numbers of rules, systems and controls. Eventually, the 'game' in the organization turns to meeting budgets and acquiring control of internal organizational units rather than pursuing new opportunity.

To maximize the amount of entrepreneurial activity or to rebuild that initial entrepreneurial activity:

● focus people on opportunity, growth and renewal. Demand performance, even on both profit and turnover

● open the information infrastructure; ensure that withholding information is not a source of individual managerial power. Encourage individuals to share knowledge, technology and skills in pursuing and exploiting opportunity

● distribute some resources throughout the organization. Make them accessible to individuals who wish to develop opportunities

● make sure individuals and teams have the training and coaching needed to support them in their activities

● let go of some of the central desire to take decisions. Often, successful entrepreneurs are their own worst enemies because they feel they have to be at the centre of every new process to develop new opportunities. Let entrepreneurs throughout the organization promote entrepreneurship! ■

❖ CASE STUDY

Siemens Nixdorf's new dynamism

Mark Maletz describes how Siemens Nixdorf accepted the challenge of becoming a more entrepreneurial company.

The challenge of change – managing it, enacting it and leveraging it – has become one of the most important topics on today's corporate agenda. Twice each year, top executives from many of Germany's most important companies meet, under the sponsorship of the senior teams from BMW, Deutsche Bank and Siemens Nixdorf, to discuss the challenges that they face in building more competitive skills and organizations.

Specific change challenges discussed at these workshops are highly varied – ranging from new organizational structures to the role of leadership. Issues associated with new behaviors and with the emerging role of behavior as a competitive advantage have surfaced at every meeting.

One clear conclusion is that flexibility, responsiveness, innovativeness and openness are the characteristics that today's corporations require and that they should replace control, rigidity, predictability and caution. This entails a transformation for many companies from bureaucracy to entrepreneurship. Through such transformation, companies can better leverage their people, at all levels, to help to design the change itself and then to become on-going leaders of innovation. The more turbulent the industry and change, the more urgent the need for this transformation becomes.

Discussion in the workshops frequently refers to US cases when describing the ways in which highly entrepreneurial companies deal with change. Initially, participants responded to such cases with some skepticism, explaining that it is easy to be entrepreneurial when one is situated in the heart of Silicon Valley.

There, companies are surrounded by some of the world's most entrepreneurial organizations with easy access to talent, capital and technology. A more rigorous test, they decided, was whether the transformation towards entrepreneurship could succeed in Germany – with the associated logic that success in Germany would mean that success was possible anywhere.

One of the sponsors of the change workshops, Siemens Nixdorf, accepted this challenge. It operates in

© FT Pictures

Gerhard Schulmeyer: his experience of cultural and structural change enabled him to lead Siemens Nixdorf's transformation.

the high-technology arena and competes directly with its Silicon Valley counterparts and therefore faces the challenge in any case. The remainder of this article will address the key elements of the transformation to entrepreneurship using Siemens Nixdorf as a living case study.

Siemens Nixdorf is the result of a merger between Siemens AG's computer unit, Siemens Dateninformationssysteme and Nixdorf Computer AG in 1990. There were significant expectations at the time of the merger concerning the new company's ability to be both disciplined and innovative but these expectations failed to be realized. Between the time of the merger and the summer of 1994, the company lost hundreds of millions of Deutschmarks every year.

In response to these mounting losses and a 'loser image' in the marketplace and within the Siemens parent, the company retreated into precisely those behaviors that made it difficult for it to compete in its marketplace – bureaucracy, command and control, parochialism and inward focus.

Finally, in the summer of 1994, top management at Siemens AG hired a new CEO for Siemens Nixdorf, Gerhard Schulmeyer, and asked him to restore the company to competitiveness. Schulmeyer had been responsible for the Americas operations at ABB where he had established a highly effective matrix organization. He had previously been a key executive at Motorola where he was instrumental in the creation of Motorola University and in Motorola's cultural shift towards quality and process improvement. The combination of these experiences with culture and structural change uniquely positioned Schulmeyer to lead Siemens Nixdorf's transformation.

The change agenda was clear – create a highly profitable, entrepreneurial enterprise capable of operating in the global, high-technology marketplace. To accomplish this, broad-based cultural and structural changes were required based on four key dimensions:

● A shift in the organizational culture to first nurture and later demand entrepreneurial behavior from all employees.

● A new organizational architecture that would facilitate entrepreneurial behavior.

● An investment in developmental activities (focusing on both behaviors and skills) that would prepare individuals at all levels of the organization to operate in the new culture and structure.

● New systems (management and information) to support the transformed organization.

Pursuing this required committed and visible leadership from the top of the organization. Schulmeyer reshaped the company's top team, recruiting executives capable of role modelling the behaviors required for the new company culture and of using and mentoring others in the use of the tools and techniques of entrepreneurship. The new top team consisted of more than a dozen executives from some of the most entrepreneurial and successful companies in Europe.

However, a dozen executives, no matter how talented, cannot lead transformational change alone. They require the pro-active support of senior managers from across the company. The new top team therefore convened a group of more than 100 senior managers from every part of the company and asked them to lead the transformation in partnership with the top team. This group became the company's executive management team.

They met regularly (roughly quarterly) to monitor the company's progress and held themselves accountable for progress from meeting to meeting. This represented an important role modelling of the performance and results orientation that world-class entrepreneurs invariably learn and demonstrate.

Culture change

Siemens Nixdorf's culture change program mobilized thousands of employees as co-producers of the company's new culture in partnership with executive management. The program was punctuated with four meetings in Hanover between December 1994 and October 1996. Each meeting was attended by 300 to 400 (different) employees interested in helping to shape and catalyse the culture change. The four meetings were organized around distinct, but related, themes.

Hanover I: the voice of the employees
It provided employees with an opportunity to reflect on the new values and behaviors that were needed by Siemens Nixdorf and then to establish action teams (59 in total) that would move the company towards these values.

Hanover II: the voice of the customers
The theme added 54 key customers to the gathering of 350 employees, ensuring that customers would have a voice in the company's transformation. The customers also participated in the follow-up work of the 20 action teams launched at Hanover II.

Hanover III: the voice of the partners
Here, 40 key business partners also attended the event, ensuring their voice in the transformation process as well. This was important in the light of the company's commitment to dramatically increase its partner-related revenue. Again, as in Hanover II, the partners were fully-fledged participants in the event and the follow-on action teams.

Hanover IV: institutionalizing the capability to change
This meeting focused on preparing the 400 employees in attendance to institutionalize the change skills and tools that the first three Hanover events had introduced into the company.

Each of these Hanover events prepared employees to behave in a highly entrepreneurial manner and to accept the responsibilities and accountabilities inherent in entrepreneurship. For example, each action team was committed to some results within 90 days of the Hanover event and substantial business impact within 180 days.

In parallel with the Hanover events, the company launched an innovation initiative designed to discover, assess and fund innovative business ideas. This included the formation of an internal venture capital fund for use by internal entrepreneurs with business plans for new products, services and solutions. A key element was the development of a network of internal resources that could support entrepreneurial business development. For example, an employee with a business idea but no financial background could be linked with an entrepreneurial financial analyst.

A key characteristic of successful entrepreneurs is the ability and courage to reflect, learn and adapt. To encourage this behavior across the company, Siemens Nixdorf launched a 'Friday forum' in which natural workgroups across the entire company would meet regularly (generally once a month) to discuss matters of mutual interest. These forums regularly provided opportunities to learn from successes and failures and to make modifications to on-going business and change activities. These sessions also enabled employees to learn to more effectively support one another and to draw on the resources and knowledge in the workgroup.

Because successful entrepreneurs have keen insight into the business environments within which they operate, Siemens Nixdorf also launched benchmarking activities focused on the best companies in the market. This included numerous visits to companies around the world, including regular visits to Silicon Valley.

The Hanover events and related culture change initiatives introduced new behaviors that Siemens Nixdorf required for its transformation to entrepreneurship. These activities also mobilized employees to drive the transformation itself.

The new organizational architecture at Siemens Nixdorf was based on a high degree of decentralization and conformed to six principles:

New organizational architecture

● One face to the customer. Customers want a direct answer to a simple question: 'Who is my representative at Siemens Nixdorf?' They should never be confused by the company's internal organization.

● Unbroken processes that begin and end with the customer. There will be no more internal negotiations over transfer prices. Any salesman the customer sees has to be part of a unified process that does the total job from design to delivery.

● Delegation of authority and responsibility to the lowest level. The real decision-makers must be the business-unit entrepreneurs in the field. The regional managers and world-wide business leaders are primarily coaches, mentors and enablers.

● Bet the future on businesses that have a defendable core competence. To prosper, a business unit must hold a clear leadership position in Germany, be one of the market leaders in Europe, and be a player elsewhere in the world.

● Customers of equal importance have equal access to the company's resources. This does not mean that all customers, regardless of size or needs, have an equal claim on the company. But one of the legacies of the company's German orientation is that strategic customers outside Germany did not always enjoy the same access to the company.

● Different business units require different structures. The company consists of service, solution and product businesses; each with distinct structural requirements. The structures for these different businesses should be designed on their unique requirements (consistent with the other five principles).

Adhering to these design principles resulted in a network structure of approximately 250 business units – each with a geographic customer focus and a line of business focus (for example, a unit might focus on the Spanish PC business). This two-dimensional structure was intended to be a first step towards a dynamically reconfigurable network model. The organization would first learn how to operate in a two-dimensional matrix and then the static matrix structure would be relaxed and business units would be dynamically reconfigured in response to customer demands and innovation.

Unlike many matrix organizations in which those in the middle of the matrix feel caught between two managers with relatively little real authority, the unit manager for each business unit was given full profit and loss responsibility for his or her unit. The regional manager and line of business manager above a unit manager served as a virtual board of directors, coaching the unit manager while empowering him to manage his business unit.

An interesting lesson learned when first preparing the matrix involved the risk of using 'entrepreneur' as a title. The original plan was to name each manager responsible for a business unit an 'entrepreneur.' Initial testing of this idea indicated that those named as entrepreneurs would protect this as a special label – resulting in no more than 250 entrepreneurs in the company. The title was therefore shifted to unit manager so that any employee could become an entrepreneur. A key mark of an effective unit manager would be the ability to develop new entrepreneurs within the business units.

Developmental activities

The greatest concern was the question 'Do we really have 250 middle managers capable of behaving as entrepreneurs and experienced enough to manage their own business unit?' Part of the answer to this question came from the culture change program, which demonstrated that a broad cross-section of employees were capable of behaving entrepreneurially when given the chance.

The other part of the answer came through the introduction of an 'entrepreneurship development program', attended by every prospective unit manager. The program was led by faculty from Babson College, INSEAD and IMD and was conducted in a highly experiential format. Participants carried out self-assessments throughout the program and decided whether they were ready to assume unit management responsibilities during the final week.

Another important developmental activity was the management development program, a week-long program open to any key manager and designed to prepare managers to operate in the entrepreneurial company that Siemens Nixdorf was becoming.

New systems

Entrepreneurial management often requires better information than other forms of management. Moreover, moving from a two-dimensional matrix to a dynamic network model also requires sophisticated information systems. At Siemens Nixdorf there were four key system improvements that accompanied the transformation towards entrepreneurship and a dynamic networked organizational form:

● Introduction of an integrated financial management package to provide business unit profit and loss information.

● Development of a business assessment methodology to be used throughout the company for purposes of portfolio management (across business units) and business model optimization (within a business unit).

● Introduction of balanced scorecards of performance and new incentive systems across the company. These scorecards emphasized both business performance and behavioral competencies.

● Development of new channels to make information and communication available across the entire enterprise in order to encourage networking across business units and to support the dynamic nature of the organizational model. This included advanced Intranet work and the placement of new media (including electronic discussion forums) on the Intranet.

At the end of 1996 Siemens Nixdorf's transformation towards entrepreneurship had been underway for about two and a half years. During this time, the company has achieved a break-even financial position, dramatically improved its customer orientation and image in the marketplace and conceived and developed many new business opportunities.

An important example of the pursuit of new business opportunities is the creation of an array of Internet-enabled lines of business. Several groups of entrepreneurial employees launched new lines of business in the Internet arena. One group provides customers with Internet-related services, leveraging the competencies that the company developed to meet its own needs. Customers are given the opportunity to benefit, in an accelerated manner, from the Internet learning curve that Siemens Nixdorf mastered. Other groups developed service and solution offerings in the areas of Internet security and electronic banking.

In Siemens Nixdorf's mainframe business, a team of natural entrepreneurs launched a new product, code-named 'Sunrise', that would transfer the BS2000 operating system to a client server platform – a vital issue in the diminishing mainframe market. Soon after launch the product had already attracted substantial customer interest.

Such successful entrepreneurial developments provide evidence of the possibility and reality of change within the company. While at the time of writing the journey may not be complete, it is clear that Siemens Nixdorf has substantially met the challenge of entrepreneurial transformation that surfaced at the change workshops for senior executives. ∎

10

Harvesting

Contents

Contributors

Rod Selkirk is Director of venture capitalist group NatWest Ventures.

Chris Harrison is a partner in Ernst & Young and national head of its UK entrepreneurial services practice.

Elizabeth Tashjian is Associate Professor of Finance at the Eccles School of Business, University of Utah.

Benoît F. Leleux is Assistant Professor and holds the Zubillaga Term Chair in Finance and Entrepreneurship at Babson College. He is also Visiting Professor at INSEAD.

Lawrence A. Weiss is Associate Professor of Accounting and Control at INSEAD.

Introduction

Part 10 brings us to the end of our story and to the exit route. We ask what are the various ways in which entrepreneurs can 'harvest' their investment by taking some or all of the value out of the business. We ask the question, when should this happen or is there a right time? Of course, not all can make this choice and we explore the problems of bankruptcy and failure. For the rest, we then look at the two main voluntary exit routes of trade sale and initial public offering.

Harvesting at the right price

Sue Birley looks at the complex question of when – and whether – an entrepreneur should sell out of the business he or she has created.

'Even the farmer must judge exactly when to harvest.'

© FT Pictures

Harvesting enterprise: what does it mean and when should it be done? For farmers, it is easy – when the grapes are ready or the corn is ripe. Or is it? Even the farmer must judge exactly when to harvest. Too soon and the crop will fail to reach expectations; too late and the weather could ruin it. So it is with business. Too soon and the value will not have reached the optimum; too late and competition may have destroyed profits. So what do we mean by harvesting? Quite simply, it is the sale of some or all of the equity of a company. This can be through a number of possible 'exit routes':

● A trade sale to another company (*see* p. 356)

● The sale of the investment to another corporate investor such as a venture capitalist (*see* Part 3, p. 82)

● The sale of equity to another individual – such as a 'business angel' or a fellow shareholder – or through a management buy-out or buy-in (*see* Part 3, p. 86 – buy-outs and buy-ins are covered in Part 8)

● The sale of equity to 'the public' through an IPO (initial public offering) on a stock exchange (*see* p. 360).

For the investor or venture capitalist, this would seem to be a relatively straightforward decision – just a matter of finding the right time to sell, deciding the exit route and agreeing a price with the purchaser. Not quite. In a private company, there may be restrictions on the ability to sell – the owner-manager may be required to offer to the existing shareholders, who cannot or will not buy. He or she may be a minority shareholder and so have no power to make a decision to sell the entire company. Many venture capitalists call these the 'living dead' investments.

Even assuming the entrepreneur is free to seek buyers for his or her shares, the value of minority holdings can be considered as worthless to prospective buyers, though there may be an agreed, and binding, exit mechanism, which includes a pricing formula. This is analogous to agreeing the divorce settlement prior to the wedding – always difficult but sometimes well worth it.

For many entrepreneurs, all this is even more complicated by the fact that they may be both owner and manager and so have two possible 'exit' decisions. The first, that of delegating managerial responsibility to others, we have dealt with elsewhere. The latter, that of realizing your financial investment, is what we are concerned with in this part of *Mastering Enterprise*. However, it may be that both arise at the same time – for example, the entrepreneur may have no obvious family successor and so may wish to retire by selling the company. Whatever the situation it will not be easy, either technically or emotionally.

The decision to sell, always assuming that it is a voluntary decision, is almost certainly related to the price that you expect to receive for your equity – and that is a lifestyle decision. You will be juggling two interlinked questions in your mind:
- what is the company worth?
- will this give me sufficient capital to enjoy the rest of my life in the manner to which I wish to be accustomed? Of course, this will be related, in part, to whether you already have a company pension plan and how you intend to invest the proceeds of the sale.

That in turn relates to two more factors:
- the size and profitability track record of the company.
- the state of the market.

Either way, it is not a decision that you can usually make overnight, nor without advice. Valuation, as we have seen earlier in *Mastering Enterprise*, is much more an art than a science. Certainly, human nature being as it is, an owner is probably likely to be more optimistic than others about the value of the company.

What does this mean? Well, that the value to you of the income stream generated by your company may be greater than that to a purchaser. It can be hard for someone who has spent many years of their life building a business to be told that while they think it is worth, say, £5m, a buyer may only value it at £3m. Of course, it does not always work that way. Sometimes the value is significantly higher than expected – getting to that point is the trick. But that is just the start. Unfortunately, sellers are not necessarily in control of the timing of the sale. For example, preparing the documentation for flotation can take six months and bulls can transform into bears overnight.

A trade sale may be ideal but no-one is interested in small fast-food franchise chains – at the moment. But even before that companies need to be prepared for a sale – the house put in order, a respectable track record in place. Indeed, though, sometimes they can be over-prepared with the balance sheet and profit and loss account presented in the very best light.

Potential buyers who are skilled in this field know this and will be looking to strip out the 'managerial toys' and 'organizational patching' that may clutter the balance sheet so that they can understand the underlying strengths of the company. Think of it as buying a house. How easy it can be to miss the crack in the wall, the poor electrical wiring, the sagging roof, particularly when it has been recently decorated (perhaps in anticipation of the sale) unless you are a professional or have professional help.

So the questions to be answered are:

- Do I wish to realize all or only part of my investment?
- Do I wish to continue to be associated with the company after the sale?
- What form of payment do I want from the sale – equity in another company, cash on deferred terms, a pension, a consultancy retainer?
- Which exit route will give the greatest return?
- If I decide to float, what will it cost and who will help me?
- If I decide to seek a trade sale or sale to a third party, how do I find a buyer?

These are not easy questions and most people only do this once. Think long and hard about why you are doing it, what you want afterwards, what is a reasonable price – and seek advice. ■

The two main routes to a company sale

Rod Selkirk looks at the choices open to a business owner when he or she decides to make an exit.

The poet T.S. Eliot was thinking about something very different from the world of venture capital when he wrote that 'the end is where we start from'. But his observation holds true for our business: investors and managers who participate in buy-outs and other venture capital deals have to start thinking about exits before they even make their entry.

Those who provide most of the equity finance for a buyout – including venture capital companies and pension funds and other financial institutions whose money the venture capitalists invest – need to know how and when they are likely to realise their investments before they commit any funds. That is because we invest not for eternity but on average for three to seven years, after which we expect to make a profit that reflects the scale of the risk we have taken on in making our investment. This puts us on the same side as management, whose financial stake in a deal is unlikely to be as large as ours in absolute terms but invariably represents a big personal risk, with a corresponding opportunity to make substantial rewards.

Management and venture capitalists thus have a common interest in growing the capital value of the business and working out ways of crystallizing that value within a medium-term time frame. So when management, advisers and financial backers such as ourselves come together to hammer out the terms of an investment, drawing up an exit strategy is an integral part of the business plan.

There are basically two types of exit route – the sale to a trade buyer or a flotation on the stock-market. (These are covered in detail on pages 356 and 360.) There are other exit strategies, and I will return to these later, but the principal choice for management and backers is whether to float or to sell. **Two roads**

Take flotation first. There is a great deal of razzmatazz associated with going public and we counsel that management takes a sober, unemotional look at the pros and cons of such a big step.

On the positive side, flotation gives a company the opportunity to raise further capital via the equity market, often the cheapest source of finance available. It allows it to finance acquisitions by issuing shares, thus allowing it to grow more quickly than if it relied solely on organic growth and bank borrowings. Furthermore, it enables management to remain on board as directors and shareholders, thereby ensuring that they participate in the company's future growth.

From a more negative perspective, flotations can be expensive in terms of advisers' fees, and directors of publicly quoted companies have to busy themselves with ongoing obligations that may distract from the day-to-day running of the business, for example maintaining relationships with institutional investors.

Many managers like the idea of being directors of public companies but often perfectly sound businesses do not lend themselves well to flotation. One reason is size: shares in smaller quoted companies often lack liquidity, making it more difficult to raise capital and for shareholders to realize their investment, thereby negating the main reasons for having a stock-market listing in the first place.

Another consideration is the volatility of the stock market. Factors well beyond the control of management teams can have an impact on the valuation a company can achieve by way of flotation. These include general market conditions – a rise in US interest rates could dampen institutional investors' appetite for new issues of any description. Often valuations in specific stock market sectors reflect fashion as much as fundamentals. **Market volatility**

Our decision to postpone the planned flotation of the Principal Hotel Group, a Leeds-based hotel chain into which we bought three years earlier, is a case in point. We had originally hoped to float the company in the first half of 1996 but, together with the management team we backed, we took the decision to delay the market debut for a year or so. The reason was that, in our judgement, institutional investors had had their fill of hotel issues in the previous couple of years – there had been half a dozen of them in that time – meaning that we would not necessarily have been able to achieve the best price for a company we believed to be markedly more attractive than most other quoted hotel groups.

By the time we revive the flotation, we believe that investors will have got over their indigestion and will have renewed appetite for hotel stocks. This decision is

*'Just the ticket:
Greater Manchester
Buses South'*

that much more palatable because there is no pressure from any quarter for a flotation or any other kind of exit – we are confident that the company's value will continue to rise and, in the meantime, it is not short of the capital resources required to finance its growth.

A big company such as Pubmaster, the pub retailing group we and others bought from Brent Walker in November 1995 for £171m, is an obvious candidate for flotation. With nearly 1,700 pubs and £17m of operating profits in 1995, it dwarfs its quoted competitors in terms of size and has a healthy track-record of profits growth despite being starved of investment over recent years. As of early 1997 the plan was for current management to upgrade the quality of its assets with a view to floating the enlarged group in about three years.

Clean exit

For every Pubmaster in our portfolio, there are many companies for whom a trade sale may provide a more appropriate exit route. Trade sales attract less pronounced headlines than flotations but can be the best way for management and venture capital backers to realize the value of their investments.

A trade sale represents a 'clean' exit, for venture capitalists and management alike, in a way that a flotation does not. It involves the sale of all of the company's equity, whereas management and backers will tend to retain a significant stake when a company is floated. Whether a company achieves a better price by way of a trade sale rather than a flotation depends on a number of factors. One is the unpredictable question of stock-market valuations, as we have seen in the case of Principal Hotels.

There may be special synergies and opportunities for cost-cutting that mean that a trade buyer will put a higher value on the business than stock-market investors. Or the company may present an opportunity for strategic diversification, as in the near-£20m sale of LivingWell Health and Leisure, one of the leading health club operators in the UK, to the Stakis hotel and casino group. Stagecoach's purchase of GM Buses South, the south Manchester bus company we backed in an employee buyout in 1994, shows how a business may have a special strategic appeal to a company already active in the sector.

In practice, however meticulous the planning process, it pays to be opportunistic about how and when to achieve the exit. Indeed, the way in which the exit is achieved can be completely at variance with what was planned at the outset of the investment, as the GM Buses South case shows. Back in 1994, had you asked the fitter in the bus depot or the driver on the 192 route to Hazel Grove who would end up buying the company, the answer would not have been Stagecoach.

The original deal created an unlikely alliance of bus drivers and venture capitalists. After lengthy haggling, we at NatWest Ventures and the bus company's 2,000 employees won the £25m bid for the company in March 1994. The deal was structured to give employees majority control and no one imagined selling the business less than two years later – especially not to Stagecoach.

During the protracted negotiations to buy the company on the employees' behalf, the chief opposition to our bid came from Stagecoach. We had always assumed that the employees would end up buying us out but before too long Stagecoach came back with a bid. It proved irresistible for the bus company's employees, who turned their initial £1,000 investment into £10,000 in little more time than it took to negotiate the transaction in the first place.

The Cara computerized payroll business that we bought from Aer Lingus also shows the importance of being flexible in achieving an exit route. When we first took the stake, we were interested primarily in the potential of a small hi-tech subsidiary in Germany, which we thought one day could well be a candidate for flotation. By the time we came to sell Cara, to Bull Information Systems, it was the payroll processing business that was booming and the principal attraction to Bull.

Other exits

I have covered flotations and trade-sales, the two main types of exits, but there are others. It may be, for example, that owner-managers of businesses want to realize part of their investment while retaining an active role in the management of the company they have helped to build.

This was the case at The Car Group (formerly Motorhouse), the Midlands-based retailer of nearly-new cars. It has now floated but, prior to this, we engineered a £32m transaction that allowed Chris Bowen, the founder of the group, to sell part of his shareholding. We were confident that his remaining investment in the company was big enough to ensure that he would remain committed to the enterprise.

He stepped down as chairman, staying on as head of the buying function, while two new directors came on board. The refinancing that was part and parcel of the deal, together with the injection of fresh management blood, was designed to prepare the company for flotation, the next stage in its development.

There is also a growing number of secondary buy-outs, transactions that enable one set of institutional investors to realise their investments while management stays on with the backing of new investors. Such deals are coming about chiefly because many venture capital funds set up in the late 1980s are approaching their termination dates – when they have to be wound up – obliging the original investors to sell out. They are replaced by fresh investors prepared to make a new medium-term commitment to the company. An example from our portfolio is the 1995 £70m Sheffield Forgemasters deal. We took a 29 per cent stake in this engineering and specialist metals group when one of the original venture capital funds reached its termination date and needed to exit.

However, secondary buyouts and The Car Group-style transactions are still relatively rare; most exits will come through either a flotation or a trade sale. No management team can enter a deal without giving plenty of thought to which of these it prefers, though it is essential to be flexible about the way in which the exit is finally completed. In practice, the choice of exit route will reflect market conditions and the preferences of management and other investors. There are no hard and fast rules but it is true to say that the better the company, the fewer problems management and venture capitalists will have finding an exit route. ∎

Navigating a course off the rocks

Elizabeth Tashjian and **Lawrence Weiss** discuss the complex details of business failure and bankruptcy laws.

In our favorite Bible story, Pharaoh has strange dreams of cattle and corn, which Joseph, the hero of the tale, interprets for him. Seven fat, or good, years will be followed by seven lean, or bad, years. The lesson of the tale, still true today, is to save in good times to survive the bad times. Unfortunately, many managers either lack the opportunity or foresight to save for the lean years.

This article explores how modern society deals with companies that are unable to repay their debts. We will first discuss why bankruptcy rules exist in their current form and then describe what the management of a failed business is likely to experience.

What is bankruptcy?

Corporate bankruptcy occurs after an enterprise defaults on its financial obligations. When a company fails to repay its debt according to schedule, the debt-holders have certain legal rights to obtain payment, including seizing the company's assets. In effect, once an organization is unable to meet its debt obligations, the debt-holders become the owners of the concern.

Without debt there can be no bankruptcy. Why, then, do companies issue debt? First, as we have already seen in *Mastering Enterprise*, debt is less costly than equity because interest payments for debt are tax-deductible and because debt is supposed to be repaid before equity in the event of financial distress. Second, debt requires less costly monitoring than equity. Since equity holders are entitled to whatever value remains in the business after creditors are paid, equity holders bear the entire cost of any corporate waste in a healthy company. Equity holders can reduce the amount of waste by closely monitoring managerial actions.

The fixed-payment schedule associated with debt also restricts the ability of management to act inefficiently by providing an early warning: failure to make a scheduled debt payment is a clear warning signal. Thus, to avoid bankruptcy and safeguard their jobs, managers must avoid violating the terms of debt contracts.

Why have bankruptcy laws?

Most jurisdictions grant creditors the right to seize the assets of a debtor who fails to adhere to the terms of a loan agreement. Outside of bankruptcy, claims against a debtor's assets are processed in the order they are filed by creditors with the local judiciary. Thus, the first creditor to file may receive full payment while the last to file may receive nothing. Just as in a bank run, the first depositor in line may receive full payment and the last nothing.

This 'first in time, first in line' rule means each creditor will expend excessive resources to position itself to win any race for an insolvent organization's assets. Collectively, the creditors should forgo the expense of this monitoring and agree instead to share all assets equitably with other creditors of the same priority. Such an arrangement increases the total value of the creditors' investment by the amount of expenses of the avoided race. Unfortunately, such mutually beneficial agreements are difficult at best because it is of no advantage to the creditor who is first in line to co-operate once financial distress occurs.

Another problem, outside of bankruptcy, is the possible dismembering of a viable company when creditors fail to co-operate and race to grab a distressed business's assets. The creditors collectively lose the difference between the value of the company as a going concern and its piecemeal liquidation value.

Bankruptcy law also reduces the amount of asymmetric information between managers and the company's creditors. Supposing a company is trying to renegotiate the terms of its debt outside of bankruptcy. Bondholders are aware that managers are likely to be better informed than they are regarding the future prospects of the enterprise and are understandably suspicious of any offer. For example, if management knows the prospects for the business are strong they are unlikely to offer a debt-for-equity swap since the swap would result in excessive dilution for existing equity holders. Therefore, when management offers equity, bondholders believe the company's prospects are poor and anticipate that the equity offered by management is over-valued, thereby resulting in an unfavorable transaction for existing debt holders.

When the level of asymmetric information is high, management and creditors may be unable to agree on the terms of a restructuring out of court. However, in a court-supervised bankruptcy, information is usually shared among management and all investors in the organization, thereby mitigating the asymmetric information problem and increasing the odds that a suitable division of the assets can be agreed to by all parties.

Finally, bankruptcy law can mitigate the problem of creditors holding out for better terms. Individual creditors have the incentive to free-ride on concessions offered by other creditors. Because there is no easy way to compel participation in a restructuring out of court, creditors may refuse to participate. Bankruptcy can solve this problem by compelling all claim holders to participate on an equal footing.

Modern bankruptcy law

Bankruptcy law is meant to save viable businesses that are experiencing temporary cash flow problems by providing some breathing room and a process to help reorganize the claims on the company.

It seeks to create an efficient debt-repayment system by determining the amounts owed to various creditors, classifying creditors into groups based on repayment priority and then treating everyone in a particular group equally. This equal treatment by class eliminates any benefit to an individual creditor of being first in line to file a claim and stops the race to grab assets. Monitoring costs for creditors are reduced and enterprises are provided with a chance to restructure their debt. In addition, the process brings together all the interested parties and avoids duplication of effort in tasks such as valuing the business.

Once the claims against the company and the order in which the claims will be paid have been established, the concern must dispose of its assets so as to maximize the value of the creditors' claims. The most common methods for disposing of the assets are through liquidation or reorganization.

Liquidation and reorganization

Whether a company is liquidated piecemeal or sold as a whole, the proceeds are distributed first to those claim holders with the highest priority until they have been paid in full, then to those with the next highest priority and so on until the available funds are exhausted.

Although liquidation provides for an orderly dissolution of the organization and an equitable distribution of assets to creditors, frequently the going concern value of the business is destroyed in the process. In a court-supervised reorganization, the business continues as a going concern and claim holders reach a consensual agreement on how to restructure the company's capital.

Who decides the terms?

The problem faced by bankruptcy law is how to properly allocate what economists would call 'decision rights' – who decides what to do with an organization's assets. The correct answer is far from obvious.

Giving senior creditors the right to decide whether to continue operations or liquidate may be a poor choice, since they will probably elect for a quick disposition of the assets whenever this would repay them in full – regardless of whether it maximizes the value of the company.

Transferring the decision to any other group – junior creditors, managers, owners or employees – is likely to give that group the ability to transfer value from others to themselves. For example, junior creditors may delay payment or continue to operate a non-viable business unless senior creditors agree to provide them with funds beyond what they would otherwise be entitled to. Owners, who often have no more equity in the business and so have nothing more to lose, may engage in highly risky ventures in the desperate hope of a turnaround. Likewise, managers may risk all in a desperate attempt to save their jobs.

The issue becomes even more complex when, as is normally the case, there is a long delay in determining the creditors' claims and their related priorities. A common solution is to have the court appoint some outside expert, a trustee, to make the decision. This is what happens in the UK and most countries outside the US. In the US, the management of large concerns is usually allowed to continue operations and attempt to restructure.

Despite differences in the treatment of bankrupt companies across the world, there are similarities in typical outcomes.

Outcomes in bankruptcy

In the UK, the business is usually preserved while the corporate shell is not. In the US, over half of major organizations are reorganized in bankruptcy and re-emerge intact.

Under both systems, senior secured debt is usually repaid in full provided there is sufficient collateral. Employees usually receive wages and small trade creditors typically receive payment for some of their claims. Repayment to unsecured junior debt and the equity holders depends on the circumstances, the country and the individuals involved.

In the US, junior creditors typically receive cash and new securities worth less than half the value of their claims. Equity holders and the most junior creditors typically receive more proceeds from the organization's assets than they would receive under strict application of the priority of claims. Senior executives and board members are usually replaced either after or during bankruptcy.

Research in the US shows that about 70 per cent of top managers are replaced by the time a company emerges from bankruptcy and that future job prospects for these managers are poor. Additionally, less than 50 per cent of board members remain two years after financial distress (as compared to about 80 per cent in the absence of financial distress) and those who leave have fewer appointments on average. In the UK, where a trustee takes over control of the business, board members are automatically dismissed in the event of bankruptcy and managers seldom remain.

On average, a company that restructures out of court spends less time and money and produces a higher recovery rate for creditors than businesses that liquidate. However, companies may choose to enter bankruptcy because, given the business's unique problems, an out of court restructuring may be prohibitively costly.

In the UK, the major clearing banks often agree to work together outside of bankruptcy to try to resolve a major organization's problems in what is called the 'London Approach'. Recently in the US, companies have started filing for bankruptcy and putting forward a plan of reorganization already approved by creditors. This procedure, called a pre-packaged bankruptcy (or prepak), attempts to incorporate the conventional advantages of bankruptcy while reducing some of the costs.

Is it better to restructure outside of bankruptcy?

Most firms try to avoid bankruptcy by selling assets to pay down debt, trying to negotiate an out-of-court restructuring or both. From the company's perspective, bankruptcy can be a very expensive and disruptive option.

First, professional fees (legal, accounting, investment banking) can quickly become enormous. Second, sales may drop precipitously as customers, fearing the business will not survive, look elsewhere to assure supply and warranties. Likewise, the best employees may jump ship to ensure their long-term employment. Finally, management's time is likely to become consumed by the bankruptcy process rather than watching the competition and running the company.

Few companies 'choose' bankruptcy without exploring other possibilities first. However, the evidence is not clear whether creditors should prefer out-of-court restructuring over bankruptcy. There is research documenting the fact that enterprises that undergo court-supervised bankruptcy reorganizations emerge with lower debt and better future prospects than concerns that reorganize out of court. Indeed, at least in the US, companies reorganizing out of court frequently end up in distress again within two years.

Furthermore, on average, creditors accept less, as a percentage of the total amount they are due, in out-of-court restructuring than in bankruptcy. Unfortunately, the evidence does not show whether this would be true in absolute terms: the lower percentage accepted outside of bankruptcy may be more than compensated for by avoiding the costs of bankruptcy noted above. ■

Timing and tenacity in a business sale

Selling a business is another critical test for the entrepreneur.
Chris Harrison gives some advice on how to get the best price.

Despite the establishment in the UK of the alternative investment market (and its predecessor, the unlisted securities market) to make it easier for private companies to go public, trade sales remain the most popular exit route for business owners. This article focuses on ways in which entrepreneurs can maximize the value of their business before a sale and enhance the consideration they receive.

What is the best time to sell?

Timing can be a critical element in how easily the sale process happens and how close an entrepreneur comes to achieving his or her objectives. Above all, it is always best to sell when there is no need to, as the need to sell often weakens a negotiating position. But there are also some more specific aspects to timing.

The businesss stage of development

Most purchasers will be looking for a business with the ability to grow, so it is better to sell a business that is on the way up, not when it has reached its peak or the market has become too competitive. Sellers should not leave it until they suddenly realize that the tide has already started to turn.

The prime time for many entrepreneurs to sell is when the concept has been proved and substantial investment is now required to expand the business either nationally or internationally. This is an ideal situation for a large corporate buyer that can fund such expansion and gain the benefits of growth. Consequently, sale at such a time often provides the highest premium for the vendors.

Market timing

Here there are two main aspects to consider. The first is the market for the company's products or services – is it thriving and growing? The second concerns the market for similar types of businesses – does the business cycle mean that companies are buying (or wanting to) and are they paying premium prices? Receiving approaches from companies expressing interest is obviously a favorable sign.

Time of year

With a seasonal business an entrepreneur will need to consider the time of year when the business will look most attractive. For example, it may be sensible to time a sale to take place after the season's orders have been placed so that results can be projected with greater certainty.

Preparing your business for the sale

The key to maximizing the return from a sale is understanding where the value of a business to a potential purchaser lies and, in the period before the sale, doing whatever is possible to enhance that value. Listed below are some of the steps that can be taken to maximize the value of a business to potential buyers. Many of these steps have long lead times and buyers need to consider them well before the actual sale process begins.

Clearly a business will be more attractive if profits are rising. But sellers should probably not be tempted to boost short-term profits by, for example, reducing necessary investment or expenditure on training or marketing – remember that the business may not be sold.

Sellers should also take steps to reduce the inherent risks in the business to a potential buyer. For example, responsibilities, decision-making and account management can be devolved to second-tier managers who will remain with the business after it is sold. If possible, the customer base should also be increased so that sales are less dependent on a few key accounts.

There may be ways to increase flexibility for a new owner. For example, there may be assets in the business that are not needed and have little value to a prospective buyer. If the business owns and occupies property, it may make sense to sell it and rent it back. This could make it much easier for a new owner to integrate the business with other operations. It would also mean that the entrepreneur receives the full market value of the property rather than a discounted price from a reluctant buyer.

☛ Top 10 tips for building the value of a business

- Aim to increase the business's recurring profits
- Focus on maintaining long-term sales growth
- Enhance the 'quality' of earnings by developing relationships with key customers
- Run the business with the same degree of governance and financial reporting as if it were a public company
- Adopt transparent and conservative accounting policies that are appropriate to the business sector
- Maintain flexibility by reconsidering major capital investment and through the ability to rent (rather than own) non-core assets

- If the owner manager is personally part of what makes the business valuable but will not be continuing to manage it, consider ways of compensating for this such as bringing in new management or transferring key business contacts to existing managers
- Make sure that any questions over the value of business assets, tax or other compliance issues are resolved in advance of the sale – if it turns out something is awry, the seller will lose credibility and it can decimate the business's value
- Identify and protect your intellectual property
- Get the timing right.

Sellers should also identify and address any potential problems that could hold up the sale and reduce the consideration if they emerged during negotiations. A buyer will probably want an accountant's report, so sellers should review any problems that have arisen in recent audits and consider how they can be overcome or explained.

If the business has its own pension fund, a valuation should be carried out and any under- or over-funding addressed. Ask lawyers to identify any possible legal hurdles to the sale and to consider what warranties and indemnities might be required.

Finding potential buyers

It is usual to put together a 'selling memorandum', which is a marketing document designed to attract interest in the business. While presenting the business in a good light, it should be factually accurate and objective and not make any claims the seller would be unwilling to warrant. While highlighting the business's strengths, it should also describe its weaknesses and, where possible, present them as opportunities. Professional advisers' experience will help substantially in developing the document.

Most entrepreneurs are likely to know of a few companies that may be interested in buying their business, but there may be others, not known, who could prove much more satisfactory. Professional advisers should be able to guide on this and to identify specific companies to approach. They can approach one company at a time, but it is more normal to approach several simultaneously. It is often best to set up a controlled auction process, in which a number of potential bidders are invited to make an offer for the business on the basis of the selling memorandum; a clear-cut timetable is then imposed, giving a period for negotiations and a deadline by which offers (subject to contract) must be received.

Understanding the buyer's perspective

It is important to remember that a buyer's concerns may be somewhat different from those of the seller and different buyers will have different priorities and objectives in making an offer for the business. Their interest may, for example, lie primarily in:

- the potential of offering the concept or product to a much wider market

- acquiring people, skills or intellectual property (this is particularly likely in the IT, high-tech or life science sectors)
- the business's market position
- the ability to integrate the business into their own operations
- the desire to inject new life into the business through different management, new investment or new processes.

To a large extent, what the buyer will be looking for will depend on who they are:

- A trade competitor already knows the market and understands the business but wants to increase its market share. It may be intending to integrate and rationalize the bought business with its own, achieving increased sales and reduced costs. It may believe that the company it wants to buy does things better and wants to adopt its working practices in its own operations.
- A customer is likely to feel it can expand its business and at the same time reduce costs by owning a supply company, controlling production and possibly integrating the two companies' operations.
- A supplier's main motives are likely to be to oust other suppliers, to get closer to its markets' or to control distribution. It may also be able to reduce costs by rationalizing the two companies' operations.

In all three cases above, it is likely that the buyer will be looking for a high degree of synergy between the business up for sale and their own.

- A financial buyer or conglomerate may not be interested in business synergy. The company's main criterion will be the potential return on the investment – both the contribution to annual earnings and the gain it makes on reselling or floating the business in the future. Such buyers will be primarily concerned that the business has the right people running it after the acquisition and are likely to take a tight hold on the business immediately after the sale.
- An overseas buyer is most likely looking for the chance to break into the local domestic market. An acquisition will give immediate critical mass and the market understanding its needs.

Try to find out how determined the buyer is to complete the deal. I have seen cases where the buyer's enthusiasm has been so obvious that the sellers have been able to negotiate from a position of real strength and obtain more than they ever hoped for.

Negotiating a successful outcome

Even if the buyers do not reveal their enthusiasm, are there pressures on them to achieve a successful deal? If it is a public company, does it have a need to be seen to acquire successfully to build its market share?

Do not get carried away with the details and the emotion of negotiations but keep strategy firmly in mind. Do not accept any more conditions than are reasonable and do not let the agreement get too complicated as it could become expensive and problematic to implement. The considerations arising from earn-outs and retentions of consideration are too complex to be considered here but should be discussed in detail with professional advisers. Also take professional advice on the tax implications of proposed conditions.

Throughout the negotiations the seller should retain control by managing the timetable and, provided that the negotiating hand is strong enough, keep the process competitive, allowing him or her to go, or threaten to go, to another party if a deadline is not met or an acceptable offer is not made.

☞ Top 10 tips for optimizing the price achieved

● Consult professional advisers at the outset and use the time before the sale process begins to build the value of the business to a potential buyer

● Make sure that a sale is the best route and that all the shareholders are in agreement

● Use all available means to identify likely buyers, including those overseas

● Analyze buyers' motives and what they are looking for; identify where they will perceive the value in the business to lie

● Make sure that the selling memorandum demonstrates the business's strengths and future potential, but that it is accurate. Any inaccuracies are sure to come to light and will cause a buyer to become suspicious or drop the price

● Sell the excitement and enthusiasm of the business – and get the purchaser enthused and excited.

● Emphasize the opportunity the business presents for future growth and profits

● Manage the negotiation process actively and keep it to a strict timetable

● Keep the sale process competitive and make sure there are alternative buyers

● If the owner-manager is to remain managing the business for a period and is confident of its future health, agreeing to an earn-out may bring a higher consideration in total

● Get advice in advance on the tax implications of the sale.

Once a buyer has been chosen, draw up the heads of agreement and proceed to completion as soon as possible. The longer the buyer has to wait for the accountants report and the draft sale and purchase agreement, the more likely he or she is to have second thoughts and, if the deal falls through, the more difficult it becomes to go back to other parties. ■

Copyright © Chris Harrison 1997

A fuller version of this article may be obtained from Ernst & Young on 0171 931 2347.

Riding on the wave of IPOs

What is the fatal attraction of an initial public offering?
Benoît Leleux offers some suggestion.

1996 was an extraordinary year for initial public offerings (IPOs). The heady markets brought about the most IPOs ever in any single year, with some 692 new offerings in the US alone, including the largest offerings ever with that of Lucent Technologies Inc. Europe was not left behind, generating another spectacular year and the largest-ever offering with that of Deutsche Telekom AG.

The total amount of equity raised, well above $46bn in the US, easily surpassed the record to date. The year also brought about a wave of new capital markets targeting growth equity and markets catering to the newly found taste for emerging companies. Some of these were designed from inception as cross-national or pan-European in focus in an attempt to reach broader investment audiences and break the critical mass barrier.

Deutschland entdeckt die Aktie:
schon mehr als 1,4 Millionen Menschen
auf T-Kurs.

Und warum bist du dabei?

Weil man mit dem
Aktien Informations-Forum
auf Nummer Sicher geht.

Deutsche
Telekom

EASDAQ, the pan-European market for smaller companies started in Brussels in September 1996, brainstormed its private institutional backers to come up with a market model that would not only permit young, high-growth companies to raise much-needed equity but would also provide the trading activity and analysts' coverage essential to liquidity. National market authorities in France, Belgium, Germany and other countries also jumped on the growth bandwagon, initially targeting local clients but soon offering various forms of cross-listing arrangements.

Coming in with the tide – Deutsche Telekom made the largest ever offering last year.

IPOs are the definite talk of the town, but are they the ultimate indicators of good times ahead? Why the sudden interest in public markets to finance the entrepreneurial 'gazelles'? Are we slowly moving towards a public form of venture capital? Are we witnessing an investor-risk culture shift and if so, what are the implications for future financings? Are issuing companies suddenly more enthused by public ownership? Why would usually discreet start-ups seek exposure to public scrutiny?

This article reviews some of the fundamental concepts behind IPOs and attempts to move beyond the roadshow magic to understand the inner workings and implications of the going-public decision.

Growth generates phenomenal consumption of resources, forcing companies that espouse it as a matter of corporate strategy into chronic capital shortages. To maintain these high growth rates, regular fund injections are needed. Is an IPO the only source of money for such organizations? Far from it; and given the small percentage of businesses that actually resort to public offerings, it may not even be the most convenient or cheapest way to raise money. So, why are companies going to the public markets to raise funds?

IPOs: equity for growth or insiders cashing out?

For one thing, a publicly-listed company enjoys an aura of respectability in the eyes of various stakeholders, from investors to suppliers and customers. Such respectability can translate into easier business arrangements and better trading terms. The additional exposure and visibility can also provide much needed PR.

Beyond the publicity, the benefits of which may be difficult to quantify, public markets also provide a continuously updated valuation for the company, facilitating later rounds of financing and providing an easy currency for acquisitions and estate management. The liquidity associated with publicly-traded shares also provides an opportunity for early investors to diversify their portfolio holdings and provides a basis for rewarding crucial employees through various forms of stock-based reward programs.

All of this comes at a cost – and a steep one at that. For one thing, market regulators, always watchful of the public interest, allow the easy trading on the exclusive condition that information always be available to the trading parties. These on-going and extensive information disclosures usually go way beyond what most owners would feel comfortable parting with, what *CFO* magazine affectionately refers to as 'indecent disclosures'. In the pursuit of that same public interest, restrictions are placed on insiders' trading activities and detailed procedures are enforced for disclosure of material pieces of information. To guarantee the quality of that information, extensive auditing has to be performed by independent third parties and/or government entities.

Public equity is also far from free. If it does not carry a contractual dividend obligation, there is still the expectation by investors that returns, in the form of capital gains and dividends, will be generated to compensate for their risk taking. Are these expectations forcing a damaging short-term performance focus by public companies?

This is really a false debate. To the extent that share prices actually aggregate the long-term prospects for the organization, short-term changes in stock prices only reflect the long-term effects of current management decisions and industry changes. In other words, a bad management decision that may not have practical implications for years will translate into a price change today. On the positive side, a public listing clearly focuses management's attention on the share price and shareholder-value creation.

Finally, going public has been shown to be a tremendously expensive endeavor. These flotation costs include not only the direct costs of underwriting the issue, performing legal and accounting due diligence, and setting up adequate reporting systems but also the less visible though nonetheless material costs of having important personnel (management and scientific) tied up for months in the process of 'roadshowing' the company to potential investors across the country and abroad.

Another significant cost is the well-documented 'underpricing' of the shares, variously attributed to the underwriters' overwhelming bargaining power, the need to leave a good taste in the initial investors' mouth to entice them to later rounds of financing or another cost of the inherent uncertainty of these situations. Whatever the explanation subscribed to, an issuer selling shares at $25 that are later priced by the market at $30 left $5 on the table.

The total costs of going public can run as high as 25 per cent or more of the expected proceeds. In most circumstances, transaction costs of 25 per cent would be considered outrageous; with IPOs, investment letters will often refer to such issues as wildly successful. How can we reconcile the two apparently contradictory elements?

For one thing, lock-up agreements often prevent insiders from cashing in on the public listing. Even though such arrangements are often limited in time, the only true benefactors from the early price rises are the privileged groups of investors allocated shares initially.

With the allocation essentially left in the US to the discretion of the underwriting syndicate, the lucky few tend to have long-standing relationships with the underwriters, relationships that provide ample opportunities for generating additional fees.

Being public does ultimately facilitate the initial investors' harvesting process, providing both flexibility and high valuations. But could these costs also be seen as the entry ticket to the most exclusive financial club on earth? Based on its worldwide membership, the club of public companies is indeed quite selective and exclusive.

For many, IPOs are almost synonymous with high-growth organizations. Is that to imply that public markets are the only or the most effective way to finance growth?

Do you need the public to grow?

A survey by Leleux and Muzyka in 1996 of European companies that decided to tap the IPO markets in the US supports the view that financing growth and being able to capture new opportunities lies at the heart of the going-public decision. But is that a necessity? Far from it. A number of companies, such as Cargill in the US, and a score of European concerns, have been riding phenomenal growth waves without recourse to such source of financing. The low profile afforded by private placements and bank financings can even in some instances facilitate customer relationships by not antagonizing their own PR efforts.

Keeping a low profile in effect leaves the limelight to the customer. The freedom from day-to-day scrutiny and the pressure from stock market prices can also facilitate the implementation of riskier strategies that may not have received wide acclaim by investment analysts.

Assuming that public markets appear to offer the best alternative for raising the funds a company needs, would your company necessarily be attractive to the markets? In other words, what does it take to capture the public markets' fancy? A good starting point is having an excellent story to tell. Most successful IPO businesses approach investors with a simple, understandable concept or product that has the potential to generate excitement.

The going-public decision

When Genset went public last June on both NASDAQ (National Association of Securities Dealers Automated Quotation) and the Nouveau Marche in Paris, it showcased itself not as a world-class genomics research laboratory, which it was, but as a large-scale industrial production chain for DNA mapping, offering the potential genetics equivalent of the Ford model T for the automobile industry at the turn of the century. Despite intense competition from such powerhouses as Human Genome Sciences and Incyte Pharmaceuticals, Genset was able to generate the excitement indispensable for a successful IPO.

An interesting financial and operational track record can help but most IPO companies have their future in front of them – not concealed in historical statements. A significant percentage of the companies going public in the US have no revenues to show, let alone earnings or profits. Keep in mind that investors do not buy last year's results but the next decade's. Hence the importance of a great story, one that appeals to visions of enormous market potential and significant barriers to entry.

To increase the appearance of a real success story in the making, a top-notch management team is required. If you do not have such a team, no need for concern: managers can be brought in as hired guns to take a company public. It will cost you money, usually in the form of stock options, but is well worth the expense.

How long the team will stay depends, of course, on many factors, not the least of which being the way the vesting schedule for the option plan was designed. To go back to the Genset example, its roadshow featured not only the two eminent founders, Pascal Brandys and Marc Vasseur, but also a chief scientist of towering international repute, Professor Daniel Cohen.

To provide a form of external certification for the potential of the venture, it helps to bring along professional investors such as venture capitalists. Their experience managing the growth process in high-technology organizations is often seen as a desirable addition to the existing management team. Genset, for example, could highlight respected venture capitalists in its ownership structure, including the Sofinnova Group, affiliates from Burr, Egan, Deleage and Co., Oxford Bioscience Partners and SR One, which as a group owned more than 59 per cent of the shares of the company prior to the IPO. Of the 692 IPOs in the US in 1996, 260 were venture-capital backed, raking in some $11.8bn, 44 per cent more than the previous record established in 1995.

With a great story, an experienced management team and a high-reputation set of initial investors, a decision is still needed on which market to seek a listing and what method to use to float the shares. The choice of markets is getting larger by the week but for all practical purposes, the US and the UK still have a virtual duopoly on equity markets, with many promising Continental European companies preferring to bypass completely their own domestic markets to float abroad.

If you decide to list in the US, the question of the flotation method has been resolved for you by the National Association of Securities Dealers since early in the century: the only procedure available is a fixed-price, fixed-quantity offering. Interestingly enough, many non-US markets offer alternative procedures, including various forms of auctions. From an issuer point of view, the auction seems to offer the best prospects for selling the shares to the highest bidders/investors.

Practically speaking, though, the fixed-price approach as practised in the US by the underwriting syndicates can very much approximate the benefits of an auction. Indeed, underwriters will usually approach potential investors in the pre-market period and elicit their informal price and quantity bids in an effort to build a book of non-legally binding commitments. The latter, though, is a pure technicality since walking out of a deal would virtually guarantee your non-participation in any of the future opportunities.

IPOs as investments

The previous sections focused on the supply side of IPO markets. To create a genuine market, investors are also required. The attractiveness of IPOs as investments caught the attention of researchers very early on. Many factors contributed to the academics' excitement. For one thing, it was quite interesting to investigate the extent to which the stock markets were able to price such opportunity-rich companies, an exercise fraught with difficulties.

The extreme cycles experienced by IPO markets were also fascinating: periods of large IPO volumes tend to be followed by dramatic droughts where few organizations even attempt to sell shares to the public. These cycles have been shown to be very closely correlated with the inflation-adjusted level of the stock markets, with large IPO volumes usually occurring close to market peaks, as would be anticipated if issuers were able to time their offerings to take advantage of the market's optimism.

More troubling was the revelation in 1991 by Jay Ritter at the University of Illinois at Champaign of the significantly poor long-term performance of IPO shares. Investors purchasing such IPO shares in the open market and holding on to them for periods of up to three years would on average earn returns statistically smaller than those they could have earned on non-IPO businesses of similar size and industry over the same period.

The evidence, since repeated on most European markets and extended to longer holding periods, is interpreted as supporting the view that issuers are indeed able to take advantage of windows of opportunity in the market to float their shares at valuation that are not sustainable over the long term. This evidence has generated controversies from a methodological (are we properly accounting for the risk in these securities?) and a market efficiency point of view (if investors are rational, why did they not correct their pricing process over the years?) and is still very much at the centre of a wide-ranging debate. ∎

⚡ CASE STUDY

Unipalm

*This is a summary of Unipalm Cases A and B, written by **Fergal Byrne**, Research Associate and **John Bates**, Teaching Fellow at London Business School. Copies of the cases can be obtained from the European Case Clearing House, telephone (+44) 01234 750903; fax (+44) 01234 751125; E-mail ECCH@cranfield.ac.uk.*

In 1986, Peter Dawe had been working for Cambridge MicroComputers for seven years. During this time, he had become increasingly excited by the opportunities in computer networking – the specialized software that allowed computers to communicate. He was particularly keen on the TCP/IP software protocol developed in the USA which, he was convinced, was the most advanced on the market. Indeed, he suspected that it would emerge as the platform networking standard. Unable to convince CMC of this, he gave up his 5 per cent shareholding in the company in exchange for the rights to distribute TCP/IP software in the UK and started his own business.

Sales in the first two years were slow, but by 1988 had begun to pick up when Peter met Bob Peters, an old colleague from CMC. Bob agreed to join up with Peter and invested £14,000 for 50 per cent of the equity in the business. Unipalm Ltd was born.

Over the next few months sales grew rapidly and by the end of the year had tripled. During this period, the company had also acquired three new directors – Arthur, a salesman, Simon, a computer programmer, and Sean to develop the training activities – who between them invested more than £50,000 for 48 per cent of the equity, diluting Peter and Bob to 52 per cent.

By 1990, sales had grown to £750,000 with profits before tax of approximately £140,000. Unfortunately, this success also created problems as it slowly became clear that the directors had different expectations for the company. For example, Sean and Simon were keen to start taking money out, Bob was unclear as to what he wanted, and Peter and Arthur were keen to develop the business further. Personal relations began to deteriorate.

At the same time Peter had identified a new opportunity. He was fascinated by the rapid growth in the use of the Internet, the worldwide network that communicated using the TCP/IP protocol, and was convinced that Unipalm should expand in this market by becoming an Internet Service Provider (ISP). Unfortunately, and despite the fact that his business plan showed profits in excess of £1m after three years, his co-directors did not take him seriously and refused his request for a budget of £100,000 to develop the service.

Over the following months, matters deteriorated so rapidly that Peter decided to resign and pursue his business idea elsewhere. Whilst he was working out his notice, Bob left the company in April after a particularly acrimonious meeting described by others as a 'blood bath'. When Peter left the Unipalm offices for the last time at the end of May, he found Bob waiting for him in his car. Over a pint of Guinness they agreed to stick together. If the other shareholders wanted to buy either of them out, they would have to buy both.

By the end of November, the situation was becoming increasingly bizarre as no real offer was forthcoming and so Bob and Peter, who between them owned 52 per cent of the equity, decided to take control of matters. Early in December they called an Extraordinary General Meeting, voted themselves back on the Board and fired the other three directors. There remained the question of their equity and it was only after months of acrid negotiations that a price for the purchase of their shares was finally agreed.

Meanwhile Peter had set up the Public IP Exchange Ltd. (PIPEX) to develop the Internet project. The partners agreed that they would become joint MDs with Bob running the Unipalm business and Peter running PIPEX, a wholly owned subsidiary of the Unipalm Group Plc. However, to move forward, they estimated that they needed a financial injection of £1m. So they approached Rob Lucas, an investment director at 3i, the largest UK venture capital company. Rob was concerned about the disappointing financial performance in 1991 but Peter and Bob convinced him that the profits were artificially depressed due to a change in management and that the Unipalm business could generate operating profits of around £1m in 1992. A deal was finally agreed.

There were two conditions to the investment – that Unipalm recruit both a new full-time finance director and a non-executive Chairman. Chris Batterham, a seasoned Finance Director with considerable experience in the high tech field, and David Thorp, an ex-3i director joined the team as non-executive Chairman of the board. Peter was now able to develop the PIPEX business.

In order to become an Internet Access Provider, PIPEX needed to develop an international data network, or data backbone, comprising leased domestic and international telecommunication circuits. Subscribers would connect the PIPEX network by a leased or dial-up line to a PIPEX Point of Presence (POP), a kind of telephonic switch. This network was in turn connected to the Internet via a leased digital line.

Forecasting the development of PIPEX was a very inexact process. Chris: *'It was almost impossible to build any kind of sensible business model for the Internet – there was a fundamental problem of scaling and it was very difficult to predict the growth of the business . . . the required capacity per user was changing, as was the range of services that were being offered. PIPEX had, nonetheless, to build the telecommunications structure – POPs and international bandwidth – in advance. The situation was further complicated due to the difficulty of forecasting Unipalm's sales which were highly volatile from one month to another. Last but not least, shortly after I arrived I discovered that we did not actually know what our telecom costs were – we were receiving bills from British Telecom a year after usage . . . continued investment required a significant act of faith.'*

Nevertheless, Peter was convinced that there was a significant opportunity just waiting to happen. Returning from a trip to the USA in March 1993, he gave an impassioned presentation to the management on the future of the Internet and the need for scale and growth. Although the others were not convinced, he began to consider the possibility of selling the Unipalm business to finance PIPEX and so in June he asked Regency Associates, a specialist broker, to identify possible purchasers. However, no reasonable offer emerged and management reluctantly concluded that this wasn't a viable option.

With no buyers on the horizon, they had three alternatives: to find a strategic partner, to raise interim finance, or to seek a public flotation. They decided upon the latter and there followed six months of intensive preparation, led by Chris. He worked closely with the brokers, E. J. Hall, and the accountants, Arthur Andersen, to prepare the 'long form report', a comprehensive analysis of the business which entailed providing information on every aspect of the business.

All along, Peter was very concerned about the timing and was constantly exerting pressure on everyone to speed up the whole process. In particular, a number of high-tech flotations in September and October had made him increasingly nervous that the 'window' would soon close. As the date for flotation grew closer, tensions mounted and relations with E. J. Hall became strained. In December, Niall Stevens, the Managing Director of E. J. Hall, called a meeting.. . . *'Given the relative youth of the company and the lack of earnings visibility, we believe that . . . the management structure will need to be streamlined, with one person responsible for the entire business.'* When Peter declined to consider this, Stevens declined the role of sponsor in the flotation. That was it. Once again, Peter was left to reconsider his options.

Postscript

A £20 million offering of shares in Unipalm was successfully floated on the London Stock Exchange in early 1994. In doing so, Unipalm became the first Internet service provider to go public worldwide. The offering price of the shares was 100p.

In late 1995, UUNET Technologies, an American Internet service provider, agreed to buy Unipalm in an all-share bid which valued Unipalm at £100 million. By the time the deal had closed, UUNET's shares rose in price from $39 to $75. As a result, the realized value of the deal for Unipalm shareholders was 740p per share or roughly 500 times 1995 earnings! Not surprisingly, Unipalm was the best performing share on the London Stock Exchange in 1995.

Merger and acquisition activity in the telecommunications sector accelerated in pace in 1996. In the summer, MFS Communications, a company which had established a series of local telephone networks in the US and Europe, acquired UUNET Technologies in a deal valued at $2 billion. One month later, World Com, the fourth largest long distance carrier in the US, acquired MFS for $10 billion.

Bob retired to Florida in May 1995, Peter left to concentrate on his investments in high technology and media in May 1996, and Chris is now Managing Director, Europe, for UUNET. ∎

Indexes

Subject index

Name index

Organization index

Have you Mastered Enterprise?

We hope that you have found this book useful. If so, why let your pursuit of management excellence end here?

We will be developing a series of opportunities for executives to stay in touch with the latest management thinking. These will enable you to constantly upgrade your management skills as part of an international community of those who are **Mastering Enterprise**. Membership of this select community will give you privileged access to a range of learning opportunities, tailored to meet your needs as the world of management evolves.

To become a member of the Masters of Management Club, fill in the application form below and return it to:

Masters of Management Club
Executive Editor, *FT Mastering Enterprise*
Pearson Education, FREEPOST, 128 Long Acre, London WC2E 9AN
Fax: +44 (0) 207 240 5771

FT Mastering Enterprise

Mr/Mrs/Miss/Ms Initial_____ Last name _____

Department _____

Job title _____

Company _____

Address _____

_____

Telephone no._____ Fax no. _____

Areas of special interest: _____

1. _____

2. _____

3. _____

4. _____

5. _____

Preferred newspaper _____

Preferred business magazine _____

Any comments on *FT Mastering Enterprise* or future projects:

_____

_____

Alternatively, contact us on the Internet at http://www.ftmanagement.com